Understanding Religious Pluralism

Understanding Religious Pluralism

Perspectives from Religious Studies and Theology

Edited by
PETER C. PHAN
and JONATHAN RAY

☙PICKWICK *Publications* • Eugene, Oregon

UNDERSTANDING RELIGIOUS PLURALISM
Perspectives from Religious Studies and Theology

Copyright © 2014 Wipf and Stock Publishers. All rights reserved. Except for brief quotations in critical publications or reviews, no part of this book may be reproduced in any manner without prior written permission from the publisher. Write: Permissions. Wipf and Stock Publishers, 199 W. 8th Ave., Suite 3, Eugene, OR 97401.

Pickwick Publications
An Imprint of Wipf and Stock Publishers
199 W. 8th Ave., Suite 3
Eugene, OR 97401

www.wipfandstock.com

ISBN 13: 978-1-62032-943-6

Cataloging-in-Publication data:

Understanding religious pluralism : perspectives from religious studies and theology / edited by Peter C. Phan and Jonathan Ray.

xvi + 320 p. ; 23 cm. Includes bibliographical references and index.

ISBN 13: 978-1-62032-943-6

1. Religious pluralism. 2. Religions—Relations. I. Phan, Peter C. II. Ray, Jonathan.

BR127 U54 2014

Manufactured in the U.S.A.

Contents

Preface / vii
Introduction / ix

1 Following the Flows: Diversity, Santa Fe, and Method in Religious Studies / 1
—*Thomas A. Tweed*

2 Between the One and the Many in the Study of Religious Pluralism: A Response to Thomas Tweed / 20
—*Francisca Cho*

3 Botánicas: Sacred Sites of Plural Religious Encounter / 28
—*Joseph M. Murphy*

4 The Buddha and the Dalai Lama on Religious Pluralism / 46
—*J. Abraham Vélez de Cea*

5 The Prospects for Interreligious and Intercultural Understanding: The Jesuit Case and Its Theoretical Implications / 66
—*Charles B. Jones*

6 Paul, Practical Pluralism, and the Invention of Religious Persecution in Roman Antiquity / 87
—*Paula Fredriksen*

7 Families of Religion, Then and Now: A Response to Paula Fredriksen / 114
—*Jonathan Ray*

8 Judaism, Christianity, and Modernity: Charles Péguy and the Mysticism of the Dreyfus Affair / 119
—*Matthew W. Maguire*

9 *Lashon ha-Ra* and Jewish Practical Pluralism:
   A Case Study of *Sefer Chafetz Chaim* / 135
   —Charles Bernsen

10 The Jewish Origins of an American Idea:
   Horace Kallen's Cultural Pluralism / 151
   —Daniel Greene

11 Religious Pluralism in Islam / 170
   —Thomas Michel

12 Response to Tom Michel / 186
   —Paul L. Heck

13 One Faith, Different Rites:
   Nicholas of Cusa's New Awareness of Religious Pluralism / 192
   —Pim Valkenberg

14 Lateral and Hierarchical Religious Difference in the Qur'an:
   Muslima Theology of Religious Pluralism / 209
   —Jerusha Tanner Lamptey

15 Outside *de jure* Religious Pluralism No Dialogue:
   A Critical Socio-Theological Assessment of Christian–Muslim
   Dialogue in Post-Colonial Sub-Saharan Africa / 223
   —Marinus C. Iwuchukwo

16 The Shifting Significance of Theologies of Religious Pluralism / 242
   —S. Mark Heim

17 From Soteriology to Comparative Theology and Back:
   A Response to S. Mark Heim / 260
   —Peter C. Phan

18 What Has Renaissance Polyphony to Offer Theological Method? / 264
   —John N. Sheveland

19 Karl Rahner's "Anonymous Christianity" in Light of Pluralism and
   Contemporary Theology of Religions in Asia / 277
   —Todd E. Johanson

20 Relativism, Universalism, and Pluralism in the Age of Globalization:
   A Reflection on Raimon Panikkar's Approach / 297
   —Young-chan Ro

List of Contributors / 309
Index / 315

Preface

THE TWENTY ESSAYS THAT make up this volume originate from the conference organized by the Graduate Program in Theological and Religious Studies of the Department of Theology, Georgetown University, May 23–25, 2012, titled "Understanding Religious Pluralism: Religious and Theological Perspectives." They all have been extensively revised for publication.

Religious diversity is a growing feature of our time and presents enormous challenges to the disciplines of religious studies and theology. The conference was planned to examine some of these challenges, with particular references to Judaism, Christianity, and Islam. It was structured around four keynote addresses (Thomas A. Tweed, Paula Fredriksen, Thomas Michel, and Mark Heim), each with a response. There were concomitant sessions in which various papers on religious pluralism broadly construed were presented, some of which are selected for inclusion in this volume.

This book is built around the four keynotes that were originally commissioned to explore the central theme of the impact of religious pluralism on religious studies and theology. The volume is made up of four parts. After an introduction on religious pluralism, the first part explores the challenges of religious pluralism on religious studies; the second those on the Jewish-Christian encounter; the third those on the encounter between Christianity and Islam; and the fourth those on Christian theology, especially the theology of religions. The book ends with an epilogue on the future of religious pluralism as an object of scholarly inquiry. We are keenly aware that other religious traditions such as Hinduism, Jainism, Sikhism, and the Chinese religions have been left out of the conversation.

Our only excuse was lack of time and resources; to make amends, we pledge to give them sustained attention in future conferences.

A conference as complex as the one from which this volume originates would not have been possible without the generous financial support of Georgetown University. The largest contribution came from the Ignacio

Ellacuría Chair of Catholic Social Thought, and we are deeply grateful to the family that anonymously endowed this university-wide chair. Other contributions came from the Berkley Center for Religion, Peace, and World Affairs; the Jesuit Advisory Board for Interreligious Dialogue and Mission, US Jesuit Conference; Georgetown Department of Theology; The Dean Office, Georgetown College; Georgetown Graduate School of Arts & Sciences; and Prince Alwaleed bin Talal Center for Muslim–Christian Understanding. To all of these institutions, sincerest thanks!

Thanks are also due to the students in our Graduate Program, in particular Dr. Maureen Walsh and Dr. Melanie Trexler, who ably took charge of the logistics of the conference. Our gratitude also goes to Peter Herman for his competent work in getting the manuscript ready for publication. We are also deeply grateful to Dr. Linda Stinson for work on the index, free of charge. Finally, we owe a debt of gratitude to all the participants of the conference—seasoned scholars and graduate students—who have generously contributed to the success of the conference that we hope will be the first of many conversations on the theme of great import for our time.

Introduction

JONATHAN RAY and PETER C. PHAN

UNDERSTANDING RELIGIOUS PLURALISM IS the product of a conference held at Georgetown University in May of 2012. Recognizing that religious diversity is a growing feature of American society, the conference organizers and participants explored the question of religious pluralism, and the various challenges it poses to the disciplines of religious studies and theology. The present book examines some of these challenges, with particular references to Judaism, Christianity, and Islam. The following essays represent some of the best and most current research on the phenomenon of religious pluralism from across a spectrum of methodological approaches. They provide both a description of social realities as well as a methodological standpoint relevant to how we might process and respond to these realities. The volume is divided into four parts: Religious Pluralism and Religious Studies, Jewish–Christian Encounters, Muslim–Christian Encounters, and Christian Theologies of Religious Pluralism. Following the structure of the conference from which it arises, each section opens with a keynote chapter on a separate theme of religious pluralism followed by a short response essay, and a collection of studies that broaden and extend each theme.

As a point of departure for understanding the discourse on religious pluralism we can acknowledge that the term possesses a high degree of elasticity. Its exact definition as a category of analysis varies considerably depending on the field. Sociology of religion, anthropology of religion, history, theology, and philosophy all use it slightly differently and, adding to the complexity of the situation, rarely take note of how the term is used in other disciplines. The purpose of this volume is not to achieve a precise definition of the term, but to recognize the variety of approaches currently employed, and to seek to find some understanding in the very plurality of these diverse takes on pluralism.

Religious Pluralism begins as a call to acknowledge the diversity of religious traditions and communities as a fact of life in the twenty-first century. But it also goes beyond that. There is an effort here to recognize not only the fact of plurality, but also the intrinsic value, or at least the potential value, of more than one religious tradition. The acknowledgment of religious diversity brings with it a moral and practical challenge to find a way to live together in peace and mutual respect. Scholars of pluralism seek to avoid talking about other religions and their adherents in condescending and distancing terms. They want to begin to understand them on their own terms. However, they also want others to return the favor: by assuming a similar stance of "tolerance" and possessing similar goals of mutual understanding—of valuing heterogeneity and pluralistic harmony. Scholars of pluralism generally agree that there exists a sort of social symbiosis among religious communities today, and that a commitment to greater mutual understanding is the key to greater social tranquility. Against the criticism that such views are unnecessarily utopian, many champions of religious pluralism hold that they are, indeed, vital to the survival of civilized societies in an increasingly globalized context. There is also a shared sense throughout this burgeoning field that discussions of religious pluralism and attempts to makes sense of the claims and perspectives of other religions also inform us about ourselves.[1]

Beyond these generally shared ideals and approaches, the study of pluralism begins to follow different paths. Globalization, migration, and persistent conflicts between religious communities around the world have all contributed to an increased awareness of pluralism within the academy. Yet for all this shared awareness, scholars remain sharply divided over some of the most essential elements and general trajectory of the field. As a result, scholars across the varied landscape of theology and religious studies have come to treat pluralism as a significant social reality, but nonetheless often assume that their use of the term should be recognized as the primary working definition.

A step toward understanding the current state of the field of religious pluralism is to acknowledge the general disparity that exists between scholars of theology and scholars of religious studies—that is, those who seek to develop operative theories of pluralism, and those who observe and describe trends that emerge from pluralistic encounters. Theologians who address questions of pluralism tend to accept as potential representations of a given religious tradition anything that appears within its sacred texts or classical systems of thought, whereas their counterparts in religious studies generally

---

1. Clooney, *Comparative Theology*, 11.

focus on the interpretations of these texts and ideologies that have formed a part of the lived traditions of these religious communities. Their discussions of pluralism within a given religion can be divided between the potential (theological approaches) and the actual (religious studies approaches).

Theologians of religious pluralism seek to effect change through dialogue and self-reflection. There is now a recognition by those engaged in this discourse to begin to move from theory to praxis.[2] They have worked to affirm not only the presence, but also the inherent value of other religious communities and their doctrines, maintaining that other religious traditions possess distinctive as well as universal truths.[3] For many, the consideration of other religious traditions has challenged their interpretations of their own religious texts and traditions.[4] They argue that, in order to understand others, we must first understand our own traditions. The increased presence—or at least the raised profile—of non-Christian traditions in the West, and of Christianity in Asia, has forced many to think more critically about their own religious traditions.[5] Like the larger category of religion, theological pluralism emerges from a particularly Christian context and retains much of its pre-modern, Christian notional categories.

One of the key elements of Christianity that has remained central to Western definitions of religion is the idea of salvation. Indeed, how those outside of one's own tradition can be saved has become an enduring question for many theologians of religious pluralism. Mindful of potential for relativism, theologians of pluralism seek the means of a respectful encounter with other religions without abandoning their sense of Christian particularism (and, by extension, without demanding that adherents of other traditions need do the same). Nor is this caution with regard to the abandonment of longstanding postures limited to Christian theologians. Muslim theorists who have joined the debate on pluralism have followed this trend to engage, but also critique or reject, theories of religious pluralism that have been derived from Islamic sources. While some scholars of Islam who write in English for a primarily Western audience have noted the Qur'an allows for the possibility of salvation of those outside of Islam, others have been quick to point out that this understanding of Islamic soteriology remains at odds with traditional and current mainstream Muslim interpretation.[6]

---

2. Fredericks, *Buddhists and Christians*, 25.

3. Griffin, "Religious Pluralism, Generic, Identist, and Deep," in *Deep Religious Pluralism*, 3–38.

4. Tracy, "Creativity in the Interpretation of Religion," 290–93.

5. Tracy, *On Naming the Present*, 67–68.

6. Khalil, "Salvation and the Other," 511–19.

In contrast to those seeking to develop a theology of religious pluralism, scholars in the various fields of religious studies are more interested in chronicling and explaining the results of this plurality—of the encounter between distinct religious communities in a pluralistic context—than they are of fomenting change. Rather than creating a conceptual framework for dialogue, they tend to draw attention to the moments of encounter among religious systems and communities. They tend to see pluralism as a sort of practical accommodation to the intricacies of daily life and social interaction in heterogeneous societies. Approaches in this field have ranged from descriptive and analytical—this is how religions interact—to a more activist stance that assumes pluralism to be an intrinsic good, and a potential source of cultural strength and social and political unity. Here, scholars of religious studies share with their colleagues in theology the implicit belief that energetic engagement and dialogue among religious groups is the key to a deeper self-understanding and a stronger, richer society.

One distinguishing element of the religious studies approach to pluralism is the assertion that features of religious identity that are linked to ethnic, racial or cultural categories are every bit as determinative as are doctrinal or ideological concerns. The argument here is that, for several religious communities, ethnic and cultural loyalties often continue to dominate the discussion of religious pluralism.[7] In the Europe and North America, scholars have pointed to the existence of multiply constituted groups—groups whose identities turn on what we might term religious *and* national *and* ethnic factors—even as they recognize the relatively unstable definition of these terms.

Still other factors have come to complicate the current discourse of religious pluralism, and to force these two disparate approaches to consider one another. Perhaps most notably, discussions of religious pluralism have proliferated in recent decades to become part of a wider discourse on religion that transcends the theological and academic worlds. Pluralism, like other notoriously contested terms such as "religion" or "culture," has now entered the popular vocabulary. It has begun to color the way in which clergy, laity, and journalists speak and think about the interaction of contemporary religious communities. In other words, religious actors and observers have already begun to use a working definition, or set of definitions, of religious pluralism that may or may not show an awareness of the academic discourse on the subject. Rather than discount those views that do not conform to scholarly definitions of the subject, observers and

---

7. See the essay by Paula Fredriksen in this volume.

interpreters of religion need to highlight the different ways that pluralism is understood in the public sphere, and find meaning in these trends.

The current scholarly discussion of pluralism emerged out of a mainstream Protestant reading of Christianity, and a Western Christian stance still shapes the terms of the debate.[8] For contemporary Christian theologians, a guiding principle of religious pluralism is the rejection of religious absolutism—that only one's own religion is true or divinely inspired. Yet, not all groups that are categorized as "religions" are equally concerned with such truth claims. Judaism conceptually allows for other religions to exist, but holds that the covenantal mission of the Jews is fundamentally different than others. Indeed, in the field of Jewish Studies, the term has often been rendered as "cultural pluralism," underscoring an important distinction in conceptual categories. Similarly, Buddhist scriptures maintain that the Buddha explained the path to Buddhahood differently to different audiences, altering the focus on absolutism. Thus, while it may be true that all religious traditions encompass many of the same components and characteristics, the place that these components occupy within a given religion varies considerably. Horace Kallen, one of the founding fathers of the study of religious pluralism in the field of Jewish Studies, noted that tradition-minded Jews of nineteenth century understood the lifeblood of the Jewish community to be found in the punctilious adherence to ritual, rather than its underlying theology.[9] We might observe that, if pluralism functions as an interpretation of plurality, the fact that these interpretations often differ depending on one's own religious, philosophical or cultural perspective remains an important characteristic of this discourse.

The particular Western, Christian posture of the present study of pluralism is also evident in claims that now, and perhaps only just now, the forces of globalization and new immigration patterns have forced awareness of religious plurality and the need to engage more actively in interreligious discourse. Such approaches, while perhaps true for the dominant Christian outlook of the West, reveal a certain naïveté about lived experiences of religious minorities around the world. Long before the globalizing trends of the late twentieth century, the fact of religious plurality had come to shape understanding of the "other" in number of settings, and exerted a substantial

---

8. Hutchinson, *Religious Pluralism in America*. A critique of the Christian-centric posture of the current discourse on pluralism can be found in Fredericks, *Buddhists and Christians*.

9. Toll, "Horace M. Kallen," 62–63. While the accuracy of Kallen's characterization of Jewish Orthodoxy is open to debate, the relative importance of ritual and theology in traditional Judaism is fundamentally different than in Christianity or more modern Jewish movements.

influence on the way that religious communities conceived of their own traditions. Jews, a minority in the polytheistic world of the ancient Near East, as well as under the Christian and Muslim cultural spheres that succeeded it, have long since had to contend with the presence of larger and more dominant religious systems than their own. Similarly, European colonization of much of the globe from the sixteenth to nineteenth centuries forced a wide variety of other religious groups including Muslims, Buddhists, Hindus and Sikhs to come to terms with religious difference.

Recognition that the current debate on pluralism represents a somewhat belated awareness of the issues of religious plurality is no small caveat. It calls attention to the fact that the various religious communities with which theologians of pluralism wish to engage may well approach interreligious dialogue and encounter from very different perspectives. Indeed, while many Christian theologians have expressed a willingness to embrace (or at lest avoid denigrating) other religious traditions, they may find that members of these other groups are far more hesitant to return the gesture.[10] The reasons for this transcend theology. For religious minorities, especially those who are first or second-generation immigrants to a new country, questions of pluralism are bound up with those of civil rights and the preservation of cultural identity.

The matter of minority-majority relationship also underscores the degree to which interreligious engagement is shaped by power dynamics. Religious minorities have little choice but to engage, on some level, the majority religious cultures in which they live. But this relationship is never fully symbiotic. Traditionally, majority cultures are far less influenced by the minority cultures in their domain. Moreover, the experience of minority communities is governed by a variety of factors. Being a minority in a more pluralistic society, such as the United States, is quite different from being the principal religious minority, as with Muslims in the United Kingdom. And minorities with a long and complicated relationship with their host societies, such as the Jews in France or Christians in Egypt, face a very different dynamic than those with relatively little history with the majority culture, such as Sikhs in the United States and Canada.

Most definitions of religious pluralism acknowledge that, within the complex matrix of ideologies, traditions and practices of each religious community, there lies the potential for an authentic and mutually beneficial engagement with other communities. Diana Eck offers the important caveat that religious pluralism goes beyond mere tolerance of other religions, necessitating an honest attempt to understand other faiths on

---

10. See Gilkey, "Plurality and Its Theological Implications," 40.

their own terms.[11] However, such statements carry with them a vision of religious communities that assumes an implicit essentialism of each. That is to say, while it is admirable to strive to move beyond tolerance toward deeper mutual understanding, it is important to note that the objects of that understanding—Islam, Judaism, Hinduism, etc.—are moving targets, multifaceted and rapidly evolving. Ironically, the tendency toward privileging orthodoxies as representative voices in each of these religious systems in order to put the world religions into dialogue with one another threatens to obscure the plurality of traditions within each religion.[12]

The post-modern turn has emphasized that religious communities, like the cultures with which they often overlap, can no longer be seen as essential and fixed. Rather, they are dynamic, changing systems that are internally fragmented, and whose borders are porous. The location of personal religiosity within each religious system varies significantly. Therefore, even the most sincere efforts to engage other religions in a profound and meaningful way must eventually confront the fact that each religion exists along a variable spectrum of practice and interpretation that supports multiple communities of believers and adherents.

So then, where do we stand? What are we to make of the notion of pluralism if we cannot agree on terminologies and basic perspectives? Perhaps it is precisely the diversity of approaches and concerns with regard to religious pluralism that suggests a starting point for the journey toward greater understanding. To enter the current debate on pluralism is to accept a certain degree of inconsistency and confusion regarding what we mean by the term, and the various ways it is used. In sum, to understand religious pluralism requires that we recognize certain governing principles of this growing field. First, that the plurality of religious communities in the North America and elsewhere, and the wide-ranging debates that this plurality has engendered, are features of contemporary society that are here to stay. Second, that these debates remains every bit as dynamic and diffuse as the broader discourse on the nature of religion, and every bit as compelling. Finally, that the current discussion on the nature and development of religious pluralism has been unmistakably Christian, but that this orientation is rapidly changing. To this end, the essays in this volume are meant to signal, if not fully encompass, the multiplicity of perspectives on pluralism. They are offered as a step forward in our ongoing understanding of the phenomenon of religious interaction, dialogue and coexistence.

---

11. Eck, "Is Our God Listening," 193.

12. Cobb, "Some Whiteheadian Assumptions," 247–48; and Bender and Klassen, *After Pluralism*, 9.

BIBLIOGRAPHY

Bender, Courtney, and Pamela Klassen, eds. *After Pluralism: Reimagining Engagement*. New York: Columbia University Press, 2010.

Clooney, Francis X. *Comparative Theology: Deep Learning across Religious Borders*. Malden, MA: Wiley-Blackwell, 2010.

Cobb, John B. Jr. "Some Whiteheadian Assumptions about Religion and Pluralism." In *Deep Religious Pluralism*, edited by David Ray Griffin, 243–62. Louisville: Westminster John Knox, 2005.

Eck, Diana. "'Is Our God Listening?': Exclusivism, Inclusivism, and Pluralism." In *Encountering God: A Spiritual Journey from Bozeman to Banaras*, 166–99. Boston: Beacon, 1993.

Fredericks, James L. *Buddhists and Christians: Through Comparative Theology to Solidarity*. Maryknoll, NY: Orbis, 2004.

Gilkey, Langdon. "Plurality and Its Theological Implications." In *The Myth of Christian Uniqueness*, edited by John Hick and Paul F. Knitter, 37–50. Maryknoll, NY: Orbis, 1987.

Griffin, David Ray, ed. *Deep Religious Pluralism*. Louisville: Westminster John Knox, 2005.

Hutchinson, William R. *Religious Pluralism in America: The Contentious History of a Founding Ideal*. New Haven: Yale University Press, 2003.

Khalil, Mohammad Hassan. "Salvation and the Other in Islamic Thought." *Religion Compass* 5 (2011) 511–19.

Toll, William "Horace M. Kallen: Pluralism and American Jewish Identity." *American Jewish History* 85 (1997) 57–74.

Tracy, David. "Creativity in the Interpretation of Religion: The Question of Radical Pluralism." *New Literary History* 15 (1983–84) 289–309.

———. *On Naming the Present: Reflections on God, Hermeneutics and the Church*. Maryknoll, NY: Orbis, 1994.

1

Following the Flows
Diversity, Santa Fe, and Method in Religious Studies

THOMAS A. TWEED

Figure 1.1. Ben Shahn, **Self Portrait among the Churchgoers**, *w/c on paper (1939)*. Used by permission: Art © Estate of Ben Shahn (1898–1969)/Licensed by VAGA, New York, NY; Private Collection /Photo © Christie's Images/Bridgeman Art Library.

2 Understanding Religious Pluralism

IN THIS 1939 WATERCOLOR by Ben Shahn, a Lithuanian-born American artist who also snapped federally funded photographs of everyday life, the observer positions himself—and his camera—near a doorway where soberly dressed congregants leave and enter a modest church (figure 1.1).[1] Beyond the observer's vision, the sign to his far right announces today's sermon: "Is the Government Fostering Irreligion in Art?" The minister will discuss, pedestrians presume, the US government's efforts to ease the Great Depression's suffering by sponsoring various public work projects, including by commissioning more than 164,000 black-and-white photographs between 1935 and 1943. Although Shahn and many of those commissioned photographers actually offered a visible record of religious practice, the photographer portrayed here points his camera toward the secular happenings in the street and away from the pious worshipping in the church, so this left-leaning artist of "social realism" playfully answers the sermon's question affirmatively.[2] The observer seems comically and intentionally inattentive to religious practice at that turbulent time when the faithful and their leaders not only were encountering the secularizing and pluralizing forces of modernity—including Freudian psychology and Marxist politics—and struggling to respond to transnational economic crisis and global political upheaval. In America and elsewhere in 1939, the religious did not agree about how to deal with any of the shared problems, including the impending war; and, like one American Protestant minister, some asked aloud *Must We Go to War?*[3] It would be two years more before the Japanese military bombed Pearl Harbor and Adolf Hitler declared war on the United States, thereby bringing the nation into the global conflict. Many would die in that war that touched all corners of the world, though economic recovery and religious resurgence followed in the United States after 1945. By the Cold War Fifties, a prayer room would be added to the Capitol Building and

---

1. I want to thank my fellow participants, and our hosts, at the Georgetown University conference on "Understanding Religious Pluralism" for their comments and suggestions. I also tried out different versions of this as part of plenary addresses to two other audiences in 2012: the conference on "Religion and the Trans" at Northwestern University, and the conference on "Religious Pluralism in Europe and Asia: Conditions, Modes, and Consequences," which was cosponsored by the University of Texas at Austin and the Käte Hamburger Kolleg at Ruhr-Universität Bochum. Those conversations helped refine my thinking. Many other friends and colleagues helped in various ways too, including Janet Davis, Oliver Freiberger, and Katie Lofton. I also am grateful to my research assistant, Elena Kravchenko, for help getting the permission for the art work I use in this chapter.

2. McDannell, *Picturing Faith*. Ben Shahn's painting was displayed as part of the exhibition, "Shared Intelligence: American Painting and the Photograph," May 20–September 11, 2011, Georgia O'Keefe Museum, Santa Fe, New Mexico.

3. Page, *Must We Go to War?*, 182–86.

"under God" would be added to the pledge of allegiance, as a confidently triumphant nation settled in—or so many Americans hoped—for a period of prosperity and peace.

Today that post-war period seems quite distant. At an historical moment when globalizing forces have intensified and two apparently competing trends are at work—the world seems both more and less religious—it's important to consider not just *why* the study of religion is important for all those who aspire to be an informed citizen today but also *how* we might do it effectively and responsibly. When we're dealing with religion—a subject that starts conflicts and settles them—that sort of judiciousness is crucial. Some might complain that the stakes are not very high. After all, the academic study of religion does not seem to have direct effects as, say, medicine and aeronautics do. It's true that if the interpreter of religion gets it wrong—misinterprets a Christian idea of *just war* or a Muslim notion of *jihad*—a patient won't flatline on the operating table and a jet plane won't fall from the sky. But interpretations—and misinterpretations—matter. Really matter. Inspired by causes that seem as certain as they are ultimate, devotees have stopped hearts from beating and planes from flying. It doesn't matter whether you personally find religion compelling or whether your town or nation seems to be growing more secular. What matters is that billions around the world practice a faith— and they *act* from their faith. It shapes how they enter the world and how they leave it, how they eat, dress, marry—and raise their children. It shapes their assumptions about who they are and who they want to be. It draws national borders. It affects law, economy, and government. Whether you notice it or not, religions play a role in how billions conduct their lives.

We are called, then, to understand this important factor in human life today—and in the past. And if we don't understand what *happened* we won't understand what's *happening*. Unlike Shahn's camera-toting observer, who overlooks the vital religious activity around him, it's important to know what to observe and how to observe it. It's morally urgent to take on the difficult questions and answer them in a way that considers not only the latest academic research about religion's past and present but also our shared world today, with its global interconnections, rapid transit, and instantaneous communication. Positioning ourselves in the middle of all those flows—and where else could we stand?—we can ask how to analyze this vital force. Some of the questions seem boring, though they are crucial to ponder: Which sources should we use? What should we do with those sources? Just as important, we have to ask other questions, even tougher questions, that raise blood pressure and start debates: What should be the interpreter's goal? How would we know if we've succeeded or not? Which standards of evidence and modes of argumentation seem appropriate when we are talking about religion? How much should we consider the perspectives of participants themselves, both those striding toward the church entrance and those strolling the secular streets? What about the investigator's perspective? As we consider this vital and volatile area of human life, what are our professional obligations and how are our (epistemic, aesthetic, and moral) values enacted at each stage of the research process? Which virtues should we try to cultivate, in ourselves and in others? Should we try to be fair to those we study, and what would "fairness" mean? What about our obligations to those who encounter our representations in the classroom and in public media? Should we aim to convert everyone to our point of view, whether that is unapologetically secular, devoutly religious, or incontrovertibly ambivalent? Work for social justice? Or be somewhat more subdued yet practical: try only to keep everyone from blowing each other up?[4]

I will not try to address all these issues in this chapter. Rather, I'll gesture toward only a few of them as I reflect on religious diversity in the United States and consider its implications for specialists who identify as scholars of Religious Studies.[5] Scholars' awareness of diversity increased

---

4. I do not have space to address the complicated questions about values and obligations I raise here. I have addressed some of those questions in previous work and plan to address them more fully in the future. In my theory of religion, I argued that all scholars enact epistemic, moral, and aesthetic values in their work: Tweed, *Crossing and Dwelling*, 26–27, 246n1. In that book I also discussed scholars' role-specific obligations (17, 27, 30–33, 53); and I reconsidered the issue in my response to four reviews of *Crossing and Dwelling*. There I proposed that "reciprocal generosity," the ability to both give and receive, is a key virtue to cultivate for those who want to formulate an ethic of civic engagement and a program for enacting social change. Tweed, "Crabs, Crustaceans, Crabiness, and Outrage," 454–57. On that virtue see Coles, *Beyond Gated Politics*. In a later piece, I also considered the "moral implications" of my theory: Tweed, "Theory and Method in the Study of Buddhism," 26–28. In affirming all this, I am suggesting that whatever the differences between Religious Studies and Theology, those cannot be framed simply as theologians enact values and make normative claims and religious studies scholars do not. In my pragmatic perspective, everyone engaged in the academic study of religion does that, as Thomas A. Lewis also has argued persuasively. Further, my position on the nature of religious studies aligns me more closely with the position of Atalia Omer, who suggests scholars are "critical caretakers," rather than with that of Russell McCutcheon, who sharply distinguishes scholars as either "critics" or "caretakers." Lewis, "On the Role of Normativity in Religious Studies," 168–185. Omer, "Can a Critic Be a Caretaker Too?," 459–96.

5. By using the term *diversity*, rather than *pluralism*, I am signaling that my focus here is the social fact of diversity—the presence of those with different religious, ethnic, linguistic, and cultural backgrounds—and not a particular attitude toward that social fact. Both of those terms have been used in multiple ways, of course, and there is a large scholarly literature. William R. Hutchison offered one historical account: *Religious Pluralism in America*. Some recent volumes reframe the issue in helpful ways: e.g., see Seligmann and Weller, *Rethinking Pluralism*; Cohen and Numbers, *Gods in America*; Weiner, *Religion Out Loud*.

during and after the 1960s, even if the predominant story told in textbooks and in classrooms still featured elite, white, male, Anglo-Saxon Protestants' religious beliefs, denominational institutions, and public power. By the 1980s and 1990s an acrimonious debate was underway. Using the binary categories provided by historian R. Laurence Moore's *Religious Outsiders and the Making of Americans*, assuming a static and consensualist view of culture, and presupposing a spiritual cartography that mapped concentric circles of distance from an imagined mainline Protestant center, some disputants reasserted the need to foreground the "insiders" who exerted pubic power.[6] In his survey of US religion, for example, the prominent historian of evangelical Protestantism, George Marsden, articulated a common view: "The story of American religion, if it is to hang together as a narrative, must focus on the role played by certain groups of mainstream Protestants who were for a long time the insiders with disproportional influence in shaping American culture."[7] Others disagreed. Some of those academic dissenters concentrated on producing rich case studies documenting diversity and gave up on telling a coherent narrative.[8] Or they refocused the conversation on religion as it is practiced, rather than the prescriptive beliefs of elites, and on diverse everyday spaces, from the street to the home, rather than just worship centers and the public square.[9] Some of those disquieted by the traditional account struggled to include a wider cast of characters in their narratives, while not ignoring mainline Protestants' indisputable clout in the public arena.

I cannot pretend to stand on neutral ground as I recount these developments, since I was in the middle of this scholarly scuffle. I took sides. I edited a volume, *Retelling U.S. Religious History*, that emphasized diversity and proposed new stories.[10] I wrote about Asian religions in America and studied the "embodied practices" of Latino Catholic migrants, as in my book *Our Lady of the Exile*.[11] Emphasizing transnational migration—one of the primary sources of America's religious diversity, along with regional variation and the First Amendment's non-establishment clause—I also began my theorizing about religion by attending not to Anglo-Saxon Protestant elites but to ordinary devotees at a Cuban Catholic shrine in Miami. In *Crossing*

---

6. Moore, "Insiders and Outsiders"; Moore, *Religious Outsiders and the Making of Americans*.

7. Marsden, *Religion and American Culture*, 5.

8. Many scholars in the field took this path. Robert A. Orsi was among the most influential. See Orsi, *Madonna of 115th Street*; Orsi, *Thank You, St. Jude*.

9. Hall, *Lived Religion in America*.

10. Tweed, *Retelling U.S. Religious History*.

11. Tweed, *Our Lady of the Exile*. Tweed and Prothero, *Asian Religions in America*.

and Dwelling, the theoretical work that resulted from that reflection on ritual and artifacts at that transnational devotional center, I proposed that "religions are confluences of organic-cultural flows that intensify joy and confront suffering by drawing on human and suprahuman forces to make homes and cross boundaries."[12]

In this chapter, I want to extend and apply that theory, as I shift from questions about *what* religion is to questions about *how* we might study it, especially if we are concerned to attend to diversity in all its forms. At the end of *Crossing and Dwelling* I asked "if we take this metaphor [about flows] seriously what are the methodological implications for the study of religion?"[13] My chapter title, which uses one of the two orienting metaphors that inform my theoretical reflections, hints at my primary point about method: religions are confluences of flows—emerging from the swirl of biological, psychological, cultural, economic, social, and political currents—and our task is to follow those flows wherever they lead. But saying that hardly settles things. You might be thinking that the talk about flows is fine. It suggests religion—and culture—is like a stream. Sure. But that's still too vague. What, exactly, are we being asked to do: jump on an inner tube and head for a rippling creek? The flows we're talking about are not exactly like the currents of a river, are they? So how do we follow the flows and what are the challenges we face along the way?

Santa Fe: An Illustrative Case Study

I will give an abbreviated answer to those questions about *how* we might follow the flows. Rather than focus on the port cities that I have researched previously (Miami, Boston, and San Francisco), I employ that aquatic metaphor *flow*—along with the spatial trope, *crossing*—to analyze diversity and contestation at an inland site, Santa Fe, and illustrate my methodological suggestions. That New Mexican town has a complex religious past and an intriguing spiritual present, and the altar of the oldest continuously used church in the region, San Miguel's Chapel (1599), is an apt symbol of the scholars' interpretive tasks (see figure 1.2); and other features of the local cultural landscape—including the Soldier's Monument and annual Fiesta—illustrate the variety of possible sources and corresponding methods available to the academic scholar of religion.[14]

---

12. Tweed, *Crossing and Dwelling*, 54.

13. Ibid., 171.

14. For a helpful overview of the history of Santa Fe, see Noble, *Santa Fe: History of an Ancient City*.

Figure 1.2. San Miguel's altar with view of archeological excavations in 2011. Photograph by the author.

In 1955, archeologists uncovered layers of an Analco Indian sacred site that dates to 1200 CE beneath the Catholic altar; and the commissioning religious order, the Christian Brothers, chose to display that history by placing four transparent windows across the altar's floor, so devotees at the communion rail could gaze down at the site's long past.[15] While Paleoindian remains in New Mexico suggest the presence of inhabitants more than eleven thousand years ago, ancestors of the contemporary Pueblos had settled near Santa Fe by 600 CE; and the Catholic worship space also was destroyed in the Pueblo Revolt of 1680 and later was associated with five national flags over its long history: Spanish, Mexican, Confederate, Union, and US (see figure 1.3). To add to the region's contested spiritual and political history, the Catholic settlers who reconquered Santa Fe in 1693 attributed their victory to the intercessory power of a Marian statue that had been made in Spain and transported from Mexico and had come to be called *La Conquistadora*. Her role in the reconquest is memorialized each year in the longest continuous festival in the United States, a multi-day celebration dedicated to her—and criticized by many local Pueblo Indians in recent years, as a 1992 documentary film

---

15. Stubbs and Ellis, *Archeological Investigations at the Chapel of San Miguel*. On that chapel, which has been run by the Christian Brothers, see also Lewis, *Story of San Miguel*; and Lindsley, *San Miguel Mission*.

showed when an Indian participant in the sacred drama wept on camera and said he regretted his participation in the ritual.[16]

Figure 1.3. San Miguel Chapel. Santa Fe, New Mexico, in 2011. Photograph by the author.

That year, and every other year, the fiesta's procession passed through Santa Fe's downtown streets, and in its central plaza also is a material reminder of the complications, and moral urgency, of studying present and past religious practices: *The Soldier's Monument*, dedicated in 1867 to Union troops who died in New Mexican battles during the Civil War and to New Mexicans who died fighting Indians (see figure 1.4). That sandstone obelisk with its four sides of Italian marble at its base has been a recurring source of local controversy.[17] The first debate erupted in 1909 when offended Southerners demanded that the word "rebel" be erased and replaced with "Confederate." Some called for the removal of the monument during the 1950s, and things really heated up in 1973, when members of the American Indian

16. De Bouzek, *Gathering Up Again: Fiesta in Santa Fe*.

17. Simmons, "Trail Dust." Simmons's was one voice among many in the local controversy, however. For a sense of the diverse reactions, see the collected letters to the editor for these two issues of the local newspaper: *New Mexican* (Santa Fe), August 5, 2000; *New Mexican* (Santa Fe), August 28, 2000. For an art historical perspective on monuments and memorials, see Young, "Memory/Monument." On memorialization, and angry reactions to public displays, see Doss, *Memorial Mania*, 313–76.

Movement (AIM), an activist group with "a spiritual base," declared that another phrase on the memorial was racist: "to those who have fallen in various battles with *savage* Indians," a passage legislators had added when appropriating $300 to complete the monument in 1867.[18] In the 1973 debate, the City Council initially sided with AIM but reversed their decision when the Santa Fe Historical Society threatened a lawsuit, although the following year a "vandal," a young man with a ponytail and presumed to be an Indian, stepped over the low iron fence in broad daylight and chiseled out the offending term "savage" (see figure 1.5).

Figure 1.4. **The Soldier's Monument** *(1867) in the Plaza, Santa Fe, New Mexico in 2011. Photograph by the author.*

Local controversy broke out again in 2000, only two years after another impassioned debate had erupted north of Santa Fe, when someone chopped off the right foot of a bronze statue of Juan de Oñate, whom many Hispanics celebrated as the first territorial governor of New Mexico but whom many Native Americans remembered as a brutal conqueror who in 1599 had amputated one foot of two dozen warriors from the Acoma Pueblo.[19] With that nearby dispute still in local memory, the 2000 controversy

18. Because the 1973 controversy involved AIM, it also got national coverage. E.g., see "American Notes: Revisionist History," *Time*, September 17, 1973, 22.

19. Doss, *Memorial Mania*, 313–16. As Doss notes, the public conversation in the

about the monument in Santa Fe Plaza was especially charged. Local NAACP leaders meeting at a local church suggested that the obelisk be replaced by a monument that would "make public space sacred" and "reconcile us with our Native American brothers and sisters."[20] Some Pueblos seemed offended that others—however well intended—were again speaking for them; in a letter to the newspaper's editor, for example, Nathan Youngblood argued for the memorial's preservation since the offending word already had been erased and "I have never been attacked by this monument and hold it no malice."[21] In an attempt to acknowledge and ease the recurring conflict, an additional freestanding plaque now stands in the Plaza and explains to visitors that "monument texts reflect the character of the times."

Figure 1.5. The erasure of "savages" from the **Soldier's Monument**, *Santa Fe, New Mexico, 2011. Photograph by the author.*

Santa Fe's newspaper, *The New Mexican*, included the voices of Native Americans, including P. J. Lopez, who wrote in a letter to the editor: "I'm part of the Acoma Pueblo, a descendent of those who were dishonored many years ago . . . If taking the foot off a statue was needed to make sure the whole story of Oñate was heard than [sic], so be it." Lopez, letter to the editor, *New Mexican* (Santa Fe), January 22, 1998. The statue, by the way, was repaired with a new foot.

20. Wanda Ross Padilla, letter to the editor, *New Mexican* (Santa Fe), August 5, 2000. The writer, a Santa Fe resident, identified herself as affiliated with the NAACP and directly challenged the views of local historian Marc Simmons.

21. Nathan Youngblood, letter to the editor, *New Mexican* (Santa Fe), August 5, 2000. The author identified himself as a "Native American."

That monument, and many other sites in the Santa Fe region, helps us to notice not only religious, ethnic, and linguistic diversity but also the array of potential sources and corresponding methods. Scholars from a variety of disciplines—including American studies, archeology, history, folklore, geography, cultural anthropology, art history, ethnic studies, media studies, and religious studies—have employed different approaches to study that well-document area.[22] And they've used an impressive variety of sources, not only that contested civic memorial, but also laws regulating the Plaza, letters by colonial clerics, performances of plays, interviews with local residents, debates in (Spanish-language) newspapers, art created at Protestant-sponsored Indian schools, and the many sites of indigenous religious life that extend beyond the Santa Fe Plaza.[23] Those include ancient archeological sites to the south near Clovis and not far from where the Arch Lake Woman was ritually interred more than 11,000 years ago, and, northeast of Santa Fe, *El Santuario de Chimayó*, a sacred site for descendants of Tewa- and Spanish-speaking ancestors, as well as the Puye Cliffs and Taos Pueblo, places of religious practice for centuries.[24] All these spaces, practices, and artifacts offer helpful hints about the many sources available to the scholar of religion—from archived colonial texts to contemporary pilgrim web pages, everyday domestic objects to collective public rituals, from excavated Paleoindian burial goods to vandalized war memorials.

And Religious Studies scholars have pondered varied sources and what to do with them. They have offered surveys of approaches,[25] thematically focused methodological proposals,[26] and collections of methodological essays.[27] Those works serve important functions, as does the web page

---

22. The relevant scholarly literature is large, but consider just a few studies by, in order, specialists who have affiliations with religious studies and anthropology, geography, folklore and ethnic studies, and American studies: Grimes, *Symbol and Conquest*; Mitchel and Staeheli, "Turning Social Relations into Space"; Lamadrid, *Hermanitos Comanchitos*; Meléndez, *Spanish-Language Newspapers in New Mexico*; Hahn, "Studio of Painting at the Santa Fe Indian School."

23. The sources I cite here are among the many used in the works I mentioned in the above note. The source by the colonial cleric is Juan De Escalona, letter to the Viceroy in Mexico City [1601].

24. Owsley et al., *Arch Lake Woman*. Gutiérrez, "El Santuario de Chimayó." One primary source among many others for the study of Taos Pueblo is the brochure they distribute there to fee-paying tourists, *Welcome to Taos Pueblo*.

25. E.g., Capps, *Religious Studies*.

26. E.g., Knott, *Location of Religion*; and Taves, *Religious Experience Reconsidered*. Lincoln, "Theses on Method."

27. E.g., Whaling, *Theory and Method in Religious Studies*; and Antes et al., *New Approaches to the Study of Religion*, vol. 1.

for "postgraduate students" on "Research Methods in the Study of Religion," which is especially useful on qualitative and quantitative social scientific approaches.[28] A recent volume, *The Routledge Handbook of Research Methods in the Study of Religion*, is the most comprehensive guidebook to appear.[29] Its 543 pages include thirty-three entries that offer advice on everything from "Auditory Materials" to "Videography." That sophisticated book, which is aimed at specialists, advances the conversation in many ways. However, I think it also might help to have a more accessible and brief introductory proposal about how we might draw on multiple sources and methods to make sense of religion.

Toward that end, and as a first step in that larger effort, I want to use the Santa Fe case study and my theory's guiding images to reimagine the interpretive process and propose methodological principles. If you will forgive me for flooding you with still more riverine metaphors, we might imagine the religious studies scholar's tasks as akin to getting in and out of a stream—looking around (*planning*), jumping in (*research*), and getting out (*representation*). Setting aside the first and third tasks—and the question of how values are enacted at each stage of the process—let me propose ten guiding methodological principles that describe the second task—research—and explain what "following the flows" might entail.[30]

TEN METHODOLOGICAL PRINCIPLES FOR THE STUDY OF RELIGION

Follow the Flows: Toward Deep and Broad History

We should not begin by presupposing the chronological or geographical scope of our study. We start somewhere and follow the flows *wherever* they lead. That will mean expanding the study of US religion.[31] In some cases, this

---

28. "Research Methods for the Study of Religion," University of Kent, available at http:www.kent.ac.uk/religionmethods, accessed May 12, 2014. The website was designed by Professor Gordon Lynch, the project's co-coordinator, but the entries were written by multiple scholars of religion.

29. Stausberg and Engler, *Routledge Handbook of Research Methods in the Study of Religion*.

30. These ten principles are an expansion and revision of the five "axioms" I offered in Tweed, "Theory and Method in the Study of Buddhism," available at http://www.globalbuddhism.org. See also Tweed, *Crossing and Dwelling*, 171–74. I affirm but do not defend the claim here that values are enacted at each stage of the research process, but on the larger question of values and the study of religion, see note 4 above.

31. For my fuller proposal, see Tweed, "Expanding the Study of U.S. Religion."

principle will lead us to do "deep history," as San Miguel's altar with its view of the excavated past reminds us, and "broad history," as the multiple flags that flew over the region and its many transregional connections demand.[32]

Chart the River: Consider Varying Scales—Neural Pathways to Global Trade Routes

To follow the flows and expand the scope means that we should consider the multiple and overlapping scales of analysis that impact what we are trying to trace. That might mean, for example, considering both the brain's neurological pathways and the relevant cognitive capacities (e.g., for imaginative play, social cooperation, or figurative language) that can explain the ritualized burial of the Arch Lake Woman's eleven thousand year old corpse as well as the nearby excavated objects—including sea shell beads—that demonstrate transregional trade networks that extended down the Rio Grande and to the Gulf of Mexico.

Cross the Borders: The Transdisciplinary Study of Religion

This third methodological principle emerges from the second, just as the second emerged from the first. To follow the flows by doing deep and broad history that analyzes varying scales requires that we cross disciplinary boundaries. To track the movements of people, things, and practices in the Santa Fe region requires collaboration with specialists in the natural sciences, the behavioral and social sciences, and the arts and humanities. For example, we need to be in conversation with scholars who do DNA testing of buried remains and radiocarbon dating of excavated artifacts, those who study the legal, political, and religious texts of colonial representatives and the material culture of Indians, Hispanics, and Anglos in the nineteenth century, as well as analysts who can observe contemporary practices, interpret new media, and understand the recent pathways of tourists and migrants.

---

32. Some advocates of "deep history" see it as opposed to religious history: Daniel Lord Smail has suggested that we "build a human history that breaks free from the grip of the sacred." Obviously, I disagree. Smail, *On Deep History and the Brain*, 11.

Observe Who Crosses: Documenting the Itinerant, the Settled, and the Absent

As we document those that move we need to recall that some stay put. This methodological principle, then, reminds us to notice the full range of diverse peoples. Some crossings are forced, as with Atlantic World slavery, and some crossings are blocked, as with Mexican migrants approaching the US border. Some characters in our stories move constantly, or seasonally, while others—prisoners, children, the disabled, the enslaved, the poor—sometimes cannot move when they want. Further, some are absent, either rendered invisible by our categories, sources, and methods or actually excluded from the site we are studying by legal constraints or moral codes, as with women in many public spaces in many historical periods. In short, notice who's there and who's not there.

Sense the Ripples: Toward the Multi-sensorial Study of Religion

As scholars notice who is present and absent they might employ all their senses and, in turn, attend to the ways that religious practice is more than visual. That might be obvious to anyone present at Santa Fe's annual festival amidst the jostling crowd, the sound of music, the sight of sacred theater, and the aroma and taste of food from street vendors. It can be exceptionally difficult to recover all the senses in the distant or recent past, but study of the diet of the earliest itinerant inhabitants, of the feel of the Pueblo's adobe walls, the scent of the hillside vegetation that greeted Spanish colonists, or of San Miguel Church's acoustics might yield a more textured account of religion as it was practiced.

Trace All Currents: Studying Religion's Multiple Expressions

We cannot ignore the elite's prescriptions as we analyze ordinary devotees' practices, yet we also should not give beliefs and values—even those sanctioned by institutions and enforced by leaders—more causal force than they warrant. That focus obscures much of religious life and many of the diverse participants. We should attend to the full range of religious expressions, including but not only tropes, emotions, rituals, and artifacts. In Santa Fe, the metaphor of conquest, the festival's rituals, San Miguel's architecture, the plaza's monument—and its impassioned "defacing"—provide important hints that we should not overlook.

Watch for Boats: Note Technology's Role

Technology mediates all those multiple expressions of religion; in particular, transportation and communication technologies *channel* religion's aquatic, terrestrial, and virtual flows.[33] A Spanish sailing ship transported the Marian image that became *La Conquistadora*; a web page informed devotees about the schedule for the 2011 festival in her honor.[34] We should notice the ways that technology allows and constrains modes of affiliation, practice, and exchange as we note the differences among biped, quadruped, galleon, and jet-plane religion as well as printing-press, telegraph, radio, and digital religion.[35]

Notice How Flows Start, Stop, and Shift: Attend to Power as well as Meaning

Religions negotiate power as well as make meaning, and the kinetics of dwelling and crossing are mediated not only by transportation and communication technology but also by institutional structures. All space is marked by the traces of social power wielded by institutions and their prescriptive codes and disciplinary mechanisms. So there are no unimpeded flows. The flows—of people, things, and practices—are propelled, compelled, and blocked by institutions. Extending the aquatic metaphor to explain how institutional power—as well as individual agency—is at work, we might say that institutions channel and regulate religious flows, functioning like a dam.[36] In those hydrodynamic engineering systems, walled structures divert the water's direction and "control valves" modulate its rate of flow. A large organization—a state or a corporation—usually constructs and maintains the dam, yet that collectivity also authorizes a particular person, who is subject to transmitted codes that constrain individual choice, to turn the valve and control the flow. Similar processes are at work, I suggest, as social institutions, including political states and ecclesiastical organizations, divert and modulate religions' organic-cultural flows. To understand Santa Fe's history, then, we would need to attend to the ways that itinerant bands, chiefdoms, empires, and states organized people and trace how churches,

---

33. I made this argument in Tweed, *Crossing and Dwelling*, 124–27.

34. *La Fiesta de Santa Fé*, sponsored by Santa Fe Festival Incorporated, available at www.santafefiesta.org.

35. Tweed, *Crossing and Dwelling*, 124–27.

36. I made this argument in Tweed, "Theory and Method in the Study of Buddhism," 26.

confraternities, religious orders, and other institutions directed religious flows and produced asymmetrical power relations.

Seek the Turbulence: Identify Devotees' Contestations and Sources' Reception

The asymmetries produced by meaning-making practices and enforced by power-wielding institutions suggest that—as in Santa Fe—contestation is more likely than consensus. To interpret the Plaza's memorial but ignore the erasure of the word "savage" would be to miss much. At the same time, to overlook Nathan Youngbood's competing view—just let the monument stand—would also obscure a great deal. There was—and is—no single viewpoint among Pueblo Indians—or among the other residents and participants. We should document the divergence as well as our sources allow. That does not mean, however, we search only for conflict and ignore surprising instances of convergence. This principle only reminds us to not grant any single source more authority than it deserves; it reminds us that we cannot determine a source's wider reception by pinpointing its origin or by considering a single reaction.

Avoid the Rocks: Anticipate Objections and Acknowledge Blind Spots

To seek the turbulence is not to cultivate self-destructive impulses. As we navigate the stream, we still need to notice the hazards and try to avoid them. The other nine methodological principles mark those hazards—or some of them—and at the end of the research process it can help to frankly acknowledge that, as I argued in *Crossing and Dwelling*, all theoretical itineraries and itinerant interpreters have their "blind spots."[37] That is inevitable. The aim, then, is to be as self-conscious and fair-minded as possible. Toward that end, it might help to review the other nine principles and reconsider our tentative approach and our emerging conclusions. We can ask if we unwittingly presupposed our project's geographical or chronological scope, overlooked a relevant analytical scale, or failed to engage an academic subfield that might correct a blindness. We can make sure that we carefully considered religion's material and institutional meditations. We can end the research process by asking if we have taken notice of *all* those present—and absent—and the varied multi-sensorial expressions of piety.

37. Tweed, *Crossing and Dwelling*, 14–15, 21–22, 28, 60–61, 171–78.

As this tenth principle reminds us, we are all a bit like the camera-toting observer in Shahn's watercolor, missing something crucial in our midst (see figure 1.1). Whether our positioned interpretations are benignly humorous or morally dangerous—and they can be both—it can help to think more systematically about how to study religion. My proposed methodological principles do not correct all blind spots or meet all challenges. They might help, though, even if they only provoke arguments about the research process or generate alternative lists of methodological guidelines. But, I hope, some of my ten principles—especially the suggestions to *observe who crosses, sense the ripples, trace all currents*, and *seek the turbulence*—might be especially useful for those of us who want to include diverse peoples, places, and practices in our narratives about religious life.

BIBLIOGRAPHY

Antes, Peter, et al., eds. *New Approaches to the Study of Religion*. Vol. 1, *Regional, Critical, and Historical Approaches*. New York: de Gruyter, 2004.
Capps, Walter. *Religious Studies: The Making of a Discipline*. Minneapolis: Fortress, 1995.
Cohen, Charles L., and Ronald L. Numbers, eds. *Gods in America*. New York: Oxford University Press, 2013.
Coles, Romand. *Beyond Gated Politics: Reflections for the Possibility of Democracy*. Minneapolis: University of Minnesota Press, 2005.
De Bouzek, Jeanette. *Gathering Up Again: Fiesta in Santa Fe*. Documentary Film. 46 minutes. Color. BetaSP. Santa Fe: Quotidian Independent Documentary Research, 1992.
De Escalona, Juan. Letter to the Viceroy in Mexico City. 1601. Reprinted in *Don Juan de Oñate, Colonizer of New Mexico, 1595–1628*, by George P. Hammond and Agapito Rey, 2:692–95. Albuquerque: University of New Mexico Press, 1953.
Doss, Erika L. *Memorial Mania: Public Feeling in America*. Chicago: University of Chicago Press, 2010.
Grimes, Ronald L. *Symbol and Conquest: Public Ritual and Drama in Santa Fe, New Mexico*. Ithaca, NY: Cornell University Press, 1976.
Gutiérrez, Ramón. "El Santuario de Chimayó: A Syncretic Shrine in New Mexico." In *Feasts and Celebrations in North American Ethnic Communities*, edited by Ramón Gutiérrez and Geneviève Fabre, 71–86. Albuquerque: University of New Mexico Press, 1995.
Hahn, Milanne Shelburne. "The Studio of Painting at the Santa Fe Indian School: A Case Study in Modern American Identity." PhD diss., University of Texas at Austin, 2011.
Hall, David D., ed. *Lived Religion in America: Toward a History of Practice*. Princeton: Princeton University Press, 1997.
Hutchison, William R. *Religious Pluralism in America: The Contentious History of a Founding Ideal*. New Haven: Yale University Press, 2003.
Knott, Kim. *The Location of Religion: A Spatial Analysis*. London: Equinox, 2005.

Lamadrid, Enrique R. *Hermanitos Comanchitos: Indo-Hispano Rituals of Captivity and Redemption*. Albuquerque: University of New Mexico Press, 2003.

Lewis, B. *The Story of San Miguel, Oldest Chapel in the U.S.* Santa Fe: San Miguel Church, 1968.

Lewis, Thomas A. "On the Role of Normativity in Religious Studies." In *The Cambridge Companion to Religious Studies*, edited by Robert A. Orsi, 168–85. New York: Cambridge University Press, 2012.

Lincoln, Bruce. "Theses on Method." *Method and Theory in the Study of Religion* 8.3 (1996): 225–227.

Lindsey, Richard Mark. *San Miguel Mission*. Eight-page pamphlet. Santa Fe: San Miguel Chapel, n.d.

Marsden, George. *Religion and American Culture*. New York: Harcourt Brace Jovanovich, 1990.

McCutcheon, Russell T. *Critics Not Caretakers: Redescribing the Public Study of Religion*. Albany: State University of New York Press, 2001.

McDannell, Colleen. *Picturing Faith: Photography and the Great Depression*. New Haven: Yale University Press, 2004.

Meléndez, A. Gabriel. *Spanish-Language Newspapers in New Mexico, 1834–1958*. Tucson: University of Arizona Press, 2005.

Mitchell, Don, and Lynn A. Staeheli. "Turning Social Relations into Space: Property, Law, and the Plaza of Santa Fe, New Mexico." *Landscape Research* 30 (2005) 361–78.

Moore, R. Laurence. "Insiders and Outsiders in American Historical Narrative and American History." *American Historical Review* 87 (1982) 390–412.

———. *Religious Outsiders and the Making of Americans*. New York: Oxford University Press, 1986.

Noble, David Grant, ed. *Santa Fe: History of an Ancient City*. Santa Fe: School for Advanced Research Press, 2008.

Omer, Atalia. "Can a Critic Be a Caretaker Too? Religion, Conflict, and Conflict Transformation." *Journal of the American Academy of Religion* 79 (2011) 459–96.

Orsi, Robert A. *The Madonna of 115th Street: Faith and Community in Italian Harlem, 1880–1950*. New Haven: Yale University Press, 1985.

———. *Thank You, St. Jude: Women's Devotion to the Patron Saint of Hopeless Causes*. New Haven: Yale University Press, 1996.

Owsley, Douglas W., et al. *Arch Lake Woman: Physical Anthropology and Geoarcheology*. College Station: Texas A&M Press, 2010.

Page, Kirby. *Must We Go to War?* New York: Farrar & Reinhart, 1937.

Putnam, Hilary. *The Collapse of the Fact/Value Dichotomy and Other Essays*. Cambridge: Harvard University Press, 2002.

Seligmann, Adam B., and Robert P. Weller, eds. *Rethinking Pluralism: Ritual, Experience, and Ambiguity*. New York: Oxford University Press, 2012.

Simmons, Marc. "Trail Dust: Soldiers Monument on Plaza Has Survived Repeated Controversies." *New Mexican* (Santa Fe), October 14, 2000.

Smail, Daniel Lord. *On Deep History and the Brain*. Berkeley: University of California Press, 2008.

Stausberg, Michael. "The Study of Religion(s) in Western Europe (I): Prehistory and History until World War II." *Religion* 37 (2007) 294–318.

Stausberg, Michael, and Steven Engler, eds. *The Routledge Handbook on Research Methods in the Study of Religion*. London: Routledge, 2011.

Stubbs, Stanley A., and Bruce T. Ellis. *Archeological Investigations at the Chapel of San Miguel and the Site of a Castrense, Santa Fe, New Mexico.* Monographs of the School of American Research 20. Santa Fe: School of American Research, 1955.

Taves, Ann. *Religious Experience Reconsidered: A Building Block Approach to the Study of Religion and Other Special Things.* Princeton: Princeton University Press, 2009.

Tweed, Thomas A. "American Occultism and Japanese Buddhism: Albert J. Edmunds, D. T. Suzuki, and Translocative History." *Japanese Journal of Religious Studies* 32 (2005) 249–81.

———. *America's Church: The National Shrine and Catholic Presence in the Nation's Capital.* Oxford: Oxford University Press, 2011.

———. "Crabs, Crustaceans, Crabiness, and Outrage: A Response." *Journal of the American Academy of Religion* 77 (2009) 454–57.

———. *Crossing and Dwelling: A Theory of Religion.* Cambridge: Harvard University Press, 2006.

———. "Expanding the Study of U.S. Religion: Reflections on the State of a Subfield." *Religion* 40 (2010) 250–58.

———. *Our Lady of the Exile: Diasporic Religion at a Cuban Catholic Shrine in Miami.* Oxford: Oxford University Press, 1997.

———, ed. *Retelling U.S. Religious History.* Berkeley: University of California Press, 1997.

———. "Space." Special issue on "Key Words in Material Religion." *Material Religion: The Journal of Objects, Art, and Belief* 7 (2011) 116–23.

———. "Theory and Method in the Study of Buddhism: Toward 'Translocative' Analysis." *Journal of Global Buddhism* 12 (2011) 17–32.

Tweed, Thomas A., and Stephen Prothero, eds. *Asian Religions in America: A Documentary History.* Oxford: Oxford University Press, 1999.

Weiner, Isaac. *Religion Out Loud: Religious Sound, Public Space, and American Pluralism.* New York: New York University Press, 2014.

Welcome to Taos Pueblo. Six-page tourism brochure. Taos, New Mexico: Taos Pueblo Tourism, 2011.

Whaling, Frank, ed. *Contemporary Approaches to the Study of Religion.* Vol. 1, *The Humanities.* New York: Mouton, 1983.

———, ed. *Contemporary Approaches to the Study of Religion.* Vol. 2, *The Social Sciences.* New York: Mouton, 1985.

———, ed. *Theory and Method in Religious Studies: Contemporary Approaches to the Study of Religion.* New York: de Gruyter, 1995.

Young, James E. "Memory/Monument." In *Critical Terms for Art History*, edited by Robert S. Nelson and Richard Shiff, chap. 16. 2nd ed. Chicago: University of Chicago, 2003.

2

Between the One and the Many in the Study of Religious Pluralism
A Response to Thomas Tweed

FRANCISCA CHO
Georgetown University

THOMAS TWEED'S VISION OF the study of religion mandates that we recognize the diversity and multiplicity of flows that make up the stream of a single "religion" such as Christianity, Buddhism, and so forth. He enumerates ten methodological principles for negotiating the complexity of these putative wholes, but his central and organizing directive seems to be contained in the sixth principle of "trace all currents." Here we are urged to go beyond the normative texts and formal prescriptions of a tradition to examine its robust range of religious participants and expressions. It is here in the multiplicity of such expressions, with their convergences, tensions and contestations that one can "seek the turbulence," as mandated by Tweed's ninth principle, and the role of institutions and power, as instructed by the eighth principle. Moreover, it is by putting a face on these diverse expressions that we can attempt to observe, in accordance with the fourth principle, *all* of those who move and cross between these flows—as well as to ask after those who are absent. And it is the task of interpreting these multiple expressions that move us to cross disciplinary borders (third principle), encompass multiples scales of analysis (second principle), appreciate the multi-sensory nature of religion (fifth principle), and discern the role of technology in enabling ever new forms of expression (seventh principle).

I appreciate Dr. Tweed's ambition to "trace all currents" because the phrase "religious pluralism" points not only to the fact that there are many religions in the world, but that each religion is an amalgamation of many diverse currents, some of which are parallel and rarely meet, some of which directly counteract each other, and some of which converge for awhile to mingle and diverge again into reconfigured flows. Nor are these diverse currents all internally generated. Some cross over from other religious as well as non-religious flows, reminding us that what we call "Christianity" or "Buddhism" or "Islam" are abstractions we create for the purpose of discourse, whose boundaries can be endlessly redrawn depending on the purpose and scale of our analysis. The metaphor of flowing water reminds us that religions are *processes* rather than *things*, ever malleable and in motion.

Having noted these critical insights that Dr. Tweed brings to our attention, I would like to take a step further by bringing out some of the challenges that "tracing all currents" presents, and some necessary mitigating observations. Dr. Tweed describes the contentious process in the study of American religions in which one coherent narrative of religion was opened up to include religion as it is practiced rather than only preached; to include religion in everyday spaces in addition to centers of worship and authority; and to include a wider cast of agents than traditional accounts have allowed. This process of becoming more inclusive has in fact affected the study of all religions. This greatly complicates our ability to make sense of things and even leads, as Prof. Tweed notes, to giving up on telling a coherent narrative at all. To many scholars nurtured in postmodern and postcolonial theory, this incoherence is a good thing and a necessary corrective to the universalizing narratives that have obliterated diversity or cast it as a deviation.

I count myself among those who embrace the expansion of the stories we tell, but I also fear the fragmentation that can result as we collect and document an ever-growing body of data and multiply the subdisciplines that are required for tracing all of these diverse currents. So even as we commit to expanding what we take into account, we must simultaneously affirm that the study of religion, as a human science, requires more than the sheer accumulation of data. Accumulation alone means the analysis of increasingly particulate phenomena that are stranded into self-contained islands of knowledge. This creates difficulty in getting a picture of large-scale phenomena and offers a specious completeness via the assembly of microscopic facts. We must retain the ability to explain all that information, and that requires some explicit thinking about the nature and conditions of knowledge. Natural history began as an inventory of biodiversity, and was commonly denigrated as mere "stamp collecting" until the theory of evolution gave it a unifying framework. The study of religions also requires unifying frameworks in order to shape and give meaning to our proliferating information.

What I advocate here, however, should not be confused with another quite different and still continuing conceit of completeness in our knowledge of things—the universalizing theory. This pitfall consists in putting undue trust in any single theory or interpretation of religion as the key that unlocks the religious universe. In referring to the domain of biology above, I do not advocate a religious studies equivalent to the theory of evolution, with the overarching role it plays in framing, making sense of, and even generating multiple domains of biological information. Religion is much more complex than biology because it includes much more than biological phenomena. The deep and broad history that Dr. Tweed calls for in his first principle covers everything, as he notes, from the neurological to global cultural and environmental flows. The study of religion indeed implicates and benefits from these multiple layers of analysis. Therefore the study of religion requires a diversity of theories, rather than a unifying explanation, in order to attend to the complexity of religion.

I make this point because the proliferation of information regularly prompts the search for a theory that appears to makes sense of it all. In an earlier age, such theories abounded, but they tend to make the synecdochic error of taking one part for the whole, whether that part comes from social scientific insights into the psychological, economic, or social structural nature of religion, or the abstract and ideal pictures provided by canonical texts. Currently, the effort known as the cognitive science of religion (CSR) dominates theorizing about religion. Although the experimental data from cognitive psychology generating this subdiscipline is new, exciting, and revealing, the often overreaching claims about its ability to explain the whence and whither of religion based on limited and preliminary insights is a familiar move.[1] To be sure, thinking about certain aspects of religion relative to demonstrable cognitive mechanisms evolved by the brain for apparently

---

1. Stausberg, *Contemporary Theories of Religion*, offers fifteen review articles of the most prominent recent books that offer theories of religion. Thomas Tweed's own *Crossing and Dwelling* (2006) is reviewed by Aaron Hughes. But more apropos of my current point, the vast majority of the books reviewed have a cognitive scientific focus, such as E. Thomas Lawson and Robert McCauley's *Rethinking Religion* (1990), Stewart Guthrie's *Faces in the Clouds* (1993), Pascal Boyer's *Religion Explained* (2001), Ilkka Pyysiäinen's *How Religion Works* (2003), Daniel Dennett's *Breaking the Spell* (2006). Yet others share the focus on evolutionary explanations, such as Scott Atran's *In Gods We Trust* (2002) and David Sloan Wilson's *Darwin's Cathedral* (2002), and on the brain, such as David Lewis-Williams and David Pearce's *Inside the Neolithic Mind* (2005).

evolutionarily adaptive purposes is useful and explanatory in certain ways. But in too many instances of such theorizing, there is no reflection on the limits of what the theory can explain, and the phenomenon of "religion" is shrunk to ignore or eliminate whatever falls outside the theory's purview.[2]

This problem is implicitly recognized in Dr. Tweed's tenth and final principle: acknowledge the blind spots. To reiterate his words: "all theoretical itineraries and itinerant interpreters have their 'blind spots' . . . The aim, then, is to be as self-conscious and fair-minded as possible." This council readily applies to all past and present theories of religion. We need to affirm that a productive explanation of any phenomenon must self-consciously disavow the claim to account for all of the data. Talk of brain states, for example, cannot fully account for the poetic, the social, and the semiotic nature of religious experiences. This must be understood so that no single theory is allowed to diminish what we can take into account for the sake of a specious completeness. I trust that I am preaching to the choir as far as this point is concerned.

But we also need to exercise this self-consciousness and fair-mindedness when it comes to the opposite and perhaps more dominant current tendency to eschew the universal theory for the many localized differences. Professor Tweed suggests that we can mitigate our blind spots by increasing the information we take into account. We must be conscious of the fact, however, that this is not an alternative path to accounting for everything there is. On the contrary, sustained pursuit of the particular shows us that it is impossible to attain completeness in any knowledge domain, no matter how small or delimited. Any system involving humans is so informationally dense we can extract only a microscopic portion of what is going on. This is true of the totality that we call religion, but also of minute subsystems such as the single individual. Even a single person is too complex to fully encompass, meaning that we must be satisfied with partial accounts. For any sufficiently complex system, no complete description can be significantly smaller than the system itself. Therefore, major aspects of the system's

---

2. Another notable aspect of much CSR literature is that it expresses the ideological view that scientific explanations comprise a level of discourse that transcends and corrects religious ones, in that religion is the unintended consequence of automatic brain functions whereas science unmasks and therefore liberates itself from these same functions. This new version of the standard "science versus religion" dichotomy not only drags CSR into this modern Western culture war, it embodies all the mythologies that come with it. For a recent statement of the ascendancy of science over religion from a CSR author, see Robert McCauley's *Why Religion Is Natural and Science Is Not* (2011), as well as my own response to its agenda in "Unnatural Comparisons: Commentary on Robert McCauley's *Why Religion Is Natural and Science Is Not*," forthcoming in *Religion, Brain and Behavior*, March 2013.

behavior will be incorrectly described or inferred. Any humanly tractable analysis or discussion is therefore necessarily incomplete and ad hoc. We are forever in this situation regardless of what we study: the system itself and what we are able to observe of it are two different things. This must be understood so that we do not replace the specious completeness of universalizing theories with the illusion of thoroughness given by voluminous descriptions of particulates.

We are not helpless as a result, however. In fact, the study of complex systems requires limiting what we take into account at any given time. Any system can be simplified, neglecting the majority of information present either due to limitations in our observational capacity or deliberate selectiveness for the sake of manageability. Simple properties can be extracted from these systems. For example, one could abstract from all human activity and estimate the average mass of the individual, ignoring everything else, and derive a highly reliable universal property. Whether or not this is interesting information depends on the context and the questions being asked. The point is that a careful selection from the endless available information about humans is the mechanism with which we can discover knowledge.[3]

An example from the natural sciences perhaps helps to illustrate and clarify this point. In the case of planetary motion, observational limitations did the information filtering for us, in that the only thing one could observe during the time of Tycho Brahe, Johannes Kepler, Nicholaus Copernicus and Issac Newton were the angular positions of planetary bodies. The result was a distillation into the more interesting model of Newtonian mechanics, which reveals relational properties of the system in a concise manner that summarizes a large collection of individual observations. This modeling makes the information meaningful by making visible the stable relationships between planetary entities. This relational knowledge is conceptually enlightening, provides explanatory power, enables predictions, and is prescriptive for designing and implementing systems.

The same insights apply to religious systems. There is certainly a time and place for cataloging the diversity of liturgical practices within Christianity, or the many versions of emptiness doctrine in Buddhism. But an equally important task is to articulate what knowledge is gained from this data. This knowledge is not predicated on the completeness of the data but rather the ability to answer specific questions. Very simple questions can be asked and answered from mere compilations of data, as with the example of the average mass of human beings. Interesting and complex questions, on

---

3. For more detailed discussion of how insights from systems theory can be applied to the study of religion, see my article, "Religion as a Complex and Dynamic System," coauthored with Richard K. Squier.

the other hand, require creativity in which we construct conceptual entities by abstracting from the particulars and looking for causal or systemic relationships between them.

Some of the key conceptual entities constructed by Newtonian mechanics are mass, gravitational action, and momentum. The greater complexity of human behavior allows for many more conceptual entities, such as belief, ritual, embodiment, experience, gender, rationality, culture, and so forth. The most important point, however, is that these conceptual entities, and the relationships between them, cannot be found in the data itself. They are the frameworks we impose for the purposes of our understanding. This necessarily means stripping out, summarizing, and boiling down our raw data to reveal systematic properties embedded in the whole. Incompleteness of information does not make explanation and knowledge impossible. In the absence of both unifying theories and complete descriptions, we can abstract out interesting systems and make reliable sense of them by considering questions that the system can meaningfully address.

Every meaningful question requires abstractions, but we must simultaneously recognize that every abstraction is limited in its applicability and in what it enables us to know. Therefore no single abstraction can speak to every question we have. An unfortunate legacy of Newtonian mechanics, with its milestone status in the history of science, was the resulting belief in the possibility of complete knowledge of the physical universe. But as time went by and more observations were made, more complexity was discovered and the Newtonian picture was rendered less complete and less universal. Pierre-Simon Laplace's postulation of a single formula that could account for the past, present and future of the universe has been cast into shadow in light of the complexity of the world.[4] What this lesson bodes, in terms of self-consciousness and fair-mindedness, is that the knowledge we construct results primarily from our own questions rather than the completeness of

---

4. Pierre-Simon Laplace wrote in 1814, "We may regard the present state of the universe as the effect of its past and the cause of its future. An intellect which at a certain moment would know all forces that set nature in motion, and all positions of all items of which nature is composed, if this intellect were also vast enough to submit these data to analysis, it would embrace in a single formula the movements of the greatest bodies of the universe and those of the tiniest atom; for such an intellect nothing would be uncertain and the future just like the past would be present before its eyes" (Truscott and Emory, *Philosophical Essay on Probabilities*, 4). Aside from the fact that Laplace's intellect is not humanly possible due to our limited computational powers, the chaotic nature of the universe limits its predictability, thermodynamic entropy and the consequent irreversibility is an apparent fact of life, and finally, quantum mechanics postulates a fundamental unpredictability.

our observations. The important issue becomes, then, what questions we choose to ask and why.

In the process of tracing all currents, we must have a clear understanding of why we are undertaking this effort. Certainly, representing those who have been ignored is both a moral and an empirical good. But these varied and diverse voices are much more than the means of augmenting an ongoing census of the religious life on our planet. If we understand our task to be the formulation of questions and frameworks of interpretation that create knowledge that is important to us, then we must trace diverse currents because they can help us to formulate these questions and frameworks. These currents are not merely our data but voices that impinge on our own thinking process. These voices help us to see the limits of our previous questions and help us to formulate new ones. These voices are not only the objects of our scholarship but our partners in determining the significant abstractions that form our knowledge itself.

Dr. Tweed's metaphors of streams and currents convey one very important way in which religious pluralism urges us to change the way we think about religion and the questions we ask about it. What we observe suggests that our traditional conception of religions as bounded entities that sustain themselves by maintaining their separateness from other religious and non-religious communities limits what we can know about them. In contrast, to think about religions as porous processes that can be visualized only in relation to adjacent processes with which they interact, converge, and diverge, opens up a whole new arena of questions, conceptual abstractions and research possibilities. This allows us to reimagine the past history of religions through the lenses of what is more readily apparent today—that "otherness" is the stuff from which tradition is made. This also changes our value system, in which our standard notion of religious syncretism, borrowings, and contamination as forms of deviation are flipped into the norms of religious systems. This is an insight that comes directly from tracing those currents that have not traditionally been represented in the study of religions.

In closing, I return to the observation that both the pursuit of the one grand theory and the many local details are prone to the fallacy of completeness, through the conceit that it is possible to sufficiently account for what there is in the world. Wherever one's work may fall on the spectrum between the one and the many, it is important that the study of religious pluralism not fall prey to the temptation and specter of completeness, which breeds either the conceit of success or the reactive response of simple bean counting. Hence I have taken this opportunity to flesh in Dr. Tweed's prime directive of "tracing all currents" to mean first and foremost a self-consciousness that it is the power of our imaginations that determines what religion is, and a fair-mindedness about the many different quarters and many different ways in which that imagination is realized.

BIBLIOGRAPHY

Atran, Scott. *In Gods We Trust: The Evolutionary Landscape of Religion*. New York: Oxford University Press, 2002.
Boyer, Pascal. *Religion Explained: The Evolutionary Origins of Religious Thought*. New York: Basic Books, 2001.
Cho, Francisca "Unnatural Comparisons: Commentary on Robert McCauley's *Why Religion Is Natural and Science Is Not*." *Religion, Brain and Behavior* 3 (2013) 119–125.
Cho, Francisca, and Richard K. Squier. "Religion as a Complex and Dynamic System." *Journal of the American Academy of Religion* 81 (2013) 357–98.
Dennett, Daniel. *Breaking the Spell: Religion as a Natural Phenomenon*. New York: Viking, 2006.
Guthrie, Stewart. *Faces in the Clouds: A New Theory of Religion*. New York: Oxford University Press, 1993.
Lewis-Williams, David, and David Pearce. *Inside the Neolithic Mind: Consciousness, Cosmos, and the Realm of the Gods*. London: Thames & Hudson, 2005.
McCauley, Robert. *Why Religion Is Natural and Science Is Not*. New York: Oxford University Press, 2011.
McCauley, Robert, and E. Thomas Lawson. *Rethinking Religion: Connecting Cognition and Culture*. New York: Cambridge University Press, 1990.
Pyysiäinen, Ilkka. *How Religion Works: Towards a New Cognitive Science of Religion*. Cognition and Culture Book Series 1. Boston: Brill, 2003.
Stausberg, Michael, ed. *Contemporary Theories of Religion: A Critical Companion*. London: Routledge, 2009.
Truscott, F. W., and F. L. Emory, eds. *A Philosophical Essay on Probabilities*. Translated by Pierre Simon from the 6th French ed. Dover, 1951.
Wilson, David Sloan. *Darwin's Cathedral: Evolution, Religion, and the Nature of Society*. Chicago: University of Chicago Press, 2002.

3

Botánicas
Sacred Sites of Plural Religious Encounter

JOSEPH M. MURPHY

BOTÁNICAS ARE SHOPS THAT sell "religious goods" in Latino neighborhoods throughout the United States. The MANTA business directory lists over 1300 stores in the United States with "botánica" in their names, and there are likely many more without it. Botánicas are at once retail stores, religious shrines, and places of spiritual counsel. The merchandise of the botánica reflects the needs of immigrants and other marginalized peoples who often lack access to adequate health care and legal protection. At the botánica, patrons can find spiritual help for all manner of practical problems with health or with relationships or with money. As the name implies, botánicas sell herbs that can be prepared to treat an illness or protect the home. The power of the herbs is believed to lie in the spiritual power of *santos*, a Spanish word that includes the English meaning of "saints" but implies something more like invisible healing agencies. Supplementing their herbal remedies, the botánica sells religious statues and candles for use on home altars dedicated to an extraordinarily diverse pantheon of *santos* of European, African, Asian and Native American origin. These devotions have intertwined for hundreds of years among Latin American peoples in their homelands and have more recently been brought together in new combinations at botánicas in the United States.

In this paper I will discuss the notion of religious pluralism as it is lived by urban American Latinos. From their rich and multiple religious heritages they have constructed functioning spiritualities that sustained them in their homelands and continue to inspire them in the United States. By examining the ways in which they have organized and juxtaposed symbols from these multiple traditions, insight into religious comparison and plural coexistence may be realized. I am arguing that the complex inter-relationships among religious traditions that have been forged by Latinos may provide a useful model for on-going discussions of pluralism by theologians and students of religion. The example of people actually leading fulfilling religious lives derived from multiple religious sources can be seen as a compelling and vital resource for understanding pluralism as it is practiced in America today.

RELIGIOUS ROOTS OF THE BOTÁNICA

The religious roots of the botánica may be traced to the momentous cultural encounters stemming from the European discovery and conquest of the Americas. Fortified by centuries of religious militancy in the reconquest and re-Catholicization of Iberia, Spanish and Portuguese adventurers set out to the new world to claim souls and riches for Cross and Crown. In a declaration of 1493, Pope Alexander VI divided the new lands for Christian mission. The famous papal bull states:

> Among other works well pleasing to the Divine Majesty and cherished of our heart, this assuredly ranks highest, that in our times especially the Catholic faith and the Christian religion be exalted and be everywhere increased and spread, that the health of souls be cared for and that barbarous nations be overthrown and brought to the faith itself.[1]

The spread and exaltation of the Catholic faith in the Americas was carried out with the violent overthrow of the indigenous nations of the Taino, Arawak, Mexica, Maya, Inca and a host of others. Dominican friar Bartolomé de Las Casas accompanied the first wave of conquistadores and chronicled the devastation they wrought in the Caribbean. He tells of Hatuey, a Taino chief (*cacique*) who had fled to Cuba to escape the depredations of the Spanish. Captured and awaiting execution for his resistance to the conquest, Hatuey experienced this encounter with the Christian message. Las Casas writes:

> When tied to the stake the cacique Hatuey was told by a Franciscan friar who was present, an artless rascal, something about

---

1. "Inter Caetera Divinae," in Davenport, *European Treaties Bearing on the History of the United States*, 40.

the God of the Christians and of the articles of the Faith. And he was told what he could do in the brief time that remained to him, in order to be saved and go to Heaven. The cacique, who had never heard of any of this before, and he was told he would go to Inferno where, if he not adopt the Christian Faith, he would suffer eternal torment, asked the Franciscan friar if Christians all went to Heaven. When told that they did he said he would prefer to go to Hell. Such is the fame and honor that God and our Faith have earned through the Christians who have gone out to the Indies.[2]

The dreadful toll on the native populations from conquest, forced labor, and old-world diseases prompted European entrepreneurs to import slaves from Africa to work in the mines, plantations, and shipyards of the growing colonies. Between 1492 and 1860 some nine million enslaved African men, women, and children were shipped to Latin America bringing with them their own histories, cultures, and religious traditions.[3]

As with the indigenous populations of the Americas the enslavement of Africans was often justified by the commandment to bring Christianity to them, offering the eternal life of salvation for a temporal life of servitude. While the Spanish and Portuguese evangelizers can justly boast of heroic and compassionate missionaries such as Fra Bernardino de Sahagún among the Mexica of New Spain and Pedro Claver with Africans in Cartegena, the Native and African experience of Christianity was characterized far more often by coercion and repression. Conversions were carried out in situations of forced labor and enslavement. The Inquisition in New Spain executed "idolaters" who had returned to Native religious practices and the Cuban government suppressed African "*brujería*" or "witchcraft" where they could find it.[4] In response to this imposition of Christianity "from above" Native and African peoples developed initiatives "from below." In addition to outright resistance to Spanish conquest and evangelization such as that of Hatuey, Native and African peoples employed other strategies. In a remarkable document written in Spanish by the indigenous historian Titu Kusi in 1570, the last Incan emperor, Manku Inka, addresses his people with this advice concerning the Christian advance:

> You must do this: if there should come a time when they tell you to adore what they adore—what they say is Wiraquchan [the

---

2. Las Casas, *Devastation of the Indies*, 45.
3. Curtin, *Atlantic Slave Trade*.
4. See Moreno de los Arcos, "New Spain's Inquisition for Indians from the Sixteenth to the Nineteenth Century," and Ortiz, *Los Negros Brujos*.

Creator] are but painted clothes, and when they say to adore them as waka [sacred], which is but cloth, do not obey. Instead, adore what we hold dear, for, as you can see, the Willkas [divinities] speak to us; and the Sun and the Moon, see them through our own eyes and what they speak of we do not see well. I believe that at some point, by force or deceit, they will have you adore what they adore. When you cannot resist any longer, make the motions before them but never forget our own ceremonies. And if they tell you to shatter your wakas, and do so by force, show them what you must and hide the rest. In this, you will greatly please me.[5]

Here we see Native initiatives at work. First Manku tells his people not to adore the "painted clothes" that the Spanish worship, but to hold fast to the indigenous *willkas*. Yet he anticipates that they will be forced to adore the Spanish divinity(ies) and so he counsels them to make the motions of worship before the Spanish, but to continue to worship the indigenous powers in secret. Thus we have a kind of basic bi-religiousness: an overt participation in Christian worship and a covert commitment to the indigenous divinities.

This double cultural and religious situation was described by Robert Redfield in his studies of the Yucatan as an interactive relationship between a "great tradition" brought from Europe and imposed from above and a "little tradition" developed by indigenous peoples in response to the "great tradition."[6] The universal, official and theological Christianity of the Roman Catholic Church is, of course, the great tradition in the lives of most Latin American peoples. The Church formed the "sacred canopy" that legitimated the social order in the Spanish and Portuguese colonies. The various little traditions are, by contrast, plural, developed in each community with its own unforgotten ceremonies and spiritual powers. As the great tradition seeks to impress local communities into the colonial order, the little traditions offer complex forms of both resistance and accommodation to the great tradition. And as the great tradition tends toward universalizing, philosophical religion concerned with salvation and the afterlife, the little traditions are localizing, practical religions that address the everyday concerns of survival and health.[7]

In the "little traditions" of Latin America evangelized peoples developed correspondences between the religion imposed "from above" and the

5. Yupanqui, *Titu Cusi: A Sixteenth-Century Account of the Conquest*, 171.

6. Redfield, *Little Community and Peasant Society and Culture*.

7. See Leach, *Dialectic in Practical Religion*, and Yoder, "Toward a Definition of Folk Religion."

indigenous religious traditions preserved "from below." Perhaps the most famous of these religious parallelisms is the relationships that were created between the Catholic saints and the African spirits called *orishas* by enslaved Yoruba peoples in Cuba and Brazil. Forced as the Native peoples had been into venerating the Catholic saints, enslaved Yoruba men and women created direct and thoughtful correspondences between the Spanish and African spirits. Santa Barbara, the virgin martyr and patroness of soldiers was paralleled to Changó, the mighty *orisha* of royal power. La Virgén de la Caridad del Cobre, the be-jeweled patroness of Cuba was juxtaposed with Ochún, the *orisha* of riches and sweet water. Thus on the feast days of the Catholic saints, in the churches and street processions and home altars, enslaved and free Africans could venerate their *orishas* before the icons of the appropriate Catholic saints. Fernando Ortiz documented this phenomenon in Cuba in the early twentieth century:

> In Cuba and in Brazil, the same logic is shown in the way Blacks assimilate their *orishas* with the Catholic saints. Shangó is equivalent to Santa Bárbara. Both divinities are patrons of thunder and lightning . . . The sorcerer Bocú defended himself skillfully before the tribunal that had condemned him, saying that the altar that he had in his house was dedicated to a Catholic divinity, to Santa Bárbara, and so, therefore, he was not a sorcerer.[8]

Yet while this parallelism of Christian and African religious symbols served to disguise the veneration of the *orishas*, something more subtle than simple disguise is going on. First the Africans chose actual religious figures—*santos*—to correspond to the *orishas* and so recognized between them similarities of religious status, patronage functions, and styles of worship. This concentration on *santos* is the reason why the tradition of parallelism is often called "Santería," the "way of the *santos*." The emphasis on at least the outward iconography of Catholicism would indicate that it has some force in order to represent the religion of the *orishas*. Next, the correspondences between *santo* and *orisha* are thoughtful rather than arbitrary. The two share attributes in iconography and narrative. Santa Barbara and Changó, as we have seen, are both associated with the lethal power of thunder and lightning. La Virgén de la Caridad and Ochún share concerns with water, riches, and childbirth.[9] The evangelized Yoruba in the Americas did not pick saintly correspondences arbitrarily but carefully, and the closer that one looks at the functions and attributes of the corresponded figures, the

---

8. Ortiz, *Los Negros Brujos*, 33.

9. Joseph M. Murphy, "Yéyé Cachita: Ochún in a Cuban Mirror," ch. 7 in Murphy and Sanford, eds., *Osun Across the Waters*.

more thoughtful they seem. Finally we can look at this parallelism as more than a disguise, since they have carried through to these relatively liberated times when the police power of church and state are no longer brought to bear on idolaters and sorcerers. Latin American peoples touched by Santería continue to maintain the parallelism when their religious oppression has been lifted.[10] And so I am arguing that we have a genuine juxtaposition of religious symbols, living together in a dynamic, mutually enhancing relationship in the lives of many Latin American peoples and patrons of the botánicas in the United States. It is to this multiple religious participation that we will return when we consider the "pluralism" of the botánica. For now let us visit the stores and see the spiritualities on display.

RELIGIONS OF THE BOTÁNICA

While most of the "little traditions" of Latin America were brought to the United States in the twentieth century, it should not be forgotten that one third of the territory of the continental United States was once "Latino" and that Latin American religious traditions have been on what is now US soil far longer than those from the English-speaking world. As Mexican-American filmmaker and writer Luis Valdéz has said, "We did not, in fact, come to the United States at all. The United States came to us."[11] Through annexations of Mexican territory and the spoils of the Spanish American War, the United States developed sustained interrelationships with several Latin American peoples whose labor in fields and factories became crucial to the US economy. While Cuba achieved its independence in 1902, Puerto Rico became a US territory and its peoples declared American citizens in 1917. In the cities of the Northeast, particularly the city of New York, Puerto Ricans became a permanent part of the city's ethnic landscape and the "little tradition" of Puerto Rican *espiritismo* a thriving religious movement in El Barrio, East Harlem.[12] Migene González-Wippler says that the name "botánica" was coined by Puerto Ricans in New York as the nickname of a store in East Harlem called "Botanical Gardens" that sold fresh herbs and herbal remedies.[13]

---

10. See Afro-Cuban priest and musician Felipe Garcia Villamil's defense of the Catholic correspondences in *orisha* traditions in Vélez, *Drumming for the Gods*, 141.

11. Quoted in Rumbaut, "Americans: Latin American and Caribbean Peoples in the United States," 279.

12. See Wakefield, *Island in the City*, and Pérez y Mena, *Speaking with the Dead*.

13. González-Wippler, *Santería: The Religion*.

US policies and interventions in the latter half of the twentieth century have led to massive migrations of other Latin American peoples, notably Cubans, Guatemalans and Salvadorans. Each people has brought its own "little tradition" of accommodation and resistance to Catholicism calling upon indigenous and African *santos* in distinctive iconographies and ceremonies. It is these traditions, each a plural construction in itself, which have been transplanted at botánicas today where they are building new correspondences among themselves and among new influences in the American religious milieu.

Amid the variety of traditions at the botánica it will be useful to look at the devotions to two representative *santos* in order to convey a sense of the organization of multiple religions. As we have said botánicas are at once retail stores, sites of consultation, and active shrines to *santos*. They sell herbal and herb-derived remedies for all manner of practical problems of health or relationships or money. Each herb has its patron *santo* who endows it with its power and whose supplication makes it effective.[14] Most botánica owners are skilled diviners who use a variety of techniques to determine the spiritual situation of their clients and prescribe the herbal and devotional remedies. Each client has his or her own array of patron *santos* and the diviner can determine which of these *santos* is appropriate to the client's problem and what the *santo* may require in order to solve it. The client will then make a *promesa* to the *santo*, a holy vow that in return for help, he or she will do something to glorify the *santo*. This can be a pilgrimage to a sacred site associated with the *santo*, or a *novena*, a nine-day cycle of prayer and penance. Most *promesas* involve a promise to embellish the home shrine of the *santo*, and the botánica provides a full array of statues, candles, and other adornments to make many home shrines elaborate and beautiful testimonies to the power of the *santo*. Many botánica owners construct shrines at their stores presenting exemplary models of and for the home shrines. These displays reveal the stores as sacred sites in their own right, as patrons come to make offerings at places within the store itself. Botánica shrines are often more elaborate and resplendent than are practical at devotees' homes since they accumulate the elaborations of many devotees, and they may become public gathering places for devotions.

Two Washington-area botánicas have built shrines for *santos* that reveal the ways in which multiple religious traditions cohere in the lives of many American Latinos. Botánica Yemayá y Changó in the Adams-Morgan neighborhood of DC and Botánica El Salvador del Mundo in the Maryland

---

14. For the fullest treatment of the interrelationships between *santos* and healing plants, see Cabrera, *El Monte*. An excellent shorter treatment is Brandon, "Uses of Plants in Healing in an Afro-Cuban Religion, Santería."

suburbs reflect respectively the Caribbean and Central American traditions of local Latinos. We will look first at the shrine to Nuestra Señora de la Caridad del Cobre at the DC store and then move to San Simón's shrine in Maryland.

La Virgen de La Caridad del Cobre—"The Virgin of Charity of (the Eastern Cuban town of) El Cobre"—is the most popular advocation of the Virgin Mary in the Latin Caribbean. In the early years of the seventeenth century she is said to have appeared to three mariners on the bay of Nipe in eastern Cuba. These "three Juans" were in a small canoe and a terrible storm had burst upon them. They prayed to the Virgin for their lives and the seas miraculously calmed. Resting on a floating plank nearby they found a small statue of the Virgin with Child. Carved into the wood were the words "Yo soy La Virgen de la Caridad/ I am the Virgin of Charity." The men took the statue to the local authorities who built a chapel for it. The statue miraculously moved itself to the mining town of Cobre and it was determined that this was the spot at which the Virgin wished her shrine to be built. Stories of the miraculous powers of the image spread all over the island and people came to petition the Virgin for all manner of problems, particularly those of conception and childbirth. As the crowds came the chapel was continually embellished and the image adorned with beautiful clothes and jewels. By the eighteenth century Bishop Morell de Santa Cruz wrote to the King to say that the sanctuary of Cobre was "the richest, most visited and devout of the Island, and the Lady of Charity, the most miraculous effigy of all that are venerated."[15]

The devotion to La Caridad del Cobre became particularly important to the growing Afro-Cuban population. The image itself is said to be *morenicita*, "a little dark," and the "three Juans" were not Spanish but people of color, Indian and African. Afro-Cubans enlisted La Caridad in their struggle for freedom, first in the Cobre mines and later in the two wars of independence in the later nineteenth century. They called her *Negrita*, "Little Black One," and "La Virgen Mambisa," an African title indicating a fierce warrior.[16] And the Virgin's qualities of watery origins, miraculous powers, and golden riches were not lost on the enslaved Yoruba men and women who worked in the mines of Cobre and the sugar plantations throughout the island. For these attributes were those of the *orisha*-spirit Ochún, for whom a Yoruba song goes: "The crowned woman . . . the ruler of the riverbed . . . She who has children listens for their crying, so she may take them up, tranquilly."[17]

---

15. Quoted in Marrero, *Los esclavos y la Virgen del Cobre*, 28.
16. Benítez-Rojo, *Repeating Island*, 291n22.
17. Collected in Gleason, *Leaf and Bone*, 166.

It is not known when the correspondences between *orishas* and saints were codified but they were in place when Swedish traveller Fredrika Bremer visited Afro-Cuban assemblies in Havana in the 1850s. On seeing the images of the saints there she wrote:

> Here also were several Christian symbols and pictures. But even here, also, the Christianized and truly Christian Africans retain somewhat of the superstition and idolatry of their native land.[18]

It is interesting that Bremer speaks of both "Christianized" and "truly Christian" Afro-Cubans as retaining African traditions in their veneration of the saints. She sees "true" Christianity and African practices as not incompatible but functional in the lives of the Afro-Cubans she meets. Like the *orisha* and the saint there seems to be not a merging of identities but rather a complex parallelism.

Today at botánicas throughout the United States the images of the Catholic saints are ubiquitous, and that of La Caridad del Cobre often holds pride of place. At Botánica Yemayá y Changó there is a magnificent shrine with a large statue of Caridad enveloped in gold satin and surrounded by offerings of flowers and fruits, candles and currency. Beneath her are sculpted the "three Juans" gazing upward in awe. The informed observer will note however a number of elements in the display that indicate another symbol system at work. Sharing the golden enclosure with the statue is a shelf with two large lidded vases. These contain sacred stones that are considered to hold the presence of the *orisha* Ochún and are lovingly bathed and fed on ceremonial occasions. Draped about the neck of the statue, and adorned with dollar-bill offerings is a huge beaded necklace strung with thousands of yellow and gold beads. This is a *collar de mazo*, a necklace worn at the time of initiation into Ochún's priesthood and so implying that the Virgin herself is a priestess of the *orisha*. The ornaments of the shrine include fans alluding to Ochún's river breezes, pumpkins for her seed-filled fertility, and honey for her sweetness.

Devotees at the botánica are not confused by the presence of the two symbol systems at the shrine. Caridad's powers and Ochún's powers are juxtaposed in a dialectic of association. The tranquility, sweetness, and fertility of one inform those qualities of the other. Both Caridad and Ochún are gentle mothers and fierce warriors who fight for their children and their spatial and devotional togetherness deepens their devotees' understanding of maternal sacred power.

---

18. Bremer, *Homes of the New World*, 383.

A second example of Latino multi-religiousness can be found at Botánica El Salvador del Mundo in suburban Maryland. Here the Latino base is Central American and the *santo* enshrined is Guatemalan. San Simón speaks at several levels to many Central Americans both in their homelands and in the United States. Depending on whether he is addressed in Spanish as San Simón or in Mayan as Maximón or Rilaj Mam, he connects devotees alternately with the biblical stories of Jesus's disciples Simon Peter and Judas and with the divine cosmology of the Mayan calendar.[19] Simon Peter and Judas are sometimes conflated by San Simón's devotees as it is their role of both companionship with and betrayal of Jesus that connect with the traditional Mayan world view. The Maya recognize, as have many other Christians, that the drama of Christian salvation requires an oppositional agent. The serpent in the Garden of Eden, the Advocate roaming the earth, and the disciple/betrayer of the Messiah are necessary catalysts for the saving actions to unfold. In traditional Mayan religions this crucial role was played by Maximón who destabilizes the cosmos by shape-shifting between male and female, and tempting gods and humans to disorder.[20]

The correspondence between the Catholic Simon Peter / Judas and the Mayan Maximón was most influentially made among the Tz'utujil Maya peoples of the Guatemalan highlands. Far from the Spanish centers of power in the years after the conquest, Tz'utujil Maya were relatively free to maintain *costumbre*—traditional beliefs and practices—while conforming to Spanish expectations of Christian worship. Robert Carlsen writes of the system of Christian confraternities (*cofradías*) among the Mayan villagers:

Evading the scrutiny of their pious overlords living in distant towns, many communities have used the *cofradía* system to transfer aspects of pre-Conquest religious ritual, refabricating the institution in the process ... Whereas enough of the accoutrements of Catholicism are generally present in the *cofradías* to deflect direct intervention, at the same time the system can constitute a "barrier," the occult side of which offers a venue for the celebrations of characteristically indigenous religious expressions.[21]

A principal concern of traditional Mayan religions was the orderly transitions of the calendar in cycles of seasons, years, and epochs. Human ceremonial activity was crucial to the proper progress of time and the "delicate times" between seasons demanded careful rites to insure the fertility of all nature. Into this cosmic concern the story of the death and resurrection

---

19. Pieper, *Guatemala's Folk Saints*, 55–56.
20. Vincent Stanzione, "Maximón," in Jones, *Encyclopedia of Religion*.
21. Robert S. Carlsen, "Meso-American Religions: Contemporary Cultures," in Jones, *Encyclopedia of Religion*, 5925–26.

of Jesus was woven. Every Good Friday the *cofradías* of the town of Santiago Atitlán in the Guatemalan highlands reenact the passion of Jesus in correspondence with the death of the dry season and the rebirth of the rains. As the image of dead Christ is processed through the town square, an image of San Simón is carried up to confront it. San Simón, like Judas Iscariot a companion and betrayer of Jesus, repeatedly bumps into the Christ image, inseminating the dead Christ with the life-giving force of the incipient rains.[22] Peter Canby witnessed the ceremony in the 1990s and wrote:

> The core paradigm of Maya religion is that everything evolves into its opposite. The *atitecos* [residents of the town] divide the year into two halves: a female half that has to do with gestation, dryness, and death, and a male half that has to do with rebirth. The transition between the two is now, at the equinox, just before the rains start, when the world is half male and half female. That's Maximón's power. He's the attraction of opposites: day to night, wet to dry, male to female.[23]

Canby here uses Maximón's Mayan name to show his role in the indigenous religion of cyclical transitions. For the *cofradías* of Santiago Atitlán the *santo* is both the biblical agent of the Christian passion as well as the traditional agent of transition. They are the same figure and a different one, functioning in different narrative and ritual contexts in which they operate. San Simón devotee Juan Serrato explained to me that San Simón was a "reincarnation" of Maximón in the time of Jesus, and that is why he looks White and dresses like a European.

The oldest images of Maximón were bundles of cloth impregnated with the presence of the Mayan kings. Apolinario Chile Pixtun, one of the foremost traditional leaders of the highland *cofradías* devoted to Maximón, says that the name of the *santo* is derived from the Mayan word *Ximon* or *shum* meaning "bundle" or "tied up." He explains the evolution of the *santo*'s image in this way:

> In the classic epoch of the Mayans... the forms of ancestors were made of tied-up leaves, wood, or bark... The original Maximón was not in this [current anthropomorphic] form, but in the energy of the first bundles that were here among the Mayans... The Catholic missionaries came, and they gave him blue eyes, and a big mustache, another form, because they had burned the original. Maximón was originally a Mayan. The Spanish burned him three times... so they [the Mayans] made him different

22. Carlsen, *War for the Heart and Soul of a Highland Maya Town*, 152.
23. Canby, *Heart of the Sky*, 317.

each time so that the missionaries wouldn't recognize him and burn him . . . to look like a Catholic saint instead of an Indian.[24]

While cloths are still an important part of Maximón's iconography it is the anthropomorphic form that is most common among US Latinos. His shrine at Botánica El Salvador del Mundo is just as spectacular as the one for La Caridad in DC. The shrine is set off from the store in a separate room painted brilliant green. San Simón's statue is of life-like resin, nearly life sized, and seated on chair. His features are distinctly European, pale luminous skin, a luxuriant mustache, and he wears a business suit and shirt and tie. Atop his head is a conservative black fedora. A lighted cigarette is placed in his mouth and smoke from many such offering fills the room. At each hand is a large staff, one golden with red stripes and the other massive and beaded. Stuck in San Simón's hands and the pockets of his suit are bristling dollar bills, and surrounding the statue dozens of glass-sheathed votive candles flicker. The *santo* shimmers in the reflections of the flames against the bright walls and glowing smoke. At least a dozen bottles of rum ring the statue and plates of tortillas and huge, crude *puro* cigars lie at its feet.

Once again the informed observer can see the two religious symbol systems at work. The statue is European-featured, representing the Maya's idea of the European origins of Christianity. The candle and money offerings reflect the Catholic conventions of shrine veneration. But the seated *santo* with hat and staff are restatements of the Mayan trickster divinity called by scholars God L, whose images can be found on pre-Columbian carved reliefs. The tobacco, tortillas, and rum—or its traditional equivalent agave beverage—are appropriate offerings to the Mayan divinities. The staff is a symbol of authority that is transferred from male to female, dry to wet, world cycle to world cycle. Maximón as the "delicate" *santo* of transitions holds the staff in readiness of the cosmic transformations.

The Latinos of Botánica El Salvador del Mundo are also maintaining a dynamic, interrelated bi-religiousness. Their parallelism of the biblical figures of San Simón and Judas Iscariot with Maximón shows insight into the dynamics of both traditions. For each cosmology to work there must be an oppositional figure, a "trickster" if you will, who simultaneously subverts the order and makes it actual. By juxtaposing the story of the death and resurrection of Jesus with the transitions of the Mayan calendar the devotees of San Simón/Maximón are deepening the symbolic power of both. As the correspondence of Caridad and Ochún revealed a profound appreciation of divine female power, so that of San Simón and Maximón shows a sophisticated grasp of the religious meanings of death and rebirth.

24. Quoted in Pieper, *Guatemala's Folk Saints*, 54.

These are but two examples of the multiple religious correspondences being celebrated at botánicas in the United States. As Latinos of Caribbean and Central American backgrounds are meeting each other, and also meeting the extraordinarily diverse spiritualities in the United States, new parallelisms are being forged. I have seen a shrine where San Simón is juxtaposed with Eleggua, the Afro-Cuban *orisha* of transition. And there is a display in Virginia where the sacred vases of Ochún rest next to a statue of the Virgin of Guadalupe. Two botánicas in the DC area have shrine to Pu-Tai Buddha, one with the offering due to the *orisha* Changó, the other placed at the threshold beside the liminal *orisha* Eleggua. These devotional constructions on the part of ordinary believers deserve attention from scholars of religious pluralism as they are active, creative responses to multiple religious traditions. In a final section of this paper I will suggest how understanding the "pluralism" of the botánica may be helpful in understanding religious pluralism in general.

RELIGIOUS PLURALISM

It is unusual to call the religious phenomena that we have been examining "pluralism." The usual term, of course, is syncretism. Yet an examination of the meanings and applications of "syncretism" reveals problems in the study of religion that have important implications for understanding religious pluralism. *Syncretism* comes from the Greek συν *syn* "together" and χρητίζειν *kretizein* "mixture." Its meaning is preserved in the English "idiosyncrasy" which calls to mind a peculiar mixture of traits in an individual. "Syncretism" is given a suggestive if unlikely etymology by Plutarch who writes that the term has its origin in the temporary alliance of quarrelsome Cretans who banded together against a common enemy: thus *syn Kretoi*.[25] The suggestion is that "syncretism" refers to things that are not usually and perhaps not successfully "mixed together." The modern use of "syncretism" has its origins in the theological controversies of the Reformation when attempts to harmonize divergent Protestant and Catholic doctrines were labeled "syncretism" by their critics. They saw these theological reconciliations as improper mixtures of ideas that should be kept separate. The term took on added meaning as Christian missionaries saw many indigenous peoples' appropriation of the Christian message as unacceptably mixed with their native paganism. The term continues to be used pejoratively to

---

25. Stewart and Shaw, *Syncretism/Anti-Syncretism*, 3. See also Martin, *Hellenistic Religions*, 11.

distinguish "pure" religions from those that are "mixed" with the further implication that they are "mixed up."

To avoid the depreciatory connotations of syncretism and to be more precise about its varieties scholars have used a variety of alternative terms that speak to similar dynamics in the uses of religious symbols from diverse sources. "Symbiosis" is derived from biology and points to mutual "living together." Looking at phenomena similar to those of the botánica, Haitian scholar of religion Leslie Desmangles has developed the notion of religious symbiosis to refer to situations where people practice two religions that interpenetrate but do not fuse.[26] "Hybridity" has its origin in genetics and refers, in Homi Bhaba's words, to "the interstitial passage between fixed identifications."[27] Hybrid religions are tools whereby the colonized reappropriate the colonizers' religion to subvert its authority and access its power. "Creolization" has been borrowed from linguistics and describes a new religious "language" which has been constructed from the elements of "languages" in contact. Depending on the historical circumstances one language may act as a "substrate" for the other and so organize the vocabulary of one into the grammar of the other. In a much-quoted passage linguist Suzanne Comhaire-Sylvain says of Haitian créole:

> We are in the presence of French poured into the mould of African grammar or, since languages are generally classified according to their grammatical parentage, of a Ewe language with French vocabulary.[28]

A creole religion, therefore, would be a construction of a "grammar" and "vocabulary" of religious symbols from different sources brought together into a structured, meaningful arrangement of elements that communicates in a religiously plural culture.

Each of these synonyms for syncretism is useful in describing a people's construction of the relationship of elements of diverse origin in their religious lives. Each term suggests different avenues of exploration in understanding the "mixed-togetherness" of different religious traditions in the lives of communities and individuals. Nevertheless the notion of religious "togetherness" connoted by syncretism or its synonyms remains problematic for those interested in religious pluralism. Pope Benedict XVI preached against syncretism as a "relativistic concept" which poses a danger

26. Desmangles, *Faces of the Gods*, 8.
27. Bhabha, *Location of Culture*, 4.
28. Quoted in Philip Baker and Peter Mühlhaüsler, "Creole Linguistics from Its Beginnings, through Schuchardt to the Present Day," in Stewart, *Creolization: History, Ethnography, Theory*, 94.

to interreligious dialogue.[29] Protestant theologian James Wiggins also sees a "threat of syncretism" when interreligious dialogue blurs religious borders.[30] These negative views of syncretism have undermined its utility as a descriptive term and historians of religions such as Robert Baird have advocated abandoning "syncretism" entirely. He argues that as a theological term it implies an ahistoric and faith-based notion of purity that is belied by history. All religious formations, argues Baird, are the products of multiple religious sources and so syncretism is a universal process in the formation of religion and thus has no explanatory power. He writes:

> Historically speaking, to say that "Christianity" or the "mystery religions" or "Hinduism" are syncretistic is not to say anything that distinguishes them from anything else and is merely the equivalent to admitting that each has a history and can be studied historically.[31]

More recently a number of scholars have promoted a revival of the term precisely because it foregrounds the issues of the construction and contestation of religious borders.[32] The disparagement of "syncretism" points directly to critical problems in the conception of what constitutes "religion" in general and "a religion" in particular. In the interests of understanding religious pluralism it will be helpful to examine briefly some of these issues.

I think that the problem with many discussions of religious pluralism is that they make assumptions about what "a" religion is, and therefore, how "religions" are conceived to relate to each other. These assumptions are based on restricted aspects of "a" religion and so scholars of pluralism are forced to exclude many kinds of religious phenomena from the discussion. For example, David Ray Griffin in his critical overview of the scholarship on religious pluralism states confidently that adherents of religions affirm "saving truths and values" and that the problem for pluralists lies in affirming that other religions also have these salvific truths.[33] He and the writers he speaks of, such as Knitter, Hick, and Cobb, seem agreed that religions are ways of salvation, each differently conceptualized. However, this depiction of religion as soteriology is problematic because the notion of salvation

---

29. Benedict XVI, "Message of His Holiness Benedict XVI to Bishop Domenico Sorrentino."

30. Wiggins, *In Praise of Religious Diversity*, 64.

31. Baird, *Category Formation and the History of Religions*, 146.

32. See André Droogers, "Syncretism: The Problem of Definition, the Definition of the Problem," in Gort et al., *Dialogue and Syncretism*, 7–15, and Stewart and Shaw, *Syncretism/Anti-Syncretism*.

33. Griffin, *Deep Religious Pluralism*, 3.

must be stretched far if it is to include the goals of all the things that we are used to label "religion." Even among the "world religions" that concern pluralist writers it is difficult to say that devotion to Shiva or adherence to the Confucian value of *li* is a way of "salvation" without stretching the meaning of the word to include the material benefits of Shiva's beneficence or social harmony in Confucian society. The idea of salvation is so thoroughly rooted in Christian theology that those elements that cannot be recognized as centered on salvation tend not to be part of the discussion. When we turn to religions that are usually not considered in this conversation, such as those of the botánica, it is still more difficult to say that salvation is what motivates devotees of Caridad/Ochún or San Simón/Maximón unless we extend the concept to include any ordinary betterment of their lives. In their own testimony botanica patrons say that they seek the help of the *santos* in order to meet the ordinary problems of life. Botánica owner and priestess of Changó Nicole Rivera says that her religion offers her "victory" in the battle of life. One way to understand these "non-soteriological" religions is to recognize that class and culture play a role in people's religious views. We have already spoken of a "philosophical" religion of the elite concerned with beliefs and "otherworldly" benefits, and a "practical" religion of the folk, concerned with practices and "this-worldly" aid.[34] As Susanne Rostas and André Droogers point out there is

> a practical problem-solving intention in popular religion. In the case of lower-class people, seeking for meaning often involves searching for a solution to problems of survival. Religions offer resources for this quest, and popular religions particularly so.[35]

Given this orientation it is not surprising that the religious borders that concern elites are so easily crossed by the folk, both within and without the "world religions." In the quest for "victory," ordinary people turn to spiritual powers that are effective. And people with plural religious heritages connect these powers into efficacious assemblages.

So what is "a" religion and where do its borders lie? In defending the distinctiveness of the world religions Griffin wishes to affirm "versions of religious pluralism that are truly Buddhist, versions that are truly Confucian, versions that are truly Hindu, versions that are truly Jewish, versions that are truly Islamic, and so on."[36] Who is to determine what "true" Buddhism or Judaism may be and what criteria are we to rely upon to distinguish them

---

34. Leach, *Dialectic*, and Yoder, "Toward a Definition."
35. Rostas and Droogers, introduction to *Popular Use of Popular Religion in Latin America*, 5.
36. Griffin, *Deep Religious Pluralism*, 4.

from each other, or distinguish them from "untrue" or inauthentic expressions of these religions? I think that the answers lie for most scholars concerned with religious pluralism in the textual formulations of elites, wherein religions are organized into systems of salvation and all other religious experience tends to be excluded as irrelevant, inauthentic, naïve or, perhaps, syncretistic.

An examination of the "syncretisms" of the botánica reveals thoughtful and carefully constructed examples of what might be called, if we were to broaden the scope of the discussion, religious pluralism. The devotions to La Caridad/Ochún and San Simón/Maximón show two (or more) religions "together" in people's lives. But they are not merged or mixed up. They are deliberately, creatively, and dynamically juxtaposed. Devotees recognize an active dialogue of religious meaning between the juxtaposed symbols that both points to their identity and preserves their distinctiveness. This to me is an exciting version of religious pluralism constructed by ordinary people often under duress. And it offers a model of pluralism that can inform the discussions of scholars as they wrestle with the category of "religion" and the many "religions" to which it pertains.

BIBLIOGRAPHY

Baird, Robert D. *Category Formation and the History of Religions*. The Hague: Mouton, 1971.
Benedict XVI. "Message of His Holiness Benedict XVI to Bishop Domenico Sorrentino on the Occasion of the 20th Anniversary of the Interreligious Meeting of Prayer for Peace." http://www.vatican.va/holy_father/benedict_xvi/letters/2006/documents/hf_ben-xvi_let_20060902_xx-incontro-assisi_en.html.
Benítez-Rojo, Antonio. *The Repeating Island: The Caribbean and the Postmodern Perspective*. Translated by James Maraniss. Durham: Duke University Press, 1992.
Bhabha, Homi. *The Location of Culture*. New York: Routledge, 1994.
Brandon, George. "The Uses of Plants in Healing in an Afro-Cuban Religion, Santería." *Journal of Black Studies* 22 (1991) 55–76.
Bremer, Fredrika. *The Homes of the New World: Impressions of America*. Translated by Mary Howett. Harper, 1853. Reprint, New York: Negro Universities Press, 1968.
Cabrera, Lydia. *El Monte*. 1954. Reprint, Miami: Ediciones Universal, 1975.
Canby, Peter. *The Heart of the Sky*. New York: HarperCollins, 1992.
Carlsen, Robert S. *The War for the Heart and Soul of a Highland Maya Town*. With a contribution by Martín Prechtel. Austin: University of Texas Press, 1997.
Curtin, Philip. *The Atlantic Slave Trade: A Census*. Madison: University of Wisconsin Press, 1969.
Davenport, Francis Gardiner, ed. *European Treaties Bearing on the History of the United States and Its Dependencies to 1648*. Washington, DC: Carnegie Institution of Washington, 1917.

Desmangles, Leslie G. *The Faces of the Gods: Vodou and Roman Catholicism in Haiti.* Chapel Hill: University of North Carolina Press, 1992.
Gleason, Judith, ed. *Leaf and Bone: African Praise Poems.* New York: Viking, 1980.
González-Wippler, Migene. *Santería: The Religion.* St. Paul: Llewellyn, 1994.
Gort, Jerald, et al., eds. *Dialogue and Syncretism: An Interdisciplinary Approach.* Grand Rapids: Eerdmans, 1989.
Griffin, David Ray, ed. *Deep Religious Pluralism.* Louisville: Westminster John Knox, 2005.
Jones, Lindsay, ed. *Encyclopedia of Religion.* Detroit: Macmillan, 2005.
Las Casas, Bartolomé de. *The Devastation of the Indies: A Brief Account.* Translated by Herma Briffault. 1542. Reprint, Baltimore: Johns Hopkins University Press, 1992.
Leach, Edmund R., ed. *Dialectic in Practical Religion.* Cambridge: Cambridge University Press, 1968.
Marrero, Levi. *Los esclavos y la Virgen del Cobre: Dos siglos de lucha por la libertad de Cuba.* Miami: Ediciones Universal, 1980.
Martin, Luther. *Hellenistic Religions.* New York: Oxford University Press, 1987.
Moreno de los Arcos, Roberto. "New Spain's Inquisition for Indians from the Sixteenth to the Nineteenth Century." Chapter 2 in *Cultural Encounters: The Impact of the Inquisition in Spain and the New World,* edited by Mary Elizabeth Perry and Anne J. Cruz. Los Angeles: University of California Press, 1991.
Murphy, Joseph M., and Mei-Mei Sanford, eds. *Osun Across the Waters: A Yoruba Goddess in Africa and the Americas.* Bloomington: Indiana University Press, 2001.
Ortiz, Fernando. *Los Negros Brujos: Hampa Afro-Cubana.* 1906. Reprint, Miami: Ediciones Universal, 1973.
Pérez y Mena, Andrés Isadoro. *Speaking with the Dead: Development of Afro-Latin Religion among Puerto Ricans in the United States.* New York: AMS, 1991.
Pieper, Jim. *Guatemala's Folk Saints.* Los Angeles: Pieper, 2002.
Redfield, Robert. *The Little Community and Peasant Society and Culture.* 1956. Reprint, Chicago: Phoenix, 1968.
Rostas, Susanna, and André Droogers, eds. *The Popular Use of Popular Religion in Latin America.* Amsterdam: CEDLA, 1993.
Rumbaut, Rubén G. "The Americans: Latin American and Caribbean Peoples in the United States." Chapter 12, in *Americas: New Interpretive Essays,* edited by Alfred Stepan. New York: Oxford University Press, 1992.
Stewart, Charles, ed. *Creolization: History, Ethnography, Theory.* Walnut Creek, CA: Left Coast, 2007.
Stewart, Charles, and Rosalind Shaw, eds. *Syncretism/Anti-Syncretism: The Politics of Religious Synthesis.* New York: Routledge, 1994.
Vélez, María Teresa. *Drumming for the Gods: The Life and Times of Felipe García Villamil, Santero, Palero and Abakuá.* Philadelphia: Temple University Press, 2000.
Wakefield, Dan. *Island in the City: The World of Spanish Harlem.* New York: Arno, 1975.
Wiggins, James. *In Praise of Religious Diversity.* New York: Routledge Chapman & Hall, 1996.
Yoder, Don. "Toward a Definition of Folk Religion." *Western Folklore* 33 (1974) 2–15.
Yupangui, Diego de Castro. *Titu Cusi: A Sixteenth-Century Account of the Conquest.* Translation and notes by Nicole Delia Legnani. Cambridge: Harvard University Press, 2005.

4

The Buddha and the Dalai Lama on Religious Pluralism

J. ABRAHAM VÉLEZ DE CEA

THIS ARTICLE INTRODUCES THE XIV Dalai Lama's method to foster interreligious harmony and puts it into dialogue with the Buddha of the *Pāli Nikāyas*, the oldest collection of Buddhist texts available. The first section examines the Dalai Lama's understanding of exclusivism, inclusivism, and pluralism, and explains his proposal to uphold with integrity an exclusivist perspective called "one truth, one religion" together with a pluralist perspective called "many truths, many religions." The second section clarifies the typology exclusivism-inclusivism-pluralism by distinguishing between views and attitudes, and compares the approaches to religious diversity of the Dalai Lama and the Buddha.

THE DALAI LAMA'S MODEL OF RELIGIOUS DIVERSITY

In his book *Towards True Kinship of Faiths: How the World's Religions Can Come Together*, his holiness the XIV Dalai Lama discusses the teachings of Hinduism, Christianity, Islam, and Judaism. He explains the basic teachings of these religions and compares them to Buddhism. He suggests that the compassion-centered ethic of religions is a "tremendous shared resource," and that universal compassion is the ultimate ideal of all religions. Religions, for the Dalai Lama, can be a source of good for this planet, and they "can help overcome prejudices, deal with conflicts, and give succor for the poor and the week."[1]

The ideal of interreligious harmony is, for the Dalai Lama, possible, but it must be based on mutual understanding and the explicit recognition of real differences. Religious diversity is a good thing. From a theistic perspective, the Dalai Lama says, differences among the religions represent the beauty of God's infinite wisdom, and, from a non-theistic perspective, the richness of the human spirit.

In order to achieve this ideal of interreligious harmony based on mutual understanding and recognition of real differences, the Dalai Lama proposes four types of interreligious dialogue: (1) dialogue among scholars of religion at the academic level about doctrinal similarities and differences, with emphasis on the purpose of religions; (2) dialogue among genuine spiritual practitioners about deep religious experiences; (3) dialogue among leaders of religions to speak and pray from one platform; (4) joint participation in pilgrimages to holy sites and rites of other religions.

Besides advocating interreligious dialogue based on mutual understanding and the explicit recognition of real differences, the Dalai Lama calls for "the emergence of a genuine spirit of religious pluralism."[2] The Dalai Lama's tries to reconcile the tension that many people perceive between deep commitment to one's own tradition and acceptance of other religions as legitimate. The Dalai Lama explains that for many people accepting the legitimacy of other faiths somewhat compromises the integrity of their own tradition. In his words:

> A devout Buddhist may feel that acceptance of other spiritual paths as valid suggests the existence of ways other than of the Buddha toward the attainment of enlightenment. A Muslim might feel that acceptance of other traditions as legitimate would require relinquishing the belief that God's revelation to the Prophet, as recorded in the Qur'an, represents the final revelation of the highest truth. In the same vein, a Christian might feel that accenting the legitimacy of other religions would entail compromising the key belief that it is only through Jesus Christ that the way to God is found.[3]

---

1. Dalai Lama, *Towards True Kinship of Faiths*, 128.
2. Ibid., 146.
3. Ibid., 145.

The Dalai Lama contends that unless we are able to balance the acceptance of religious diversity with commitment to one's own tradition, there will not be interreligious harmony. Before advancing his proposal to achieve the aforementioned balance, the Dalai Lama discusses three basic responses to other religions: exclusivism, inclusivism, and pluralism.

The Dalai Lama defines exclusivism as "a position that one's own religion is the only true religion and that rejects, as if it were by default, the legitimacy of other faith traditions." Inclusivism, on the other hand, considers other faith traditions as partially valid, "but maintains that their teachings are somehow contained within one's own traditions." The Dalai Lama acknowledges that inclusivism is more tolerant than exclusivism but equally problematic because it entails that other traditions are ultimately redundant. The Dalai Lama defines pluralism as the acceptance of other religions as valid. For the Dalai Lama, the pluralist accords validity to all faith traditions.[4] This conception of pluralism does not imply relativism. Other traditions are valid as long as they are able to provide a foundation for ethical and spiritual practices, and as long as they can generate in their followers spiritual qualities such as love, compassion, simplicity, patience, forgiveness, and so on.

The Dalai Lama suggests that achieving the ideal interreligious harmony requires the adoption of some form of pluralism. However, not all conceptions of pluralism are acceptable. For instance, the Dalai Lama rejects the "multiple rivers" view of religious diversity because it presupposes the ultimate oneness of all religions, and this "demands a precondition that remains impossible for the majority of adherents of the world's great religions."[5] Instead, the Dalai Lama proposes a form of pluralism that recognizes and respects differences among the traditions. This recognition of diversity at the ultimate level "is not only essential but also the first step toward creating deeper understanding of each other."[6]

Another conception of pluralism that the Dalai Lama finds problematic is the one that seeks a universal religion. Whether this universal religion is a totally new religion or one of the old ones, is irrelevant. For the Dalai Lama, the idea of a universal religion is "simply unfeasible." First, because given the diversity of mental dispositions and spiritual inclinations, a single set of spiritual teachings will not serve everyone. Second, because given the history of religions, they are already adapted to specific cultures and

---

4. Ibid., 147.
5. Ibid., 148.
6. Ibid.

environments, thus making the spread of one religion to all cultures and environments virtually impossible.

Thus, a plurality of religions seems unavoidable and accepting such religious diversity is indispensable to fostering peace and human happiness. Religious diversity, for the Dalai Lama, is consistent with the way things are in reality, whereas exclusivism or the denial of religious diversity "represents a perspective that is not in accord with reality."[7]

For the Dalai Lama, in order to achieve interreligious harmony we need to practice interreligious dialogue and be pluralists in the sense of truly accepting the reality and value of other faith traditions,[8] that is, respecting their ultimate legitimacy.[9] The main reason for accepting and respecting other religions is that they serve and benefit human beings. More specifically, the ultimate reason for accepting and respecting other faith traditions is that "they, too, engender the beautiful qualities of the human heart and foster compassion and loving kindness—exactly the qualities one is striving to attain through one's own faith."[10]

After clarifying what he means by pluralism, the Dalai Lama distinguishes between three aspects of religions: (1) ethical teachings, (2) doctrines or metaphysics, and (3) cultural specifics. Among these three, ethical teachings are, for the Dalai Lama, the essence of religions. For the Dalai Lama, there is a profound convergence of the world's great religions on the level of ethical teachings. All religions share the same ethical purpose, which the Dalai Lama describes as the betterment of humanity and the creation of more compassionate and responsible human beings. The Dalai Lama claims that the ethical teachings of religions are essentially the same, as well as the fruits of such teachings, namely, love and compassion.[11]

On the level of culture and metaphysics, however, there are many differences, some of them fundamental and unbridgeable. There are differences about the concept of afterlife, the concept of well-being that takes place in the afterlife, the origin of the universe, the methods to achieve well-being in the future life, and about what exactly constitutes the ultimate truth. Any attempt to find convergence on this doctrinal and metaphysical level is, for the Dalai Lama, bound to fail.[12]

---

7. Ibid., 149.
8. Ibid., 144.
9. Ibid., 149.
10. Ibid., 150.
11. Ibid., 151.
12. Ibid., 152.

For the Dalai Lama, however, the fundamental differences that exist on the doctrinal and metaphysical level have a purpose. In order to explain this purpose, the Dalai Lama uses "a Buddhist hermeneutical principle," namely, the concept of *upāya* or skillful means. For the Dalai Lama, the Buddha taught divergent, even contradictory teachings, depending on the context, the needs, and the spiritual level of his listeners. The Dalai Lama extrapolates this understanding of the Buddha's teachings to the teachings of all religions. In the same way that the Buddha teaches many divergent and contradictory teachings depending on the needs and the capacity of his disciples, many religions teach different and even contradictory things because there are many people with diverse mental dispositions, diverse spiritual and philosophical inclinations.

According to the Dalai Lama, the teachings of religions are like medicines. In the same way that it does not make much sense to prescribe one medicine for all kinds of illness, the idea that there should be only one religion or only one teaching for all beings is untenable. We can say "this is the best teaching" or "this is the best medicine," but always from a particular context. We cannot evaluate a teaching or a religion as "the best" independently of specific contexts: "Therefore, a Buddhist cannot say, when relating to the Buddha's teaching, 'this is the best teaching,' as if one can make such evaluations independent of the specific contexts."[13] Similarly, when we talk about religions in general we have to qualify our claims of superiority and say that a religion is the best for us, but not necessarily the best for everybody. The Dalai Lama definitely believes that Buddhism is the best for him, but he does not consider Buddhism the best for all.[14] Likewise, we can say that this specific medicine is the best for this particular ailment and for such and such patients, but we should never claim that it is the best medicine in absolute and universal terms independently of the context.

Rather than seeing religious diversity as a threat to one's own tradition, religious diversity should be seen as something to be embraced, appreciated, and even celebrated. The Dalai Lama acknowledges that this understanding of religions as medicines and skillful means undermines the urge to convert others and leads to the acceptance of other religions as legitimate. In the Dalai Lama's words:

> Understood thus, the urge to convert others to one's own faith loses its force. In its place arises a genuine acceptance of the reality of other faith traditions. Then, instead of seeing others as an aberration, or at worst as a threat, one can relate to others out

13. Ibid., 155.
14. Ibid., 158.

of a sense of deep appreciation for their profound contribution to the world.[15]

According to the Dalai Lama, pluralists need to take seriously the concerns of exclusivists. The concern of exclusivists is that accepting other religions as legitimate may involve the relativization of the truths found in one's own religion. In order to avoid such relativization, the Dalai Lama proposes we uphold two distinct perspectives in two different contexts.

The first perspective is to be adopted in the context of individual religious practice and the second perspective in the context of society and religious diversity. The first perspective is called "one truth, one religion," and the second "many truths, many religions." The first perspective corresponds to the view of religious diversity held by one's own tradition, which, for the Dalai Lama, involves some form of exclusivism. In his words:

> As many religious believers feel, I would agree that some version of exclusivism—the principle of "one truth, one religion"—lies at the heart of most of the world's great religions. Furthermore, a single-pointed commitment to one's own faith tradition demands the recognition that one's chosen faith represents the highest religious teaching. For example, for me Buddhism is the best, but this does not mean that Buddhism is the best for all. Certainly not. For millions of my fellow human beings, theistic forms of teaching represent the best path. Therefore, in the context of an individual religious practitioner, the concept of "one truth, one religion" remains most relevant. It is this that gives the power and single-pointed focus of one's religious path. At the same time, it is critical that the religious practitioner harbors no ego-centric attachment to his faith.[16]

If I understand the Dalai Lama correctly, he seems to be suggesting that a version of exclusivism in the context of individual religious practice is not only unavoidable but also indispensable to have single-pointed commitment to one's own tradition.

Whereas the first perspective in the context of individual practice is exclusivist, i.e., "one truth, one religion," the second perspective in the context of society is pluralist, i.e., "many truths, many religions." If the exclusivist perspective allows us to be committed to one's own tradition, the pluralistic perspective allows us to accept, respect, and even celebrate religious diversity.

---

15. Ibid., 156.
16. Ibid., 158.

For the Dalai Lama, there is no conflict between these two seemingly contradictory perspectives.[17] The two perspectives can be combined without contradiction because they relate to two distinct contexts, i.e., individual and social. Thus, by distinguishing between the exclusivist perspective of individual practice and the pluralist perspective of social relationships with other religions, the Dalai Lama is able to achieve two goals: (1) facilitating the acceptance of other religions as legitimate, and (2) avoiding the relativization of doctrinal claims that traditions consider definitive truth. In other words, the adoption of the aforementioned two perspectives fosters interreligious harmony because it balances the tension that many people feel between commitment to one's own tradition and acceptance of religious diversity. The Dalai Lama's distinction between two perspectives also contributes to interreligious harmony because it avoids disputes on the level of doctrines and metaphysics, while promoting respect and appreciation for religions on the level of ethics and spirituality.

It should be noticed that the doctrines and metaphysical beliefs of one's own tradition are never relativized but rather relegated for pragmatic reasons to the perspective or context of individual practice. In other words, in order to achieve interreligious harmony, the Dalai Lama advocates three things: (1) the practice of diverse forms of interreligious dialogue; (2) keeping doctrinal and metaphysical claims outside the social context of religious diversity or perspective of many truths, many religions; (3) acknowledging the overall common ground and positive contribution of religions on the level of ethics and spirituality.

Although the Dalai Lama does not equate the individual perspective with the private sphere nor the social perspective with the public sphere, in practice the implication seems to be that the doctrinal and metaphysical claims of religions belong in the "private" sphere of one's own community or, as the Dalai Lama puts it, in the context of individual practice.

The Dalai Lama concludes his discussion of the two perspectives by offering two reasons for respecting religious diversity: (1) religions provide solace, spiritual development, and a system of ethics for millions of people, (2) despite the doctrinal differences between religions, their teachings ground in strikingly parallel and praiseworthy ways the ethical conduct of their followers.

---

17. "In the context of society, however, the concept of 'many truths, many religions' not only becomes relevant but also necessary. In fact, where there is more than one person, already the pluralistic perspective of 'many truths, many religions' becomes critical. Thus, if we relate these two seemingly contradictory perspectives to their differing contexts of society and the individual we can see no real conflict between the two." Ibid., 159.

The Dalai Lama acknowledges that in order to uphold the two perspectives with integrity a creative approach is needed. As an instance of this creative approach, the Dalai Lama speaks about two complementary psychological attitudes toward religions: faith and respect. Faith relates to cognitive states such as "belief" as well as to affective states such as "trust" and "confidence." Respect, on the other hand, relates to mental states such as "appreciation" and "reverence." The Dalai Lama explains that in the Sanskrit Buddhist tradition faith and respect are interrelated. The term faith (śraddhā) can be understood as having three senses: admiration, conviction, and emulation. Faith in the sense of admiration is similar to respect or reverence, whereas faith in the sense of conviction relates to belief, trust, and confidence.

The Dalai Lama seems to suggest that faith in the sense of belief, trust, and confidence should be reserved for one's own tradition because faith in this sense of belief pertains to truth, especially doctrinal truths. This faith in the sense of belief in the truth of one's own tradition, however, does not prevent us from cultivating faith in the sense of admiration, that is, respect and reverence for other traditions. For the Dalai Lama this form of faith as admiration "can be fully extended to other religions."[18]

The Dalai Lama's proposal is simple yet profoundly practical. Since religions are not going to agree with each other on the level of doctrines and metaphysical claims, it is better to set aside such claims and keep them outside the social context of religious diversity. By keeping doctrinal and metaphysical claims outside the social context of religious diversity, we can be pluralists without compromising the exclusivist claims of our tradition. In other words, for the Dalai Lama, being a pluralist on the social sphere is compatible with being an exclusivist on the context of individual practice. The doctrinal and metaphysical claims of other religions may be challenged and rejected, but not their ethical and spiritual contribution. The exclusivist rejection of other religions on the level of doctrine and metaphysics is compatible with the pluralist acceptance of religious diversity on the level of ethics and spiritual practice. That is, the Dalai Lama is not suggesting that we accept other religions only on the public domain while we reject them on the private context of individual practice. Quite the contrary, religious diversity is to be accepted, respected, and even celebrated both on the individual and the social contexts, not because their doctrinal and metaphysical might be true but rather for practical reasons. First, because for many people, religions provide the foundation for ethical conduct and promote the cultivation of spiritual qualities such as love and compassion. Second,

---

18. Ibid., 161.

because there are many different kinds of people with diverse sensibilities and, therefore, it is unrealistic to believe that only one religion, like only one medicine, can be the best for everybody at all times and in all contexts.

It is this therapeutic understanding of religions what allows the Dalai Lama to accept religious diversity and accord them validity on the ethical and spiritual levels. For the Dalai Lama, being a pluralist consists in accepting other religions as legitimate, not on doctrinal grounds, but rather on ethical and spiritual grounds. The pluralist accords ethical and therapeutic value to religions despite their incommensurable doctrinal differences. Yet, a pluralist in this sense can simultaneously hold some form of exclusivism about the ultimate or definitive truth of one's own tradition on the level of individual practice.

COMPARING THE BUDDHA AND THE DALAI LAMA

Before comparing the approaches to religious diversity of the Dalai Lama and the Buddha, it is necessary to clarify the typology exclusivism-inclusivism-pluralism.[19] I understand approaches to religious diversity in terms of openness. I distinguish between two kinds of openness: openness in theory (views) and openness in practice (attitudes). There are four main views (exclusivism, inclusivism, pluralistic-inclusivism, and pluralism) and three main attitudes (exclusivistic, inclusivistic, and pluralisitic). These views and attitudes can be combined in different ways. For instance, someone can have an exclusivist view of religious diversity, e.g., salvation is unique to Christianity, and at the same time display genuine inclusivistic attitudes.

Each view entails a claim about the existence of OTMIX among the religions and presupposes a particular kind of openness. The acronym OTMIX stands for "our tradition most important X." X may refer to different things but it always functions as the most important within a given context and for a particular tradition or set of traditions. What functions as the most important may be an ultimate reality, goal, ideal, concern, teaching, revelation, truth, value, practice, etc. For instance, in some contexts and for some traditions, X may refer to God, Salvation, Specific Revelation. However, in other contexts and for other traditions X may refer to the Dharma, Emptiness, Nirvana, Tao, Brahman, liberation, highest holiness, spiritual practice, mystical union, and so on.

- Exclusivists in terms of view claim that OTMIX is unique to their tradition, and therefore, are open to the existence of X only in their tradition.

19. Vélez de Cea, "Cross-Cultural and Buddhist-Friendly Interpretation."

- Inclusivists in terms of view claim that OTMIX may be found in other traditions as well, but believe that X in other traditions is always similar to OTMIX. Therefore, inclusivists in terms of view are open to the existence of X in other traditions, but only as long as X is similar to OTMIX.

- Pluralistic-inclusivists in terms of view also claim that OTMIX may be found in other traditions besides one's own, but believe that X in other traditions need not be always similar to OTMIX. However, they believe that X in other traditions can never contradict, challenge, or supersede OTMIX. Therefore, pluralistic-inclusivists are open to the existence of X in other traditions, even when X is different from OTMIX, but only as long as X in other traditions is compatible with and subordinated to the fundamental teachings of one's own tradition. In other words, pluralistic-inclusivists in terms of view are open to both similar and different instances of X in other traditions, but constrained by nonnegotiable doctrinal claims about what is true and good.

- Pluralists in terms of view agree with pluralistic-inclusivists in that X in other traditions may be different from OTMIX, but, unlike pluralistic-inclusivists, pluralist do not think beforehand that X must always be compatible with and subordinated to the fundamental teachings of one's own tradition. That is, pluralists in terms of view do not reject the possible existence of X in other traditions that may contradict, challenge, or supersede OTMIX. Like pluralistic-inclusivists, pluralists are open to both similar and different instances of X in other traditions. Similarly, the openness of pluralists, like that of pluralistic-inclusivists, may be constrained by standards and doctrinal claims about what is true and good. However, unlike pluralistic-inclusivists, pluralists do not consider such standards and doctrinal claims nonnegotiable by definition. In other words, unlike the openness to X of pluralistic-inclusivists, the openness of pluralists is not dogmatically constrained, i.e., no doctrinal claim or standard is in principle or *a priori* nonnegotiable.

Each of these four aforementioned views of religious diversity may be combined with at least one of three main attitudes. There are correlations but not a necessary connection between views and attitudes. For instance, exclusivistic attitudes are likely to be associated with exclusivist views but exclusivist views can also be associated with inclusivistic and even pluralistic attitudes. Views influence and condition attitudes and vice versa, but this mutual influence is to be understood as a form of conditioning, not determinism.

It might be the case that one tradition and even one practitioner may hold a certain view in some contexts that lead to a certain attitudes, but in other contexts, the same view may lead to a different attitude. For instance, in some contexts exclusivist views may be associated with inclusivistic attitudes, but in other contexts the same exclusivist view may give rise to exclusivistic attitudes. In other words, religious traditions and individuals are not monolithic either in terms of views or attitudes. That is, traditions and individuals do not always display the same attitudes in all contexts even when their views of religious diversity remain unchanged. Conversely, traditions may change their views of religious diversity over time without necessarily modifying their basic attitude. For instance, a tradition or an individual may remain faithful to its original inclusivistic attitude even after shifting from an exclusivist view to an inclusivist one.

Unlike views, which presuppose different claims about the existence of OTMIX among the religions, attitudes presuppose distinct practical dispositions. Specifically, dispositions to accept, respect, and dialogue with other traditions.

- Exclusivistic attitudes: fail to accept the existence of other religions, and tolerate them at best. There is not genuine respect but rather political correctness. Dialogue with other religions is avoided or usually confrontational and intended to proselytize their members.

- Inclusivistic attitudes accept the existence of other religions with ambiguities and often as mere stepping stones towards one's own tradition. There is genuinely respect for the teachings of other religions if and only if they are similar or compatible with the teachings of one's own tradition. Dialogue with other religions is usually the monopoly of experts and official representatives, and ultimately dispensable if it is not subordinated to mission and proclamation.

- Pluralistic attitudes accept other religions unambiguously and without assuming that they are skillful means or stepping stones toward one's own tradition. There is genuinely respect for the teachings of other religions even when they are different from and not fully compatible with the teachings of one's own tradition. Dialogue with other religions is encouraged without subordinating it to other goals, not even agreement or conversion. Dialogue is an intrinsically valuable and open-ended process indispensable for promoting mutual understanding and harmony.

Having clarified that exclusivism, inclusivism, and pluralism may refer to views and attitudes, we can compare the Dalai Lama and the Buddha.

In terms of attitude both the Dalai Lama and the Buddha can be said to display pluralistic attitudes. Both accept religious diversity unambiguously as a matter of principle, not simply tolerate others, which is characteristic of exclusivistic attitudes, or accept other religions with ambiguities and reservations, which is common among people with inclusivistic attitudes.

Similarly, the Buddha and the Dalai Lama genuinely respect other traditions without necessarily agreeing with all their teachings. Unlike people with exclusivistic attitudes, the Buddha and the Dalai Lama do not assume that non-Buddhist traditions and their teachings are useless if not harmful. Unlike people with inclusivistic attitudes, the Buddha and the Dalai Lama do not reduce other traditions the mere stepping stones conducive to one's own tradition. Religious diversity has a purpose and it is there to stay. Finally, both the Buddha and the Dalai Lama dialogue with other traditions without necessarily seeking agreement or conversion, which are the ultimate reasons for dialogue among people with exclusivistic and inclusivistic attitudes. That is, the pluralistic attitude does not subordinate interfaith dialogue to mission and proclamation but rather to mutual understanding and the cultivation of harmonious relationships among religions.

It should be noted that the Dalai Lama's pluralistic attitude goes far beyond the inclusivistic attitude characteristic of his Geluk school of Tibetan Buddhism. The traditional Geluk attitude toward other Buddhist traditions tends to be inclusivistic rather than pluralistic because it reduces other traditions to mere stepping stones towards the highest, i.e., Geluk presentation of emptiness.

In terms of view, however, neither the Buddha nor the Dalai Lama can be considered pluralists. I have defined the pluralist view in terms of non-dogmatic openness to other traditions, that is, openness to OTMIX in other religions, but without nonnegotiable doctrinal constraints. Both the Dalai Lama and the Buddha approach other traditions with nonnegotiable standards about what they consider ultimately true and valuable. Likewise, neither the Buddha nor the Dalai Lama can be considered pluralists if by pluralism it is meant a postmodern and relativist ideology that celebrates diversity to the point of endorsing relativism. Neither the Buddha nor the Dalai Lama would celebrate the existence of ways of life that foster greed, hate, and ignorance. However, if celebrating diversity simply means welcoming the positive ethical contribution of religions, then the Dalai Lama is clearly a pluralist and the Buddha could be interpreted as one because he does not object to the existence of religious diversity as such, only to specific doctrines and practices found in some traditions.

For the Dalai Lama as well as for the Buddha, religious diversity does not pose any theological problem. Neither of them thinks that his tradition needs to eventually replace or subsume all the others. In both, the belief in karma and rebirth serves as a foundation for their overall positive approach to religious diversity. Given that people have different karma (inclinations, capacities, contexts) as well as many lives ahead of them in order to travel the spiritual path, it is only natural to accept the existence of many teachings and many traditions, each one suitable for different kinds of individuals in different contexts and at different stages of spiritual development. This genuine acceptance and respect for religions does not entail relativism or uncritical acceptance of any doctrine and spiritual practice. Both the Dalai Lama and the Buddha agree in that not all paths lead to the same goal, and that certain doctrines and practices are less effective than others to attain liberation and highest holiness.

Regarding commitment to one's own tradition, both the Dalai Lama and the Buddha of the *Pāli Nikāyas* approach other traditions with unshakeable commitment to what they consider ultimately true, the Dharma in the case of the Buddha, the teachings on emptiness of the Geluk tradition in the case of the Dalai Lama. For the Dalai Lama, the teachings about the ultimate truth found in his Geluk tradition are definitive, and, therefore, nonnegotiable. Similarly, for the Buddha, aspects of the Dharma such as selflessness, dependent origination, and the four noble truths, are never questioned, and, in this sense at least, also nonnegotiable. Here, however, there are crucial differences that should be noted.

The Dalai Lama suggests that some version of exclusivism is necessary in the context of individual practice. It is unclear what exactly the Dalai Lama means by exclusivism because he does not distinguish between views and attitudes. Exclusivists, for the Dalai Lama, seem to be those who do not accept other religions as legitimate and therefore, do not respect their integrity and accord them any value. I distinguish between four senses of exclusivism: (1) the "exclusivist view," which is a claim about the existence of OTMIX: "OTMIX exists only in one's own tradition"; (2) the "exclusivistic attitude," which primarily consists in failing to accept and respect other religions; (3) the "exclusivist way of thinking," which is a tendency to apply an absolutist black or white logic to all aspects of reality even when there are gray areas; and (4) "specific exclusivism," which is the rejection of particular doctrines and practices found in other traditions, i.e., those that contradict the teachings of one's own tradition.

What the Dalai Lama says about exclusivism corresponds to what I call "the exclusivistic attitude." Exclusivistic attitudes, however, are characteristic of fundamentalists, and it would be unfair to attribute them to all those who hold exclusivist views of OTMIX. For instance, most evangelical Christians believe that other religions do not provide means of salvation (exclusivist view) yet they accept and respect other religions because they contain some elements of general revelation (vague knowledge about God, basic morals). Thus, it is simply not the case that those who hold an exclusivist view of salvation fail to accept and respect religious diversity. Most exclusivists are not fundamentalists and people with exclusivist views need not display exclusivistic attitudes. In order to differentiate people with both exclusivist views and attitudes from people with exclusivist views but inclusivist attitudes I distinguish between exclusivistic-exclusivists and inclusivistic-exclusivists. Most Buddhists and Christians can be interpreted as inclusivistic-exclusivists, that is, they combine an exclusivist view of OT-MIX with a sincere inclusivistic attitude that accepts other religions to some extent and genuinely respects similar elements of truth and goodness found in them.

Even the Dalai Lama, at least when he speaks about other Buddhist traditions as an orthodox member of the Geluk school, can be interpreted as an inclusivistic-exclusivist. In many texts in which he discusses the teachings of other Buddhist traditions, the Dalai Lama reduces them to mere stepping stones toward his Buddhist tradition, thus displaying an inclusivistic attitude rather than the pluralistic attitude he demonstrates in his latest book on religious diversity. Maybe the ideas of the Dalai Lama about other religions have evolved; maybe he speaks differently depending on his audience, in more pluralistic way when he talk to Westerners and about world religions, or in a more inclusivistic way when he talks to fellow Geluks about other Buddhist schools. Be it as it may, the Dalai Lama combines either an inclusivistic or pluralistic attitude with an exclusivist view of liberation. For the Dalai Lama, liberation is exclusive to Buddhism and the highest understanding of emptiness is the monopoly of his Geluk school of Tibetan Buddhism. More specifically, only emptiness as taught by the Prāsaṅgika-Madhyamaka philosophical school leads to the ultimate end of liberation. In the Dalai Lama's words:

> Liberation in which "a mind that understands the sphere of reality annihilates all defilements in the sphere of reality" is a state that only Buddhists can accomplish. This kind of mokṣa or nirvāṇa is only explained in the Buddhist scriptures, and is achieved only through Buddhist practice...The mokṣa which is described in the Buddhist religion is achieved only though the practice of emptiness. And this kind of nirvāṇa or liberation, as I have defined above, cannot be achieved even by Svātantrika

Mādhyamikas, by Cittamātras, Sautrāntikas or Vaibhāṣikas. The followers of these schools, though Buddhists, do not understand the actual doctrine of emptiness. Because they cannot realize emptiness, or reality, they cannot accomplish the kind of liberation I defined previously.[20]

Unlike the Dalai Lama's view of liberation, the Buddha's view is not exclusivist.[21] The Buddha's view of religious diversity is more consistent. That is, there is no tension between the individual and the social perspectives of the Buddha because, unlike the Dalai Lama, he does not hold an exclusivist view of liberation that is somewhat silenced in the social context of religious diversity.

For the Buddha, liberation and highest holiness are not tradition-specific. The early concept of *paccekabuddha* (self-enlightened being) demonstrates that someone who has never met the Buddha, heard his teachings, and practice under the guidance of his disciples, can and does attain liberation and highest holiness. In other words, for the Buddha, liberation and highest holiness are not necessarily confined to his teaching-and-discipline because there are beings, i.e., *paccekabuddhas*, who reach the ultimate end of the spiritual path without taking refuge in the Buddha, the Dharma, and the Sangha, that is, independently of Buddhas and Buddhists.

It is true that there is an absolutist claim underlying the Buddha's approach to religious diversity, namely, that there is only one ultimate end. However, this absolutist claim about *nibbāna* is an instance of what I call "specific exclusivism," not an instance of the exclusivist view. Making truth-claims about the ultimate end necessarily entails the rejection of specific doctrines that contradict such truth-claims. The Buddha rejects many doctrines and practices including wrong doctrines about what constitutes the ultimate end (specific exclusivism), but he does not claim that only Buddhists attain the ultimate end (exclusivist view).

The Dalai Lama's view of religious diversity combines two distinct perspectives: the exclusivist view of liberation in the context of individual religious practice, and the pluralistic attitude that accepts other traditions as legitimate, respects them and accords them value due to their ethical and spiritual contribution. Within the context of individual practice, the Geluk perpective of one truth, one religion, the Dalai Lama holds an exclusivist view of the ultimate end, Buddhahood, which is attainable only through the

---

20. H. H. the 14th Dalai Lama, "'Religious Harmony' and Extracts from *The Bodhgaya Interviews*," 169.

21. For a justification of this interpretation, see Vélez de Cea, *Buddha and Religious Diversity*.

Geluk presentation of emptiness. Yet, within the social context of religious diversity, the public perspective of many truths, many religions, the Dalai Lama displays a most exemplary pluralistic attitude.

The Dalai Lama can uphold the individual and the social perspectives with integrity because he legitimizes the validity of religions only on the level of ethics and spirituality, not on the level of doctrines and metaphysics. Other religions are legitimate and worthy of respect because they provide a foundation for ethical conduct and help to generate qualities such as love, compassion, and so on.

The Dalai Lama acknowledges that traditions make divergent and contradictory claims about doctrinal and metaphysical matters, but, on the social context, he makes no attempt to either legitimize or delegitimize such claims as true, false, or indifferent. He legitimizes religions as useful methods or skillful means to morally improve human beings and society, never as true, not even as relatively true or true from a particular perspective, as Mark Heim's model seems to do. This point is crucial to understand that the Dalai Lama is not replicating Heim's model of religious diversity.

The Dalai Lama does not judge the truth of religions on the doctrinal level from the social perspective. From the individual perspective, however, which is the perspective of his own Geluk tradition, the Dalai Lama cannot but judge other traditions on doctrinal grounds and make exclusivist claims about his tradition. Otherwise, the Dalai Lama would not be upholding the perspective of his tradition with integrity.

I interpret the Dalai Lama as an orthodox follower of the Geluk school and, therefore, he cannot legitimize the contradictory teachings of other traditions on the level of ultimate truth. This legitimation would put such teachings on par with the Geluk teachings on emptiness, and more important, would relativize the Geluk teachings as being true only for those who share the Geluk perspective. However, then the individual perspective of the Geluk school would be contradicted and relativized, which is what the Dalai Lama's model tries to avoid in the first place.

In order to uphold with integrity the individual perspective of his Geluk school, the Dalai Lama cannot claim at the social level that Geluk teachings about the ultimate truth are only true for him or just for members of the Geluk tradition. This is why, when the Dalai Lama says that Buddhism is the best for him, he must be referring to matters of practice or method, not to matters of ultimate truth or wisdom.

For the Geluk school, only their doctrinal claims about the ultimate truth are definitive, and this is so for everyone, not just for those who share the Geluk perspective. If the Dalai Lama went as far as to claim that the teachings of the Geluk tradition about the ultimate truth are true only for him, then he would not be faithful to the individual perspective of the Geluk tradition and he would no longer be an orthodox Geluk, but rather a Geluk with a postmodern outlook. In order to remain committed to his own faith tradition, the Dalai Lama must limit his pluralist acceptance of other traditions to the ethical level or the level of method, never to the doctrinal level of ultimate truth or level of wisdom.

This limited acceptance of religious diversity merely on the level of method or ethical teachings renders the Dalai Lama's model problematic. The problem is that religious traditions that make universal claims of truth cannot in good conscience keep such claims within the context of individual practice, as if such context had nothing to do with the social context of religious diversity. The individual context of traditions and practitioners is also part of the social context of religious diversity. We can choose not to judge the doctrinal claims of other traditions on the social level, and this is an excellent way of being politically correct and avoid religious conflicts, but we cannot pretend that the universal truth claims of our traditions are only true for us without at the same time undermining the truth of such claims.

The Dalai Lama's concept of two distinct perspectives is nonetheless a brilliant solution to the tension many people perceive between commitment to one's own faith tradition and acceptance of religious diversity. The Dalai Lama legitimizes the existence of many religions without downplaying their doctrinal differences and without relativizing their doctrinal claims about the ultimate end and the ultimate nature of reality. However, many traditions may object to the Dalai Lama's attempt to keep exclusivist claims out of the social context of religious diversity. For these traditions, the context or the perspective of individual religious practice is inseparable from the social context or perspective of religious diversity.

The Buddha of the *Pāli Nikāyas* is less politically correct than the Dalai Lama. For the Buddha, we cannot separate wisdom and method, individual and social perspectives, as well as the level of doctrines and the level of ethical teachings. Theory and practice are interrelated in the *Pāli Nikāyas*: views condition attitudes and deeds; conversely, attitudes and deeds condition views. The way things are requires the observance of certain practices and practices presuppose assumptions about the way things are.

From the perspective of the *Pāli Nikāyas*, we can distinguish but never separate right view from other factors of the path. That is, the level of ethical teachings and the level of doctrines or views are intertwined. Right view includes doctrinal claims such as the doctrine of karma and the distinction between the wholesome and the unwholesome. Thus, ethical teachings presuppose doctrinal claims and doctrinal claims considered right view involve ethical teachings. Likewise, the doctrines of selflessness and dependent origination and the ethical and spiritual practices associated with these doctrines are inseparable.

Although the Buddha of the *Pāli Nikāyas* does not speak about two perspectives, it is possible to distinguish between two aspects in the Buddha's approach to religious diversity: his pluralistic-inclusivist view and his pluralistic attitude. These two aspects can be compared to the Dalai Lama's exclusivist view (context of individual practice) and his pluralistic acceptance of religions (social context).

The Buddha's view of other traditions is best interpreted as a form of pluralistic-inclusivism. This simply means that the Buddha is genuinely open to religious diversity yet with ethical and doctrinal standards. These standards are nonnegotiable because they are aspects of the Dharma, which is stable and regular, i.e., structurally unchangeable. What changes is our knowledge of the Dharma and the particular representations of the Dharma traditions make in different contexts and times. In my reading, the Buddha would be open to new representations of the Dharma in the future and new knowledge about the Dharma. Yet the Buddha's openness would be critical and constrained by the nonnegotiable ethical and doctrinal standards found in the *Pāli Nikāyas*.

Such standards of the Dharma would constrain the Buddha's openness to other traditions, but without limiting the existence of OTMIX to the Buddha's teaching-and-discipline (exclusivism), nor without reducing OTMIX in other traditions to just the same thing that is already found in the Buddha's teaching-and-discipline (inclusivism).

The Dalai Lama's view of religions is qualitatively different. Yes, the Dalai Lama's openness to other traditions is also constrained by nonnegotiable ethical and doctrinal standards, but this does not make him a pluralistic-inclusivist like the Buddha. The Dalai Lama's view of OTMIX is exclusivist, at least when X refers to liberation, Buddhahood, and the highest presentation of emptiness. Unlike the Buddha, the Dalai Lama is not really open to the existence of OTMIX in other traditions. The Dalai Lama considers the Geluk teachings about the ultimate truth not only the definitive truth, i.e., nonnegotiable, but also (and this is where he parts company with the Buddha) exclusive to a particular school of Tibetan Buddhism. Whereas for the Buddha liberation and highest holiness are not to be understood in tradition-specific terms, for the Dalai Lama they cannot be attained without the presentation of emptiness that exists only in the Geluk school of Tibetan Buddhism.

Another key difference between the Buddha of the *Pāli Nikāyas* and the Dalai Lama is that, unlike the Dalai Lama, the Buddha does not advocate "some version of exclusivism" in order to show "commitment to one's own faith tradition." For the Buddha, the Dharma is not tradition-specific and, therefore, commitment to the Dharma cannot be understood in sectarian terms as adherence to the doctrinal tenets of a particular school, be it Theravāda or Geluk.

Even though the Buddha's view is best understood as a form of pluralistic-inclusivism, his advice to his disciples to investigate teachings critically, including his own teachings, requires the adoption of a pluralist view free from dogmatic constraints.

It is true that the Dalai Lama, like the Buddha, recommends that people investigate critically the Buddha's teachings. Like many Tibetan Lamas, the Dalai Lama quotes the Buddha as saying "Monks and scholars should well analyze my words, like gold [to be tested through] melting, cutting and polishing, and then adopt them, but not for the sake of showing me respect."[22] However, it is difficult to understand how this invitation to think critically about the Buddha's words can be reconciled with commitment to the dogmatic tenets of one's own Buddhist tradition. If the context of individual Buddhist practice requires someone to assume that the teachings of only one Buddhist school are the definitive truth, and if Buddhist practitioners are taught first and foremost that they need to remain committed to the doctrinal tenets of their own school or lineage, then I fail to see how they can put into practice the Buddha's advice to think critically even about his own teachings. Thinking critically about the Buddha's teachings and never questioning the dogmatic tenets of one's own Buddhist school does not seem to me compatible.

On the contrary, the Buddha of the *Pāli Nikāyas* does not demand from his disciples "dogmatic" commitment to any particular faith tradition including his own. Those who consider the *Pāli Nikāyas* authoritative know that for the Buddha certain teachings are never questioned by him, and this seems to indicate that they are nonnegotiable aspects of the Dharma. The Buddha, however, never asks his disciples to have faith in such teachings or to follow them out of respect for the Dharma, him or his teaching-and-discipline. Rather, the Buddha encourages his disciples to investigate such nonnegotiable teachings critically until they see for themselves that they are true, i.e., in accordance with the Dharma.

Moreover, the Buddha of the *Pāli Nikāyas* does not demand that his disciples hold an exclusivist view of liberation and highest holiness. Commitment to the Buddha's teaching-and-discipline has nothing to do with holding exclusivist claims and believing in the unique superiority of a particular presentation of Buddhism. Similarly, commitment to the Buddha's

---

22. Dalai Lama, *Buddhism of Tibet*, 55.

teaching-and-discipline has nothing to do with what some people may perceive as patronizing inclusivistic attitudes toward other forms of Buddhism disguised as the pluralist acceptance of religious diversity. Rather, commitment to the Buddha's teaching-and-discipline has to do with practicing the Dharma, and this cannot be done without keeping an open mind free from dogmatic constraints, be they Theravādin, Geluk, or otherwise.

BIBLIOGRAPHY

Dalai Lama. *The Buddhism of Tibet*. 3rd ed. Ithaca, NY: Snow Lion, 2002.

———. "'Religious Harmony' and Extracts from *The Bodhgaya Interviews*." Chap. 12 in *Christianity through Non-Christian Eyes*, edited by Paul Griffiths. Maryknoll, NY: Orbis, 1983.

———. *Towards True Kinship of Faiths: How the World's Religions Can Come Together*. New York: Three Rivers, 2010.

Vélez de Cea, Abraham. *The Buddha and Religious Diversity*. London: Routledge, 2012.

———. "A Cross-Cultural and Buddhist-Friendly Interpretation of the Typology Exclusivism, Inclusivism, Pluralism." *Sophia* 50 (2011) 453–80.

5

The Prospects for Interreligious and Intercultural Understanding
The Jesuit Case and Its Theoretical Implications

CHARLES B. JONES

INTRODUCTION

For the past several years, I have been reading and translating anti-Jesuit polemical literature and Jesuit apologetic responses of the late Ming and early Qing dynasties (roughly 1600–1724). In the course of the research I have read through much literature by Western and Chinese scholars, and I have found in their writings not only their analyses of the historical facts, but also their judgments upon the Jesuit missionaries. These generally fall into three patterns in accordance with the authors' particular horizons:

1. Jesuit and some American historians such as George Dunne and Liam Brockey tend to judge the Jesuits favorably. For them, the missions were successful both in making converts and in initiating a cultural exchange between East and West. In David Mungello's reading, they are the forefathers of modern sinology.[1]

    Chinese authors such as Yu Liu, Ping-yi Chu, and Qiong Zhang, render more negative judgments of the Jesuits as cultural interlopers.

---

1. See Dunne, *Generation of Giants*; Brockey, *Journey to the East*; Mungello, *Curious Land*.

Since missionaries assume *a priori* that other cultures need their gospel before they know anything about them, they cannot be anything but intruders. Some believe that the Jesuits' friendly demeanor masked more sinister intentions. For example, Liu says,

> Like ... other Europeans, Ricci was animated by "a will to conquer and proselytize." Unlike them, however, he recognized and accepted the limitations of European power in China. ... When he refashioned himself in 1595 as a Confucian scholar-official, he revealed in addition his newly acquired sense of how accommodation could be best utilized for his evangelical purposes.[2]

2. The language of conquest recurs throughout Liu's article, and in his conclusions, Liu avers that Ricci would have preferred the use of force to dominate China had it been possible, but chose dissimulation and accommodation as a fallback plan.[3]

3. European scholars such as Erik Zürcher and Jacques Gernet also looked unfavorably upon the Jesuits for similar reasons. In their judgment, the Jesuits were doomed to fail because the Chinese represented a superior culture which the Jesuits never understood.[4]

In this chapter I propose to leave the first category aside and examine possible reasons for the two negative judgments. In the next section, I will focus on two systematic arguments that hold that true intercultural communication is impossible in the nature of things regardless of the skill, sensitivity, and goodwill of the practitioners. Following that, I will list some practical arguments that specify only why *in this case* communication did not take place. Finally, I will argue that the Jesuit missions to China were a qualified though incomplete success and offer methodological suggestions for assessing other instances of interreligious encounter.

SYSTEMATIC CRITICISMS OF THE JESUITS

European and Chinese scholars generally hold that the Jesuits did not understand their host culture and its long history of philosophical-religious thought. Although rarely explicit, one may discern behind their opinions certain theories of intercultural exchange which deny the possibility of

---

2. Liu, "Intricacies of Accommodation," 466.
3. Ibid., 480.
4. See Zürcher, "In the Beginning," 163.

mutual understanding even under the best of circumstances. These are the theories of linguistic relativity and incommensurability.

Linguistic Relativity

The theory of linguistic relativity goes by many names, including "linguistic determinism," "the Sapir-Whorf hypothesis," or the "guidance and constraint hypothesis."[5] This theory has a long pedigree, and although it is frequently associated with the anthropologist Edward Sapir (1884–1939) and the linguist Benjamin Whorf (1897–1941), the basic idea goes back at least to Friedrich Schleiermacher's (1768–1834) essay, "On the Different Methods of Translating" ("Methoden des Übersetzens," 1813).[6] Simply stated, this theory holds that language determines thought and worldview so that people coming from different language groups will construe the world in significantly different ways. A weak version of the hypothesis posits various discrete areas of mutual unintelligibility while allowing for overlaps in worldview that permit some level of communication. In stronger versions, the worldviews will be so incompatible with each other that no true understanding or interlinguistic communication is possible. If one accepts this, then it would follow that the Jesuits, whose minds were formed completely by European languages, would never be able to comprehend Chinese thought, couched as it is in an alien and unrelated language.

It cannot be our purpose to detail all the "strong" and "weak" versions of this theory or the attempts to test it experimentally, but that does not really matter, since most scholars who give appraisals of the Jesuits in China do not make a sophisticated use of it. Erik Zürcher, for example, simply says this: "The subject of this paper has been yet another dialogue of misunderstandings: a clash of beliefs that never developed into a real exchange of views, mainly because the basic concepts and assumptions were so far apart that they did not belong to the same universe of discourse."[7] The assertion

---

5. Wardy, *Aristotle in China*, 11.

6. An English translation of Schleiermacher's essay is found in Schulte and Biguenet, *Theories of Translation*, 36–54. On linguistic relativity, Schleiermacher says, "Every human being is, on the one hand, in the power of the language he speaks; he and his whole thinking are a product of it. He cannot, with complete certainty, think anything that lies outside the limits of language. The form of his concepts, the way and means of connecting them, is outlined for him through the language in which he is born and educated" (38). While Schleiermacher did believe good translation was possible, this statement articulates a fairly strong version of linguistic relativity. For Whorf's statement of the hypothesis, see Whorf, "Relation of Habitual Thought and Behavior to Language."

7. Zürcher, "In the Beginning," 163. He made this the theme of his 1962 inaugural

that "universes of discourse" can be so different that a "real exchange of views" becomes impossible is a form of linguistic relativity, here expressed without elaboration. We thus must present some of the hypothesis' salient points, and then proceed to an evaluation of its utility for analyzing the Jesuits in China.

Benjamin Whorf based his version of the theory on observations of deep differences in the ways that various languages allowed their speakers to relate to the world. He pointed to studies of Hopi language that purported to show that they had a very different conception of time than did speakers of European languages, and suggested this meant they lived in a thought-world where time had a different texture and feel to it. It was not punctuated into moments of past, present, and future, but rather confronted Hopi speakers with a world that stretched along a timeless continuum. In addition, he pointed out that the Inuit had far more words words for "snow" than Western languages to illustrate the way that a people's environment can constrain their language.[8] In the case of Chinese versus European worldviews, others have argued that Chinese (spoken and classical) has no way of expressing counterfactuals, with the result that Chinese people cannot articulate ideas in the subjunctive mode or raise hypothetical situations. Examples such as these are often given as supports for the strong version of the theory, which would imply the untranslatability of one language, and therefore one worldview, into another. If this is true, then one might suppose that the Jesuits were never going to understand the Chinese worldview and vice versa. How strong are this hypothesis's warrants?

While some empirical studies do demonstrate differences in worldview that correlate well with the structure of language, the theory does not hold up in its strongest form that insists that languages (and cultures) are radically untranslatable. The data upon which Whorf based his hypothesis have been shown to be dubious. Geoffrey Pullum's 1991 book *The Great Eskimo Vocabulary Hoax*, among other works, demonstrated that native northern Alaskan languages have no more words for snow than any European language, especially if one takes into account phrases as well as words (e.g., English terms like "drifting snow" or "wet/dry snow").[9] In addition,

---

address, *Dialoog der misverstanden*. In it, he uses the term "*misverstanden*" in Dutch with the sense of two parties talking past one another with no real understanding or connection. I thank Wilhelmus Valkenberg for reading this piece with me and explaining the nuances of this term.

8. See Whorf, "Relation of Habitual Thought and Behavior to Language" for other examples.

9. Pullam, *Great Eskimo Vocabulary Hoax*. See also Martin, "Eskimo Words for Snow."

Ekkehart Malotki's monograph *Hopi Time* provided translations from Hopi language such as the following epigraph to his book: "Then, indeed, the following day, quite early in the morning at the hour when people pray to the sun, around that time then he woke up the girl again."[10]

As to the case of the supposedly missing Chinese counterfactuals, Robert Wardy points to Confucius' *Analects* 3:9. Here is the text with James Legge's translation:

> The Master said, "I could describe the ceremonies of the Xia dynasty, but Ji cannot sufficiently attest my words. I could describe the ceremonies of the Yin dynasty, but Song cannot sufficiently attest my words. (They cannot do so) because of the insufficiency of their records and wise men. If those were sufficient, I could adduce them in support of my words."[11]

If Chinese cannot articulate counterfactuals, then the last two statements would directly contradict one another: "They *cannot* do so because of the *insufficiency* of their records and wise men. They *are sufficient*, and thus I *can* adduce them in support of my words." For the text to make sense, the latter sentence must be translated as a counterfactual.[12] The principle of charity, as Donald Davidson reminds us, requires that when someone utters a sentence that they believe to be true, we must assume that it relates to a truth that we could also accept. Otherwise, we have to assume that anyone who says something that we cannot understand is mad.[13] In order to grant that Confucius did not mean to contradict himself, we must assume he is using a counterfactual.

One sustained scholarly critique of the theory of linguistic relativity, happily enough, deals directly with the China Jesuits. In *Aristotle in China*, Robert Wardy presents extracts from the *Mínglǐ tàn* 名理探, a 1631 Chinese translation of Aristotle's *Categories* published by Francisco Furtado and Li Zhizao 李之藻. He found that, no matter how abstruse or technical the philosophical arguments, and even when the argument was based on Greek and Latin word morphology without parallel in literary Chinese, the translators succeeded in conveying the meaning. In some cases, Wardy judged the Chinese even clearer than the original Greek![14] Thus, it appears that Chinese is not as inhospitable to European thought in translation as a hard version of the Sapir-Whorf hypothesis might hold.

10. Malotki, *Hopi Time*, n.p.; cited in Wardy, *Aristotle in China*, 14.
11. Legge, *Chinese Classics*, 1:22. Romanization modified.
12. Wardy, *Aristotle in China*, 29n102.
13. Davidson, "On the Very Idea of a Conceptual Scheme," 19.
14. Wardy, *Aristotle in China*, 120.

All this, I think, erodes the claim that the "universes of discourse" inhabited by European missionaries and Chinese intellectuals were so different as to preclude adequate mutual understanding. However, as Gadamer noted, translation is only the first step in understanding.[15] After successful translation, further obstacles to understanding lie in wait, which we may group under the rubric "incommensurability."

Incommensurability

The idea of incommensurability is similar to that of linguistic relativity, but covers a broader terrain with less precision.[16] While I examined the theory of linguistic relativity above as a way of evaluating narrowly focused questions of translatability, here I will look at incommensurability to widen the inquiry beyond translation problems.

The concept of incommensurability was first enunciated in the early 1960s by philosophers of science Thomas Kuhn and Paul Feyerabend. Borrowing the term from mathematics, in which it signifies the failure of one unit of measure to indicate the dimension of another unit without remainder (e.g., the incommensurability of the radius and circumference of a circle), they used it to indicate the inability to transfer information from one scientific paradigm to another. Both men received scholarly criticism for the term's lack of precision, and Kuhn reformulated the idea several times.[17] In a 1982 article, Kuhn proposed a "very modest form" of incommensurability, which he said applied not only to scientific communities and specializations, but to anthropology and other cross-cultural pursuits as well.

First, Kuhn distinguished between "translation" and "interpretation," something he held philosophers such as Quine had mistakenly conflated. "Translation" always involves two languages and the transfer of text from one to another; "interpretation" need not involve another language, although it might.[18] An anthropologist might hear a native word and employ one of a number of strategies to make it meaningful in his or her own language. First, there might be an exact equivalent for the word in English, such as "dog," making the meaning very clear. Second, lacking such an exact equivalent, the anthropologist might describe the phenomenon in clear English. Neither of these two instances exemplifies incommensurability between the two languages or cultures. However, in a third instance the native manner

---

15. Gadamer, *Truth and Method*, 180.
16. Bernstein, *Beyond Objectivism and Relativism*, 79.
17. See Chen, "Thomas Kuhn's Latest Notion of Incommensurability," 257–58.
18. Kuhn, "Commensurability, Comparability, Communicability," 672–73.

of conceptualizing the phenomenon might be embedded in such a different way of categorizing things that not even a description can convey the sense of the term; this would be an instance of incommensurability.[19] This reduces the concept of incommensurability to another version of the Sapir-Whorf hypothesis, since it posits linguistic or conceptual frames as the impediment to understanding, and hence is subject to the critique given above.

Other authors use the word differently. Paul Griffiths put forward an "incommensurability thesis" according to which a religious community's insiders hold not only doctrines but also the criteria by which they judge doctrines to be sensible and useful or not. Members of competing communities cannot pass valid judgments on the sense and utility of one another's doctrines, simply because they bring different criteria to bear. In short, no community's beliefs may legitimately be assessed by external critics.[20] Garrett Green cites several authors who describe people as "imprisoned" within conceptual worlds in such a way that they cannot meaningfully communicate with people who inhabit other conceptual prisons.[21] Green himself draws upon Clifford Geertz's classic distinction between "world view" and "ethos" to point out that religions and cultures do not merely propound doctrines (the "world view"), but also inculcate distinctive moods, motivations, ethical systems, and aesthetic styles that contribute to mutual incomprehension as well.[22] Richard Rorty put the matter thus:

> By "commensurable" I mean able to be brought under a set of rules which will tell us how rational agreement can be reached or what would settle the issue on every point where statements seem to conflict. These rules tell us how to construct an ideal situation, in which all residual disagreements will be seen to be "noncognitive" or merely verbal, or else merely temporary—capable of being resolved by doing something further.[23]

I will take the claim of incommensurability to mean that, not only are languages untranslatable, but that the concepts contained within two linguistic-cultural complexes are so disparate that they could not even be *explained* outside their own circles. In other words, not only could one not translate a text from another language into one's own; one could not even explain its contents in one's own words to others of one's community. One may perhaps account for this by appeal to the concept of "orientation" put

19. Kuhn, "Commensurability, Comparability, Communicability," 673.
20. Griffiths, *Apology for Apologetics*, 27–28.
21. Green, "Are Religions Incommensurable?," 226.
22. Ibid., 224.
23. Quoted in Bernstein, *Beyond Objectivism and Relativism*, 61.

forward by Nicholas Rescher. For him, an "orientation" is a fundamental way of seeing the world, a way that undergirds and provides a framework for the views we articulate, but of which we may not be conscious. If so, it would be s source of mutual incomprehension that would be very difficult even to detect, let alone overcome.[24] It would render almost impossible the production of an annotated translation or a basic commentary.

Some Chinese authors have made such claims. Ping-yi Chu argues that the Aristotelian basis of Jesuit teachings made them incomprehensible to their Chinese readership. The story of Jesus' birth to a virgin seemed heretical, and Confucian scholar-officials could never accept that Jesus deserved reverence after being condemned as a rebel by the competent political authorities.[25] He concludes: "This was a vain attempt at a dialogue between two incommensurable world views."[26] Yuming Sun, after describing the depiction of Jesus as the incarnation of the Lord of Heaven (*tianzhu* 天主) in artwork that the Jesuits brought with them, declares that the Chinese would not have been able to make sense of such a depiction, since Heaven and the "Sovereign on High" (*shangdi* 上帝) were incorporeal and suprasensible in their classical texts. He concludes, "Here is a classic example of cultural untranslatability."[27] In sum, the incommensurability thesis would hold that the Jesuits and their Chinese interlocutors never had a chance of understanding one another; their intellectual, historical, and cultural backgrounds were too different to have allowed that.

Evaluation

On such bases as these, some critics of the Jesuit missions hold that, in theory, any European-Chinese dialogue was doomed to failure because their modes of thought and expression inhabited irreconcilable universes of meaning. While, as Wolfgang Kubin says, such theories may be a useful tonic against the other extreme view, namely that accurate translation and adequate understanding occur easily and quickly,[28] we must not let them

---

24. Rescher, "Philosophical Disagreement."
25. Yang, *Budeyi* 不得已 [I cannot forebear], 450a, is a good example.
26. Chu, "Technical Knowledge," 100.
27. Sun, "Cultural Translatability," 468. Sun does not use the word "incommensurability," but since he is not speaking of the translation of texts and modifies the word "translatability" with "cultural," I believe he means something very like "incommensurability" here.
28. Kubin, "Importance of Misunderstanding," 257.

pass without careful thought. I will raise four objections to these theoretical qualms.

First, these theses put forward an unrealistic standard for communication, one that accepts only an ideal transfer of meaning, affect, and connotation into the target language. The evidence shows that attempts to meet such a standard rarely succeed, and indeed may not need to. For example, Wardy acknowledges that Li and Furtado took many liberties with the text of Aristotle's *Categories*, but notes that they did so in order to ease the path to understanding. A strict translation with all the proper names of other philosophers, couched in syllogistic formalisms, and conveying Aristotle's ironic tone, might not have been accessible to a Chinese reader. The liberties and ellipses of the translation not only did not alter or diminish the ideas being communicated; they actually provided a better avenue to understanding.[29] In some places, Wardy considers the Chinese rendering of particular philosophical points clearer than in the original text.[30] Wardy gives many specific examples of philosophical points made in the *Categories*, such as the original text's presentation of four different ways of thinking about substance, and judges that in each case, Furtado and Li found ways to transmit the ideas adequately and even elegantly into Chinese.[31] Wardy concludes that the *Mingli tan* 名理探 generally succeeded in rendering even Aristotle's most technical distinctions into Chinese.

What about translation in the other direction, i.e., from the Chinese thought-world to the European? Even as they translated European scholastic thought into literary Chinese, the Jesuits were also translating the Chinese classics into Latin. One of the earliest results of their efforts was the *Confucius Sinarum Philosophus* of 1687, a publication that Thierry Maynard has examined in detail and rendered into English. In the introductory material, Maynard appraises the Jesuits' grasp of the meaning of the texts of three of the canonical *Four Books* (*si shu* 四書) of Confucianism: the *Analects* (*Lunyu* 論語), the *Great Learning* (*Daxue* 大學), and the *Doctrine of the Mean* (*Zhongyong* 中庸). While acknowledging that some modern scholars such as Jacques Gernet, David Hall, and Roger Ames, considered the Chinese and European systems of thought incommensurable, Maynard says, "The two traditions were so commensurate that a true dialogue occurred and a new meaning was created."[32] These two examples should be adequate to demonstrate that translation and interaction between cultures

---

29. Wardy, *Aristotle in China*, 83, 84.
30. Ibid., 120.
31. Ibid., 127–38.
32. Maynard, *Confucius Sinarum Philosophus*, 27.

can achieve real communication even when they do not attain the level of precision demanded by a strict theory of commensurability.

Second, as Paul Griffiths argues, the incommensurability thesis assumes that the doctrines and ideas of any culture or religion are held only for *causes*, never for *reasons*. That is to say, the cultural, historical, or intellectual matrix within which people hold to beliefs are the *cause* of those beliefs. A different set of matrices would *cause* adoption of a different set of beliefs. If that were true, then no dialogue would indeed be possible, as the causal matrices out of which the partners spoke would be incapable of rendering the others' views intelligible. However, if people do in fact hold their beliefs and teachings for *reasons*, then there is a very good chance that, given enough time for continued dialogue, they will eventually come to understand one another's reasons for believing as they do.[33]

Third, such theories show little regard for translation theory, in which genre matters. Straightforward technical instructions, such as those for assembling furniture, are extremely easy to translate with great accuracy. Poetry occupies the opposite end of the spectrum. Philosophical works are somewhere in between. Indeed, George Steiner commented that philosophical texts are the second-easiest type to translate successfully after technical manuals.[34] Critics must take into account the genre of literature under consideration when assessing the success or failure of any given translation. Perhaps the poems in E. E. Cummings' *73 Poems*, so abstract and gnomic that they can hardly be considered English, would present insuperable difficulties of translation, but surely the "Life of Christ" books and the catechisms that the Jesuits published for popular consumption communicated their teachings in Chinese effectively. The refutations of these works that I have seen in Chinese polemical literature demonstrate that the critics had no trouble grasping European concepts.

Finally, Ping-yi Chu, one of the scholars who assert the incommensurability of Counter-Reformation European and Ming-Qing Chinese culture, makes the salient observation that one may make a claim of incommensurability as a means of establishing a boundary between cultures, a useful strategy when one culture feels another is encroaching on it.[35] Mario Biagioli demonstrated that one side in a debate may even make an asymmetric declaration of incommensurability, as when Galileo claimed that his philosophical rivals, lacking his knowledge of mathematics, made arguments incommensurable to his, while he, being conversant with their

33. Griffiths, *Apology for Apologetics*, 28–29.
34. Steiner, *After Babel*, 326.
35. Chu, "Technical Knowledge," 93n24.

philosophy, could absorb their views quite readily.[36] Such claims may function to lay down markers to keep others out or to refute their claim to an insider's understanding, but they are hardly rigorous theoretical statements.

Thus, we must reject any theory that asserts the *a priori* untranslatability or incommensurability of the Jesuit message into Chinese or of Chinese thought to Europeans as both theoretically unsound and empirically unproven.

PRACTICAL CRITICISMS OF THE JESUITS

Not all criticisms of the Jesuits are systematic in nature. Some are practical, and argue that *this particular group of representatives* from the West did not succeed in gaining a true understanding of late Ming-early Qing Chinese thought. The first such critique holds that missionaries in general cannot comprehend other cultures and religions because their very evangelical mandate precludes understanding. We will examine this broad claim and then its specific application to the Jesuits. The second critique eschews such broad assertions and focuses narrowly on the Jesuits as would-be cultural usurpers lacking legitimacy.

Missionaries Cannot Understand Other Religions

One often encounters the assertion that dialogue and evangelization are incompatible; one can practice one or the other but not both, and individuals must therefore choose one or the other function when encountering other religions. This idea can even be found in official church pronouncements, such as the Vatican document *Dialogue and Proclamation*, in which the Catholic magisterium declared that the church ought to engage in both activities, but should prioritize evangelization over dialogue.[37] According to this way of thinking, missionaries, as church representatives who follow the vocation of evangelization, cannot fruitfully participate in interreligious dialogue.

The broad assertion that evangelization is contrary to dialogue, which entails the conclusion that missionaries can never really understand their host culture, does not stand up to empirical testing. Galen Amstutz, in his book *Interpreting Amida*, asked why Westerners looking for religion in Japan were blind to the presence of the Pure Land schools of Jōdo Shū 淨土

---

36. Biagioli, "Anthropology of Incommensurability."
37. Pontifical Council, *Dialogue and Proclamation*, §75–81.

宗 and Jōdo Shinshū 淨土真宗 in Japan, even though these were the largest, wealthiest, and most active religious organizations on the scene. To boil his complex analysis down to summary terms, he found that Pure Land did not suit the spiritual needs of Western seekers or the academic interests of scholars. Missionaries, however, did see the Pure Land schools for what they were, assessed their importance correctly, and described their beliefs and practices accurately.[38] Having their own religious commitments already in place, missionaries seek to understand the competition as realistically as possible. In addition, they often remain on the scene for long years, learn the local language, and cultivate networks of educated informants. Thus they prove less likely to distort the data than the other two groups.

Other missionaries proved as attentive as the Jesuits to their religious surroundings. James Legge (1815–1897), a nineteenth-century Protestant missionary to south China, preached the Gospel to be sure, but he also produced critical translations of key Confucian texts of such high quality that they are still widely consulted. He also became Oxford's first professor of Chinese. Ernst J. Eitel (1838–1908), an Evangelical Lutheran missionary to China produced the *Handbook of Chinese Buddhism Being a Sanskrit, Chinese Dictionary* (1888), one of the first reference tools on Chinese Buddhism ever published.[39] Thus, we have no reason to think that the nature of their vocation prevents missionaries from understanding the religions of their host cultures.

What about the specific contention that the Jesuits themselves failed in both dialogue and understanding? On the face of it, it seems unlikely that some of Europe's most intelligent and educated men, after living in China for decades, mastering its language, studying its literature, and having many conversations with highly educated friends and converts, would consistently miss the point of Chinese thought. Jacques Gernet himself, after articulating this view, provides clues that they actually understood their hosts quite well by quoting letters that Nicolò Longobardo sent to Rome which evince quite an adequate grasp of Confucian philosophy.[40]

Erik Zürcher gives a somewhat more nuanced critique of the Jesuits in a lecture in which he compared their efforts to those of the Buddhists several centuries earlier. Buddhist monks, he says, infiltrated China slowly and as individuals. Having left their home countries behind, they did not communicate with any central authority back home (indeed no such authority existed), leaving them free to adapt their religion to local conditions.

---

38. Amstutz, *Interpreting Amida*, chaps. 4 and 5.
39. See Girardot, *Victorian Translation of China*.
40. Gernet, *China and the Christian Impact*, 207, 211.

Buddhism thus successfully penetrated China. The Jesuits, on the other hand, maintained contact with and loyalty to Rome, and the strict, doctrinaire religion of the Catholic Counter-reformation bound their hands and prevented them from achieving a successful adaptation.[41]

It is difficult to credit these critiques. Gernet undercuts his own assertions by the evidence that he himself presents. Zürcher's comparison of the Jesuits with the earlier Buddhist missionaries rests on inadequate foundations. He compares Buddhist missions from a period spanning five centuries with only the first century of the Jesuit missions. If one looked at only the first century of Buddhism's presence in China, one would find a comparable difficulty of translation and a high degree of mutual misunderstanding. If one looked at Catholic missionary efforts in China for a period of five hundred years (taking it well into the twentieth century), one might find that Christianity's adaptability to Chinese circumstances compares more favorably with that of Buddhism. In the end, then, I find the specific criticisms of the Jesuits' abilities to understand the Chinese and adapt to China unconvincing.

The Jesuit Mission as Illegitimate Cultural Incursion

As noted in the introductory section, some scholars regard the Jesuits as uninvited cultural interlopers who, before ever coming to China, had decided that the Chinese needed their message. Aside from the quotation from Yu Liu given earlier, we also find this criticism in Qiong Zhang's 1996 Harvard dissertation. Near the end, she appraises the Jesuits as men who believed that their Scholastic philosophy and theology was the pinnacle of human achievement, and who thus came to China already believing that it needed both Christianity and Western learning to "upgrade" it from its entanglement in idolatry and inferior philosophy.[42] She further speculates that the encounter may have been more fruitful for both sides had the Jesuits been more receptive to the insights of China's philosophical heritage.[43] Certainly many of the anti-Jesuit writers of the late Ming and early Qing periods harbored their own suspicions about the Jesuits' motives, connections with Western powers, and intentions. Ouyi Zhixu 澫益智旭 (1599–1655), for example, exclaimed in his *Pixie ji* 闢邪集 [Collected refutations of heterodoxy]:

---

41. Zürcher, *Bouddhisme, christianisme et société chinoise*, 29–37.
42. Zhang, *Cultural Accommodation or Intellectual Colonization?*, 290–92.
43. Ibid., 291.

Alas! Who knew that Wang Mang, so modest and respectable, would be a usurper of the Han court? Or that [Wang Anshi's] "new learning" was actually a parasite of the [Northern] Song period. Your intentions are also very wicked![44]

However, one could take a softer view. Missionaries in other parts of the world, and even in China itself, came with a greater show of military power that enabled them to impose their presence upon a resisting population. One may recall the Dutch in Taiwan, for instance, who outlawed the practice of religions other than Christianity and flogged violators.[45] The Protestant missionaries who arrived in the latter half of the nineteenth century were enabled to travel without let or hindrance throughout China because of the presence of Western gunboats and the "unequal treaties" whose memory still arouses resentment. The Jesuits, in contrast, had no such power base and could not impose their presence. They relied only upon their command of the language, their literary creations, their scientific and technological novelties, and their powers of persuasion.

This is more a question of legitimacy than of success in understanding Chinese thought. However, a few observations are appropriate here. As Nicholas Standaert has pointed out, such a polemical stance assumes a level of helplessness and passivity of the populations among which Western missionaries worked. In the academic environment of post-colonial studies, this may be a valid concern when missionaries depend upon a significant power imbalance to gain access and pursue their mission in other lands, but the Chinese were hardly helpless in this situation. In addition, scholars such as Standaert and Monika Übelhör have demonstrated that exchanges and conversations between the Chinese and the Jesuits were not infrequently initiated by the Chinese intelligentsia in pursuit of their own interests, and they certainly had an active hand in determining how the Jesuits' teachings and publications were disseminated and received.[46]

In the final analysis, this critique stems from a value judgment rather than from questions of evidence. Perhaps we can boil the matter down to this: One may judge that anyone who enters foreign territory intending to effect changes in native culture, whether religious, ideological, or political, displays arrogance at the very least. More important for us, perhaps, is the observation that such an attitude does not lead to the *praxis* of dialogue as understood by Hans-Georg Gadamer and Richard Bernstein. Absent such

---

44. Ouyi Zhixu 蕅益智旭, *Pixie ji* 闢邪集, 19:11807. Translation mine.
45. Jones, *Buddhism in Taiwan*, 3, 4.
46. Standaert, "Study of the Classics by Late Ming Christian Converts," 19; Standaert, *Handbook of Christianity in China*, 601.

praxis, the encounter of cultures and religions cannot bear the kind of fruit that a true exchange would produce. Others may judge differently, and assert that even missionaries, in spite of their intentions for the mission field, can still display good will and openness enough to understand their hosts well enough. The question remains open.

ANOTHER WAY OF LOOKING AT THINGS

Most, if not all, of the views on the Jesuit encounter with Chinese religion canvassed above suffer from a grave methodological defect. They take a historical encounter between two highly evolved cultures that has lasted until the present day and try to boil it down into simple binary judgments such as success/failure or legitimate/illegitimate. Such an encounter, involving many actors and spanning several centuries, surely cannot be analyzed in any fruitful way by such crude metrics. As an alternative approach, I want to make the following methodological suggestions:

1. *Distinguish between description and interpretation in appraising interreligious understanding.* As Galen Amstutz points out, Jesuits in Japan understood Pure Land Buddhism quite well, even though they interpreted it through the lens of Christianity.[47] Following his lead, I will suggest that we distinguish questions of factual understanding from questions regarding appropriate interpretation of local religious traditions, and evaluate the two separately. Using this measure, we could say that the Jesuits in early modern China understood the Neo-Confucianism of their hosts quite well on the factual level. We may then consider the appropriateness of their overall Christian-Thomistic framework for interpreting this tradition and the missionary impulse that brought them into contact with it as a separate matter.

   At this point one may cite Hans-Georg Gadamer's dictum that mutual understanding equals agreement and conclude that any disagreement even about the interpretation of Chinese thought by the Jesuits entails misunderstanding.[48] I do not believe such a criticism applies here. Throughout *Truth and Method*, Gadamer assumes that the interpreter is engaging with *his or her own tradition*. Whether or not one can understand *another* tradition and its literature is a question he does not address.

---

47. Amstutz, *Interpreting Amida*, 45–46.
48. Gadamer, *Truth and Method*, 180.

The Prospects for Interreligious and Intercultural Understanding 81

2. *Use multigenerational, long-range time frames as the basis for evaluation rather than immediate understanding.* The vast majority of the scholarship on Jesuit encounters with Neo-Confucian thought centers on the early generations of missionaries. Matteo Ricci gets the lion's share of coverage; second-generation Jesuits such as Giulio Aleni get far less; late seventeenth-century figures such as Johann Adam Shall von Bell and Ferdinand Verbiest somewhat less. A very late missionary such as Alexandre de la Charme (1695–1767) gets almost none at all. As intelligent and diligent as the early Jesuits were, and as remarkable as their achievements in coming to grips with Chinese thought were, it is unreasonable to expect that they would get everything right in all details within one or two generations. It would be more realistic for us to acknowledge that the encounter between East and West and the drive toward mutual understanding is an ongoing process in which we are still very active. We continue to stand on the shoulders of all who have gone before us as we press ahead.

3. *Understand that the cultures and religions that are trying to understand one another are not static entities, but are ever-developing systems whose courses will be altered by the encounter itself.* As an example of this, one frequently hears that the concept "religion" did not exist in early China, and that the term used nowadays for this concept, *zongjiao* 宗教 was a nineteenth-century Japanese neologism coined specifically to convey this Western idea. The concept is not native, but was thus grafted into East Asian thought and language.[49] However, we must not fail to acknowledge that the word has long since been "naturalized," and is part of East Asian discourse now. One may easily find literature on interreligious dialogue (*zongjiao duihua* 宗教對話), find departments of religion (*zongjiao xi* 宗教系) in Chinese universities, and engage in religious studies (*zongjiao xue* 宗教學). An appendix in Lydia H. Liu's book *Translingual Practice* lists around 500 such vocabulary items that began as translations of Western terms but have since become part of Chinese language.[50] Thus, intercultural and interreligious understanding is not a matter of one static entity studying another and trying to get it right; it is an enterprise the very engagement in which creates and then takes place within a trajectory of mutual transformation. The Japanese Protestant theologian Seiichi Yagi's work bringing Buddhist

---

49. But see Campany, "On the Very Idea of Religions," for an argument that a concept very like "religion" did exist in traditional China.

50. Liu, *Translingual Practice*, 284–98.

thought into Christian theology provides an example of this process carried out intentionally.[51]

4. *See interreligious and intercultural encounter as an asymptotic process.* Anyone who has studied a foreign language knows that one may get better and better at it the longer one sustains one's efforts, but the likelihood of "going native" is remote. The same applies to habituation to a new culture; one may eventually become quite comfortable within another culture, but may still occasionally find oneself in difficult situations in which only the guidance of a native will do. Mastery of another language and culture is never either-or, and lauding the sojourner as either getting everything right or criticizing him for getting nothing right is a bootless endeavor.

5. *Understand that all parties in the exchange, both host and guest, are involved in the process of creating representations.* Edward Said, in his influential book *Orientalism*, was careful not to argue that European colonial powers created a false picture of the Middle East and its peoples; such an argument assumes an essentialized "Arab" (or, for us, "Chinese") susceptible to misrepresentation. He acknowledged that both colonizers and colonized were involved in creating representations both of themselves and of the other. The real issue is that *all* systems of discourse constitute their subjects, no matter who is representing and who is represented.[52] The task, then, is not to determine if this representation is right while that one is wrong, but to analyze the power relations that make one representation dominant while suppressing others. Mutual representation that takes form in a dialogical situation marked by unprejudiced curiosity and a balance of power may be the most desirable, but as we have seen from the examples raised by Amstutz, good representation can occur in competitive contexts as well.

6. *Do not let the discourse of power relations between guest and host obscures the highly collaborative nature of interreligious encounter.* Academics such as myself have grown accustomed to producing translations alone in our offices, surrounded by our reference books and online resources. We must remember that, in the past, much translation was done collaboratively, whether by the Kuchean monk Kumarajīva rendering Sanskrit texts into Chinese orally while Chinese scribes polished the final drafts, or Jesuits working with educated Chinese partners, as when Li and Furtado worked together to translate Aristotle's

---

51. Swidler and Yagi, *Bridge to Buddhist–Christian Understanding.*
52. Said, *Orientalism,* 325–26.

Categories. The Jesuits applied this method consistently from the earliest collaborations of Matteo Ricci with Chinese literati.[53] It is harder to criticize one side of the process of translation and interpretation when one realizes how much the other side cooperated in the venture.

CONCLUSIONS

So did the Jesuits understand the religion and philosophy of their literati hosts? We have seen that there is no *a priori* reason to think that they could not have done so. We have also seen that there was nothing about their missionary vocation or circumstances that would have precluded them from doing so. However, I want to be clear: While I do think one side in this centuries-old debate has a stronger case than the other, and believe that the Jesuits did a good job of engaging with Chinese thought, I do not wish to go so far as to say that they were entirely correct from the very beginning.

If we apply my six methodological suggestions, then I think we arrive at the more modest conclusion that they did as well as anyone could have. They arrived on an intellectual scene that was already buzzing with controversies and factions; native understandings abounded in great profusion. The Jesuits themselves could not agree on the most appropriate approach to take. Nevertheless, I think it fair to say that they got off to a good start, and helped to launch a period of East-West encounter whose fruits are still developing. Our two cultures and their native religious traditions are a pair of moving targets whose very proximity, beginning with European explorations and contact, has engendered continuous mutual change. Modern Western scholars are still busy studying and interpreting Chinese culture. The project will never be complete, but we can keep getting better and better the longer we stay engaged.

BIBLIOGRAPHY

Amstutz, Galen. *Interpreting Amida: History and Orientalism in the Study of Pure Land Buddhism*. Albany: SUNY Press, 1997.
Bernstein, Richard J. *Beyond Objectivism and Relativism: Science, Hermeneutics, and Praxis*. Philadelphia: University of Pennsylvania Press, 1983.
Biagioli, Mario. "The Anthropology of Incommensurability." *Studies in History and Philosophy of Science Part A* 21 (1990) 183–209.
Brockey, Liam Matthew. *Journey to the East: The Jesuit Mission in China, 1579–1724*. Cambridge: Harvard University Press, 2007.

---

53. He 何,"譯者的消失與僭越," 58; see also Li 李, 明末耶穌會翻譯文學論, chap. 5, for another account of Jesuit-Chinese cooperation in translation.

Campany, Robert Ford. "On the Very Idea of Religions (in the Modern West and in Early Medieval China)." *History of Religions* 42 (2003) 287–319.

Chen, Xiang. "Thomas Kuhn's Latest Notion of Incommensurability." *Journal for General Philosophy of Science / Zeitschrift für allgemeine Wissenschaftstheorie* 28 (1997) 257–73.

Chu, Ping-yi. "Technical Knowledge, Cultural Practices and Social Boundaries: Wannan Scholars and the Recasting of Jesuit Astronomy, 1600–1800." PhD diss., University of California, Los Angeles, 1994.

Cummings, E. E. *73 Poems*. New York: Liveright, 1963.

Davidson, Donald. "On the Very Idea of a Conceptual Scheme." *Proceedings and Addresses of the American Philosophical Association* 47 (1973/74) 5–20.

Dunne, George H. *Generation of Giants: The Story of the Jesuits in China in the Last Decades of the Ming Dynasty*. South Bend: University of Notre Dame Press, 1962.

Gadamer, Hans-Georg. *Truth and Method*. 2nd rev. ed. Translated by Joel Weinsheimer and Donald G. Marshall. New York: Continuum, 1989.

Gernet, Jacques. *China and the Christian Impact: A Conflict of Cultures*. Translated by Janet Lloyd. New York: Cambridge University Press, 1985.

Girardot, Norman J. *The Victorian Translation of China: James Legge's Oriental Pilgrimage*. Berkeley: University of California Press, 2002.

Green, Garrett. "Are Religions Incommensurable? Reflections on Plurality and the Religious Imagination." *Louvain Studies* 27 (2002) 218–39.

Griffiths, Paul J. *An Apology for Apologetics: A Study in the Logic of Interreligious Dialogue*. Maryknoll, NY: Orbis, 1991.

He Zhihe 何致和. "譯者的消失與僭越—晚明耶穌會傳教士與二十世紀華人作家的非母語書寫" ["Loss and usurpation of translators: Late-Ming Jesuits and twentieth-century Chinese writing in non-native languages"]. *Zhongguo wenzhe yanjiu tongxun* 中國文哲研究通訊 86 (2012) 55–71.

Jones, Charles B. *Buddhism in Taiwan: Religion and the State, 1660–1990*. Honolulu: University of Hawai'i Press, 1999.

Kubin, Wolfgang. "The Importance of Misunderstanding: Reconsidering the Encounter Between East and West." *Monumenta Serica* 53 (2005) 249–60.

Kuhn, Thomas S. "Commensurability, Comparability, Communicability." *PSA: Proceedings of the Biennial Meeting of the Philosophy of Science Association* 2 (1982) 669–88.

Legge, James, trans. *The Chinese Classics*. 5 vols. London: Trübner, 1861.

Li Shixue 李奭學. 明末耶穌會翻譯文學論 [A discussion of Jesuit literary translations in the late Ming]. 翻譯史研究論叢 1. Hong Kong: Chinese University Press 中文大學出版, 2012.

Liu, Lydia H. *Translingual Practice: Literature, Culture, and Translated Modernity—China, 1900–1937*. Stanford: Stanford University Press, 1995.

Liu, Yu. "The Intricacies of Accommodation: The Proselytizing Strategy of Matteo Ricci." *Journal of World History* 19 (2008) 465–87.

Malotki, Ekkehart. *Hopi Time: A Linguistic Analysis of the Temporal Concepts in the Hopi Language*. Trends in Linguistics, Studies and Monographs 20. Berlin: de Gruyter, 1983.

Martin, Laura. "Eskimo Words for Snow: A Case Study in the Genesis and Decay of an Anthropological Example." *American Anthropologist* 88 (1986) 418–23.

Maynard, Thierry. *Confucius Sinarum Philosophus (1687): The First Translation of the Confucian Classics*. Monumenta Historica Societatis Iesu, n.s., 6. Rome: Institutum Historicum Societatis Iesu, 2011.

Mungello, David E. *Curious Land: Jesuit Accommodation and the Origins of Sinology*. Studia Leibnitiana, Supplementa 25. 1985. Reprint, Honolulu: University of Hawai'i Press, 1989.

Ouyi Zhixu 溢益智旭. *Pixie ji* 闢邪集 [Collected refutations of heterodoxy]. In *Ouyi dashi quanji* 溢益大師全集 [The collected works of Great Master Ouyi], 19:11771–11818. Taipei: Fojiao chubanshe 佛教出版社, 1989.

Pontifical Council for Inter-religious Dialogue. *Dialogue and Proclamation: Reflection and Orientations on Interreligious Dialogue and the Proclamation of the Gospel of Jesus Christ*. Rome, 19 May 1991. http://www.vatican.va/roman_curia/pontifical_councils/interelg/documents/rc_pc_interelg_doc_19051991_dialogue-and-proclamatio_en.html.

Pullam, Geoffrey K. *The Great Eskimo Vocabulary Hoax and Other Irreverent Essays on the Study of Language*. Chicago: University of Chicago Press, 1991.

Rescher, Nicholas. "Philosophical Disagreement: An Essay towards Orientational Pluralism in Metaphilosophy." *Review of Metaphysics* 32 (1978) 217–51.

Said, Edward W. *Orientalism*. New York: Vintage, 1978.

Schulte, Rainer, and John Biguenet, eds. *Theories of Translation: An Anthology of Essays from Dryden to Derrida*. Chicago: University of Chicago Press, 1992.

Standaert, Nicholas, ed. *Handbook of Christianity in China*. Vol. 1, 635–1800. Handbook of Oriental Studies. Section Four, China 15. Leiden: Brill, 2001.

———. "The Study of the Classics by Late Ming Christian Converts." In *Cheng—All in Sincerity: Festschrift in Honour of Monika Übelhör*, edited by Denise Gimpel and Melanie Hanz, 19–40. Hamburg: Hamburger sinologische Gesellschaft, 2001.

Steiner, George. *After Babel: Aspects of Language and Translation*. 3rd ed. Oxford: Oxford University Press, 1998.

Sun, Yuming. "Cultural Translatability and the Presentation of Christ as Portrayed in Visual Images from Ricci to Aleni." In *The Chinese Face of Jesus Christ*, edited by Roman Malek, 2:461–98. Sankt Augustin, Germany: Institut Monumenta Serica / China-Zentrum, 2002.

Wardy, Robert. *Aristotle in China: Language, Categories and Translation*. Cambridge: Cambridge University Press, 2000.

Whorf, Benjamin Lee. "The Relation of Habitual Thought and Behavior to Language." In *Language, Thought, and Reality: Selected Writings of Benjamin Lee Whorf*, edited by John B. Carroll, 134–59. Cambridge: Technology Press of MIT, 1956.

Yagi, Seiichi, and Leonard Swidler. *A Bridge to Buddhist–Christian Dialogue*. New York: Paulist, 1988.

Yang Guangxian 楊光先. *Budeyi* 不得已 [I cannot forebear]. Manuscript dated 咸豐八年 [1858]. Reprinted in *Xùxiū Sìkù Quánshū* 續修四庫全書 [Complete library in four divisions, supplemental edition], 1033:443–501. Shanghai: Shanghai gu ji chu ban she 上海古籍出版社, 2002.

Zhang, Qiong. *Cultural Accommodation or Intellectual Colonization? A Reinterpretation of the Jesuit Approach to Confucianism during the Late Sixteenth and Early Seventeenth Centuries*. PhD diss., Harvard University, 1996.

Zücher, Erik. *Bouddhisme, christianisme et société chinoise*. Paris: Conférences essais et leçons du Collège de France, 1990.

———. *Dialoog der misverstanden: Rede uitgesproken bij de aanvaarding van het ambt van hoogleraar in de geschiedenis van het Verre Oosten aan de Rijksuniversiteit te Leiden op 2 maart 1962*. Leiden: Brill, 1962.

———. "'In the Beginning': 17th-Century Chinese Reactions to Christian Creationism." In *Time and Space in Chinese Culture*, edited by Chun-Chieh Huang and Erik Zürcher, 132–66. Sinica Leidensia 33. Leiden: Brill, 1995.

6

Paul, Practical Pluralism, and the Invention of Religious Persecution In Roman Antiquity

PAULA FREDRIKSEN

MODERN SCHOLARS ARE AT several disadvantages when we try to orient ourselves with the religious world of Mediterranean antiquity.[1] For one thing, antiquity had no category corresponding to what we call "religion." Relations between heaven and earth were commonly configured along ethnic lines,[2] a point to which I shall return below. Second, our historical retrospect risks giving to the emergent identities of religious traditions—"paganism," "Judaism," and "Christianity"—a kind of coherence and a notional "essence" that the phenomena themselves, in context, belie.[3] Further,

---

1. This essay draws substantially on a longer piece, "Retrospect Is the Mother of Anachronism: How Later Contexts Affect Pauline Contents," which is forthcoming.

2. For a general discussion of this point, see Fredriksen, *Augustine and the Jews*, 6–15. This generalization holds true for all such groups in Mediterranean antiquity, though because of the current question of how to translate *Ioudaios* (whether as "Jew" or as "Judaean"), the relationship(s) of ancient "ethnicity" to "religion" have recently received much attention. See in particular the reflections of Miller, "Meaning of *Ioudaios*," and "Ethnicity Comes of Age," with literature cited.

3. For this reason, some historians hesitate to use the word "Christian" at all for the first generation of the movement; see most recently on this historiographical point Marshall, "*Sonderzeit* Paul," 5–7; and Arnal, "Collection and Synthesis." Judaism in the late Second Temple period evinces such diversity that some scholars have advocated speaking of "Judaisms." For problems with "pagans," the classic essay is O'Donnell, "Demise of Paganism."

what we think of as individual traditions often display great diversity, even when—perhaps especially when—their spokesmen insist on internal homogeneity. And finally, these traditions all interact with the broader shared culture and with each other: boundaries are porous, intrinsically unstable, in fact often notional rather than actual. The historical situation that we seek to describe resists the clarity that we would like to ascribe.

False clarity is one of the perils of retrospect. One way to compensate for our perspectival difficulties as historians—thus, as committed retrospectators—is to try to imaginatively place ourselves in the world of gods and humans as ancient people themselves conceived it. It was, first of all, a world *full* of gods. To phrase the same thought differently: for *all* ancient people, *all* gods exist. Different groups might argue for the relative importance or power of one deity or another; philosophers might systematize relations between deities; particular cities might promote particular cults. But the existence of all gods was a fact of life presumed both by pagans and by those two whom we confusingly designate "monotheists"—that is, by ancient Jews and Christians. In other words, in antiquity, all monotheists were polytheists. Ancient Jews and Christians might in principle restrict their worship to a single deity, but they knew that other deities existed as well, exerting real effects on human lives.[4]

Part of the evidence for the various gods' existence was the humans who worshiped them: in antiquity, gods and humans formed family groups. The ethnic bonds between gods and peoples was often configured as descent, whereby the offspring of a primordial divine/human coupling conferred semi-divine status on a much later ruler. Thus Alexander descended from Heracles; and the Julian house, via Aeneas, from Venus. (More metaphorically, Jews mobilized the same idea to describe the relationship between their god and rulers of the house of David, e.g., Ps 2:7; 2 Sam 7:12, 14.) But whole populations might descend from a god, and such lineages could be put to practical political uses: Hellenistic and Roman diplomats, negotiating treaties between cities, would establish shared kinship, traced through lines

---

4. For the full argument, Fredriksen, "Mandatory Retirement," 241–43; for different arguments making the same point—that "monotheist" and "polytheist" suit the ancient context too poorly to be of much use as descriptive or analytic terms—see also the essays assembled in Mitchell and van Nuffelen, *One God*, especially those by Markschies ("The Price of Monotheism"), Chaniotis ("Megatheism"), and Belayche ("*Deus deum . . . summorum maximus*"). On Paul's acknowledgment of and struggles with pagan gods, Fredriksen, "Judaizing the Nations," 240–41. All of my own articles cited in the current essay may be found in PDF format on my Boston University web page, www.bu.edu/religion/faculty/fredriksen.

Paul, Practical Pluralism, and the Invention of Religious Persecution 89

of descent back to a god, or to his or her offspring. This ancient bond of shared "blood" served to stabilize current agreements.[5]

Cult, then, was thus an ethnic designation, and ethnicity was a cult designation. What we think of as "religion" ancient people considered an inheritance, "ancestral custom": *paradoseis tōn patrikon, ta patria ēthē, mos maiorum, hoi patrioi nomoi.* "In the Roman world, religion and ethnic loyalties were inseparable."[6] This was true at the micro-level of family gods and ancestors, and true at the macro-level of city gods and cosmic divinities. *Eusebeia* or *pietas* ("piety") did not measure what we think of as sincerity or strength of "belief" so much as attentiveness in the execution of inherited protocols of worship. This was for good reason: improper cult made gods angry. Proper cult demonstrated respect, pleased the gods, and inclined them to be gracious. So also *pistis* and *fides*: often translated as "belief," *pistis* indexed conviction, that is, confidence that the ancestral protocols in fact pleased the god; *fides* (often translated "faith") attested to loyalty to ancestral traditions and scrupulousness in performing them.

All gods exist, their existence witnessed in part by the existence of their humans; gods and humans form family groups, hence cult is an ethnic designation and ethnicity is a cultic designation. If we accept these two descriptions of ancient divine/human relations, then we can venture a third, a description of ancient empire. An anthropological definition of empire ("the greatest number of peoples under a single government") can be restated theologically: "the greatest number of gods under a single government." That different peoples had their own gods and, thus, customs was a commonplace of ancient ethnography and a fact of ancient culture.[7] Mediterranean empires, whether Hellenistic or Roman, were in consequence extremely commodious in terms of what we think of as "religion." To label all of this religious breathing space as "religious tolerance" is to

---

5. On Israel as God's "son," e.g., Exod 4:22; Jer 31:9; also Rom 9:4; on the association of the *ethnē* with their own pantheons, e.g., Mic 4:5; on a city's citizens being of one *genos*, e.g., Acts 18:24, said of the Alexandrian Apollos. Further on the family connections between peoples, gods and Greek cities, see especially Jones, *Kinship Diplomacy*. Gentile Christians eventually will avail themselves of the same kinship trope, becoming "sons by adoption" in the Pauline locution: see above, p. 00.

6. Isaac, *Invention of Racism*, 500. As these terms attest, cult itself was envisaged as a type of family association.

7. "In [the Roman] empire," notes the second-century Christian apologist Athenagoras, "different nations have different customs, and no one is hindered by law or by fear of punishment from following his ancestral customs, no matter how ridiculous these may be" (*Legatio* 1). Similarly, the pagan Celsus comments that Jews "observe a worship which may be very peculiar but at least it is traditional. In this respect they behave like the rest of mankind, because each nation follows its particular customs" (*Contra Celsum* 5.25).

misdescribe it with a word drawn from our own later civil societies. *Ancient empire embodied pragmatic pluralism.*[8] If all peoples have their own gods, if all gods exist, if cult makes gods happy, and—perhaps the most important point of all—if *any* god is more powerful than *any* human, then such a posture simply made good sense.

What becomes difficult to account for, given the cultural presuppositions that I have just sketched, is not antiquity's practical pluralism, but rather its unquestionable episodes of religiously motivated persecution, the use of force to compel cultic conformity and to quell religious difference, perceived as (dangerous) deviance. How, within a context of pragmatic pluralism, did religious persecution ever arise?

To explore this question, I would like to consider the particular and peculiar case of the apostle Paul. Paul repays investigation on this issue for many reasons. First, we have the evidence of his own letters, wherein he presents himself both as both a (former) persecutor and as someone who is persecuted. Second, his double experience as persecutor and as persecuted actively involves him with most of the other populations in our ancient picture: fellow Jews both within and without the Jesus-movement, Judaizing pagans, pagan Christ-followers, straight-up pagans both Greek and Roman, and also and most significantly, pagan gods. Finally, by considering Paul and by identifying the factors specific to his circumstances, we can gain some insight as well, I shall argue, into the reasons behind two later instances of more wide-flung religious persecution: that of gentile Christians from roughly 100 to 300 CE in the days of the pagan Roman empire, and that of gentiles both pagan and *especially* Christian, from the late fourth century on, in the days of the Christian Roman Empire.

1.

Before we turn to Paul himself, we need first to consider his context. Paul was a Jew of the western Diaspora whose language was Greek, whose biblical tradition was the Septuagint (LXX), and whose ambit was the cities of the eastern Empire. To understand him and the evidence related in his extant letters, we have first to understand this western diaspora Jewish population.

Unlike the Jewish community outside of the empire, in Babylon, Jews of the western Diaspora had resettled voluntarily, pulled in part by the

---

8. Same point, different vocabulary: "Rome was interested in keeping the urban masses under control and in checking initiatives of too political a nature. For the rest, Roman authorities just let people be. . . . Tolerance was only a by-product of Rome's administrative measures" (Rutgers, "Roman Policy toward the Jews," 111).

Paul, Practical Pluralism, and the Invention of Religious Persecution 91

Macedonian Diaspora occasioned by the conquests of Alexander the Great. These Mediterranean Jews in time came to view their diaspora communities as "colonies" (*apoikiai*) of their *metropolis* (*mater-polis*), Jerusalem; their cities of residence, however, they viewed as their *patria*, their fatherland, their inheritance, and their home.[9] Greek, the English of antiquity, became their vernacular; the gods of the *ethnê* no less than the *ethnê* themselves, their immediate neighbors.

How did Jews get along with their neighbors, both human and divine? The humans could be factious. Urban unrest in Alexandria notoriously took the form of inter-ethnic violence, which had a "religious" cast: Jewish sites might be defiled (as with the emperor's cult image) as well as destroyed.[10] Cities in Asia Minor, in the decades of Rome's bumpy transition from republic to empire, sometimes seized Jewish cash contributions to the temple in Jerusalem for use in temples and liturgies closer to home—a practical move motivated by economy, but expressed in terms of cult. The principled Jewish avoidance of paying public cult to foreign gods prompted irritation in classical ethnographers, who then complained about Jewish separateness (*amixia*), impiety (*asebeia*), and "foreigner-hating lifestyle" (*misoxenos bios* or *misanthrôpia*; cf. Tacitus' *adversus omnes alios hostile odium*, "hostile hatred against all outsiders," *Hist.* 5.5,1[11]). Taken at face value, this evidence can suggest that in the Diaspora, Jews lived as a people apart, *ceterarum gentium communione discreta*.[12]

---

9. For this *mater/pater* interplay, see Philo, *In Flaccum* 46. My summary here draws especially on the work of Barclay, *Jews in the Western Mediterranean Diaspora*, and of Gruen, *Heritage and Hellenism* and *Diaspora*. On Jewish communities in Asia Minor in particular, Ameling, "Die jüdischen Gemeinden." Roman Jews in late antiquity were no less attached to their hometowns than their first-century Hellenistic forebears had been. When the Jews of Magona, on Minorca, were faced with the choice of conversion or exile in 418 CE, one of them observed that "whoever does not abandon his *patria* will not be able to retain his *fides patrum*" (*Letter of Severus* 18.19).

10. One of the problems with the Jews' expectation of being treated as full citizens, the Egyptian Apion observed, was that "the Jews do not worship the same gods as the Alexandrians" (*c. Apionem* 2.65). Cf. *AJ* 12.126, for similar complaints from cities in Asia Minor. For more on the riots of 38 CE, Schäfer, *Judeophobia*, 136-60; cf., for a rosier interpretation, Gruen, *Diaspora*, 54-83.

11. For a quick prosopography of classical writers' anti-Jewish accusations, Schäfer, *Judeophobia*, 15-33; for analysis of insults, Feldman, *Jew and Gentile*, 107-76.

12. For Josephus' discussion of the seizure of Jewish sacred funds in Asia Minor, *AJ* 14. The complaints of the ethnographers and the observations of the satirists are collected in Stern, *Greek and Latin Authors on Jews and Judaism* (hereafter *GLAJJ*); see also Isaac, *Racism*, 440-91 (anti-Jewish aspersions) and 492-500 (these insults within the broader context of hostile classical ethnographies). On the expulsions from Rome, cf. Barclay, *Jews*, 282-319, and Gruen, *Diaspora*, 1-53; also Rutgers, "Roman Policy toward the Jews," 93-116. Augustine, quoting this OT passage (given above)

Against this conclusion, however, and against the hostile ethnographic rhetoric that it rests upon, other data mass, data attesting to Jews voluntarily in gentile places, and gentiles (whether pagan or, eventually, Christian) voluntarily in Jewish places.[13] In other words, on the ground in the ancient Graeco-Roman city we see the effects of antiquity's practical pluralism.

These sites of inter-ethnic mingling are at once "cultural" (thus, ethnic), "social," and "religious" (thus, again, ethnic). For example, before 66 CE, whether as tourists or as worshipers (or both), pagans could be found at the Temple in Jerusalem, where the largest courtyard was reserved for them.[14] And in the Diaspora, we have inscriptional and literary evidence both of pagan gentiles and, later, of Christian gentiles within Jewish community structures (the "synagogue"). The Diaspora data often refer to such gentiles as "godfearers" or as "Judaizers," labels that can be confusing. Gentile god-fearers were *not* converts.[15] God-fearers did *not* renounce their native gods: they associated with Jews while remaining loyal to their own gods as well. (Julia Severa, a synagogue patron, was a priestess in the imperial cult;[16] Luke's centurion Cornelius, another synagogue patron, even if fictive, would have been understood to actively worship Rome's gods as part of his position as an army officer; Acts 10.) The synagogue, a type of ethnic reading-house,[17] was part of the urban landscape, not only architecturally (as at Sardis), but socially.

This outsider presence in Jewish community activities was voluntary and ad hoc.

Interested pagans display a range of behaviors, from occasional drop-ins (such as magicians, who garble biblical stories when picking

---

against Faustus the Manichaean, insisted that Jews had always lived separate from other peoples and untouched by the worship of foreign gods, *c. Faust.* 12.13. Pace Augustine, I will argue against this description.

13. The following paragraphs condense material laid out in Fredriksen and Irshai, "Christian Anti-Judaism: Polemics and Policies"; also Fredriksen, "Judaizing the Nations," 235–40. "Pagan" or "Gentile" is no happier a solution to designate all of these other ethnic groups than is "Jew" for *Ioudaios*, but I can think of no better option: "Polytheist" is too misleading to help, because (as noted above, p. 00) ancient Jews and, eventually, Christians shared the conviction with pagans that many gods exist.

14. Schürer, *History of the Jewish People*, 2:309–13 (hereafter *HJP*).

15. Cohen, *Beginnings of Jewishness*, 171, misidentifies "god-venerators" (i.e., god-fearers) as ex-idolators, "denying or ignoring all other gods"; so too Esler, *Conflict and Identity in Romans*, 106. On the contrary, god-fearers remained active pagans while adding Israel's god to their own particular pantheons.

16. On Julia and other pagan synagogue patrons, Levine, *Ancient Synagogue*, 111, 121, 476–83.

17. Thus Young, *Biblical Exegesis*, 13.

up important information in order to invoke the Jewish god in spells) to extravagant patronage (such as Julia Severa's construction of the *oikos* in Acmonia) to co-celebrating the translation of the LXX (Philo, *Life of Moses* 2.41–42) to personally adopting some Jewish ancestral practices (like Juvenal's famous god-fearer, who rests on the Sabbath, *Sat.* 14.96). Magicians in particular were partial toward the Jews' god, relying on him to cast effective spells.[18] Donor plaques and mosaics proclaim the many benefactions to the Jewish community of sympathetic pagans.[19] And literary evidence from the first century BCE to the fifth century CE, from gentiles both pagan and Christian, bespeak their adoption and adaptation of Jewish practices and their presence, thus active interest, in synagogue communities.[20]

Some of these pagans did, weirdly, "become" *ioudaioi*, in effect changing ethnic groups, an act that went against a commonsense construal of "blood." What moderns designate "conversion," given ancient divinity's ethnic embeddedness, hardly made sense. The closest Roman analogues were adoption and marriage, both of which ritually created a bond of (legal but fictive) kinship, obligating the adoptee, or the wife, to new deities, rituals, and ancestors.[21] While a pagan's worshiping the gods

18. For one such recipe, see *Paris Magical Papyrus* ll. 3007–85. Origen notes that the names of the patriarchs are "so powerful when linked with the name of God that the formula 'the God of Abraham, the God of Isaac, the God of Jacob' is used not only by members of the Jewish nation in their prayers to God and when they exorcise demons, but also by almost all those who deal in magic and spells" (*c. Cel.* 4.33). See further Alexander, "Jewish Elements in Gnosticism and Magic."

19. This display of respect might have had as much to do with local intra-human politics as with local divine-human ones: distinguishing between the two motivations is impossible from the evidence. Pagan benefactions to synagogue projects account for a significant portion of our inscriptional data, on which see Levine, *Ancient Synagogue*; also Reynolds and Tannenbaum, *Jews and God-Fearers at Aphrodisias*. Recently, Chaniotis, "Jews of Aphrodisias," has redated the inscriptions from the third century to the fourth-fifth, raising the interesting possibility that some of the non-Jewish town councilors mentioned might be Christians as well as pagans.

20. Pagan complaints about pagans' frequenting synagogues, collected in *GLAJJ*, are discussed in Fredriksen and Irshai, "Christian Anti-Judaism," 985–98; see ibid., 1005–7, for comments about Christian Gentiles in Jewish places. Chrysostom's infamous sermons in 387, *Against the Judaizers*, catalogue the Jewish practices of John's gentile Christian congregation, who attend synagogue on the Sabbath and the high holy days (1.5; 8.8), go to hear the "trumpets" (Rosh haShanah; 1:5), fast on Yom Kippur (1.2), and join in "pitching tents" (that is, erecting *sukkot*, 7.1). Wilken notes that John, Theodoret of Cyrus, and the Apostolic Constitutions likewise criticize gentile Christians for frequenting *mikvaot*, *John Chrysostom and the Jews*, 75; see too Kelly, *Golden Mouth*, 63–66.

21. "It is becoming for a wife to worship and to know only those gods whom her husband esteems" (Plutarch, *Moralia* 140D). On Roman adoption—presided over by a *pontifex*—Beard and North, *Pagan Priests: Religion and Power in the Ancient World*, 38.

of other peoples had no necessary effect on his relationships with his own gods, and while a pagan's decision to honor the god of Israel along with his own gods was an available option, a pagan's "becoming" a Jew was tantamount to changing his own past, reconfiguring his ancestry, deserting his own pantheon, family, and *patria*. For these reasons, hostile pagan witnesses considered what we call "conversion" an act of cultural treason, and they criticized pagan Judaizing or "god-fearing" as the beginning of this slippery slope (again, see Juvenal *Sat.* 14).[22] How many of these interested pagans did indeed convert to Judaism in antiquity? We have no way of knowing, of course; and, absent data, some scholars have postulated huge numbers.[23] But as we shall see when considering the social consequences of the mission of the early Jesus-movement in the Diaspora, the likelihood of truly numerous conversions is low.

Ancient pluralism worked both ways, though pagan complaints about Jewish separateness do not prepare us to see this. In the Diaspora, Jews also frequented pagan places. Foremost, the ancient city was itself a religious institution, its governance and its wellbeing dependent upon good relations with its god(s). Within these cities, we find Jews everywhere: in the theatres and in the courts, in town councils and in gymnasia and schools, in the baths and at the races. These Graeco-Roman urban structures were all sites of worship, their activities initiated by and dedicated to honoring the god(s).[24]

In other words, Jews in the Diaspora acknowledged the existence and the power of gods other than their own, showing respect to them and thus, importantly, to their humans. The existence of these gods was attested, first of all, in Jewish scriptures, most especially in Psalms. The Septuagint's translators acknowledged these deities with some deference, suggesting

22. For an analysis of Juvenal's jibe, which targets "conversion" as well as god-fearing, *GLAJJ*, 2:94–107; cf. also Tacitus' complaints, *History* 5.1-2, on "conversion" as cultural treason.

23. Feldman holds the numbers to have been in the hundreds of thousands, *Jew and Gentile*, 290–93; cf. Fredriksen, "What Parting of the Ways?," 49–51; Rutgers, *Hidden Heritage of Diaspora Judaism*, 200–205. Paget, "Jewish Proselytism at the Time of Christian Origins," provides a road map for the whole controversy.

24. Tertullian floridly laments—and thus narrates—the embeddedness of these divinities in urban culture in *de spectaculis* and *de idololatria*, while the near-contemporary Mishnah Avodah Zara outlines ways for (rabbinic?) Jews to avoid the idolatrous entanglements of urban living: see Fredriksen and Irshai, "'Include Me Out': Tertullian, the Rabbis, and the Graeco-Roman City." If we can trust our variegated inscriptional material, however, not all Jews were bothered by such involvement, while later writings—Tertullian's high rhetoric; sermons; church canons—complain of Christian nonchalance. On Jews' showing respect for—but not cult to—foreign gods, Fredriksen, "Judaizing the Nations," 236–37 and notes.

that relations with them should be handled gently, when they changed the Hebrew of Exodus 22:27, "Do not revile God," to the Greek of 22:28 LXX: "Do not revile the gods" (*tous theous*). Commenting on this passage, Philo of Alexandria salutes its wisdom, since "reviling each others' gods always causes war" (*Questions and Answers in Exodus* 2.5). Philo goes on to note that Jews ought also to respect pagan rulers, "who are of the same seed as the gods" (2.6).[25] We find Jews invoking pagan gods on votive plaques and in synagogue manumission inscriptions; they showed respect to them in funding dedicated athletic competitions. And they participated in Hellenistic kinship diplomacy by conjuring distant unions between patriarchal families and Greek gods: in this way, Spartans and Jews discovered that they were "cousins," linked by common descent from the union of Heracles with a granddaughter of Abraham's.[26]

It is true that Jews generally seem to have drawn the line at actively participating in public cult but, depending on their roles in their cities, they would have been at least present, demonstrating respect and civility, when such cult was offered. In brief, diaspora Jews participated vigorously in majority culture socially, politically, and intellectually (this last achieved through *gymnasia* educations) by coming to terms as well with that culture's gods. In many ways, except for their general demurral regarding public pagan cult, Jews were *not* all that separate. A high degree of social integration coexisted, for them as for other groups, with religious—better, ethnic—distinctiveness. Every time our ancient evidence presents us with a Jewish ephebe, a Jewish town councilor, a Jewish soldier or a Jewish actor or a Jewish athlete, we find a Jew identified as a Jew who obviously spent part of his working day demonstrating courtesy to gods not his.[27]

---

25. See van der Horst, "Thou Shalt Not Revile the Gods," 1–8; by the same author, more recently, "Judaism in Asia Minor," 321–40, with bibliography.

26. "After reading a certain document," announces a Spartan king to the Jewish high priest, "we have found that Jews and Lacedaemonians [Spartans] are of one *genos*, and share a connection with Abraham" (1 Macc 12.21). This *suggeneia* also appears in 2 Macc 5.9 and in Josephus, *AJ* 12.226; for Heracles' union with Abraham's granddaughter, *AJ* 1.24–41. Analysis of this tradition in Jones, *Kinship Diplomacy*, 72–80; Gruen, "Jewish Perspectives on Greek Ethnicity," 361–64. Paul will also avail himself of this idea of Abraham as "the father of many nations," Rom 4:11–18; Gal 3:7–14; cf. Gen 17:5; Stowers, *Rereading Romans*, 227–50.

27. The most recent review of Jewish diaspora acculturation to Hellenism is Bloch, *Moses und der Mythos*. Inscriptional materials are organized and analyzed in Williams, *Jews among the Greeks and Romans*, and in Levinskaya, *Book of Acts in Its Diaspora Setting*; also Donaldson, *Judaism and the Gentiles*, 437–66. On Moschos Ioudaios and his obedience to the gods Amphiaraos and Hygieia, Schürer, *HJP*, 3:65; on Pothros' manumission inscription, Levinskaya, *Acts* 111–16 (with the full text of the inscription on 239); cf. Levine, *Ancient Synagogue*, 113–23.

Showing respect for each other's gods—which went far toward keeping the city's religious ecosystem in balance—does not mean that pagans and Jews shared each other's view of their respective gods. But, intriguingly, often they did share a common conceptualization, the idea that divinity was organized along a power gradient of higher and lower. Lower gods were *daimones*. Demonic divinities tended to be local, involved in the lower material cosmos (whether terrestrial or celestial), and partial to blood sacrifices. For this reason, gentiles (whether pagan or Christian) might construe the Jews' god as a *daimon*: his involvement in the organization of the material universe, his penchant for blood sacrifices, his patronage of one particular ethnic group, his location in Jerusalem and, especially after 70 CE, his defeat by the gods of Rome all suggested as much.[28] Jews, meanwhile, subordinated the gods of majority culture to the god of Israel by using this same idea: "The gods of the nations are *daimonia*," sang the Psalmist in Greek (Ps 95:5 LXX).[29]

This demonic interpretation of pagan deity was supported in part by a peculiarity of Jewish theology, which pressed a singular and paradoxical claim. Despite their confidence in their god's ethnic loyalties, Jews also insisted that theirs was a universal deity, the supreme or highest god. Such a position stood in tension with the canons of philosophical paideia, according to which the highest god was radically transcendent, ethnically nonspecific, radically acorporeal, and certainly above any involvement in matter,

---

28. On Jerusalem's fall as the god of Israel's defeat, e.g., M. Felix, *Octavius* 10.4; cf. the Christological explanations offered by Tertullian, *Apology* 26.3, Origen, *c. Celsum* 4.32. Origen will insist against Celsus that "the supreme god is called the god of the Hebrews even by people alien to our faith," 5.50, but a great number of Christians (in particular Valentinians and Marcionites) distinguished between the two deities, the high god and the Jewish god; see Fredriksen, *Sin: The Early History of an Idea*, 64–79. In the late fourth century, Faustus (also Christian) could still identify the Jews' god as an ethnic demon, *c. Faust.* 18.2. On the particular link between blood sacrifices and demons—much exploited in Christian rhetoric *contra Iudaeos*, specifically against the Temple cult—see, e.g., Justin, 2 *Apology* 5; *Trypho* 19, 22, 43, and frequently. The idea that high gods neither need nor want sacrifices, but lower gods do, was originally pagan: thus Porphyry's reference to Theophrastes, *On Abstinence* 2.27, 1–3.

29. Pagan *daimones* could be either good or evil; see Chadwick, on Plutarch and Porphyry, "Oracles of the End"; Rives, "Human Sacrifice among Pagans and Christians," 80–83; Kahlos, *Debate and Dialogue*, 172–81. Some Hellenistic Jews (such as the author of *Wisdom*; also Paul) took daimones as exclusively evil, bound up as they were with the worship of images. Cf. Augustine's remark on "demons" as lower [pagan] gods: "If the Platonists prefer to call these 'gods' rather than 'demons,' and to count them among those whom Plato their master writes about as gods created by the highest god, let them say what they want . . . for then they say exactly what we say, whichever word they may use for them" (*civ. Dei* 9.23).

time, and change.³⁰ Educated Hellenistic Jews squared this circle through several strategies. They generated allegorical understandings of their own sacred text, the LXX, which cushioned its depictions of divine activity. They deployed *angeloi* as the high god's agents, thereby also insulating him from any compromising behavior.³¹ Some Jews subordinated pagan gods to their own god by identifying pagan gods with celestial bodies, as did Philo in his commentary on Genesis. The firmament, he says there, is "the most holy dwelling-place of the manifest and visible gods" (*theôn emphanôn te kai aisthêtôn, de opificio mundi* 7.27): manifest and visible gods are "lower" than the highest, invisible god.³²

Two very ancient cultic peculiarities of Judaism further facilitated Yahweh's Hellenistic makeover. The first was cultic aniconism: Jewish tradition forbade making visual representations of their god. Such aniconism facilitated their identification of their god with the acorporeal high god of philosophy. The second peculiarity was cultic specificity: though prayer could be offered anywhere, *latreia*, the sacrificial cult, was in principle restricted to the temple in Jerusalem.³³ Jews distant from Jerusalem thus (again, in principle) did not offer sacrifices to their god. Instead, they contributed annually for the up-keep of the cult, the so-called temple tax. This practice—

---

30. Hence Justin's complaints about—and philosopher's incredulity at—the Jews' insistence that Scripture revealed the activities of the high god, 1 *Apology* 63, cf. *Trypho* 60. To Justin it was clear that the deity active in the LXX could only be a lower god, the high god's pre-incarnate Son (e.g., *Trypho* 56). For a comparison of pagan, Jewish, and Christian theological *paideia*, Fredriksen, *Augustine and the Jews*, 41–78.

31. Hellenistic Judaism employed many divine mediating figures to bridge the gap between God and the world: various angels especially, but also God's Sophia ("Wisdom") and his word ("Logos"); two books by Alan Segal, *Paul the Convert* and *Two Powers in Heaven*, give good orientations in the relevant material. Justin Martyr was comfortable referring to Christ as God's *angelos* (*Trypho* 56, 59). Pagans also deployed their cosmic gods as "messengers." The famous Oenoanda inscription presents Apollo speaking of the highest deity (*theos hypsistos*) while referring to himself and to the other lower gods as "angels": "Born of itself, without a mother, unshakable, not contained in a name, known by many names, dwelling in fire, this is God. We, his *angeloi* [messengers] are a small part of God . . ." For more on this hexameter hymn and the pagan cult of the highest god, see Mitchell, "Cult of *Theos Hypsistos*"; the inscription is given in full on 82.

32. When Paul identifies these gods with cosmic *stoicheia*, he might be making the same move, Gal 4:3–9: these forces are not "gods by nature" (4:8), but subordinate, inferior entities. Synagogue zodiac mosaics similarly represent pagan sidereal divinities, whose very visibility would place them "below" the high (that is, the Jewish) god.

33. I say "in principle" because, since the mid-second century BCE, another temple also functioned in Egypt, at Leontopolis. In consequence of the first Judean revolt in 66–73 CE, Rome destroyed this temple, too. See discussion in Schürer, *HJP*, 3:47–48, 145–47.

or, perhaps better, this absence of an all but universal practice—combined with their avoidance of local pagan cult, meant that diaspora Jews were the only non-sacrificing population in the early first-century empire. Even so unsympathetic an outsider as Tacitus, on the basis of the Jews' aniconism and lack of sacrifice, could be persuaded: by worshiping *sola mente*, without offerings or images, he said, Jews paid homage to the high god.[34]

Socially, intellectually, and practically, then, many diaspora Jews—perhaps *most* diaspora Jews—accommodated the gods of majority culture as part of their daily reality. But this irenic posture could coexist with a vigorous critique of the pagan worship of "idols," that is, of the visual representations of their gods. "How miserable, their hopes set on dead things, are those who give the name 'gods' to the works of human hands!" exclaimed the author of *Wisdom of Solomon* sometime in the first century BCE (Wis 13.10). Bad religious practices made for bad people: pagans, claimed this author, kill children and indulge in profligate sexual relations; they deceive and murder; they lie, cheat and steal (14.23–31; Paul echoes this critique in Rm 1.18–34). Apocalyptic writers in particular looked forward to the day when pagans would destroy their idols, and the universal worship of the god of Israel would prevail.

Yet many Jewish apocalyptic traditions are, in their idiosyncratic way, also pluralistic. That is, these texts express the conviction that when God at last establishes his kingdom, he would include more than just Jews. Gentiles too (and even their gods, as we shall shortly see) also have a place in God's kingdom. In the Final Days, proclaim prophetic and intertestamental texts, the nations will *turn from* their gods, destroy their idols, and *turn to* the worship of the god of Israel.[35] *Not* "convert": there is no cosmic, End-

---

34. *History* 5.4; for comment, *GLAJJ*, 2:43.

35. Since Jewish apocalyptic eschatology is a big and baggy tradition, I sum up its main themes here, via a pastiche from the classical prophets, the Dead Sea Scrolls, various non-canonical writings from 200 BCE–200 CE, and various New Testament writings. Events marking the End of the Age include:
- Travails; persecution of the righteous
- Celestial and terrestrial catastrophes (earthquakes, plagues, falling stars)
- Final battle between Good and Evil, led by God, or by a commanding angel, or by an anointed king
- Destruction of the wicked (foreign kings, wicked gentiles, apostate Jews, esp. those whose views differ from the writer's)
- Resurrection of dead, vindication of the righteous. In-gathering of exiles (Lost Tribes)
- Return to the Land, gathering at rebuilt or renewed Temple
- Pagans bury their idols, turn to worship the god of Israel
- The nations will stream to Jerusalem and worship together with Israel (Isa 2:2–4 / Mic 4)

time, universal propogation of Juda*ism*. Israel's god, not Israel's ancestral practices, at the End reigns surpreme. All the nations, say these texts, will acknowledge him.

Who are these "eschatological gentiles"? They are a purely hypothetical construct, one of the elements of Jewish apocalyptic speculation. They conform to neither of the other two kinds of actual gentile affiliation with (quotidian) Judaism that we have already considered. *Like* god-fearers, these eschatological gentiles would remain gentiles; *unlike* god-fearers, they would not worship their native gods. *Like* converts, these eschatological gentiles would worship the Jewish god alone; *unlike* converts, they would not assume Jewish ancestral, thus ethnic, practices. *Eschatological gentiles* in other words are *neither converts nor god-fearers*. They represent a unique— and, again, a theoretical—category. In the Last Days, these people would enter God's kingdom *as gentiles*, but they would not worship idols any more. *Jewish apocalyptic thought, in other words, severed antiquity's normal and normative correspondence of ethnicity and cult.*

With all this as his context, let us turn to Paul.

2.

In his letters Paul presents himself as a former persecutor, while at the same time proclaiming his excellence both as a Jew (Gal 1:13–14; see too v. 23) and as an apostle to pagans (1 Cor 15:9–10). Whom did he "persecute," and how? Taking the evidence of the epistles over that of Acts, thus also

- They will together eat on the Temple mount the feast that God will prepare (Isa 25:6)
- Gentiles will accompany Jews at the Ingathering (Zech 8:23)
- Gentiles will themselves carry exiles back to Jerusalem (Ps Sol 7.31–41)
- Gentiles will bury their idols and direct their sight to uprightness (1 Enoch 91.14)
- Many nations will come from afar to the name of the Lord God, bearing gifts (Tobit 13.11); after the Temple is rebuilt, all the nations will turn in fear to the Lord, and bury their idols (14.5–6)
- God called upon to restore J'lem, so that "all who are on the earth" will know that he is the Lord God (Sirach 36.11–17)
- At the coming of the Great King, the nations will bend knee to God (Sib Or 3.616), the nations will go to the Temple, and renounce their idols (715–24), from every land they will bring incense and gifts to the Temple of the great god (772).
- Peace, universal acknowledgment of god of Israel

For a review of these traditions, see Donaldson, *Judaism and the Gentiles*; on the ways that they relate to Paul's mission, Fredriksen, "Judaism, the Circumcision of Gentiles, and Apocalyptic Hope."

taking "persecution" to mean, not "execution" (Luke's picture) but flogging (2 Cor 11:24), we infer the following: that sometime within a few years of Jesus' execution, the gospel of the risen and returning Christ reached Paul's synagogue community in Damascus. Within this synagogue community were Judaizing pagans ("god-fearers") as well as Jews. Evangelizing apostles, themselves Jews, would have formed a Christ-following subgroup, an assembly (*ekklēsia*) drawn from the synagogue's Jews and god-fearers both. Paul-as-persecutor[36] would then have participated in having (only) the Jewish members of this ekklesia flogged (2 Cor 11:24) to the maximum degree (*kath'huperbolēn*, Gal 1:14) allowed by the Law, that is, thirty-nine lashes.[37] Later, as an apostle, he would receive the same treatment himself (2 Cor 11:24).

Why? Different NT scholars have offered different explanations. Some have conjectured that the message of the new movement—a *crucified* messiah—would have occasioned a deep religious offence, since such a messiah would have died a death "cursed by the law"—Deut 21:23, by way of Gal 3:13. Others infer legal offense: these itinerant apostles (often associated with the "Hellenists" of Acts), lax in their own law-observance, offended the host synagogue as "sinners" (Deut 25:1–3 LXX), and thus were subjected to "the" thirty-nine lashes (in mishnaic idiom, *makkot arba'im*). Others conjecture that the Damascus synagogue would have been offended by the apostles' novel social intimacy with "impure" gentiles—eating together and praying together without first requiring that these gentiles be circumcised, that is, convert to Judaism. Still others, finally, have argued that the message of a crucified messiah would have put the host community at political risk, alienating the local representatives of Roman government. The wider Jewish community would have responded by repudiating the message, subjecting its messengers to disciplinary flogging, up to the maximum number allowed by the Law (*makkot mardut*).[38]

---

36. Paul must have been in some official capacity within the synagogue to have done so: he could not have administered disciplinary lashing on his own authority.

37. As Sanders famously observed, punishment implies inclusion, *Paul, the Law, and the Jewish People*, 192. This means not only that the objects of Paul's actions would have been Jews (whether the sojourning apostles, the Damascene Jews, or some combination of both), but also that the ekklesia would have formed *within* the synagogue community: had this group separated from the synagogue, the synagogue would have had no authority over it. This observation holds true also for Paul's own later experience, when he was lashed on five different occasions (2 Cor 11:24): he would not have received this punishment, and accepted it, had he not continue to move within synagogue circles. For the argument that "persecution" means "lashing," Hultgren, "Paul's Pre-Christian Persecutions."

38. All of these explanations are presented with bibliography, analyzed, and (save

These same reconstructions then serve to explain why Paul, later, was himself persecuted: his message of the crucified messiah caused religious offense, as would his personal laxity about the law, perhaps even his principled apostasy *from* the law. Paul's social practices in re gentiles "shatters the ethnic mould" of synagogue Judaism; the new social entity of the ekklesia "transgresses the boundaries of the Diaspora synagogue"; "Paul's assimilating practices and his lax (or at least inconsistent) observation of the law earned him suspicion, opposition, and even punishment" in the synagogue.[39]

All of these reconstructions, but especially the last, require that the earliest Christian message be somehow in principle irreconcilable with traditional Jewish practice. The ekklesia's ready inclusion of uncircumcised gentiles (*sic*) is held up as one of the proofs of this. But as we have seen, pagans had participated in synagogue life well before the introduction of the Jesus-movement; and gentiles both pagan and Christian would continue to do so for centuries thereafter. The mixed population of the tiny, new ekklesia, then, cannot in and of itself have moved Paul to persecute, or to be persecuted.

What about persecution because Jesus-following Jews abandoned Jewish practices? This to me seems to impose a much later, *gentile* Christian construction of a "law-free gospel" upon the earliest days of the movement. Gentiles-in-Christ, Paul will teach—intemperately in Galatians, more measuredly elsewhere—are not obligated to Jewish law. *But what Jew, of any stripe, would disagree with him?* This is true of gentiles universally, whether within the movement or outside of it: only Jews were obligated to Jewish law (Rom 9:4). To make the same point differently: these Christ-following gentiles' not living according to Jewish custom gives us no reason to think that Christ-following Jews did the same thing. We cannot in fact infer *anything* about the Jewish apostles' level of Jewish observance on the basis of the ekklesia's *gentile* members' not keeping most of the Jewish observances. *Gentiles are not obligated to Jewish ancestral practice, period.*[40]

"Gentile impurity" is also an unlikely source of offense or concern to Jews for a number of reasons. First, the Levitical purities/impurities that shaped access to the temple—in other words, that were part of Jewish law—were not relevant to gentiles: these states of impurity, highly contagious, related solely to Jews. And, second, as the very architecture of Herod's

---

for the last position) dismissed in Fredriksen, "Judaism, the Circumcision of Gentiles, and Apocalyptic Hope," 548–56. The last explanation was advocated *loc. cit.* 556; *retractandum est.*

39. Barclay, *Mediterranean Diaspora*, 393.
40. For the full argument, Fredriksen, "Retrospect and Anachronism."

temple lets us know, gentile impurity (whatever that was and howsoever we construe the term) was not contagious, therefore again of no direct consequence to Jews: Jews walked through the outermost court—and therefore bumped into gentiles—whenever they made their way to their own areas of worship. Third, the synagogue, itself not a site of sacrifice, was not regulated by Temple purity codes.[41] Finally, as I hope that I have by now demonstrated, diaspora synagogues frequently received pagan gentiles (sic) *qua* god-fearers into their midst, evidently without the least concern for purity. Why then should the ekklesia's gentiles offend the synagogue on this score?

Paul himself suggests that circumcision (thus, "Christian" policy toward admitting gentiles) has something to do with the reason why he is persecuted. ("If I still preach circumcision, why am I still persecuted?" Gal 5:11: *note that he does not say by whom.*) And he suggests that his circumcising apostolic competition in Galatia advocates circumcising Christ-following gentiles so that they themselves might avoid being persecuted. ("Those who would . . . compel you to be circumcised . . . [do so] only in order that they may not be persecuted for the cross of Christ," Gal 6:12: *note, again, that the agents of such persecution are not named.*) As long as we restrict the "persecution" endured by Paul to *makkot*, lashing, and as long as we restrict the reasons for these contentions to issues arising primarily from the practice of Jewish custom, we restrict both the identity of Paul's persecutors *to* Jews and the reasons for his persecution (both giving and getting) to issues internal to Judaism.

But Paul names more than synagogue harassment in his list of woes in 2 Corinthians 11.[42] He is also "persecuted" by Roman government officials, he says (three times beaten with rods, v. 25). Contrary winds, weather, and water—the domain of the lower, cosmic gods—impede his mission (vv. 25–26). Paul was "in danger from my own people and *in danger from gentiles*" (pagans who are not Romans?), as well as in danger from "false brethren" (that is, I assume, from other apostles-in-Christ whose *euangeliai*

---

41. For a detailed discussion of Jewish purity laws and customs in the first century, Sanders, *Jewish Law from Jesus to the Mishnah*, 29–41, 131–254 (Pharisees), 258–71 (diaspora communities); on impurity and gentiles, Klawans, "Notions of Gentile Impurity in Ancient Judaism"; and Hayes, *Gentile Impurities and Jewish Identities*.

42. "I am a better servant of Christ, . . . with far greater labors, far more imprisonments, with countless beatings, and often near death. Five times I have received at the hands of the Jews forty lashes less one. Three times I have been beaten with rods, once I was stoned. Three times I have been shipwrecked; a night and a day adrift at sea; on frequent journeys, in danger from rivers, from robbers, from my own people, and from Gentiles; danger in the city, in the wilderness; danger at sea, danger from false brethren; in toil and hardship, through many a sleepless night, in hunger and thirst, without food, in cold and exposure" (2 Cor 11:23–27).

are different from Paul's, v. 26; cf. Galatians, passim). Who are all these "persecutors"? And what has motivated them?

The answer to all these questions emerges only once we consider Paul's *entire* social world—that is, not only its humans but also its gods. From the moment that the early mission first moved out into the Diaspora, the Jesus movement encountered these gods as it encountered their people. The diaspora synagogues' long-standing and socially stable practice allowed pagans *qua* god-fearers to worship Israel's god while continuing in their native cults. Significantly, the apostles set the bar much higher: (male) pagans joining the ekklesia could no longer sacrifice to their gods.[43] "Indeed there are many gods and many lords," Paul says to his gentile community in Corinth, "but *for us* there is one god, the Father, . . . and one Lord, Jesus Christ," (1 Cor 8:5–6). If a "brother"—that is, a baptized Christ-following gentile—continues to worship idols, he is to be shunned (5:11). "Formerly, when you did not know God, you were in bondage to beings that by nature are no gods" (Gal 4:8). "Beloved"—this again to the Corinthians—"shun the worship of idols," (1 Cor 10:14). "You turned (*epestrepsate*) to God from idols," Paul tells his gentiles in Thessalonica, "to worship the true and living god," (1 Thess 1:9).

This image of the nations "turning"—a good prophetic locution—appears both in Paul and in Acts 15. It derives from Jewish apocalyptic traditions, preserved variously in prophetic texts and in intertestamental writings. At the End of time, so say these passages, the nations will *turn from* their native gods, destroying their images, and they will *turn to* the god of Israel. "Turn (*epistraphate*) to me!" (Isa 45:22 LXX, addressed to "the nations"). "All the nations will turn (*epistrepsousin*) in fear of the Lord God . . . and will bury their idols" (Tobit 14.6). "We should not trouble those of the gentiles who turn (*epistrephousin*) to God," says James (Acts 15:19 RSV; cf. 15:3, where *epistrophēn* is translated wrongly as "conversion").[44]

In other words, Jewish apocalyptic traditions provide the textual location of gentiles who eschew their idols, who turn to make an exclusive commitment to the god of Israel, and who do *not* assume Jewish ancestral practices, a.k.a. "the Law" (circumcision, food laws, Sabbath, and so on). Such "eschatological gentiles" had long been an imaginative construct, their exclusive commitment to the god of Israel one of any number of anticipated end-time events. Once the Jesus movement begins to establish itself in the Diaspora, they become a social reality. This apocalyptic tradition, then,

---

43. His thinking of public cult means that Paul is speaking mainly about men. His expectations of Christ-following women whose spouses are still pagan is much more flexible and circumspect: see Hodge, "Married to an Unbeliever."

44. Fredriksen, "Judaizing," 241–43.

is what informs the first generation's (improvised) "gentile policy," which James, Peter and John confirmed for Paul when he went up to Jerusalem (Gal 2:1–10), and which was operative even in those gentile ekklesiai founded independently of Paul (such as the one at Rome). Knowing what hour it was on God's clock (Rom 13:11), racing in the (for all they knew) brief wrinkle in time between Christ's resurrection and his Parousia (1 Cor 15), seeing in the pneumatic behavior of their new gentile members confirmation of their own eschatological convictions, these Jewish apostles welcomed gentiles as *adelphoi*: brothers adopted into God's people *kata pneuma*, still distinct and different *kata sarka*—as is the case with all human adoption. And these Jewish apocalyptic convictions in their Christian iteration cohered with the broader Mediterranean construction of divine/human relations: gods and their humans form family groups. If the nations, through an eschatological miracle, now worship Israel's god alone, then even though *they remain ethnically distinct, they are spiritually adopted*. They too, like Israel, can call God "Abba, Father" (Rom 8:15; Gal 4:6).

We see here in the earliest mission's message the social birth of what had previously been an apocalyptic trope, and an apocalyptic hope. These gentiles' "Law-free" inclusion therefore tells us nothing about the Jewish observance of Paul and of his fellow Jewish apostles. The dual source of gentile "law-free-ness" was, first, the normal Jewish construal of Jewish law and, second, this particular element of Jewish apocalyptic tradition; it had nothing to do with prevenient apostolic apostasy. And the source of the apostles' unprecedented demand to these gentiles ("shun the worship of idols") was these same apocalyptic traditions. At the End of the Age—which is where the first generation of the Jesus-movement thought it stood—gentiles would destroy their idols, spurn their gods, and worship Israel's god alone.

But the gods struck back. These lower cosmic deities, the *archontes tou aiônes toutou*, had crucified the son of Paul's god (1 Cor 2:8); now they persecuted Paul and Paul's Christ-following gentiles, all of whom thereby shared in the sufferings of Christ. The *theos tou aiônes toutou* blinded the minds of those who refused Paul's message (2 Cor 4:4). Paul acknowledges the gods' hostility but also holds them in contempt: their power, after all, has been broken by Christ. The beings formerly worshiped by his congregations, he says, were not "gods by nature" but simply cosmic light-weights, *stoicheia* unworthy of fear or worship (Gal 4:8–9). Such gods in fact are mere *daimonia*, subordinate deities, "demons," (1 Cor 10:20–21, nodding to Ps 95:5 LXX). Soon, however, Paul teaches, these lower powers—every *archê* and every *exousia* and every *dunamis*—will themselves acknowledge the god of Israel. The returning Christ will defeat them and establish the kingdom of his father (15:24–27).⁴⁵ In the End, these superhuman beings wherever they are—above the earth or upon the earth or below the earth—will "bend knee" to Jesus (Phil 2:10). The *parousia* of Christ, Paul absolutely believed, besides raising the dead and transforming the living (1 Cor 15:23, 51–54), would bring about the *Götterdämmerung* of antiquity's cosmos. In the ever-shortening meanwhile before the Kingdom came (Rom 13:11), those "in Christ" had only to endure this divine anger, and to wait.

The Jewish Jesus-movement's non-negotiable proviso to interested gentiles—their absolute cessation of traditional worship—well explains the anger of their gods. And this divine anger in turn explains why Paul initially persecuted the movement, and why, later, he was persecuted after joining the movement. We see this more clearly if we glance ahead to the second and third centuries, to the pagan persecutions of gentile Christians.

The fact that ancient gods ran in the blood meant that people were born into their obligations to particular deities—family gods, civic gods, and (a special case) imperial gods. If these pagans became Christ-followers, ceasing to honor these gods with cult, they denied honor to the emperor and risked alienating heaven. This is why so many of the pre-Constantinian martyr stories turn upon the magistrates' efforts to coerce cultic conformity. At issue was not "belief," but the public display of respect. "Hilarianus said: 'Offer the sacrifice for the welfare of the emperors.' 'I will not,'" (*Perpetua* 6.3). "'Will you offer sacrifice?' the proconsul asked. 'No.' 'Offer sacrifice,' said the proconsul. 'I will not.' 'Do you attend to the air? Then offer sacrifice to the air!' 'No'" (*Pionius* 19). "'Swear by the genius of our lord the emperor.' 'I do not recognize the empire of this world'" (*Scillitan Martyrs* 5–6).⁴⁶

Because these non-sacrificing pagans of the Christian movement refused to honor their gods, the Tiber might overflow or the Nile might not, the earth might move or the sky might not (Tertullian, *Apol.* 40.2). "No rain, because of the Christians!" (Augustine, *civ. Dei* 2.3). Divine wrath risked havoc. Gods could strike with flood, famine, and earthquake, with drought

---

45. For the lexicography on these terms as astral agents, see Bauer, Gingrich, Danker, *Greek-English Lexicon of the New Testament*; cf. the "principalities and powers" of Eph 6:12.

46. Martyrdom as "discursive practice"—identity-confirming Christian narratives—currently dominates historical scholarship, and the historicity of events retailed by martyr stories, absent Roman evidence for persecution, "means that a historical narrative of legal persecution and prosecution cannot be re-created" (Moss, *Ancient Christian Martyrdom*, 12); see ibid., 1–22, for a good critical introduction to the historical and historiographical problems. Around 247 CE, Origen of Alexandria said that the number of Christians martyred "could easily be counted" (*c. Celsum* 3.8). However few the episodes of actual pagan persecution of Christians, then, the *idea*, amplified in martyriological literature, dominates ancient constructions of Christian identity.

and disease; they could cease protecting their cities, or allow foreign armies to invade. For this reason, uncoordinated local initiatives pre-250, and occasional imperial ones during the "crisis of the third century," attempted to coerce gentile Christians' cultic conformity. These unprecedented persecutions were motivated, quite simply, by piety—that is, by fear of the gods.[47]

Conversion to Judaism—which had the same effect in terms of sacrificing as becoming Christian did—was tolerated, if resented, because Judaism itself was familiar, as well as widely recognized as both ancient and ancestral, the two criteria of respectable cult. This fact, I think, provides the context for Paul's remarks that "preaching circumcision" entails no [pagan] persecution: Majority culture had long tolerated (male) converts to Judaism, who as part of the process would have received circumcision.[48] But by these same criteria of antiquity and ancestry—especially early on, in the middle decades of the first century—"Christianity" was, precisely, nothing.[49] Not requiring complete, or ethnic, affiliation with Judaism via circumcision, insisting that native cults nonetheless be renounced, the early apostles walked these Christ-fearing pagans into a social and religious no-man's land. The apostles themselves as well as their gentiles may not have been too worried: after all, Christ was on the verge of returning, of gloriously summing up the ages, and of submitting the cosmos and

---

47. "From Britain to Syria, pagan cults aimed to honour the gods and avert the misfortunes which might result from the gods' own anger at their neglect," notes Robin Lane Fox. "Any account of pagan worship which minimizes the gods' uncertain anger and mortals' fear of it is an empty account" (*Pagans and Christians*, 39). "The best that humans could hope for was that they could keep the gods in a good mood" (Potter, "Martyrdom as Spectacle," 134). Roman piety combined with patriotism, since the proper execution of traditional cult "is not only of concern to religion, but also to the well-being of the state" (Cicero *de legibus* 1.12.30). See Isaac, *Racism*, 467 and nn121–27 for citations to many Roman expressions of this view. Christians no less than pagans were aware that divine wrath was the consequence of neglecting cult, and for this reason they blamed these gods, qua evil *daimones*, for inspiring persecution against them, Reed, "Fallen Angels." For fear of divine anger as a root cause of the so-called "Great Persecution" begun under Diocletian (303–311 CE), Digeser, *Threat to Public Piety*; cf. the reconstruction by Rives, "Persecution of Christians."

48. For a different reconstruction of the meaning of Paul's remark, which also takes seriously the ethnic specificity of his commitments, see Runesson, "Inventing Christian Identity," esp. 80–84.

49. "Since they were neither Jew nor pagan, they were isolated, without a recognizable social identity" (Sanders, "Paul's Jewishness," 67; see too n26). For the same reason, we have no Jewish term for these people either: they fit no actual social category. Paul calls them either *hagioi* ("sanctified" or "set-apart" ones), or *adelphoi* ([adopted] "brothers"), or (since this is what they are), *ethnē*, which translates both as "pagans" and as "gentiles"; Fredriksen, "Judaizing the Nations," 242–44, 247–50; cf. Hodge, *If Sons, Then Heirs*, 43–66, 202n1.

everything in it to his divine father (1 Cor 15). But the pagan majority in these diaspora cities *was* worried. The gods' anger could shatter the common weal. Ancestral obligation, not particular beliefs—what people did, not what they thought—was what mattered.

Jews who were Christians in later centuries are invisible in the evidence for pagan persecutions: Jews had long had the option not to sacrifice to the gods of the majority. (For this reason, reports Eusebius, a gentile Christian during a period of pagan persecution had considered converting to Judaism, in order to be spared harassment, *Church History* 6.12,1.) But in the early decades of the new movement, Jewish apostles *were* targeted—hence Paul's being beaten with rods three times, a Roman punishment—precisely because they were raising pagan anxieties by drawing pagans away from their ancestral practices, *something that the synagogues had never done with their god-fearers*. For this same reason—the early movement's success at turning gentiles to the exclusive worship of the god of Israel—diaspora synagogues subjected Jewish apostles to disciplinary flogging, *makkot mardut*.[50] Such a destabilizing and inflammatory message, radiating from the synagogue, could make the Jewish urban community itself the target of local anxieties and resentments. Alienating the gods put the city at risk;[51] alienating the pagan majority put the diaspora synagogue at risk—especially when the behavior occasioning that risk, an exclusive commitment to the god of Israel, was so universally and uniquely associated with Jews themselves.

To sum up: Jewish apostles of the movement's first generation were persecuted in the Diaspora by fellow Jews, by pagans, and by Roman officials, but for second-order, not first-order religious reasons. These Jews (and only *these* Jews) were persecuted for the threat that they represented to disturbing the peace (riling anxiety in the pagan majority; potentially placing the local Jewish community at risk). We have no way of knowing for how long after the first generation of the movement such persecutions continued.[52]

---

50. The forty lashes (*makkot arbaim*) was a punishment meted out for violation of a biblical prohibition (m Makkot 3). *Makkot mardut*, on the other hand, was discretionary lashing, with no fixed number of lashes except for its upper limit, thirty-nine; see Hare, *Jewish Persecution in the Gospel of Matthew*, 42–46. The earliest attestation of *makkot mardut* is in the Mishnah, but the traditions upon which the Mishnah rests antedate the late second/early third century. Perhaps then (to close this circle), 2 Cor 11:24, which lacks the article *hoi* in Greek (cf. the RSV's translation, "*the* forty lashes less one") is our earliest attestation of *makkot mardut*.

51. Historians of Rome seem to have an easier time seeing this than do historians of Christianity: see, e.g., Barnes, "Legislation against the Christians"; Millar, "Imperial Cult and the Persecutions," 145–75; Lane Fox, *Pagans and Christians*, 419–34.

52. Mark 13:9—"They will deliver you up to councils; and you will be beaten in

Christ-following gentiles, by contrast, when persecuted (however sporadically) by fellow gentiles, suffered because they were deviant pagans. Their impiety endangered their own communities. The motivation for this persecution was *explicitly* religious. Each side knew that the god(s) of the other side existed, but neither side feared to disregard them. Christian gentiles thought the pagan gods mere demons: they could inflict harm, but fundamentally their power had been broken by Christ. Pagan gentiles thought the Jewish god defeated by the gods of Rome, and they rarely held Jesus to be other than a crucified man. Disrespecting Christian claims, thus the Christian god, bore no risk. As a result, the gentile forms of this new religious movement fell outside the parameters of antiquity's practical pluralism.[53]

Truly wide-scale and long-lived anti-Christian religious violence had to wait till the fourth century. It was practiced by Christians against each other. More Christians were persecuted by the Roman Empire *after* the conversion of Constantine than before.[54] Christianity had always been internally diverse—a diversity vociferously (and simultaneously) both denied and decried by the rhetoric of orthodoxy. Constantine's surprising patronage of one church led him to disallow the churches of the "heretics."[55] His efforts to close the gap between Athanasius and Arius, between Donatus and Caecilian, only made more of a mess. Imperial efforts at consolidation actually increased Christian diversity, and that diversity was deplored—occasionally with violence—by both church and state. Eventually, post-Theodosius (d. 397), state persecution found further targets: pagans, too and Jews, could feel its sting. Ironically, such coercion stemmed from the same source as had persecution in the days of Paul: fear of angering heaven. The denomination of heaven may have shifted, but under the Christian god impiety still risked divine anger: harvests could fail and frontiers fall.[56]

---

synagogues; and you will stand before governors and kings for my sake, to bear testimony before them"—may attest to such intra-Jewish activities' continuing after the year 70.

53. Cf. Moss, *Christian Martyrdom*, 82: "It was the social and religio-politial nonconformity of early Christians, their novelty, and their challenges to established social order and power structures that made them repulsive to Roman authorities."

54. On persistent intra-Christian violence, see esp. Brown, "Christianization and Religious Violence"; more recently, Shaw, *Sacred Violence*, provides a detailed (and disheartening) panorama of late fourth- / early fifth-century intra-Christian religious persecution in North Africa.

55. See, e.g., Eusebius, *Life of Constantine* 3.64. Drake argues that such imperial utterances were more about rhetorical bark than actual bite, *Constantine and the Bishops*, 194–272; but these laid the groundwork and established a mentality for later, post-Theodosian pro-active imperial initiatives.

56. "Why has the spring renounced its accustomed charm? Why has the summer, barren of its harvest, deprived the laboring farmer? . . . Why all of these things, unless

Late antique Rome reshaped the old theological definition of empire: "the greatest number of gods under a single government" ceded to "the greatest number of people protecting a single government by worshiping the single (though triune) god in a single way." Notionally and rhetorically, and in the language of law no less than in the language of doctrine, orthodoxy triumphed. Realistically and actually, however, the old gods continued to exist. Gentiles whether pagan or Christian still frequented synagogues. Jews, Christians and pagans co-celebrated urban festivals, went to the baths together, married each other.[57] And, for a long time after Constantine, the imperial cult of the emperor continued.[58] Was all this social activity an expression of doctrinal inconsistency, normal human messiness, or a continuing practical pluralism? It is hard to say. By the fifth century, however, such pluralism as survived the Western empire's collapse took its place alongside no less well-established traditions of religious persecution.[59]

BIBLIOGRAPHY

Alexander, Philip. "Jewish Elements in Gnosticism and Magic." In *Cambridge History of Judaism*, edited by William Horbury et al., 3:1052–78. Cambridge: Cambridge University Press, 1999.

Ameling, Walter. "Die jüdischen Gemeinden im antiken Kleinasien." In *Jüdische Gemeinden und Organisationsformen von der Antike bis zur Gegenwart*, edited by Robert Jütte and Abraham P. Kustermann, 29–55. Vienna: Böhlars, 1966.

Arnal, William. "The Collection and Synthesis of 'Tradition' and the Second-Century Invention of Christianity." *Method and Theory in the Study of Religion* 23 (2011) 193–215.

Barclay, John M. G. *Jews in the Mediterranean Diaspora: From Alexander to Trajan (323 BCE–117 CE)*. Edinburgh: T. & T. Clark, 1996.

---

nature has transgressed the decree of its own law, to avenge impiety?" Theodosius II, *NTh* 3, in his constitution against pagans, Samaritans, and Jews (430 CE). Cf. his convening the IIIrd Ecumenical Council in 429, so that "the condition of the church might honor God *and contribute to the safety of the Empire*," *Acta consiliorum oecumenicorum* I.1,1,114; cf. Tertullian, *Apol.* 40.2.

57. The evidence for these continuing interactions can be traced in the irate legislation of imperial edicts and in the canons of church councils, for which the two legal compendia by Linder, *Jews in Imperial Roman Legislation* and *Jews in the Legal Sources of the Early Middle Ages*; for discussion, Fredriksen and Irshai, "Christian Anti-Judaism," 1005–7.

58. On the Christian emperor cult, MacMullen, *Christianity and Paganism*, 34–39; Bowersock, "Polytheism and Monotheism in Arabia"; see too the earlier comment in Jones, *Later Roman Empire*, 1:93. Boin promises a fresh treatment in "Imperial Cult in a Christian Empire."

59. Fredriksen and Irshai, "Christian Anti-Judaism," 1020–27, provide a quick overview.

Barnes, Timothy D. "Legislation against the Christians." *JRS* 58 (1968) 32–50.
Beard, Mary, and John North. *Pagan Priests: Religion and Power in the Ancient World.* Ithaca: Cornell University Press, 1990.
Beard, Mary, John North, and Simon Price. *Religions of Rome.* Vol. 1: *A History.* Cambridge: Cambridge University Press, 1998.
Belayche, Nicole. "*Deus deum . . . summorum maximus* (Apuleius): Ritual Expressions of Distinction in the Divine World in the Imperial Period." In Mitchell and van Nuffelen, *One God,* 141–66.
Bloch, René. *Moses und der Mythos.* Leiden: Brill, 2010.
Boin, Douglas. "Imperial Cult in a Christian Empire: Late Antique *Divi* and the Imperial Priests of the Late 4th and early 5th century B.C.E." Paper delivered at the *Society of Biblical Literature,* Chicago, 2012.
Bowersock, Glen W. "Polytheism and Monotheism in Arabia and the Three Palestines." *Dumbarton Oaks Papers* 51 (1997) 1–10.
Brown, Peter. "Christianization and Religious Conflict." In *Cambridge Ancient History,* edited by Averil Cameron and Peter Gurnsey, 13:632–64. Cambridge: Cambridge University Press, 1998.
Chadwick, Henry. "Oracles of the End in the Conflict of Paganism and Christianity in the Fourth Century." In *Mémorial André-Jean Festugière: Antiquité païenne et chrétienne,* edited by Enzo Lucchesi and H. D. Saffrey, 125–29. Geneva: Cramer, 1984.
Chaniotis, Angelos. "The Jews of Aphrodisias: New Evidence and Old Problems." *Scripta Classica Israelica* 21 (2002) 209–42.
―――. "Megatheism: The Search for the Almighty God and the Competition of Cults." In Mitchell and van Nuffelen, *One God,* 112–40.
Cohen, Shaye J. D. *Beginnings of Jewishness.* Berkeley: University of California Press, 1999.
Digeser, Elizabeth DePalma. *A Threat to Public Piety.* Ithaca, NY: Cornell University Press, 2012.
Donaldson, Terence L. *Judaism and the Gentiles: Jewish Patterns of Universalism (to 135 CE).* Waco, TX: Baylor University Press, 2007.
Drake, H. A. *Constantine and the Bishops.* Baltimore: Johns Hopkins University Press, 2000.
Esler, Philip F. *Conflict and Identity in Romans: The Social Setting of Paul's Letter.* Minneapolis: Fortress, 2003.
Feldman, Louis H. *Jew and Gentile in the Ancient World.* Princeton: Princeton University Press, 1993.
Fredriksen, Paula. *Augustine and the Jews.* New Haven: Yale University Press, 2010.
―――. "Judaism, the Circumcision of Gentiles, and Apocalyptic Hope: Another Look at Galatians 1 and 2." *Journal of Theological Studies* 42 (1991) 532–64.
―――. "Judaizing the Nations: The Ritual Demands of Paul's Gospel." *New Testament Studies* 56 (2010) 232–52.
―――. "Mandatory Retirement: Ideas in the Study of Christian Origins Whose Time Has Come to Go." *Studies in Religion/Sciences Religieuses* 35 (2006) 231–46.
―――. "Retrospect Is the Mother of Anachronism; or, How Later Contexts Affect Pauline Contents." In *Jews and Christians in the First and Second Century: Historiographical Questions,* edited by J. Schwartz and P. Tomson. CRINT. Leiden: Brill, forthcoming 2013.

———. *Sin: The Early History of an Idea*. Princeton: Princeton University Press, 2012.

———. "What Parting of the Ways?" In *The Ways That Never Parted*, edited by A. Becker and A. Y. Reed, 35–63. Tübingen: Mohr-Siebeck, 2003.

Fredriksen, Paula, and Oded Irshai. "Christian Anti-Judaism: Polemics and Policies, from the Second to the Seventh Century." In *Cambridge History of Judaism*, edited by Steven T. Katz, 4:977–1034. Cambridge: Cambridge University Press, 2006.

Gruen, Erich S. *Diaspora: Jews amidst Greeks and Romans*. Cambridge: Harvard University Press, 2002.

———. *Heritage and Hellenism: The Reinvention of Jewish Tradition*. Berkeley: University of California Press, 1998.

———. "'Include Me Out': Tertullian, the Rabbis, and the Graeco-Roman City." In *L'identité à travers l'éthique*, edited by Katell Berthelot et al. Brepols, forthcoming.

———. "Jewish Perspectives on Greek Culture and Ethnicity." In *Ancient Perceptions of Greek Ethnicity*, edited by Irad Malkin, 347–73. Cambridge: Harvard University Press, 2001.

Hare, Douglas R. A. *The Theme of Jewish Persecution in the Gospel according to St. Matthew*. Cambridge: Cambridge University Press, 1967.

Hayes, C. *Gentile Impurities and Jewish Identities*. New York: Oxford University Press, 2002.

Hodge, Caroline E. Johnson. *If Sons, Then Heirs: A Study of Kinship and Ethnicity in the Letters of Paul*. New York: Oxford University Press, 2007.

———. "'Married to an Unbeliever': Households, Hierarchies, and Holiness in 1 Corinthians 7:12–16." *Harvard Theological Review* 103 (2010) 1–25.

Horst, Pieter W. van der. "Judaism in Asia Minor." In *Cambridge History of Religions in the Ancient World*, edited by Michele R. Salzman 2:321–40. Cambridge: Cambridge University Press, 2013.

———. "'Thou Shalt not Revile the Gods': The LXX Translation of Exodus 22:28 (27), Its Background and Influence." In *The Studia Philonica Annual*, edited by David T. Runia, 5:1–8. Atlanta: Society of Biblical Literature, 1993.

Hultgren, Arland J. "Paul's Pre-Christian Persecutions of the Church: Their Purpose, Locale, and Nature." *Journal of Biblical Literature* 95 (1976) 97–111.

Isaac, Benjamin H. *The Invention of Racism in Classical Antiquity*. Princeton: Princeton University Press, 2005.

Jones, A. H. M. *The Later Roman Empire, 284–602: A Social, Economic, and Administrative Survey*. 2 vols. Norman: University of Oklahoma Press, 1964.

Jones, Christopher P. *Kinship Diplomacy in the Ancient World*. Cambridge: Harvard University Press, 1999.

Kahlos, Maijastina. *Debate and Dialogue. Christian and Pagan Cultures c. 360–430*. Aldershot, UK: Ashgate, 2007.

Kelly, J. N. D. *Golden Mouth: The Story of John Chrysostom*. Ithaca, NY: Cornell University Press, 1995.

Klawans, Jonathan. "Notions of Gentile Impurity in Ancient Judaism." *AJS Review* 20 (1995) 285–312.

Lane Fox, Robin. *Pagans and Christians*. New York: Knopf, 1987.

Levine, Lee I. *The Ancient Synagogue*. New Haven: Yale University Press, 2000.

Levinskaya, Irina. *The Book of Acts in Its Diaspora Setting*. Grand Rapids: Eerdmans, 1996.

Linder, Amnon. *Jews in Roman Imperial Legislation*. Detroit: Wayne State University Press, 1987.

———. *Jews in the Legal Sources of the Early Middle Ages*. Detroit: Wayne State University Press, 1997.

MacMullen, Ramsay. *Christianity and Paganism in the Fourth to Eighth Centuries*. New Haven: Yale University Press, 1997.

Markschies, Christoph. "The Price of Monotheism: Some New Observations on a Current Debate about Late Antiquity." In Mitchell and van Nuffelen, *One God*, 100–111.

Marshall, John W. "Misunderstanding the New Paul: Marcion's Transformation of the Sonderzeit Paul." *Journal for Early Christian Studies* 20 (2012) 1–29.

Millar, Fergus. "The Imperial Cult and the Persecutions." In *Le culte des souverains dans l'empire Romain*, edited by Elias J. Bickerman and Willem den Boer, 145–75. Geneva: Hardt, 1973.

Miller, David M. "Ethnicity Comes of Age: An Overview of Twentieth-Century Terms for *Ioudaios*." *Currents in Biblical Research* 10 (2012) 293–311.

———. "The Meaning of *Ioudaios* and Its Relationship to Other Group Labels in Ancient Judaism." *Currents in Biblical Research* 9 (2010) 98–126.

Mitchell, Stephen. "The Cult of *Theos Hypsistos*." In *Pagan Monotheism in Late Antiquity*, edited by P. Athanassiadi and M. Frede, 81–148. Oxford: Clarendon, 1999.

Mitchell, Stephen, and P. van Nuffelen. *One God: Pagan Monotheism in the Roman Empire*. Cambridge: Cambridge University Press, 2010.

Moss, Candida R. *Ancient Christian Martyrdom*. New Haven: Yale University Press, 2012.

O'Donnell, James J. "The Demise of Paganism." *Traditio* 35 (1979) 45–88.

Paget, James Carleton. "Jewish Proselytism at the Time of Christian Origins: Chimera or Reality?" *Journal for the Study of the New Testament* 62 (1996) 65–103.

Potter, David. "Martyrdom as Spectacle." In *Theatre and Society in the Classical World*, edited by Ruth Scodel, 53–88. Ann Arbor: University of Michogan Press, 1993.

Reed, Annette Yoshiko. "The Trickery of the Fallen Angels and the Demonic Mimesis of the Divine." *Journal of Early Christian Studies* 12 (2004) 141–71.

Reynolds, Joyce M., and Robert Tannenbaum. *Jews and God-Fearers at Aphrodisias*. Cambridge: Cambridge Philological Society, 1987.

Rives, James B. "Human Sacrifice among Pagans and Christians." *Journal of Roman Studies* 85 (1995) 65–85.

———. "The Persecution of Christians and Ideas of Community in the Roman Empire." In *Politiche religiose nel mondo antico e tardoantico*, edited by Giovanni A. Cecconi and Chantal Gabrielli, 199–217. Bari, Italy: Edipuglia, 2011.

Runesson, Anders. "Inventing Christian Identity: Paul, Ignatius, and Theodosius I." In *Exploring Early Christian Identity*, edited by Bengt Holmberg, 59–92. Tübingen: Mohr Siebeck, 2008.

Rutgers, Leonard V. *Hidden Heritage of Diaspora Judaism*. Leuven: Peeters, 1998.

———. "Roman Policy toward the Jews: Expulsions from the City of Rome during the First Century C.E." In *Judaism and Christianity in First-Century Rome*, edited by Karl P. Donfried and Peter Richardson, 93–116. Grand Rapids: Eerdmans, 1998.

Sanders, E. P. *Jewish Law from Jesus to the Mishnah*. Philadelphia: Trinity, 1990.

———. *Paul, the Law, and the Jewish People*. Philadelphia: Trinity, 1983.

---. "Paul's Jewishness." In *Paul's Jewish Matrix*, edited by Thomas G. Casey and Justin Taylor, 51–74. Bible in Dialogue 2. Rome: Gregorian & Biblical, 2011.

Schäfer, Peter. *Judeophobia: Attitudes toward Jews in the Ancient World*. Cambridge: Harvard University Press, 1997.

Schürer, Emil. *The History of the Jewish People in the Age of Jesus Christ*. Edited by Geza Vermes et al. 3 vols. Edinburgh: T. & T. Clark, 1973–87.

Segal, Alan F. *Paul the Convert: The Apostolate and Apostasy of Saul the Pharisee*. New Haven: Yale University Press, 1990.

---. *Two Powers in Heaven: Early Rabbinic Reports about Christianity and Gnosticism*. Studies in the Judaism of Late Antiquity 25. Leiden: Brill, 1977.

Shaw, Brent D. *Sacred Violence: African Christians and Sectarian Hatred in the Age of Augustine*. Cambridge: Cambridge University Press, 2011.

Stern, Menahem. *Greek and Latin Authors on Jews and Judaism*. 3 vols. Jerusalem: Israel Academy of Sciences and Humanities: 1974–1984.

Stowers, Stanley K. *A Rereading of Romans: Justice, Jews, and Gentiles*. New Haven: Yale University Press, 1994.

Wilken, Robert L. *John Chrysostom and the Jews*. Berkeley: University of California Press, 1983.

Williams, Margaret. *Jews among the Greeks and Romans*. Baltimore: Johns Hopkins Press, 1998.

Young, Francis M. *Biblical Exegesis and the Formation of Christian Culture*. Cambridge: Cambridge University Press, 1997.

7

Families of Religion, Then and Now

A Response to Paula Fredriksen

JONATHAN RAY

PROF. FREDRIKSEN'S CHAPTER ON religious interaction and religious persecution in late antiquity explores the nature of religious communities—indeed, of religious "families"—calling our attention to the problem of trying to separate scripture, ritual and belief from religious community and identity. By way of response, I'd like to highlight some themes that have been introduced in her study, and to consider how our current understanding of pluralism might look different in the light of these categories.

The first issue that I would like to raise has to do with demographics. In particular, how does the size (and thus potential power and potential threat) of a religious community change its relationship to other communities? Judaism did not present much of a challenge to pagan power in the Roman world, and in those instances in which Jews did (in a the form of rebellion, for instance) they were harshly punished. Similarly, as we have seen, it was primarily when Christians started drawing pagans to their community in larger numbers and thus challenging pagan hegemony, that they caused anxiety.

These power dynamics are still very much a part of the way in which religious communities relate to one another. It is perhaps the size of religious communities as much as their theological stance that accounts for the different experience of Muslims in the Middle East and their experience in nations such as the United States, the United Kingdom and France. This imbalance with regard to communal size and influence plays a central role in shaping the willingness to engage in interreligious dialogue or pluralist activities. For religious minorities, boundary maintenance is promoted as a necessary protective measure. The need to distinguish between "us" and "them," arises not only out of a difference in beliefs and concepts of salvation, but also out of a fear of assimilation here and now. While for dominant religious cultures this fear of extinction is almost nonexistent, for minority groups it can quickly come to overshadow all other motivating factors.

The relative social and political power of a community can also alter theological ideals or the interpretation of sacred texts. In the communities of the ancient Mediterranean, one could worship the god of another ethnos, but not exchange one's ethnicity and all of the ancestral ties and future destinies that went with it. Such "cultural treason" was far more important than belief, or even worship, of particular deities. For modern Jews and, perhaps, several other religious communities, ethnic and cultural loyalties continue to dominate the discussion of religious pluralism. Thus, a secular, nonobservant Jew can marry another secular, nonobservant Jew without much resistance from family and community, but marrying a secular Christian or Muslim is another matter entirely.

The next issue that I think merits consideration is the ongoing historical relationship between these, and other, ethno-religious communities, and the way this past continues to shape the present and future. Fredriksen draws our attention to the notion that, even though the gentiles of Paul's age might remain ethnically distinct, they could be spiritually "adopted" by Jews if they (in accordance with Jewish apocalyptic traditions) worship Israel's God alone. This notion is theologically intriguing, and opens up some very interesting avenues for exegesis. However, as we consider how sacred texts might be read differently, we cannot lose sight of how things have been read, and lived, and the histories that have ensued. Simply put, we need to appreciate the fact that long histories of religious exclusion and persecution continue to haunt the collective memories of many religious communities. Despite the various ways in which the religious institutions of Judaism and Christianity *might* have developed, the way in which they *did* develop matters. The Church did, in fact, come to displace paganism, and Christian society assumed a dominant position vis-à-vis the Jews who lived in their midst. Similarly, rabbinic Judaism emerged as the dominant force within Jewish society, effectively controlling the boundaries of normative Judaism until the nineteenth century. As Rome became a Christian empire, its definition of Judaism came to matter for Jews, whether or not they agreed with it. The same cannot be said of Jewish views of Christianity. Indeed, the relatively weak social and political position of late-antique rabbis vis-à-vis other Jews meant that rabbinic views of Christianity were far less entrenched within Jewish society than the views of Christian theologians among other Christians.

There is a tendency in theological and religious studies to bracket that which is difficult and dark in the historical relationships between religious communities, and to search for more hopeful signs that the way communities have interacted in the past need not be the way they interact in the future. This progressive approach is understandable, even laudable, when one considers the ease with which many become mired in seemingly endless cycles of accusation and retribution. And yet I think that the way forward requires more of us than a tacit nod to past excesses. The question of persecution that is raised in Fredriksen's study—and the way in which the persecuted can become the persecutor—is one that we would do well to bear in mind as we examine religious interaction today. In our desire to transcend some of the more upsetting moments of interreligious discord, we must be careful to avoid underestimating the potency of past relations and the scars that they have left.

The last category that I suggest that we think about is that of representation within each religious community—that is, the question of who speaks for these communities. When we approach the questions of religious pluralism, do we imagine sets of religious cultures, in which anyone can take part, or religious systems that are regulated by a particular group? Who speaks for these religious families? It may be that Jewish apocalyptic traditions in antiquity were inherently pluralistic, but it's hard to imagine these traditions having much of an impact beyond the small circles of the intellectual elite. One of the most suggestive elements in Prof. Fredriksen's study is the question of control, and the fear of dissonance within one's own community. We might consider how attitudes toward other religious groups are a reflection of internal uncertainties with regard to a group's own identities.

In the ancient Mediterranean, exclusion of the religious "other" was part of a broader process of the construction of orthodoxy and heresy that also marginalized and excluded a variety of groups, ideologies and practices within the same religious community. The religious legacy of late antiquity was not just the parting of the ways between Christians and Jews, but also the particular formulations of Christianity and Judaism that bound their adherents more closely to a central set of ideals. This process of establishing and enforcing religious boundaries served (and serves) to legitimize the authority of certain groups within each community. In arguing for religious exclusivity, rabbis and early Church Fathers alike were also asserting their own legitimacy as arbiters of religious orthodoxy. If the goal of religious pluralism is, at least in part, to foster interreligious communication, respect and acceptance, then we need to recognize that our readings of sacred texts have always been shaped by a multiplicity of factors, including the defense of clerical authority.

Rabbinic literature from this period suggests a community—or network—of scholars with a shared worldview. Thus, we can speak of rabbinic Judaism in late antiquity in the sense of an imagined community of intellectuals, perhaps akin to Hellenistic philosophical schools. But the existence of this literature does not necessarily indicate a larger society of Jews who embraced rabbinic concepts of God, community, law, etc. And even if we can determine, from other evidence, that there did exist in this period an identifiable Jewish society whose cultural norms overlap with those of rabbinic literature, it does not necessarily stand to reason that this society took the rabbis and their particular reading of Judaism as exclusively authoritative.

Crossing religious boundaries and engaging in moments of pluralism was the default setting for most people in late antiquity. Paganism was a large and pervasive system with many attractive features, and Christianity was close enough to Judaism that it is easy to see why adherents to both traditions saw great potential benefit in expanding their forms of worship of and service to the divine. Curtailment of such boundary crossing necessitated religious authorities with both the interest in and ability to keep these groups apart. Throughout much of this period, Jewish and Christian leaders struggled to assert this sort of authority. The long list of patrons, elders and communal officials in Late Antique Jewish society suggests a complex web of power relationships, with no particular group wielding much authority. Particularly noteworthy in this regard is the apparent lack of power enjoyed by rabbis, or similar clerical figures, despite their relatively exalted image in rabbinic texts of the era.

Today, the question of representation remains a relevant issue in the discourse on religious pluralism. Current events continue to spur scholars to create opportunities for dialogue and learning about different religious and ethnic groups in the hope of easing tensions and advancing mutual understanding. Thus, scholars and clergy invite Christians and Muslims to sit down together and discuss issues of mutual concern. But which members of these groups show up, and whom do they truly represent? What about those who do not wish to engage? There is, I fear, a tendency to shrug and say that we can only work with what we have—with those who are willing to engage on these issues. And perhaps when it comes to interreligious dialogue that is the case. But I'd like to propose that the questions surrounding religious pluralism transcend dialogue. Religious cultures are in constant contact, even if they are not in dialogue, and they are shaped by this contact. Polemic, violence and, as Fredriksen points out, persecution, are also forms of pluralistic encounter, and ones whose importance cannot be disregarded just because they make us uncomfortable.

Prof. Fredrikesn's incisive portrait of religious pluralism and persecution in Roman antiquity reminds us that our conceptual categories that separate Christians from Jews, and the human from the divine, are less rooted in tradition than we recognize. In other times and places the boundaries separating these groups were often notional, rather than actual. We would do well to remember these lessons, if for no other reason, to contradict the false clarity offered by those who have expunged such periods of natural religious pluralism from their memories, and from their narratives of religious history. The problems and possibilities of religious interaction in this foundational period serve as a suitably complex model for our own time. However, the long and often tragic relationship between Christians and Jews that connects that era with our own will not be overcome easily. The degree to which twenty-first-century Jews and Christians will have mutually beneficial discussions about theological commonalities and social coexistence will be governed as much by a thoughtful engagement with their shared history, as by the potential relationship that inheres in their sacred texts and divine mandates.

8

Judaism, Christianity, and Modernity

Charles Péguy and the Mysticisms of the Dreyfus Affair

MATTHEW W. MAGUIRE

AS A CRYSTALLIZING MOMENT for so many formative elements of late modern culture, the Dreyfus Affair has never ceased to fascinate its posterity. It is at once a proleptic formulation of fascism and more generally of twentieth-century ideological extremism, even as it also figures within the genealogy of contemporary notions about human rights, and perhaps the vindication of a thoroughgoing secular politics as well. It is often considered a harbinger of an especially poisonous compound of religious and racial anti-Semitism in the twentieth century, even as it is also considered an event in the intellectual genealogy of Zionism. That it is also the occasion for a breakthrough in understanding between Christianity and Judaism is now almost unknown.

It is not that Charles Péguy (1873–1914), a Catholic philosopher, journalist and poet whose account of the Dreyfus Affair is responsible for this breakthrough, has gone forever unnoticed—or that his efforts to recast Christians' understanding of Judaism have been forever obscure. It was Péguy's interreligious thinking that accounted for the theologian and resistor Henri de Lubac's acknowledgment of the ways in which Péguy proved so helpful for his own resistance journal during the Nazi Occupation of France, in particular as a way to combat the "racist contagion" that he and other

Catholic resistors fought in word and deed.[1] After the War, the great scholar of Judaism, Gerschom Scholem, gave an emphatic tribute to Péguy, declaring that Péguy "has incisively understood the Jewish condition to an extent that has been rarely achieved, and has never been surpassed by non-Jews."[2]

Yet at present, a moment when the intellectual genealogy of Christian-Jewish and specifically Catholic-Jewish relations are being written anew, Péguy's work has fallen into heavy shadow. Paula Frederikson has rightly called attention to Augustine's innovative reading of Judaism (one that was, one might add, subsequently developed by the great neo-Augustianian Pascal), but her focus is legitimately and explicitly on late Antiquity.[3] John Connelly's just-published *From Enemy to Brother* at times recklessly contends that there was no Catholic, non-supersessionist reading of Judaism before the 1930's, and what progress was made was, in his argument, almost entirely the work of converts to Catholicism, especially but not exclusively from Judaism, many of whom increasingly found themselves attracted to Judaism.[4]

In this way, despite Scholem's recognition that Péguy's work constitutes a crucial development in Christian thinking about Judaism, it threatens to become something like—if we may use a metaphor from genetics to complement the contemporary scholarly fascination with genealogy—a random mutation without consequence for Christianity's and especially Catholicism's late modern or postmodern phenotype.

Yet it is not so. Péguy exerted an enormous impact upon not just French, but European thought in the early to mid-twentieth century, attracting the admiring attention not only of de Lubac and Scholem, but of other major theologians and philosophers of religion—including Hans Urs von Balthasar, whose long, affirmative essay on Péguy emphasizes his "persistent dialogue" with Judaism and its history.[5]

Furthermore, Péguy's account of how Christianity and Judaism relate to one another gives his readers a more promising basis for interreligious

---

1. See de Lubac, *Christian Resistance to Anti-Semitism: Memories from 1940–44*, 49. To this end, de Lubac quotes the judgment of Léon Poliakov, *Bréviaire de la haine*, 340.

2. Scholem, *Fidélité et utopie*, 90. See *L'Amitié Charles Péguy: Bulletin d'informations et de recherches* 9, Jan-Mar 1980. A similarly strong endorsement of Péguy can be found in an article adapted from a lecture given by Scholem to the World Jewish Congress in 1966, printed in *Commentary*, November 1966. Unless otherwise noted, all translations are my own.

3. Fredriksen, *Augustine and the Jews*.

4. Connelly, *From Enemy to Brother*.

5. See von Balthasar, *The Glory of the Lord: A Theological Aesthetics*, vol. 3, *Studies in Theological Style: Lay Styles*, and in particular the chapter devoted to Péguy, 400–517. The cited quote can be found on 421.

dialogue than many accounts offered elsewhere. It also offers a fresh way of thinking about the complex relationship between Christianity, Judaism and secularism in modern culture, and thus about the recent flood of "modernity stories," in which contemporary scholars aspire to explain the origins of modernity to a postmodern world.

Yet what precisely is distinctive about Péguy's account of Judaism? Its singularity can be found in a series of daring inversions. It was a commonplace of historical Christian anti-Judaism that Judaism be understood with reference to the exaltation of law, to carnality, and to Good Friday (and with it, supremely, Judas). Hence an allegedly ineluctable affinity for legalism, the flesh and treason among Jews and within Judaism appears over and over again in Christian anti-Semitism, including the indefatigable bleatings of Edouard Drumont, Léon Bloy, Maurice Barrès, and other French anti-Semites writing about Judaism at the turn of the last century.[6]

In his writing about the Dreyfus Affair—above all in *Notre Jeunesse*, his famous essay about the Affair, written in 1910—Péguy transforms this anti-Semitic triad, and its opposing assumptions about Christianity, into something new. For Péguy, Judaism is a supreme instance not of a stultifying legalism, but of something altogether different, what he repeatedly calls a *"mystique"*—that is, a mystical love that makes selfless inquiry into truth and quiet, humble sacrifices on behalf of justice possible.[7] Péguy's close friend Bernard-Lazare—Jewish and fascinated by Judaism but himself an atheist, and a very early defender of Dreyfus' innocence—incarnates for Péguy a passionately lucid prophetic mysticism of justice that sacrifices personal ambition to do God's work in the world, and is faithful to that work regardless of consequences.[8] That Bernard-Lazare greets this sacrifice with a kind of patient irony about the workings of mysticism's antipode—politics—is, for Péguy, also very much a part of his distinctively Jewish way of thinking about justice and its labors through time.[9]

---

6. For example, see Drumont, *La France juive*, and for an anti-Semitic critique and elaboration upon Drumont, see Bloy, *Le Salut par les Juifs*. In Bloy's case, the emphasis on Jewish corporeality could extend to the Christian Eucharist itself: in a letter to Raïssa Maritain, he wrote: "I eat, every morning, a Jew named Jesus Christ" [je mange, chaque matin, un Juif qui se nomme Jésus-Christ]. See Burton, *Holy Tears, Holy Blood*, 80–81. For more on anti-Semitism during the Belle Epoque, see Birnbaum, *The Anti-Semitic Moment*.

7. See Péguy, *Oeuvres Complètes* (4 vols.). Henceforth, this source will be cited as "OC, Péguy," followed by volume number, manuscript title, year of publication (in the first citation) and page number. OC, Péguy, III, *Notre jeunesse* (1910), 47–52, 157–58.

8. OC, Péguy, III, *Notre jeunesse* (1910), 69.

9. Ibid., e.g., 60, 63–66, 72, 90, 93, and 95.

In now traditional postmodern language, it could be said that Péguy "essentializes" Bernard-Lazare and Judaism (this question will be addressed further below). Revealingly, however, for Péguy, Bernard-Lazare is not simply or only Jewish—he is also and simultaneously French, and Parisian, and secular in his sensibilities.[10] Yet this multiplicity of identities gives something indispensable to the effort to save Dreyfus from death and ignominy, both within and among the persons that inhabit these diverse identities. As Péguy put it, "The Dreyfus Affair, and the campaign for Dreyfus . . . was a culmination, a recovery and culmination of at least three mysticisms: Jewish, Christian, and French."[11]

If Bernard-Lazare simultaneously represented a distinctively Jewish and French mysticism at work in the fight to establish Dreyfus' innocence, for Péguy, that aspiration was developed variously, almost fugally, by several other sources of mystic nourishment. These included deep memories drawn from a French chivalric tradition of fighting cheerfully against difficult odds, from a French republican exaltation of solidarity with the oppressed drawn from the French Revolution, and from a life inspired by a Christian sanctification of sacrificial love of neighbor that accepts poverty and marginality as the privileged dwelling place of holiness and truth.

For Péguy, all three of these mysticisms—Christian, Jewish, and French—cooperated with one another to exonerate Dreyfus, and offered something unique and irreplaceable in relation to the Affair's meaning and outcome. A campaign for Dreyfus that involved only one of these three mysticisms would, he strongly suggests, have failed, since these three mysticisms were together engaged in what he calls a process of "cross-checking" that allowed for the flourishing of their respective mysticisms.[12] In this way, Péguy speaks directly of the friendship that those devoted to one or two of these mysticisms had with one another, and how this friendship involved a mutual testing that brought out what is distinctively best in each of them.

These mystiques flourished even as they simultaneously struggled with the political negation of their mystique in what Péguy calls *politique*. This *politique* was evident in the decision of some within the French Jewish community to lie low and avoid further persecution by allowing Dreyfus' persecution to continue, or in the desire of French patriots to withhold criticism of their own government and institutions even when they were clearly

10. Ibid., 64 and 74.
11. Ibid., 47.
12. Ibid., 50.

in the wrong, or in the tendency of French Catholics to avoid a scandal that would might diminish the standing of the Church in the world.[13]

For Péguy, the secret of *mystique's* numinous and extraordinary power is a willingness to inhabit with one's very body the truth of one's love for neighbor and of God. For him, mysticism is not the negation of the body, but the love that makes the body a home for truth and justice. Hence for Péguy, the word in French for what is fleshly or carnal—"*charnel*"—is not a word of disgust, and often of anti-Semitic invective, as it could be for a host of anti-Semitic contemporaries. Rather, it is a strongly, even ecstatically positive word.

Péguy's prose and poetry is full of loving references to the "carnal earth,"[14] to the ways in which the spiritual and the carnal complement and fulfill one another: Jesus himself lives a carnal life, and for Péguy, Mary's singular blessing is that "being carnal she is pure/but, being pure, she is also carnal."[15] Péguy pointedly observed that Jesus was a God-man or man-God, not an angel.[16] For Péguy it is an enormous mistake to neglect the carnality not just of Jesus but of saints, and thus, in his words, to "confuse the angel and the saint."[17] Both Incarnation and Resurrection are themselves both carnal and mystical for Péguy.[18] For him, carnal and mystical are not opposites, but natural and necessary complements in a creation that testifies to the goodness of God. As the muse of history, Clio, tells him in one of his final writings about the virtues of hope, faith and love, "it is these spiritual things that are carnal, not me."[19]

This affirmation of carnality leads to Péguy's final transformation in thinking about Judaism and Christianity. Though he writes at length about Good Friday, he shows no interest in some "Jewish responsibility" for Jesus' death, a death that is properly for him the consequence of all human sin. Rather, he thinks of the Jewish people as connected to Christ, as Christ is always connected to the Jewish people, since the Jewish people are related supremely and uniquely to Christianity not through Good Friday, but through the Incarnation and Resurrection. How does Péguy think through this relationship between Judaism and the founding commitments

13. Ibid., 50–52, 85, 149–53.
14. OC, Péguy, *Oeuvres Poétiques*, "Ève," (1913), 1028–29.
15. Ibid., "Le porche du mystère de la deuxième vertu" (1911), 576.
16. OC, Péguy, III, *Dialogue de l'histoire et de l'âme charnelle* (written in 1909), 679.
17. Ibid.
18. Ibid., 728.
19. OC, Péguy, II, *Clio, Dialogue de l'histoire et de l'âme païenne* (posthumously published—written in July 1913), 1154.

of Christian faith? It is a question that leads Péguy to reflect on human freedom, Christology, the history of Christianity, and the constitutive assumptions of modern culture with considerable care.

For Péguy, the Incarnation is a free act of God that like all acts of freedom, does not break from the past but daringly and creatively draws ever more deeply from its origin. Here Péguy draws upon the philosophy of his mentor Henri Bergson: for Bergson, freedom is a state in which, in his words, the "self lets itself live, when it abstains from establishing a separation between the present and anterior states."[20] In Bergson's philosophy, "a free act" occurs when "the self alone is the author of it, since it expresses the entire self."[21] In this Bergsonian way, for Péguy, Judaism and Christianity are neither impassive and timeless essences, nor are they contingent representations radically subject to the flux of becoming. Instead, they draw faithfully to the past to produce what is radical (in the true etymological sense of radical, that is, "from the root") and are thus both entirely faithful and astonishingly new.

For Bergson's student Péguy, Christianity must express the prior or "antecedent state" of Judaism to express itself freely and authentically. Through Bergson, Péguy expresses a way of thinking about origins and originality totally unlike that of Baudelaire, Rimbaud and other near-contemporary luminaries in late modern French culture, for whom originality could only emerge by perpetually *transgressing* or breaking with an origin and its subsequent development. Rather, for Péguy, originality comes to be through radically lucid and continuous *fidelity* to an origin. In this way, Jesus' Incarnation itself expresses its originality through fidelity to its Jewish root.

This commitment to origins discloses a distinctive feature of Péguy's thinking about the relationship between time, history and Christianity—and with it, its complicated and in historical terms, often deeply flawed relationship to Judaism. The question became an intense and complex one for Péguy, given his commitment to fighting anti-Semitism in both its modern secular and modern religious forms. In fact, while discriminatory injustice and religious prejudice have existed for centuries, Péguy claims that a comprehensive ideology of anti-Semitism is a distinctly modern development.[22] It is thus profoundly connected to the absence of love in modern Christianity and in modern secular culture alike. For Péguy, "the modern world

---

20. Bergson, *Essai sur les données immédiates de la conscience*, 67.

21. Ibid., 109 (for a broader discussion of freedom and separation from conventional demarcations, temporal and otherwise, see 109–13).

22. OC, Péguy, III, *Notre jeunesse*, 131–32.

is essentially the glorification of intellect as opposed to love."[23] Similarly, Christianity suffers in the modern world not because of some sort of alleged antagonism between itself and science or reason, but from the same absence: "it is not at all the case that reasoning is missing [from Christianity], but love."[24]

For Péguy, the Incarnation affirms human beings as both spiritual and material beings in a bond of love, at once connected to the present and eternity; the "insertion of the eternal in the temporal" through "carnal creation" is for him a supremely vivid reality.[25] Jesus' genealogy—through prostitutes, liars and illicit affairs as well as Kings—is "frightening" but the evangelist Matthew, with "that distinctively peasant honesty" is sure not to hide it.[26] Christ's life and death put carnal human life at the same value as God.[27] For Péguy, the Resurrection is itself simultaneously carnal and mystical,[28] and testifies to what for Péguy is the essence of Christianity: through the Incarnation, "God sacrificed himself for me."[29] God's "immense, infinite love"[30] for human beings in Christ had a unique effect: *"it put the infinite everywhere."*[31]

For Péguy, a genuinely Christian life of love is of course a difficult achievement in any century, since "all these twenty centuries have been...bad Christian centuries."[32] All times belong to God,[33] but saints are very often misunderstood by their Christian contemporaries, just as the prophets were misunderstood by their contemporaries in ancient Israel.[34] It is Christianity's peculiar burden, however, to struggle with the question of time, infinite love and historical change in a unique way, because the meeting of the temporal and eternal in time (i.e., with the life of Christ in ancient Israel) means that Christians can feel temporally estranged from eternity itself as generations and centuries pass.

---

23. OC, Péguy, II, *Par ce demi-clair matin* (1905), 209.
24. OC, Péguy, III, *Notre jeunesse, Cahiers*, 98–99.
25. OC, Péguy, III, *Victor-Marie, comte Hugo* (1910), 233.
26. Ibid., 238–39.
27. OC, Péguy, III, *Dialogue de l'histoire et de l'âme charnelle*, 681–82.
28. Ibid., 728.
29. Ibid., 676 and 679.
30. Ibid., 740.
31. Ibid., 703–4; italics in original text.
32. Ibid., 690.
33. Ibid., 648.
34. OC, Péguy, III, *Notre jeunesse*, 56.

For Péguy, this estrangement leads to impatience and a desire for purely temporal vindication; the source of this failing can, unsettlingly, be found in the origin of Christian teaching. As Péguy wrote in one provocative passage, "Jesus knew how to graft Jewish anxiety into the Christian body." But "Jesus was not able (or did not want) to graft Jewish patience into the Christian body."[35]

At first, Péguy's thought about Christian impatience is strikingly reminiscent of Franz Rosenzweig's reflections on Judaism and Christianity in *The Star of Redemption*, in which (to state it with starkly simplifying brevity) Christians live in a stretched, sometimes unstable linear time of eschatological expectation, whereas Jews dwell amidst a vital and immediate relation to eternity.[36] But Péguy's thought takes a different turn, since "it is by the deepest internal logic of language itself that *patience* is the virtue of the *passion*,"[37] a logic incarnated not just in the suffering of Jesus, but in the lives of saints that live Christ's passion anew.[38]

It is this forgotten passion of Christian patience—that Jesus *embodied* rather than *taught* or *made*—that for Péguy intensifies or even opens the way to many of the flaws of modern culture, including anti-Semitism.

Péguy descries two preeminent errors in Christian experiences of time, distinct from their "conservative" or "progressive" orientations in modern culture: in one, the importance of time is altogether denied in favor of God's eternal love, and human beings are encouraged to live in an atemporal nullity, as if creation were an excrescence or a mistake. In the other, the temporal distance between the Incarnation and the present—and the historical or present procession of sin in Christendom or institutional Christianity—is felt so keenly that a living sense that the present and God's eternal love are in communion is lost. This loss in turn impels a denial of the living tension between the temporal and the eternal. Those who succumb to this denial submit to the passing imperatives of the temporal, either by way of a rote, indiscriminate affirmation of the past or of the present. These various relations to time and eternity deny the transformative force of what Péguy calls "the Christian Revolution."[39]

For Péguy, whatever "side" is exalted at the cost of the other, any Christian separation of the eternal and the temporal is a catastrophe.[40] For

---

35. OC, Péguy, III, *Note conjointe sur M. Descartes* (1914), 1293.
36. See Rosenzweig, *Star of Redemption*.
37. OC, Péguy, III, *Un nouveau théologien*, 420.
38. Ibid.
39. OC, Péguy, III, *Note conjointe sur M. Descartes*, 1318.
40. OC, Péguy, III, *Dialogue de l'histoire et de l'âme charnelle*, 652–54.

example according to Péguy, it is "the temptation of great souls" to deny temporality and matter. It is, as it were, a "beautiful," "noble," and "aristocratic" way of thinking about one's experience,[41] where an immaculate empyrean alone truly exists among a world of vain and vulgar shadows. But then creation has no purpose, and for Péguy it is a "gross heresy" to claim that God created the world "to no effect."[42] The Incarnation expresses God's desire to save the world by participating in it bodily, to affirm the carnal world but not to dominate it, and certainly not to command separation or withdrawal from the world.[43]

While a certain kind of Christian falls into an incorporeal, atemporal angelism—and with it descends into an infertile rejection of the present—Péguy has little sympathy for Christians who dispense with or simply avoid the supernatural and a living, ongoing reciprocity between the temporal and eternity,[44] often in favor of politics and purely temporal concerns. This could take the form of a conservative clericalism, and Péguy wrote scathingly of what "clerical politics had done to Christian mysticism."[45] But with greater frequency in his own historical moment, it could take the form of a theological liberalism that attenuated the eternal and supernatural dimensions of Christianity. For example, when Péguy's poem "*Le mystère de la charité de Jeanne d'Arc*" [The mystery of Joan of Arc's love (1910)] was critically reviewed in *La Revue Hebdomadaire* in June 1911, Péguy memorably quarreled with the editor of the journal, Fernand Laudet, about the review's theologically liberal assumptions.

The review in Laudet's journal made a stark division between "history" and "legend."[46] It strongly implied that Jeanne had not had visions, but hallucinations; that was more or less to say, Péguy argued, that Jeanne was "a crazy woman."[47] The review claimed that we only have access to the public lives of Jesus (i.e., his ministry) and the saints. Péguy observed that this argument logically led to the conclusion not only that countless lives of saints were inaccessible to Christians, but also the Incarnation itself.[48]

Péguy could let fly once warmed to his task, and Laudet was not spared a blunt assessment of the sensibility that led to the notion that the

41. Ibid., 671.
42. Ibid., 641–42.
43. Ibid., 653–54.
44. Ibid., 674.
45. OC, Péguy, III, *Notre jeunesse*, 21.
46. OC, Péguy, III, *Un nouveau théologien* (1911), 400.
47. Ibid., 452.
48. Ibid., 400–402.

"legendary" (i.e., divine) account of Jeanne's vocation by Péguy was really redolent of childhood.[49] Péguy affirmed that many atheists are people of "good faith" and integrity, citing Anatole France as an example. But, he observed, Anatole France made no claim to believe in God. Laudet brought naturalistic and atheistic metaphysical assumptions into Christian thinking, Péguy claimed, because he was clearly embarrassed by his own faith and wished to make it conform to what he believed was a more commodious and less challenging set of opinions popular in the present. Péguy went further, referring in general terms to the man "who sells his God (for a smile, I mean to not fall under the smile of an augur from the intellectual party) . . . this man who sells his God sells Christianity as well."[50] Péguy commented dryly that "evidently the saints can appear contemptible when one has the honor of being the editor of *La Revue Hebdomodaire*."[51]

On the more general theme of theological progress, Péguy says of those "who want to improve Christianity," that it is "a little . . . as if one wanted to improve . . . the direction of the North."[52] But for Péguy, to make time the judge of all things appeals strongly to those who wish to escape the challenge of embodying the temporal and eternal together. In this way, Péguy's Clio—in his dialogue between the Clio, the muse of history, and "the pagan soul"—claims that "the modern world has made of me a poor idol."[53]

Christian impatience and its secular descendants, Péguy claimed, led both "conservatives" and "progressives" to idolize an abstract series of ideological propositions (i.e., *politique*) rather than to inhabit patiently the truth of God's infinite love and live it out in their bodies, thus wagering their lives upon the proper, mystical relation of the present with eternity. They wish to see history vindicate their beliefs for them, rather than living them out themselves, often obscurely. Seeking a purely temporal vindication for their propositions, they lack the mystical patience embodied by the Dreyfusards.

For Péguy, the Christian Revolution would not be an accommodation of divine revelation to modern impatience (conservative or progressive); still less to the presuppositions of modern cultural imperatives. Rather it would be a deep and radically patient fidelity that brings thinking and action together in strikingly new situations. For example, he claimed that, where an often brutal and extreme capitalism holds sway, the living out of

49. Ibid., 440.
50. Ibid., 453–54.
51. Ibid., 407.
52. OC, Péguy, III, *Dialogue de l'histoire et de l'âme charnelle*, 686.
53. OC, Péguy, III, *Clio, Dialogue de l'histoire et de l'âme païenne*, 1129.

the words "and forgive us our debts, as we forgive those indebted to us" from the Our Father would, "taken seriously," constitute "the greatest revolution that there could now be, for it would be a revolution within the reign of money."[54]

In this way, Christians in Péguy's account must cultivate a courageous patience, waiting for the radically new and faithful possibilities associated with the Incarnation and Resurrection to emerge. These possibilities are in turn deeply and persistently entwined with eternity *and* with their Jewish origin. Nowhere in Péguy's work is the relationship between origin and originality, temporality and eternity, Judaism and Christianity, Incarnation and Resurrection more clear than in Péguy's poem "Le mystère de la charité de Jeanne d'Arc" [The Mystery of Joan of Arc's Love, 1910], and "Le porche de la deuxième vertu" [The Threshold of the Second Virtue (i.e., hope)] written the following year.

Péguy's Jeanne is tormented by both the bodily and spiritual poverty of her people. She knows that those around her lack, as she puts it, both material and spiritual bread.[55] She also senses the burden of time's brokenness, and how little difference human action appears to make in human history, where evil is continuously present, and her patience appears to be at an end. In her words, "fourteen centuries of Christianity... and nothing, nothing, always nothing. And what reigns over the face of the earth, nothing, nothing, nothing but perdition."[56]

As Jeanne reflects on her impatience with evil and uncertainty, her own recognition of Jesus' Incarnation and Resurrection is exiguous, if not entirely absent—and with it, Judaism is absent. Early in the poem, she refers to Jesus' crucifixion as a sacrifice, but not as an explicitly carnal sacrifice, or as a victorious sacrifice—the embodied reality of Jesus' life, death and especially Resurrection are absent. Yet even as Jeanne is very nearly accusing God in her despair, she tells him, "You know what we are missing. We need perhaps something new, something that has never been seen before... after so many saints, after so many martyrs, after the passion and death of your son." At this point, Jeanne begins to spin thread, which she had stopped doing to pray. Then comes a single sentence: "In the end... my God, it is necessary that you send a woman saint [*une sainte*]... who succeeds."[57]

---

54. OC, Péguy, III, *Note sur M. Bergson et la philosophie bergsonienne* (1914), 1273.

55. OC, Péguy, *Oeuvres Poétiques*, "Le mystère de la charité de Jeanne d'arc" (1910), 399–400.

56. Ibid., 370.

57. Ibid., 372.

In a phrase, the prayer begins to receive its answer: it is Jeanne herself who will be the new *sainte*, and one who succeeds by embodying God's eternal love and justice in a new way, as a woman and a soldier who does not fight but leads others to fight with restraint and justice. When her work is once more freely assumed, the prayer ceases to be a lamentation and becomes a precise request that Jeanne herself is called to live out with hope.

As she begins to understand her life as a radical commitment to the living relation between temporality and eternity, Jeanne begins to speak powerfully not only about crucifixion and loss, but about Jesus' resurrected body, "human in its humanity, in our common humanity." This resurrected body enters into a fully embodied eternity with the Ascension, bringing human being into an unprecedented communion with time-transcendent reality.[58] Almost immediately upon that insight—not in spite but because of it—the embodied relation of Jesus to the Jewish people becomes visible to Jeanne with extraordinary sharpness: "Jesus who was Jewish, a Jew among you; race that received the greatest grace, and one that was refused to all the Christian people, mystery of grace; elected race...we are brothers of Jesus in our humanity. But you, the Jewish people, you were his brothers even in his family."[59]

The affirmation of Incarnation and Resurrection is in this way emphatically not an affirmation that implies the *denial* of fraternity with Judaism, but rather it is precisely through a full, radically patient Christian fidelity to the Incarnation and Resurrection that Christians can *enter* into true fraternity with Judaism, one that does not deny or sublate their differences but allows these differences to relate to one another as two iterations of divine truth. For Péguy, Christians and Jews had different religions, but are in different ways both particular and universal, both bodies in which God's truth lives in the world. For Jeanne, a patient, hopeful newness comes neither through an impatience with spiritual stasis nor a transgressive despair, but by embodying temporal originality in communion with the eternal original love, manifest in time through both Jewish and Christian revelation.

It is not the case that the contrapuntal fidelity to mysticism among Jews, Christians and non-believers will always have the sought-for consequences; the eternally renascent Dreyfus Affairs of history do not always end well in immediate terms. But for Péguy, with an authentically mystical love, the experience of history's brokenness is itself changed, as ideology gives way to embodiment, and history to an infinitely more fertile relationship between origins and originality, the present and eternity. In Christian

---

58. Ibid., 404.
59. Ibid., 410–11.

terms, it is this mysticism that allows Christians to embody the patience that Jesus lived. As Péguy writes in "Le porche de la deuxième vertu," Christians understand both their hope and its partial but inevitable disappointment from the perspective of eternity as well as from within time. If their faith is understood only in relation to an empty, homogenous time of past, present and future (as it is in standard notions of time in modern history), Christian hope dissolves either into an impatient, increasingly politicized frustration or a kind of vaporous abnegation of the world. But for Péguy, true Christian hope counts failure faithfully, as God does beyond time, where fidelity and newness, origins and difference are reconciled:

> For the wisdom of God.
> Nothing is ever nothing. All is new. All is other.
> All is different.
> In the eyes of God nothing is repeated.
> These twenty times that she [i.e., hope] makes us take the same road
> to arrive at the same point
> in vain.
> For human eyes it is the same point, the same road, these are the
> same twenty times.
> But they are mistaken.
> This is the wrong reckoning, and the false accounting ...
> If the way is a way of holiness
> In the eyes of God, a way of trials
> makes the one who takes it two times, two times more holy
> in the eyes of God and the one who takes it three times
> three times more holy and the one who did it
> twenty times, twenty times more holy. That is the way that God counts.[60]

Three important conclusions can be drawn from these observations about Péguy's account of Judaism, Christianity and the Dreyfus Affair. First and in strict historical terms, accuracy demands that through Péguy, the Dreyfus Affair must occupy a prominent place not just in the origins of fascism and human rights, modern anti-Semitism and Zionism, but in the history of Christian-Jewish relations, manifest in the influence Péguy exerted and the profound appreciation he elicited from Scholem, de Lubac, von Balthasar and others.

Second, Péguy asserts a unique theological complementarity between Judaism and Christianity that offers an especially promising basis for interreligious dialogue between them. That is, Péguy consistently conceives the relation between Judaism and Christianity neither in supersessionist terms

---

60. Ibid., "Le porche de la deuxième vertu," 651.

(a supersessionism that does not, for example, leave Augustine and Pascal untouched); nor does he understand that relation, à la Franz Rosenzweig and in some ways John Connelly, in what one might call pre- or ante-sessionist terms, in which Christianity appears as an etiolated and perhaps volatile outgrowth from its Jewish origin. Instead, both Judaism and Christianity relate to one another contrapuntally (to use the kind of musical metaphors of which Péguy was fond), developing what is distinct in one another in new ways that they would not take if they ceased to relate to one another, ways that for him, are nonetheless audaciously faithful to their origins.

Finally, Péguy's account of Judaism and Christianity—and more generally of the Dreyfus Affair—discloses the all too-limiting parameters of debate in the preëminent modernity stories of our time, in part because of their misprisions of time.

Modernity stories currently enjoy great intellectual prestige; they attempt, among other things, to explain genealogically how the religious pluralism, tolerance, self-government and freedom of belief and expression we in the West enjoy came to be. For Mark Lilla[61] or Jonathan Israel,[62] we owe these benisons of modernity entirely to religious skeptics like Spinoza and Hobbes, and to the skepticism they encouraged in others (in Israel's case, modernity appears to have the same relationship to Spinoza's mind as Athena has to Zeus' head). Eric Nelson's *The Hebrew Republic*[63] attributes the blessings of modern politics and culture supremely to growing interest in Judaism and Jewish thought in early modernity. Following a long procession of thinkers about modernity—Tocqueville and Nietzsche, for example—scholars like Charles Taylor seek (at least in substantial part) modernity's origins and the general course of its subsequent trajectory primarily in Christianity and its distinctive preoccupations and aspirations.[64]

In Péguy's very different account, the historical trajectory of the Dreyfus Affair required the mystical, continuous conflict and still deeper complementarity of distinctly Jewish, Christian and secular sources, devoted to diverse practical and difficult work animated by a different ways of mystically embodying truth, love and justice. Even when the focus of that labor is in part political—as it was for the Dreyfusards and for Jeanne—it is never inspired by politics or oriented by political success. These different *mystiques* and the complementarity they afforded often had to overcome the all-too-human, almost gravitational power of hastily

---

61. Lilla, *The Stillborn God*.
62. See Israel, *Radical Enlightenment*; and Israel, *Enlightenment Contested*.
63. Nelson, *The Hebrew Republic*.
64. See Taylor, *A Secular Age*.

seeking temporal vindication through *politique* among Christians, Jews, and non-believers alike.

Drawing upon Péguy's account of origins and originality, of time, eternity and history and the possibility of contrapuntal mysticisms, a more vital and relational history comes into sharp focus. The desire evident in many modernity stories[65] to assign the benisons of modernity to some disembodied, increasingly immanent, "genealogical" procession of concepts and propositions (often political ones) can distort the diverse dimensions, attachments and commitments of the past. By presenting modern persons' experience of time and history in this way, modernity stories threaten to sterilize the possibilities of the past for the present and its various futures.

Péguy's alternative allows us to see the Dreyfus Affair—an archetypal event of justice and right in late modern culture and politics—as a fascinating, consequential and complicated coproduction of secularism, Christianity and Judaism. He thus opens to his careful readers a far more nuanced and three-dimensional account of modernity than those frequently on offer in contemporary modernity stories, and one that intimates depths of understanding and historical possibility with resonances far beyond the Dreyfus Affair.

Even if we must limit ourselves to genealogies of modernity and its pluralisms, in which the relation between religions—and between religion and non-religion—figure so prominently, Péguy's thinking affords his readers an opportunity to make them truly genealogical. That is, true genealogical history should include the rich epistatic relations of genetic development, of dormant and recessive possibilities renewed after the dominance of some other phenotype, always open to surprising reappearances that are never a mere repetition, themselves open to faithfully creative growth in the future. Péguy allows us to see the possibilities of complementarity between Christianity and Judaism, time and eternity, fidelity and originality in surprising ways. This helix of now-recessive possibilities can become part of the inheritance we offer to a procession of future modernities, and to all their still more ancient faiths.

---

65. It must be said that of the authors mentioned, Charles Taylor is most appreciative of the shortcomings attending modernity stories, particularly their tendency to preclude embodied experience. Perhaps it is not surprising that his book includes an extended encomium to Péguy. See Taylor, *Secular Age*, 745–55.

BIBLIOGRAPHY

Balthasar, Hans Urs von. *The Glory of the Lord: A Theological Aesthetics*, vol. 3, *Studies in Theological Style: Lay Styles*. Translated by Andrew Louth et al. San Francisco: Ignatius, 1986.

Bergson, Henri. *Essai sur les données immédiates de la conscience*. In *Oeuvres*, edited by André Robinet. Paris: Presses Universitaires de France, 1959.

Birnbaum, Pierre. *The Anti-Semitic Moment*. Translated by Jane Marie Todd. Chicago: University of Chicago Press, 2003.

Bloy, Léon. *Le Salut par les Juifs*. Paris: Demay, 1892.

Burton, Richard D. E. *Holy Tears, Holy Blood: Women, Catholicism and the Culture of Suffering in France, 1840–1970*. Ithaca, NY: Cornell University Press, 2004.

Connelly, John. *From Enemy to Brother: The Revolution in Catholic Thinking about the Jews*. Cambridge: Harvard University Press, 2012.

Drumont, Édouard. *La France juive: essai d'histoire contemporaine*. Paris: Marpon & Flammarion, 1886.

Fredriksen, Paula. *Augustine and the Jews: A Christian Defense of Jews and Judaism*. New York: Doubleday, 2008.

Israel, Jonathan. *Enlightenment Contested: Philosophy, Modernity, and Emancipation of Man*. Oxford: Oxford University Press, 2009.

———. *Radical Enlightenment: Philosophy and the Making of Modernity*. Oxford: Oxford University Press, 2002.

Lilla, Mark. *The Stillborn God: Religion, Politics and the Modern West*. New York: Knopf, 2007.

Lubac, Henri de. *Christian Resistance to Anti-Semitism: Memories from 1940–44*. Translated by Elizabeth Englund. San Francisco: Igantius, 1990.

Nelson, Eric. *The Hebrew Republic: Jewish Sources and the Transformation of Modern Political Thought*. Cambridge: Harvard University Press, 2011.

Péguy, Charles. *Oeuvres Complètes*. 4 vols. Edited by Robert Burac. Paris: Gallimard, Bibliothèque de la Pléiade, 1987–1992.

Rosenzweig, Franz. *Star of Redemption*. Translated by William Hallo. Notre Dame, IN: University of Notre Dame Press, 1985.

Scholem, Gershom. *Fidélité et utopie*. Paris: Calmann-Lévy, 1978.

Taylor, Charles. *A Secular Age*. Cambridge: Harvard University Press, 2007.

# 9

Lashon ha-Ra and Jewish Practical Pluralism
A Case Study of Sefer Chafetz Chaim

CHARLES BERNSEN

Thou shalt not speak badly about any fellow Republican.
—Ronald Reagan, 1966[1]

INTRODUCTION

The Republican Party's "eleventh commandment" is a good place to begin this essay—and not just because it employs a powerful religious metaphor to make its point, namely that Republicans must not let internal ideological differences and power struggles undermine party solidarity. Ronald Reagan's now famous edict also neatly illustrates two points relevant to a discussion about rabbinic attitudes toward Jewish plurality.

---

1. Reagan, *American Life*, 150. Although Reagan was the first Republican to cite the eleventh commandment in public, he later credited the idea and wording to California Republican Party Chairman Gaylord Parkinson.

First, the eleventh commandment was a prescriptive response to polemical discourse among Republicans that Reagan viewed as a threat to him and his party. A vicious rhetorical battle between Rockefeller moderates and Goldwater conservatives during the 1964 presidential primary had splintered the GOP and helped precipitate one of its worst election defeats of the twentieth century. When Reagan issued the eleventh commandment two years later, he was seeking his party's nomination for governor of California and hoped to avert a similar debacle.

The second point is that while Republicans still venerate Reagan and have enshrined his edict as GOP doctrine, they nevertheless violate it on a regular basis. We need only consider the rhetoric in the 2012 GOP presidential primary or the ubiquity of the term RINO (Republican in Name Only), a pejorative employed by some party members to marginalize or exclude others whom they view as ideologically impure. It seems that in some circumstances the obligation not to speak ill of a fellow Republican is less important than the need to defend crucial political ideology or determine authority within the party.

This essay is about a Jewish version of the Republican eleventh commandment that dates back almost two thousand years: the rabbinic prohibition against *lashon ha-ra* (the evil tongue), a term that historically has referred to speech that demeans or otherwise harms another Jew. The first mention of *lashon ha-ra* occurs in the Mishnah, the foundational book of rabbinic Judaism. The concept is discussed extensively in the Babylonian and Jerusalem Talmuds as well as other rabbinic texts of late antiquity; medieval legal, mystical and ethical literature, and modern responsa and commentaries.

The premise of this essay is that the prohibition against *lashon ha-ra* is more than an ethical precept pertaining to interpersonal relationships. Because it governs what Jews may say and believe about one another, it also plays a role in delimiting Jewish collective identity and regulating Jewish power relations. In that respect, it mediates what Reuven Kimelman has described as "the peculiar problematic of Jewish unity"—the fundamental tension between the ideal of a universal Jewish commonwealth whose members are united in belief and practice and the messy reality that Jews comprise diverse and often contentious groups and societies.[2]

Although I am examining this tension in a Jewish context, the problem created by the presence of difference and autonomy is not, to use Kimelman's term, peculiar to Jews. As the example of the Republican eleventh commandment illustrates, other groups share the same ambivalence about

---

2. Kimelman, "Judaism and Pluralism," 131.

how to respond to divergence: Should it be denounced as a threat to collective identity and authority? Or should it be tolerated for the sake of unity and social stability, perhaps even encouraged as essential for a healthy, dynamic society?

In this essay I examine how this tension plays out in *Sefer Chafetz Chaim*, a legal code and commentary on *lashon ha-ra* originally published in Vilna in 1873. *Sefer Chafetz Chaim* was the first book by Lithuanian Rabbi Israel Meir Kagan, who would go on to become an important figure among Orthodox Jews. He played a key role in the founding in 1912 of World Agudat Yisrael, the anti-Zionist political alliance of East European Orthodox Jews. His *Mishnah Berurah*, a commentary on Joseph Caro's *Shulkhan Aruch*, remains authoritative among ultra-Orthodox Jews to this day. But Kagan's reputation as a "paragon of piety" widely admired for his modesty and virtue stems in large part from his authorship of *Sefer Chafetz Chaim* and two subsequent volumes on relations among Jews.[3] His first book also is the source of the sobriquet by which he is popularly known: the Chafetz Chaim.

Today *Sefer Chafetz Chaim* is the primary sourcebook for the *shmirat ha-lashon* movement, a worldwide effort to suppress *lashon ha-ra* and promote good relations among Jews. The organizational force behind the movement is the Chafetz Chaim Heritage Foundation in Monsey, New York. Although primarily an ultra-Orthodox phenomenon with messianic overtones, the movement has spread in non-messianic forms to other streams of Judaism, increasing awareness of both Kagan and the concept of *lashon ha-ra* among all Jews.

SEFER CHAFETZ CHAIM: RESPONDING TO A CRISIS IN JEWISH DISCOURSE

Lashon ha-ra is often translated as "slander" or "gossip," but for Kagan it signified any speech—true or false, public or private, malicious or innocent—that demeans or otherwise harms another Jew. Kagan states quite explicitly that he wrote *Sefer Chafetz Chaim* because the sin of *lashon ha-ra* pervaded contemporary Jewish society. "Many, many people commit it

---

3 Brown, "Yisrael Me'ir ha-Kohen," n.p. The other two books are *Shmirat ha-Lashon* (1876), a short compilation of moral and aggadic writings that elucidate the laws of *lashon ha-ra* first laid out in *Sefer Chafetz Chaim*, and *Ahavat Chesed* (1888), a commentary on the laws on interpersonal relations involving money and property.

thousands of times during their lifetimes and don't take it upon themselves to guard against it."[4] He continues:

> The matter [guarding against *lashon ha-ra*] has collapsed so completely that people are accustomed to saying whatever happens to come out of their mouths without considering whether their words are *r'khilut* and *lashon ha-ra*. Because of our many sins, we have become so accustomed to this sin that many people do not consider it wrong even if they speak unmitigated *lashon ha-ra* and *r'khilut*, for example saying something evil about one's *chaver* and purposely condemning and dishonoring him.[5]

Even allowing for hyperbole, the descriptions in these two excerpts indicate that the discourse Kagan found so problematic was neither unusual nor associated with some aberrant minority. Rather it was ubiquitous. His use of the word *chaver*, a term that describes a special socio-religious relationship among members of *klal yisrael* (the idealized community of Israel), indicates that he viewed *lashon ha-ra* as widespread among traditionally observant Jews.

In addition to the pervasiveness of *lashon ha-ra*, Kagan also describes its pernicious effect: Those who consider *lashon ha-ra* a *hefker* (trivial matter) resist rebuke and persist in speaking it until they "no longer consider [the subjects of their remarks] to be part of *klal yisrael*."[6] In Kagan's view, widespread violation of the prohibition against *lashon ha-ra* was undermining Jewish solidarity and social cohesion.

For Kagan this discourse was a theological and existential crisis. In the long Introduction to *Sefer Chafetz Chaim*, he argues that Jews who routinely speak *lashon ha-ra* potentially violate at least thirty-one specific biblical

---

4. Kagan, *Sefer Chafetz Chaim* (Vilna, 1873), preface, 8. See also Kagan, 1873, foreword, 2. A brief explanation about references to *Sefer Chafetz Chaim*: The book has two parts. The first is called *mekor ha-chaim* (the source of life), which Kagan describes as a concise summary of the law. The much longer second part is called *be'er mayim chaim* (spring of the waters of life). In it Kagan presents more complex legal arguments based on traditional rabbinic sources. The two parts appear together on the same page in the format of a main text with footnotes. There also are dozens of *hagahot* (elaborations) throughout both *mekor ha-chaim* and the *be'er mayim chaim*. When citing the *mekor* I will refer to the chapter, clause, and page. "Kagan, 1873, 1.1, 37," for example, refers to the first clause of the first chapter of the *mekor* on page 37. "Kagan, 1873, 1.1.1, 37–38" refers to the first note in the *be'er mayim chaim* accompanying the same clause on pages 37–38. An "(h)" indicates that the citation is from a *hagahah*.

5. Ibid., preface, 9. *R'khilut* is often translated as gossip. Kagan defines it as a specific kind of *lashon ha-ra* in which a Jew says something that creates animosity or discord among other Jews.

6. Ibid., introduction, 17.

commandments, a far greater number than can be found elsewhere in rabbinic literature. And while a number of rabbinic sources identify *lashon ha-ra* as the sin for which God destroyed the second Jerusalem temple and exiled the Jewish people, Kagan goes one step further. The redemption will not occur, he insists, until Jews rectify this terrible sin.

> If we search and investigate our ways for the sins that are the essential cause of our long exile, we will find many. But the sin of the tongue is the worst for many reasons. First, it is known that it was the cause of our exile as is explained in [the Babylonian and Palestinian Talmuds]. If that is the case, then how can the redemption come if there is no attempt to rectify this sin? Because this sin is such a terrible defect that it caused us to be exiled from our land, surely it prevents us from returning to our land.[7]

CONTENT AND CONTEXTS OF *LASHON HA-RA*

Because it is a legal code, much of *Sefer Chafetz Chaim* is taken up with an analysis of passages from the Talmuds and other rabbinic texts that discuss the laws pertaining to *lashon ha-ra*. But Kagan regularly breaks away from his analysis of legal precedents to comment on the context and content of the contemporary discourse he found so troubling. Many of these observations are accompanied by the formulaic phrase *ba-avonoteinu ha-rabim matzui ha-rabah m'od* (because of our many sins it is extremely common), an explicit indication that he viewed a particular kind of speech act as not just sinful but also widespread.

For instance, Kagan often portrays *lashon ha-ra* occurring in the context of financial disputes, particularly those involving employment, commerce and contracts. This makes sense given the drastic economic decline of Jewish society in Poland-Lithuania under Russian rule during the nineteenth century. Kagan also laments the widespread public criticism of *g'dolei ha-dor* (prominent people) and *tovei ha-ir*, a term that refers to Jewish communal leaders. This almost certainly reflects what Michael Stanislawski and others have described as an unprecedented rupture in fidelity toward the *kahal*, the Jewish communal government, primarily because of its complicity and perceived corruption in the conscription of Jews for the Russian army.[8] This rupture resulted in an upsurge in the number of Jews making

---

7. Ibid., preface, 7.
8. Stanislawski, *Tsar Nicholas I and the Jews*, 17.

allegations of communal corruption to the Russian government, turning to Russian courts to settle internal Jewish disputes, and even seeking to dissociate legally from the Jewish community.

More significant for this discussion, however, is that Kagan describes *lashon ha-ra* as commonplace in the most traditional of religious settings, namely the synagogue and the *beit midrash* (communal study house). He also indicates that it often was directed at rabbis and Torah scholars.

> I find it necessary to write this explicitly because I have seen that many people are accustomed to speaking [*lashon ha-ra*] about someone when he lectures in the *beit midrash*... The law forbids mocking him and saying that his *drashot* (scriptural interpretations) are without substance and not worth listening to. And because of our many sins, we see that many people erupt in this manner... According to the law, this is unmitigated *lashon ha-ra* because speech like this often causes monetary damage and sometimes distress and shame as well... [The critic] should approach [the lecturer] one-on-one after his talk to suggest that he change his method because his remarks are not being heeded ... But under no circumstance can this critic make a public mockery of the lecturer.[9]

In a related passage, Kagan tells us even more about the substance of the derisive remarks that were "erupting" in the *beit midrash*. In addition to being ridiculed "for not knowing what he is talking about," a lecturer was likely to be criticized for speaking "to satisfy his personal needs," that is, for a fee.

> Even if he wanted to collect a fee but also wanted to increase Torah knowledge and observance, he is still a righteous person ... From the perspective of truth, we are required to give the lecturer the benefit of the doubt [regarding his motives]... Maybe at the time he lectures, his basic intention is that everyone hear words of *musar* (ethics) and *yirat ha-shamayim* (fear of heaven) ... Usually this criticism [of the lecturer] comes from people who themselves have no *yirat ha-shamayim*, so criticism for lax Torah observance grates on them. The shortcomings they assign to the lecturer are really their own. Because of our many sins, the critic's ridicule stems from a hatred of the lecturer. In some instances he may be an authority who ruled against [the critic] in some civil matter. Or perhaps it is in the nature of critics to hate decent men because they disapprove of their lowly behavior ... When one carefully considers the actions of the critics

---

9. Kagan, 1873, 2.12, 53–55.

and their listeners, one will find that they violated every one of the Torah commandments cited in the Introduction.[10]

Taken as a whole, these passages describe unabashed animosity toward lecturers in the *beit midrash*. They were routinely ridiculed as not only boring and ignorant but venal as well. According to Kagan, it also was common for critics to resent moralistic critiques of Jewish society and to hold grudges against rabbinic decisors for past rulings. More important, this anger and derision were not coming from outsiders but rather from within the *beit midrash* itself. The setting and nature of the criticism are entirely traditional. Not only do they portray a lack of deference toward the scholarly elite, but they also indicate the presence of hard-edged rivalries if not outright discord *among* them and their followers.

The disputes Kagan describes can be explained in terms of the religious divergence occurring within Lithuanian Jewish society at the time. I am not speaking only or even primarily about the rise of Hasidism and the challenge it posed for traditional Lithuanian Judaism, though that certainly was an important part of it. Religious divergence and competition for religious prestige and authority were increasing even among traditional Litvaks.

The Lithuanian Yeshiva movement that began in the early nineteenth century wrested control of religious education from communal rabbis and created a network of independent scholars who competed for status and authority with each other and with local rabbis. At the same time, the prestige of communal rabbis was declining as a result of restrictions enacted by the Russian government on their salaries and duties. Immanuel Etkes has documented an interesting phenomenon during the last half of the nineteenth century that speaks to the decline of the status of the rabbinate and a corresponding rise in status of *roshei yeshivot* (heads of yeshivas) and their students. It became common for Lithuanian Torah scholars to express a deep aversion to a career as a communal rabbi so as to avoid having to use Torah as "a hoe with which to dig," a euphemism for a tool or skill for earning a living. Instead they extolled the ideal of Torah for Torah's sake alone.[11] This attitude gives us some insight into the religious differences and competition underlying Kagan's reference to criticism of those who lectured in the *beit midrash* for a fee.

In addition, at the time Kagan wrote *Sefer Chafetz Chaim*, the terms *musar* and *yirat ha-shamayim* carried a special connotation associated with a controversial religious movement that arose in Lithuania in the early 1840s. The *musar* movement did not spark a popular religious revitalization

10. Ibid., 2.12 (h), 54.
11. Etkes, *Gaon of Vilna*, 210–11.

as its supporters had hoped, but its persistence in some *yeshivot* created periodic disputes—some quite ferocious—among Lithuanian religious scholars throughout the last half of the nineteenth century. Opponents of *musar* viewed its emphasis on non-legal ethical literature and ecstatic style of study as an affront to traditional Lithuanian intellectualism. The synagogue and *beit midrash* are just where we would expect this kind of religious dispute to erupt.

We should also consider how the emergence of fundamentalism affected Jewish discourse. Many East European Jews saw the growing pressure for religious and social reform in the late 1860s as an existential threat to traditional practice and authority. As opposition to reform hardened into ideological and halachic militancy, it began to color discourse among traditionalists themselves. Even minor legal disputes over religious belief and practice were magnified into crucial battles against reform. As Yosef Salmon observes, Lithuanians were among the most vociferous participants in these disputes, which often devolved into what he describes as "a new style of argumentation based on defamation of character."[12]

Finally, these vitriolic exchanges among traditionalists often played out quite publicly in the pages of the nascent Jewish periodical press in Eastern Europe. *Sefer Chafetz Chaim* was published smack in the middle of the ten-year period (1868 to 1878) during which, according to Salmon, this public and highly polemical religious discourse emerged. Keeping this in mind, it is significant that Kagan asserts that one of the two reasons *lashon ha-ra* pervaded contemporary Jewish society was that many *ba'alei torah* (those learned in Torah) mistakenly cited leniencies that permitted derogatory or harmful remarks spoken *bifnei t'lata* (in the presence of three, meaning publicly), *b'panai* (directly to the subject or in his presence) and in response to *ba'alei machloket* (those who routinely provoke controversy).[13] The implication is that rabbis and others among the scholarly elite were sanctioning polemical rhetoric associated with public disputes and confrontations. Kagan states clearly that one of his primary aims in writing *Sefer Chafetz Chaim* was to rebut the legal basis for these leniencies.

12. Salmon, "Orthodox Judaism in Eastern Europe," 106–14.

13. Kagan, 1873, preface, 8. The other reason was that *hamon*—the Jewish public in general—did not understand that the prohibition against *lashon ha-ra* applies to truthful remarks as well as those that are false.

THE LIMITS OF KAGAN'S PLURALISM

Thus far I have argued that Kagan wrote *Sefer Chafetz Chaim* in response to polemical rhetoric among traditional Jews associated, at least in part, with religious divergence. He was espousing a practical pluralism that tolerated religious difference and autonomy for the sake of Jewish social cohesion. But there were limits to Kagan's tolerance of Jewish plurality.

"The entire prohibition against *lashon hara* applies specifically to [speech about] a person who, according to Torah law, is still *amitekha*," he writes. He then defines *amitekha* as "someone who is with you in Torah and *mitzvot*."[14] *Amitecha*, the second person possessive form of *amit*, is often translated as "your fellow Jew," but this in not quite adequate. While it's true that in the context of nineteenth-century Lithuania *amitekha* refers to another Jew, it signifies a special relationship that does not include all Jews. For Kagan, *amitekha* reflects certain ideas about what it means to be a proper Jew, a member in good standing of *klal yisrael*. When Kagan says a Jew is no longer *amitekha*, it is comparable to a twenty-first-century Republican using the epithet RINO to marginalize another party member.

One kind of problematic Jew who receives a great deal of attention in *Sefer Chafetz Chaim* is the *rasha*, or evil person. As the following passage indicates, Kagan's condemnation of the *rasha* is harsh and unambiguous.

> For example, *ha-poreik*[15] who breaks faith with the kingdom of heaven or isn't careful about avoiding a particular *aveirah* (violation of religious law) that all the rest of his people recognize as an *aveirah* (*asher kol sh'ar amo yod-im sh'hi aveirah*), whether the sin he committed on purpose several times is the same *aveirah* [the observer] wants to disclose or whether the sin he committed on purpose several times is another *aveirah* well known by everyone to be an *aveirah* (*ham'pursemet la-kol sh'hi aveirah*). As long as his actions demonstrate that he did not stray from God's path because his *yetzer ha-ra* (evil inclination) overcame him but rather that he acted willfully (*im bishrirut livo hu holeikh*) and is not afraid to oppose God in his affairs, it is permissible to shame him and relate his disgrace, whether in his presence or not. And if this person does or says something [ambiguous] that can be judged favorably or unfavorably, one must judge it unfavorably since he has shown himself to be an utter *rasha* in

---

14. Ibid., 8.5, 104.

15. In rabbinic literature, a *poreik* is someone who intentionally casts off the yoke of Torah. The Yiddish term *poreik ol* refers to a person who contemptuously refuses to live according to the *mitzvot*.

the rest of his affairs . . . It is permissible to shame him for his actions, make known his abominations and heap scorn upon him. And if he was admonished to give up [his sinful behavior] and did not, all the more is it permitted to publicize his identity, disclose his sins publicly and heap scorn upon him until he reverts to a better lifestyle.[16]

Looking beyond the condemnatory rhetoric, I want to make two important observations. First, in Kagan's view denouncing a *rasha* is not a *mitzvah* (a holy commandment or obligation). Instead he describes it as *mutar*, that is permissible. Second, the *rasha* is redeemable. The reason for publicly denouncing the *rasha* is so that he will stop his sinful behavior and thereby regain the status of *amitekha*. The significance of these observations will become clear in a moment.

We should also consider how narrowly Kagan defines the term *rasha*. The *rasha* is not someone who has undesirable personality traits such as a quick temper or who lacks certain abilities such as a good business sense. Rather he is someone who violates a religious law. But for Kagan this cannot be just any violation. Twice in this passage he says the act must be widely if not universally viewed as a violation—eating pork, for example. I would also note that in the first reference to this condition, Kagan says the violation must be one "that all the rest of his people" recognize as a violation, not "your people" or "our people." The wording implies that legal standards vary among Jewish communities and that such differences do not necessarily warrant labeling members of another group *reshaim* and thereby excluding them from the category of *amitekha*. Instead individuals are to be judged according to the legal standards and customs of their own communities.

Furthermore, in Kagan's view committing a widely recognized sin only once does not make someone a *rasha*. Even the person who repeatedly commits such a sin is not necessarily a *rasha*. Rather a *rasha* is someone who routinely commits at least one widely recognized offense and does so out of defiance rather than because he is unaware that he is sinning or unable to control his emotions or appetites. In other words, a *rasha* is defined less by specific deviant behaviors than by a defiant attitude. The *rasha* intentionally and brazenly thumbs his nose at a legal standard recognized by everyone in his community.

Finally, Kagan further narrows the category *rasha* by exempting interpersonal sins (*bein adam l'chavero*) such as stealing, as distinguished in rabbinic tradition from sins against God (*bein adam la-makom*) such as idolatry.

---

16. Kagan, 1873, 4.7, 67–68.

In regard to *bein adam l'chavero*, even if someone violates them many times, we are obligated to rebuke him [privately, not denounce him publicly] because he does not leave the ranks of *amitekha*. Only for the sin of *lashon ha-ra* does Rabbeinu Yonah (thirteenth century French Rabbi Yonah Gerondi) permit [denouncing the offender]. But this is not because [the offender] is no longer *amitekha* but rather only for the sake of truth and to help demonstrate that he is guilty [as opposed to the subject of his remarks]. But in regard to privately rebuking and loving one's companions and the rest of the obligations we owe to our *amit*, we must also extend them to [those who commit interpersonal sins, including *lashon ha-ra*].[17]

Kagan's insistence that no Jew loses the status of *amitekha* for an interpersonal sin, regardless of how widely recognized it is or how often or brazenly he commits it, is not unprecedented in rabbinic literature. However, it diverges from a number of important rabbinic authorities. The point is that he could have taken a less tolerant position in regard to interpersonal sins.

We should not conclude from all this that Kagan condoned or accepted as valid behavior that in his view violated religious law. Indeed, he contends that one must privately rebuke another Jew who sins, whether against God or another person. The relevant point is that he sharply restricts excluding Jews from the ranks of *amitekha* and protection against *lashon ha-ra* solely on the basis of non-conforming behavior, even when that behavior involves repeated violations of religious law. In that sense, Kagan can be described as tolerating a significant degree of difference in Jewish society, even what he would have called deviance.

Kagan's pragmatic approach to divergence is best exemplified by his attitude toward those who shirk their obligation to study Torah, considered by Lithuanian traditionalists to be the most important Torah commandment for men. Twice Kagan emphasizes that laxness in Torah study does not remove a Jew from the category of *amitekha*. "[The sin of not wanting to learn Torah] is not in this grave category. Because of our many sins, today's society is lax in regard to Torah study, believing that it interferes with earning a living."[18]

Kagan goes on to say that while one should privately admonish even the destitute about their obligation to study Torah, denouncing another Jew for shirking Torah study constitutes *lashon ha-ra* and is forbidden. It is fair to assume that denigrating rhetoric directed at those who were lax in Torah

17. Ibid., 10.10.30, 120.

18. Ibid., 4.2.6. 62. The implication here seems to be that financial hardship had diminished both the interest and ability of many people to engage in Torah study.

study was coming from traditionally observant Jews, probably from the scholarly elite themselves. No doubt Kagan was among those who lamented this trend. Yet he prohibits marginalizing Jews who were not fulfilling this important obligation.[19] This does not mean that Kagan considered Torah study optional or unimportant. Rather his position reflects a pragmatic tolerance of a widely held divergent attitude toward Torah study.

Kagan has no such tolerance for the person who "sins as a result of heresy (*mifnei sh'yeish bo apikorsut*), God forbid. In regard to a person like this who is not in the category of *amitekha*, we are not bound by the prohibition not to peddle gossip."[20] In regard to heretics

> it is a *mitzvah* to denounce and scorn them, whether in their presence or not, for anything one sees or hears about them . . . Someone is called an *apikoreis* if he disavows Torah and the prophecy of Israel, whether the Written Torah or the Oral Torah, even if he says the entire Torah is sent from heaven except for one sentence or one deduction or even a single distinction or point of grammar.[21]

To understand Kagan's definition of a heretic, one must know that "Written Torah" refers to the Jewish Bible and "Oral Torah" to the Mishnah, the Talmud and subsequent rabbinic literature that explains and elaborates on the Bible and Jewish law. The heretic, then, is defined not by a specific behavior but rather by the belief that scripture and the traditional rabbinic interpretations of it no longer are central to Jewish life.

To be clear, Kagan is not condemning those who have certain interpretations of scripture, only those who deny that every jot and tittle of scripture is relevant and that rabbis have the authority to determine that relevance. Significantly, it is not merely permissible to denounce a heretic. Doing so is a *mitzvah*, a holy obligation. Nor does Kagan ever indicate that the heretic

---

19. See also Kagan, 1873, 4.11 (h), 72. "It is typical in [today's] society," Kagan observes, "that when [a person] moves to a new city and meets someone from his former town, he inquires about all his old acquaintances in general and in detail, how well they are behaving, both in their relationship with God and with other people, either good or bad. In particular these inquiries are made to find out whether the youth are still studying Torah. . . There is no grounds for permitting these types of inquiry because the questioner has no intention of moving back to the first town to rebuke them [privately] and convince them to return to Torah study. This kind of inquiry and response is utter *lashon ha-ra*." This passage is further indication that laxness in Torah study was an issue of public discourse and that Kagan was trying to suppress criticism of those perceived to be shirking this obligation.

20. Ibid., 4.1 (h), 62.

21. Ibid., 8.5, 104.

is redeemable. It is quite clear, then, that he views the heretic as a greater danger to Jewish society than the *rasha*.[22]

Another kind of Jew closely identified with the heretic is the person who "goes and informs on Israel to gentiles (*holeich v'malshin al yisrael bifnei nakhrim*)." About this person Kagan says, "Most certainly his sin is terrible and hateful. As a result he enters the ranks of informants (*nikhnas al y'dai zeh bi-klal ha-malshinim*) and is equal to the *apikoreis* and those who deny Torah and the resurrection of the dead."[23]

Kagan distinguishes the *malshin* from someone who merely "denounces [fellow Jews] in front of gentiles" (*m'ganeihu bifnei nakhrim*). The informant reports derogatory or harmful information about another Jew to a gentile *authority*. Thus, his sin involves more than saying something to a gentile that endangers or demeans an individual Jew. By speaking to an authority representing the gentile collective, he commits an affront against the Jewish collective and its institutions of authority, including the rabbinate. As a result, the *malshin* is "considered to have abused and cursed and raised his hand against Torah and Moses our teacher."[24]

According to Kagan, the *malshin* is no longer *amitekha*. No Jew may believe *lashon hara* about any *adam m'yisrael* (person of Israel), he says, "except for *apikorsim* (heretics) and *malshinim* (informants) and the like who are no longer *amitekha*."[25] Although Kagan does not say that one must denounce the informant, he strongly implies such an obligation by linking the *malshin* and the *apikoreis* and by equating the informant's sin to denying Torah and the fundamental belief in resurrection. Nor is there any indication that the *malshin*, like the *rasha*, can regain the status of *amitekha*.

CONCLUSION

I would like to conclude by considering why a book like *Sefer Chafetz Chaim* emerged in Lithuania in 1873. After all, neither difference nor polemical rhetoric against it was new to Lithuanian Jewish society. Social criticism had become "an integral part of the inner life of the Jews of Eastern Europe"

---

22. Although the details are beyond the scope of this essay, there is another important difference in Kagan's attitude toward the heretic compared to the *rasha*. He establishes five conditions for denouncing the latter. For example, one may not lie or exaggerate about the nature of the *rasha*'s offenses. He says explicitly, however, that none of those conditions apply when warning others not to associate with a heretic.

23. Ibid., 8.12, 106–107.

24. Ibid.

25. Ibid., 8.13, 107. The wording implies that the heretic and the informant, although not *amitekha*, are nominally still Jews.

in the eighteenth century, and the number of edicts condemning "gossip mongers" and those who ridiculed town notables indicates that Jewish civil authorities were concerned about these critics and sought to marginalize them.[26] Likewise, the prevalence of "heresy hunting" during the last half of the eighteenth century indicates that Jewish religious leaders were intent on excluding those who did not conform or who challenged their authority to determine socio-religious norms.[27] Prominent among these efforts were the bans of excommunication issued by the Vilna Gaon in 1777 and 1781 against the emerging Hasidic movement.

In the intervening years, however, traditional Jewish society in Lithuania had gone from arguably the most secure in Eastern Europe to the most vulnerable. Despite Lithuanian opposition, Hasidism had become the dominant form of Judaism in Eastern Europe. Jewish communal institutions in Lithuania had grown weak and religious authority more diffuse and uncertain. Then, in the late 1860s, famine and a highly publicized Russian inquiry into accusations of communal corruption in Vilna created a heightened sense of economic and political crisis among Lithuanian Jews.

Like the Reagan's edict for Republicans, *Sefer Chafetz Chaim* should be understood as a pragmatic response to plurality in the context of social instability and political vulnerability. For Kagan, tolerating some degree of Jewish divergence was the price to be paid for preserving Jewish social cohesion and a place for traditionalism within an increasingly plural Jewish world.

Pragmatic pluralism has limits, however. Not *all* difference can be tolerated, even in a time of crisis and vulnerability. At some point the threat posed by religious difference and autonomy outweighs the practical social and political reasons for accepting it. While the definition of *amitekha* in *Sefer Chafetz Chaim* appears to make room within Jewish society for Hasidim, *musar* adherents and even those who shirk Torah study, it emphatically excludes *maskilim*, the Jewish enlighteners who sought to de-emphasize the role of rabbinic literature and the authority of rabbis in Jewish society. Nowhere is this dichotomy more evident than in the final clause of the last chapter, which was added to the second edition of *Sefer Chafetz Chaim* published in 1877.

26. Ettinger, "Modern Period," 766–67. Jewish artisan and craft societies, for instance, protested corruption and patronage among communal leaders and the enactment of taxes on certain goods and services. Some even organized their own synagogues and hired their own rabbis. Communal authorities tried to obstruct the societies by limiting their access to public funds, restricting their membership and, in some cases, banning them outright. Ettinger also observes that ethical literature popular among East European Jews during the eighteenth century included "a strong element of social criticism."

27. Hundert, *Jews in Poland-Lithuania in the Eighteenth Century*, 183.

Understand that everything we have written in this book about the profound importance of being careful to avoid the sin of *lashon hara* applies to [speech about] those who are counted as *amitekha*. But regarding the people who deny God's Torah—even a single letter—and who mock the words of *chazal*,[28] it is a *mitzvah* to publicize their false opinions (*daitam ha-cozevet*) for everyone to see and to condemn them so that we [those who are *amitekha*] will not emulate their evil ways.[29]

In simultaneously prohibiting and commanding the denigration of other Jews, this passage reflects the conflicting attitudes toward Jewish plurality with which rabbinic Judaism has wrestled for two millennia. One is to tolerate difference and autonomy, even if grudgingly, in order to preserve social stability. The other is to reject or marginalize those who refuse to accept certain religious ideas, practices or institutions in order to enforce social conformity and defend rabbinic authority.

Sefer Chafetz Chaim demonstrates that the rabbinic prohibition against *lashon ha-ra* is more than an ethical concept. By mediating the tension between the impulse toward practical pluralism and its limitations, it is inevitably implicated in specific socio-historical disputes about Jewish collective identity and power relations.

BIBLIOGRAPHY

Aleksandravicius, Egidijus. "Jews in Lithuanian Historiography." In *The Gaon of Vilnius and the Annals of Jewish Culture*, edited by Izraelis Lempertas and Larisa Lempertiene, 9–17. Vilnius: Vilnius University Publishing House, 1998.

Bartal, Israel. *The Jews of Eastern Europe, 1772–1881*. Translated by Chaya Naor. Philadelphia: University of Pennsylvania Press, 2005.

Ben Rafael, Eliezer, et al., eds. *Contemporary Jewries: Convergence and Divergence. Jewish Identities in a Changing World 2*. Leiden: Brill, 2003.

Brown, Benjamin. "Soft Stringency in the *Mishnah Brurah*: Jurisprudential, Social, and Ideological Aspects of a Halachic Formulation." *Contemporary Jewry* 27 (2007) 1–41.

———. "Yisrael Me'ir ha-Kohen." In *The YIVO Encyclopedia of Jews in Eastern Europe*. http://www.yivoencyclopedia.org/article.aspx/Yisrael_Meir_ha-Kohen.

Etkes, Immanuel. *The Gaon of Vilna: The Man and His Image*. Berkeley: University of California Press, 2002.

———. "Haskalah." In *The YIVO Encyclopedia of Jews in Eastern Europe*. Translated by Jeffrey Green. http://www.yivoencyclopedia.org/article.aspx/Haskalah.

28. *Chazal* is a rabbinic acronym referring to all of the sages of the Mishnaic and Talmudic periods. Thus "words of *chazal*" refers to the Mishnah, the two Talmuds and other rabbinic literature of late antiquity.

29. Kagan, *Sefer Chafetz Chaim*, 2nd ed., (1877), R9.15, 149.

———. *Israel Salanter and the Mussar Movement: Seeking the Torah of Truth*. Translated by Jonathan Chipman. Philadelphia: Jewish Publication Society, 1993.

Ettinger, Shmuel. "The Modern Period." In *A History of the Jewish People*, edited by H. H. Ben-Sasson, translated by George Weidenfeld, 727–1075. Cambridge: Harvard University Press, 1976.

Ferziger, Adam. *Exclusion and Hierarchy: Orthodoxy, Nonobservance and the Emergence of Modern Jewish Identity*. Philadelphia: University of Pennsylvania Press, 2005.

Frankel, Johnathan. "Assimilation and the Jews of Nineteenth Century Europe: Toward a New Historiography?" In *Assimilation and Community: The Jews of Nineteenth Century Europe*, edited by Jonathan Frankel and Steven Zipperstein, 1–37. Cambridge: Cambridge University Press, 1992.

Hundert, Gershon D. *Jews in Poland-Lithuania in the Eighteenth Century: A Genealogy of Modernity*. Berkeley: University of California Press, 2004.

Kagan, Israel Meir. *Sefer Chafetz Chaim*. Vilna: 1873.

———. *Sefer Chafetz Chaim*. 2nd ed. Warsaw: 1877.

———. *Sefer Shmirat ha-Lashon*. Vilna: 1876.

Kimelman, Rueven. "Judaism and Pluralism." *Modern Judaism* 7 (1987) 131–50.

Klier, John D. "The *Kahal* in the Russian Empire: Birth, Death and Afterlife of a Jewish Institution, 1772–1882." In *Yearbook of the Simon Dubnow Institute*, edited by Dan Diner, 5:33–50. Göttingen: Vandenhoeck & Ruprecht, 2006.

———. "Traditions of the Commonwealth: Lithuanian Jewry and the Exercise of Power in Tsarist Russia." In *The Vanished World of Lithuanian Jews*, edited by Alvydas Nikzentaitis et al., 5–20. Amsterdam: Rodopi, 2004.

Lederhendler, Eli. "Modernity without Emancipation or Assimilation? The Case of Russian Jewry." In *Assimilation and Community: The Jews in Nineteenth Century Europe*, edited by Jonathan Frankel and Steven Zipperstein, 324–43. Cambridge: Cambridge University Press, 1992.

Levin, Dov. *The Litvaks: A Short History of the Jews of Lithuani*. Translated by Adam Teller. Jerusalem: Yad Vashem, 2000.

Nadler, Allan. *Faith of the Mithnagdim: Rabbinic Response to Hasidic Rapture*. Baltimore: Johns Hopkins University Press, 1997.

———. "Misnagdim." In *The YIVO Encyclopedia of Jews in Eastern Europe*. http://www.yivoencyclopedia.org/article.aspx/Misnagdim.

Orbach, Alexander. *New Voices of Russian Jewry: A Study of the Russian-Jewish Press of Odessa in the Era of the Great Reforms, 1860–1871*. Leiden: Brill, 1980.

Reagan, Ronald. *An American Life*. New York: Simon & Schuster, 1990.

Salmon, Yosef. "Orthodox Judaism in Eastern Europe." In *The Gaon of Vilnius and the Annals of Jewish Culture*, edited by Izraelis Lempertas and Larisa Lempertiene, 104–15. Vilnius: Vilnius University Publishing House, 1998.

Schochet, Elijah. *The Hasidic Movement and the Gaon of Vilna*. Northvale, NJ: Aronson, 1994.

Stampfer, Shaul. "The Yeshiva after 1800." In *The YIVO Institute Encyclopedia of Jews in Eastern Europe*. http://www.yivoencyclopedia.org/article.aspx/Yeshiva/The_Yeshiva_after_1800.

Stanislawski, Michael. *Tsar Nicholas I and the Jews: The Transformation of Jewish Society in Russia, 1825–1855*. Philadelphia: Jewish Publication Society of America, 1983.

10

The Jewish Origins of an American Idea
Horace Kallen's Cultural Pluralism

DANIEL GREENE

IN HIS 1924 ESSAY "Culture and the Ku Klux Klan," American philosopher Horace M. Kallen described a nation in crisis. He wrote that the American body politic was enmeshed in a "widespread hysterical taking of stock" over "the stuff and form of the American being." This taking of stock accounted for the proliferation of Americanization programs, the nativist movement, and even the Ku Klux Klan's terrorist tactics intended to ensure white Protestant hegemony in the United States. Kallen countered this hysteria with the idea for which he is best remembered: cultural pluralism. He invoked cultural pluralism to claim that the health of a democratic society depended on its commitment to cultural diversity. As Kallen declared, "The alternative before Americans is Kultur Klux Klan or Cultural Pluralism."[1] This marked the first time that Kallen's term "cultural pluralism" appeared in print.

For Kallen, cultural pluralism was aspirational—it described the nation as he hoped to see it, rather than the nation as he saw it during the 1920s.[2] In a pluralist American nation, multiple religious and cultural groups would live in harmony, rather than in conflict, with each other.

---

1. Kallen, *Culture and Democracy in the United States*, 16, 35.

2. On pluralism as proscriptive, rather than descriptive, see Orsi, "Disciplinary Vocabulary of Modernity."

Kallen believed that cultural pluralism not only was *possible* within a democracy, but that it *defined* a healthy democracy. Cultural homogeneity, in contrast, stifled citizens' creativity and limited a society's potential for development. Being American was not singular or restrictive, Kallen insisted. It depended on "manyness, variety, [and] differentiation."[3] This was no small vision, considering that American mainstream political culture in the 1910s and 1920s was increasingly defined by prejudice against immigrants. "Hyphenated" Americans were considered dangerous to the nation's well being, and concern about dual loyalty proliferated in politics and culture. It was a time marked by fear of foreign hordes, despite Emma Lazarus's poem on the Statue of Liberty inviting "your tired, your poor, and your huddled masses yearning to breathe free" into the nation.[4]

Amid this climate, Kallen and a small cohort of Jewish intellectuals resisted the dominant tide by claiming that pluralism strengthened the nation, rather than weakened it. As a result of their efforts, cultural pluralism emerged as a theory of ethnic difference, envisioning the nation as a combination of ethnic groups in which "becoming American" did not mean casting off one's particular cultural, ethnic, or religious heritage. Yet the history of cultural pluralism in modern America is usually told in abstract terms; it has been relegated to the realm of ideas divorced from lived experience. This essay proposes instead that cultural pluralism grew out of the lived experiences of a group of second-generation American Jews at the beginning of the twentieth century.[5] Like all universalistic philosophies, cultural pluralism was articulated from a particular point of view. Intellectual concepts are not distant from the people who conceive of them; in this case, cultural pluralism was born in part as a tool of introspection for a group of Jewish intellectuals who shared concerns about the future of Jewish culture in America.

We can better understand the discourse surrounding American pluralism as imagined in the early twentieth century by returning Jewishness to a narrative in which it too often has become invisible. For American Jews, this discourse surrounding pluralism over the past one hundred years has been bound inextricably with debates about culture and ethnicity as well as about religion. Jewish culture mattered profoundly to Kallen and his peers. Indeed, Kallen and his cohort primarily intended cultural pluralism to make space for Jewish culture to thrive in the United States. Recovering

3. Kallen, *Culture and Democracy in the United States*, 35.

4. For the full text of Lazarus's "New Colossus," see http://www.poetryfoundation.org/poem/175887.

5. For a fuller articulation of this argument, see Greene, *Jewish Origins of Cultural Pluralism*.

Kallen's thinking about pluralism from the early twentieth century to mid-century also helps us to understand how Jewish intellectuals struggled to define Jewish identity in relation to categories of nation, culture, and race.

Although Kallen did not use cultural pluralism until 1924, pluralism had decades-long roots in his writings and his experiences. Since his days as a Harvard undergraduate from 1900 to 1903, Kallen had been developing the ideas foundational to cultural pluralism.[6] Throughout his distinguished academic career that included helping to found the New School for Social Research in New York City, Kallen rarely would stray far from the topic. Although he published on subjects as varied as consumerism, environmentalism, and adult education, Kallen is best remembered for his work on pluralism.

Kallen's 1924 essay in which he first used cultural pluralism echoed many of his earlier publications, especially his essay, "Democracy Versus the Melting Pot," published in the *Nation* magazine in February 1915. There, he reacted vehemently against both nativists and champions of the melting pot metaphor as he portrayed the United States as a "federation or commonwealth of national cultures."[7] He used musical metaphors to articulate cultural pluralism, describing the nation as an orchestra in which each cultural group plays its own instrument in harmony, although not necessarily in unison, with others. Kallen proposed that America's many ethnic groups should coexist in one political entity, but that political coexistence did not require cultural conformity. He pressed the point by claiming that cultural difference was not weakening the nation. In fact, just the opposite was the case. Writing in direct opposition to nativist academics—especially sociologist E. A. Ross, who was a colleague of Kallen's at the University of Wisconsin–Madison in 1915—Kallen insisted that ethnocultural difference supplied the United States with its national strength.[8]

The phrase cultural pluralism has become part of common parlance in speaking about American diversity, as have the assumptions at its foundation. Politicians and others describe the United States as "a nation of immigrants." We speak of creating "one" out of the "many." "E pluribus unum" remains emblazoned on the nation's seal. The assumption that our nation is made up of many peoples and cultures is almost taken for granted. But we

6. On Kallen, see Klingenstein, *Jews in the American Academy 1900–1940*; Konvitz, "Horace Meyer Kallen"; Konvitz, *Nine American Jewish Thinkers*; Konvitz, *Legacy of Horace M. Kallen*; Schmidt, *Horace M. Kallen*; Toll, "Horace M. Kallen."

7. Kallen, *Culture and Democracy in the United States*, 108. Reprint of Kallen's 1915 *Nation* magazine essay, "Democracy Versus the Melting Pot."

8. Ross, *Old World in the New*. Kallen opened "Democracy versus the Melting Pot" by chastising Ross as a "nervous professor," 61.

need to think deeply about the history of this idea that somehow has come to be taken for granted. Like all ideas, pluralism has a history—one that is contested, and one that is longer than many of us assume.

Cultural pluralism, of course, did not corner the market as a description for American diversity during the interwar era. Much better known, then and now, was the idea that America is a "melting pot" of diverse ethnic groups. The melting pot metaphor resurfaced in American political and popular discourse following the 1908 staging of Israel Zangwill's play titled *The Melting Pot*.[9] Opening-night attendees at the Washington, DC, premier in 1908 included Theodore Roosevelt and Jane Addams, both of whom championed Zangwill's play.[10]

The melodrama features a marriage between two Russian immigrants to the United States—one Jewish and one gentile—who overcome seemingly insurmountable differences because their experiences as immigrants in the United States effectively erase their pasts. And the differences do seem insurmountable. After David, the Jewish protagonist, falls in love with Vera, a Christian immigrant, they learn that her father orchestrated the Russian pogrom that killed his parents. Even their parents' pasts, however, cannot dampen their love for each other. The two still wed. One way to interpret the lesson of the play is that the American melting pot erases cultural difference and even family history. Love conquers all, but only because the love occurs in *America*, where all nations and races will fuse together to make the new American.

Jewish intellectuals' anxiety about the melting pot metaphor was profound. A 1909 front-page review of the play in the newspaper the *American Israelite* summed up many American Jews' reaction: "Ethnologically the Jew is doomed to extinction in America and this perhaps is the real message that lies at the heart of Israel Zangwill's great play."[11] In short, respondents to both the play and the ideas it spawned feared that, with the combination of coercive Americanization efforts and the freedom to intermarry, Jews eventually would "disappear."[12] This was just one of many competing responses to the melting pot idea in 1908, but, for the majority of Jews, it carried the day.

Alongside the melting pot were other, less accepting models of cultural diversity that coexisted with it, including one that would later be labeled

---

9. Nashon, *From the Ghetto to the Melting Pot*.
10. Sollors, *Beyond Ethnicity*, 66–75.
11. "'The Melting Pot': Will the Jew Become Merged in It and Disappear?" *American Israelite* 55 (March 4, 1909), 1.
12. Gerstle, "Liberty, Coercion, and the Making of Americans."

"Anglo-conformity." Here, the assumption was that America's culture was an Anglo culture from the days of the Puritans; therefore, "becoming American" meant conforming to Anglo norms. At an even further extreme was nativism. Nativists claimed that some immigrant and non-white groups simply were "unmeltable" and therefore should be excluded altogether from the American political and cultural spheres.[13] Though there are significant differences between these theories of Americanization, none of them allowed for the possibility that immigrants and their descendants could continue to nurture their own cultures while becoming acculturated into American society in the way that cultural pluralism did.

Kallen and his peers thought of cultural pluralism as an alternative to the melting pot. But pluralism was not solely reactive. For American Jews specifically, it represented a necessary precursor for fostering a renaissance of Jewish life in the United States based on cultural activities for college-age youth, including arts and letters and political criticism. In explaining his distaste for the melting pot metaphor, Kallen often wrote about the challenges posed by diversity in the early twentieth century that the nation's founders had not anticipated in the late eighteenth century. Kallen's primary objection to the melting pot was that he considered it antidemocratic. Even as the melting pot metaphor dominated popular understandings of what it meant to be an American, and even as "hyphenated American" became the epithet used to described immigrants who held dual (read: competing and potentially dangerous) loyalties, Kallen had the courage to declare in 1915, "Democracy is hyphenation."[14] This bold, three-word summary of Kallen's ideology effectively asked Americans to reconsider the meaning of democracy for a new century.

Horace M. Kallen's personal history informed the origins of cultural pluralism in critical ways. Knowing more about his biography helps to emphasize the point that ideas are not separate from the lived experiences of those involved in creating them. Kallen was born in Bernstadt, Silesia, in 1882. He immigrated to Boston with his father, an Orthodox rabbi, in 1887. To his father's great disappointment, Horace did not follow him into the rabbinate. Kallen rejected Orthodox Judaism during his youth. He ran away from home many times as a child, and by the time he entered college he was "very close to casting aside his Jewish identity," according to one biographer.[15] Kallen continued throughout much of his adult life to criticize his father's strict adherence to tradition and ritual.

13. Higham, *Strangers in the Land*.
14. Kallen, "Nationality and the Hyphenated American," 82.
15. Schmidt, *Horace M. Kallen*, 21.

By the time he entered Harvard as an undergraduate in 1900, Kallen was indifferent to Judaism. He earned his bachelor's degree in 1903 and his doctorate in philosophy in 1908 at Harvard. He held teaching posts at Princeton from 1903 to 1905 and at the University of Wisconsin–Madison from 1911 to 1918. Kallen later claimed that, had Princeton known he was Jewish, he likely would not have been hired. At Wisconsin he was dismissed for advocating pacifism during World War I. After leaving Madison, Kallen moved to New York City and helped to found the New School for Social Research in 1919. He taught there until 1973, a year before he died.[16]

While at Harvard, Kallen joined a cohort of Jewish students who concerned themselves with restoring pride in Jewish culture and integrating Jewish subjects into secular university curricula. In 1906, Kallen chaired the first meeting of a student club that became known as the Harvard Menorah Society. Between the 1910s and the 1930s, the society, eventually known as the Intercollegiate Menorah Association (IMA), spread to approximately eighty campuses across the nation. In 1915, the founders of the IMA began to publish an influential magazine of opinion, the *Menorah Journal*. By the 1930s, the collegiate society was supplanted by Hillel and fraternities as well as crippled by the Great Depression. The *Menorah Journal* would continue to be published until 1962. Kallen himself would remain a champion of the Menorah movement his entire life.

The thinkers and writers associated with IMA and the *Menorah Journal* were particularly well-suited to articulate a pluralistic understanding of American society at this time, for they were seeking in their own lives to develop a vibrant Jewish cultural renaissance in an American setting. Their nearly thirty-year effort to forge a Jewish cultural renaissance within a pluralist nation had broad implications and lasting significance. Indeed, a close reading of this cohort's efforts reveals that their ideas and experiences, and even the very vocabulary they originated and relied upon, remain central to contemporary understandings of both Jewish identity and American diversity.[17]

The founders of the IMA embarked on a bold project to remake Jewish life by fashioning Jewish culture in the image of the scholarly world they

---

16. On his claim regarding Princeton, see Kallen, "Promise of the Menorah Idea," and Kallen's obituary, *New York Times*, February 17, 1974, 66.

17. On the Menorah Association, see Alter, "Epitaph for a Jewish Magazine"; Fried, "Creating Hebraism, Confronting Hellenism"; Fried, "*Menorah Journal*: Yavneh in America"; Greene, *Jewish Origins of Cultural Pluralism*; Grumet, "Menorah Idea and the Apprenticeship of Lionel Trilling"; Harap, "Menorah Journal"; Joselit, "Without Ghettoism"; Korelitz, "Menorah Idea"; Krupnick, "Menorah Journal Group"; Pappas, "Picture at the *Menorah Journal*"; Strauss, "Staying Afloat in the Melting Pot"; Wald, "Menorah Group Moves Left."

had come to admire. They sought to preserve Jewish distinctiveness by better synthesizing it with mainstream American political and intellectual thought. Their goals were cerebral but they tried to accomplish them with at least a nod to the practical, forming the Intercollegiate Menorah Association, exporting the model to universities across the nation, and publishing a high-quality journal of opinion that included political and cultural criticism, poetry and literature, reviews, and visual art. During its heyday, the IMA and the *Menorah Journal* formed a vanguard in terms of social integration and participation in the academy.

As students and professors at the nation's most elite colleges, those who coalesced around the Menorah movement enjoyed access to institutions that their parents would not have imagined; in their young adulthood, they founded and edited publications that shaped public opinion. Their position as simultaneous outsiders and insiders in American cultural life allowed them to test the meanings and limits of group difference in America in specific and important ways. Their ideas about Jewish identity and cultural difference developed at a critical moment of transition, during which racial and religious definitions of Jewish identity were under siege, and in an environment where what it meant to be an American also was being contested vigorously. The men behind the Menorah movement embarked on two interrelated and strategic projects: they promoted Jewish humanities as the foundation of a modern Jewish identity and they championed cultural diversity as the essence of democracy. In other words, they simultaneously sought to refigure Jewish identity and American identity for a modern age. Their history thus is one of culture-making and nation-making.

The nation's intense debates over pluralism during the 1910s and 1920s were shaped in part by the *Menorah Journal*, and by the Menorah movement's effort to realize a pluralist ideology in three realms: first, by seeking to integrate the study of Jewish humanities on American campuses (which we may interpret as a call for Jewish studies fifty years before Jewish studies would take hold on campus); second, by writing a new Jewish history integrated historiographically and temporally with world history; and third, by publishing literature in which pluralism was embodied in idealized Jewish protagonists.

The central location for these new models of historiography, criticism, and fiction was the *Menorah Journal*, which soon after its 1915 founding became the leading journal of Jewish opinion in the English language. The journal's editors and frequent contributors, especially Henry Hurwitz, Elliot Cohen, Harry Wolfson, and Marvin Lowenthal, published acerbic critiques of interwar American Jewish cultural life, focusing their sights on excessive materialism, anti-intellectualism, and Reform rabbis. Within the pages of the *Menorah Journal* historians Cecil Roth and Salo Baron conceived of new methods for writing Jewish history. Rabbi Mordecai Kaplan tested ideas that would fill his 1934 opus *Judaism as a Civilization*, which spawned the Reconstructionist movement in the United States. The *Menorah Journal* editors introduced readers to a cohort of influential young fiction writers, essayists, and critics, including Meyer Levin, Lionel Trilling, Ludwig Lewisohn, and Anzia Yezierska. One way to view the *Menorah Journal*, therefore, is as a training ground for those who would become the cultural arbiters of the American Jewish experience by the mid-twentieth century.

Many of the individuals responsible for fashioning the Menorah movement had complicated senses of their own Jewish heritage. Most Menorah movement leaders were the children of eastern European Jewish immigrants. In seeking to integrate themselves into an academic-oriented world, however, they adopted German intellectual traditions that most could not rightly claim from their own family genealogy. The Menorah Association derived inspiration in this realm from the *Verein für Cultur und Wissenschaft der Juden* (Society for Culture and Science of the Jews), a group of Jewish intellectuals in Germany who, beginning in the 1810s, advocated scientific study of Jewish history, culture, and religion.[18] The regularity with which Menorah Association leaders described their scholarly activities as "scientific" and their frequent acknowledgement of *Wissenschaft des Judentums* (the scientific study of Judaism) pioneer Leopold Zunz and his contemporaries signals that they understood their project as a continuation of that initiated by German Jews one hundred years before them.

The IMA's vision for a Jewish cultural renaissance in the United States grew, as well, out of the context of the Haskalah (Jewish enlightenment), though the IMA's founders were less bound in their rhetoric to Haskalah than they were to *Wissenschaft des Judentums*. Nonetheless, the IMA's efforts remained indebted to those European Jews of the nineteenth century who, in Shmuel Feiner's words, "embarked on a conscious, deliberate course to change their cultural environment."[19] Haskalah's emphasis on secular Jewish culture and education, on history as constitutive of identity, and on Hebrew language all echo loudly in the Menorah Association's philosophy.[20] Like many intellectuals at the center of the Haskalah movement, those at the center of the IMA sought to reform Jewish culture and conceived of their work within a context of Enlightenment thought, both Jewish and gentile.

---

18. Meyer, *Response to Modernity*; Schorsch, *From Text to Context*.
19. Feiner, *Jewish Enlightenment*.
20. On Haskalah, see Feiner and Sorkin, *New Perspectives on the Haskalah*.

For those individuals who defined their Jewish identity by affiliating with the Menorah Association, attending college became a launching point for a highly intellectual movement based on the foundation of cultural pluralism. By embracing pluralism, they made it possible to fashion new Jewish selves based on Jewish culture. Their understanding of their Jewish selfhood would emerge out of the tension between the mutability of identity and an anxious quest to find a point of fixity in Jewish culture. Even though this cohort of Jewish intellectuals was not the most representative of wider American Jewry during the 1910s and 1920s, it did struggle with a tension between the desire for acceptance and the commitment to difference that defined the American Jewish experience of the twentieth century. Like so many American Jews who came after them, the young men at the center of the Menorah movement passionately searched for a way to fashion themselves as both American and Jewish, without apology or contradiction.

This particular worldview may sound somewhat tame today, but do not forget the context in which Kallen and the Menorah Association operated in the 1910s and 1920s. Harvard, where the Menorah Association was founded, was an unmistakably Protestant institution in 1906, as it had been for its 270-year history to that point. Although antisemitism in the United States paled in comparison with that in Europe, the heyday of the Menorah Association coincided with a rise in antisemitism unlike any other era in US history. Discrimination against Jews went far beyond elite universities seeking to keep Jewish students from enrolling. Beginning in the late 1910s, proponents of the "Red Scare" portrayed Judaism and Bolshevism as synonymous. The Ku Klux Klan experienced a resurgence in the 1920s. Henry Ford's *Dearborn Independent* aided the reissue of *The Protocols of the Elders of Zion*, a forged document "proving" Jews' intentions to dominate the world. *The Dearborn Independent* published its own hate-filled series of articles based on the *Protocols of the Elders of Zion* titled *The International Jew: The World's Foremost Problem*. Ford's book was translated into dozens of languages and circulated the globe.[21]

Within this hostile climate, the young Jewish men associated with Menorah Association and the *Menorah Journal* hoped to initiate a Jewish cultural renaissance in America. They worked on two fronts, arguing for an *inclusive* definition of American national identity to the larger American public while promoting a *cultural* definition of Jewish identity to Jewish students and readers. The renaissance of Jewish culture, in other words,

---

21. Higham, *Strangers in the Land*; Dinnerstein, *Anti-Semitism in America*; Baldwin, *Henry Ford and the Jews*.

depended on accepting pluralism—the idea that America is a compilation of many national and ethnic cultures.

The Jews who led the Menorah movement were very much a vanguard in their day. Most Jews in America were not yet thinking in the same terms as the founders of the Menorah Association, nor were most Jews feeling the same pressures to explain themselves to the broader American world. The individuals who spearheaded the Menorah movement likely are not be the first that leap to the popular imagination when picturing Jews in New York City or other urban centers during first decades of twentieth century. Their primary affiliations were not religious, but academic and cultural. Though they were not wealthy, they had some means and more opportunities than many of their peers. They were not labor activists, or union oriented in any way. Although their base of operations on 14th Street in Manhattan was within walking distance of Manhattan's Lower East Side, the needle trade shops might as well have been worlds away. The *Menorah Journal*, for example, never published a single article about Yiddish theater in its nearly 50-year run from 1915 to 1962. That was not the culture it editors intended to promote. Instead, they hoped to promote study of Hebrew language, literature, poetry, and visual art.

Zionism was integral to the movement, specifically cultural Zionism as articulated during this period by Ahad Ha'am. According to Ha'am, Zionism acted a spiritual center, with Jewish culture radiating across the globe to Jewish communities. Those in the Menorah movement never insisted or even imagined that that Jews in the United States would move to Palestine. Consider the fact that when Hebrew University opened in 1925 in Palestine, the *Menorah Journal* published articles on everything from the architecture to the curriculum of this new university.[22] The IMA, too, officially supported Hebrew University, basing its endorsement on the idea of cultural Zionism. As a center of Jewish culture, Jerusalem needed a singular institution devoted to Jewish scholarship. Moreover, Palestine needed a Jewish university as a refuge for Jewish students and professors who had been excluded from European universities. The founders of the Menorah Association also clearly argued, however, that it was *European* Jewish scholars, those being persecuted by antisemitism, who needed Hebrew University. Jewish scholars in the United States needed to be integrated into secular universities. Those at

---

22. Ben Zion Mossinsohn, "Hebrew University in Jerusalem," *Menorah Journal* 4 (1918), 330; Lewis Mumford, "Vision of the Architect," *Menorah Journal* 8 (1922) 33–36; Sol Rosenbloom, "Chief Function of the Hebrew University," *Menorah Journal* 7 (1921) 36–40; Jessie E. Sampter, "On the Mount of Olives," *Menorah Journal* 8 (1922) 36–40; William Schack, "Four Years of the Hebrew University," *Menorah Journal* 16 (1929) 325–34.

the center of the Menorah movement claimed that, if Jewish culture could win a place in the curriculum alongside that of other world cultures, the essence of cultural pluralism would be validated.

Despite its ambitious vision for diversity in the United States, cultural pluralism had significant and troubling blind spots. First, cultural pluralism envisioned cultural groups existing in silos, meaning that it imagined cultural groups operating independently of each other rather than cooperating with each other. The shorthand criticism of Kallen, for those like the educator John Dewey and the journalist Randolph Bourne who engaged his orchestra metaphor, was to ask how to achieve harmony without a conductor. Who was going to make sure these groups played a tune together, much less made an effort to learn each others' parts? In March 1915, shortly after Dewey read "Democracy Versus the Melting Pot," he congratulated Kallen. "I quite agree with your orchestra idea," Dewey wrote in a letter to Kallen. His praise came with a warning, though, that the orchestra metaphor only worked "upon [the] condition we really get a symphony and not a lot of different instruments playing simultaneously." Dewey advised Kallen that the nation would only benefit if each group developed its cultural heritage in order "to contribute to others," rather than to remain turned inward.[23]

In a letter to Kallen two weeks later, Dewey argued that Jews had a unique opportunity not only to develop their own heritage but also to learn about the cultures of other groups in America.[24] For Dewey, as for his student Bourne, a cultural group could not contribute to the improvement of American society by developing its own culture in isolation, which is where they thought Kallen's pluralism rested.[25] Without interaction among cultural groups, America would not truly become a federation of nationalities but rather a nation of distinct, non-cooperating groups.[26] Excessive particularism without cooperation, Dewey argued, eventually would prove dangerous because it would not foster understanding among different peoples who had to coexist in the same polity.

A second critical shortcoming is that cultural pluralism focused entirely on European groups. Pluralism, circa 1920, was limited to those who today are called white ethnics. Kallen sometimes made promises to address the particular cultural challenges of non-European groups, but these promises went unfulfilled until the 1950s. Consequently, many late

---

23. Dewey to Kallen, March 31, 1915. Kallen Papers, Box 7, folder 13. American Jewish Archives (AJA), Cincinnati, Ohio.
24. Dewey to Kallen, April 16, 1915. Kallen Papers, Box 7, folder 13. AJA.
25. See Bourne, "Trans-National America."
26. Westbrook, *John Dewey and American Democracy*, 212–14.

twentieth-century critics have vilified Kallen for the limitations of his pluralist vision.[27] It is important to note these limitations. Yet the limitations themselves reinforce the point that Kallen formulated cultural pluralism in large part to address concerns specific to American Jews.

It is perhaps most troubling that Kallen's pluralist logic paid little attention to similar questions being considered by African American contemporaries. In 1897, just a decade before Kallen began to publish on pluralism, his fellow Harvard graduate W. E. B. DuBois famously asked, "What after all, am I? Am I an American or am I a Negro? Can I be both? Or is it my duty to cease to be a Negro as soon as possible and be an American?"[28]

Kallen's failure to acknowledge the similarity of his concerns and DuBois's is even more glaring considering that Harvard philosopher William James was a dominant intellectual influence on both of these Harvard men.[29] The questions central to DuBois's "double consciousness" and Kallen's cultural pluralism were not identical, but the similarities are strong enough to wonder why Kallen did not write about or correspond with DuBois. Of course, DuBois was black and Kallen was white.[30] At the end of his life, when Kallen looked back to his collegiate years, he claimed to be quite aware of his white privilege as he formulated pluralism. For the purpose of understanding pluralism's Jewish origins, the absence of blacks in the pluralist model reveals both how central Jewish culture was to pluralism and how the Jewish intellectuals who articulated pluralism also sought to set the boundaries of inclusion in national culture. There is no doubt that DuBois was more of an outsider than Kallen. Perhaps, then, Kallen had little to gain by recognizing DuBois.

Kallen's blind spot was even more glaring in the case of his contemporary Alain Locke, the first African American Rhodes Scholar and one of the primary voices of the New Negro Movement, or Harlem Renaissance. While a graduate student at Harvard, Kallen worked as a teaching assistant in a class on Greek philosophy taught by George Santayana. Locke, then an undergraduate, enrolled in the class. Only many years later, in 1955, would Kallen claim that Locke was present when Kallen first used of the term cultural pluralism in this very class.[31] Their association also moved beyond

27. See Sollors, "Critique of Pure Pluralism"; Benn Michaels, *Our America*, 64–72; Posnock, *Color and Culture*.

28. DuBois asked this question in his 1897 essay, "Conservation of Races." See DuBois, *Souls of Black Folk*, 184. See also Lewis, *W. E. B. DuBois*.

29. For James's influence on DuBois, see Heinze, "Schizophrenia Americana," 242.

30. On Jews and whiteness, see Heinze, *Is It 'Cos I's Black? Jews and the Whiteness Problem*.

31. See Kallen, "Alain Locke and Cultural Pluralism." Menand notes that Locke did

Harvard Yard. In 1907, Kallen and Locke both spent the year studying at Oxford, where they occasionally socialized with each other.[32] Their essays and speeches from this era, as one scholar recently has shown, share similar phrases and metaphors, as well as a concern about how cultural groups could remain independent while integrating into American society.[33]

In addition to sharing institutional affiliations, Locke and Kallen struggled with similar questions about the boundaries of cultural difference. Locke's effort to promote African American arts and culture resembled the IMA's desired renaissance of Jewish culture that Kallen supported throughout his life. In fact, both the temporal and ideological parallels between Locke's and Kallen's thought—and thus between the Harlem Renaissance and the Menorah movement—were striking. Locke's 1925 edited collection *The New Negro* appeared just one year after Kallen coined cultural pluralism in print. Locke dedicated his book to "the younger generation," in the hope that it would liberate young blacks from feelings of cultural inferiority, just as the IMA hoped that an elite cohort of Jewish youth would. Kallen rarely wrote as eloquently as Locke, or with such a clear notion that pluralism should provide a path to cosmopolitan cooperation. Many critics seized on this as well as many other perceived shortcomings in Kallen's pluralist logic. Yet, the majority of critics were white, too, and conceived of a pluralist nation of immigrants descended from Europeans.

Although this glaring absence of non-whites in cultural pluralism of the 1920s remains troubling, it also reveals both how central Jewish culture was to pluralism and how the Jewish intellectuals who articulated pluralism also sought to set the boundaries of inclusion in national culture. These blind spots actually reinforce the contention that cultural pluralism to some extent was designed by Jews primarily to promote Jewish culture in the United States. Kallen's gaze was primarily focused on Jews, rather than on diversity more generally. He made gestures to the idea that cultural pluralism would be a model for all ethnic and racial groups, but the gestures were not well thought through.

The blind spots inherent in cultural pluralism also have informed its complicated relationship to multiculturalism. To consider pluralism's legacy, we have to remind ourselves that Kallen's pluralist thought emerged during the 1910s and 1920s in large measure out of his training as a Pragmatist. William James, the father of American Pragmatism, was Kallen's

---

not share the same memories about the first use of cultural pluralism. Menand, *Metaphysical Club*, 391.

32. On Kallen and Locke, see Whitfield, "Introduction to the Transaction Edition," 30–31; and Menand, *Metaphysical Club*, 388–91.

33. Weinfeld, "What Difference Does the Difference Make?"

dissertation advisor and one of his most profound intellectual influences.[34] James believed that ideas needed to be tested constantly to see if they retained their value and to see if they "worked" in the flux of modern American life. Even the ideas foundational to the American nation were open to testing and flux.

All this emphasis on change in Pragmatist thought serves to highlight one of the most perplexing contradictions in Kallen's logic. In his 1915 *Nation* magazine essay, "Democracy Versus the Melting Pot," in which he described the American nation as an orchestra of ethnic groups and pleaded passionately against both the logic of the melting pot and the xenophobia of the nativist movement, Kallen also treaded dangerously close to arguing that biology is destiny. After spending much of the essay explaining the potential for cultural coexistence in America, he closed with a troubling, and now infamous, assertion. Kallen wrote: "Men may change their clothes, their politics, their wives, their religions, their philosophies, to a greater or lesser extent: they cannot change their grandfathers. Jews or Poles or Anglo-Saxons, in order to cease being Jews or Poles or Anglo-Saxons, would have to cease to be, while they could cease to be citizens or church members or carpenters or lawyers without ceasing to be."[35]

This might be the most quoted cited passage from Kallen's work across his nearly sixty years of publishing. His claim that we cannot change our grandfathers was not an anomaly. In a 1913 speech Kallen said that Jewish identity was guaranteed by "inborn nature."[36] He stated the claim even more strongly in his 1918 book, *The Structure of Lasting Peace*, when he wrote: "So an Irishman is always an Irishman, a Jew always a Jew. Irishman or Jew is born; citizen, lawyer, or church-member is made. Irishman and Jew are facts in nature."[37]

These claims about the relationship between biology and identity have left contemporary readers uncomfortable with Kallen. Using these passages, scholars of American ethnic history tend to cite Kallen when they want to caution readers about the ways that we *used* to think of identity as immutable. There is no doubt that it is difficult to reconcile the claim that we cannot change our grandfather with the Pragmatists' contention that modern life is

---

34. In 1908, Kallen completed his dissertation, "Notes on the Nature of Truth," under James. The two remained in close contact after Kallen left Harvard. Before James died, in 1910, he asked Kallen to gather and prepare the writings that were published in 1911 as *Some Problems in Philosophy*. Kallen also wrote the introductory essay to the Modern Library's edition, *The Philosophy of William James*, in 1925.

35. Kallen, *Culture and Democracy in the United States*, 114–15.

36. Intercollegiate Menorah Association, *Menorah Movement*, 81–86.

37. Kallen, *Structure of Lasting Peace*, 31.

characterized by change and flux. But we can explain it in part by realizing that Kallen was anxious about a particular group—Jews—assimilating and losing their culture. And he was looking for a safety net to comfort him in the face of this anxiety.

Scholars who care about the history of pluralism will continue to debate what Kallen meant when he claimed that we cannot change our grandfathers. Those who demonize Kallen for his shortcomings, though, tend to freeze his thought in 1915, when he made the claim that we cannot change our grandfathers. If we unfreeze Kallen from that moment in 1915—and acknowledge the potential for change over time—we learn that his postwar writings on ethnicity have strong affinities with our current notions of ethnic difference. Kallen's age and his intellectual maturity matter in this case. Remember that Kallen was born in 1882; he published "Democracy Versus the Melting Pot" in 1915, when he was in his early thirties. Four decades later, Kallen understood ethnicity and Jewish identity in a remarkably different way.

While we keep Kallen's 1915 contention that we cannot change our grandfathers in the background, consider some assertions he made about the fluidity of identity in a series of lectures he delivered at the University of Pennsylvania in 1954. First, Kallen said: "Among free peoples, most such associations are what we call voluntary; they form, change, grow, dissolve, at the option of the individuals who constitute them, are creations of their consent." Next, he explained: "Even his relation to his family, which he is born into by no known choice of his own, is a function of this commitment, for he can reënforce 'accident of birth' by consent and loyalty or nullify it by withdrawal from all association with the members of the family and the refusal of family responsibility."[38] By the mid-1950s, Kallen had moved away from envisioning a pluralist society as one defined by coexisting silos of cultural groups determined by birth. Instead, he imagined overlapping affiliations determined by individual choices. At the same time, he resoundingly rejected claims based on biology.

The postwar Kallen understood that the boundaries among ethnic groups were porous, not fixed. He described commitment to a group or withdrawal from it as "decisions of the individual" rather than as "compulsions of his group." To consider identity as fixed would be stubbornly dogmatic, according to Kallen. That said, he would have been utterly inconsistent had he refused to describe his own 1915 claims about identity as dogmatic. And, to his credit, he did exactly that, writing: "The dogma that we cannot change the past is not an understanding of the process of change

38. Kallen, *Cultural Pluralism and the American Idea*, 22.

but a prejudice of our resistance to it and a static illusion symbolizing our fear of it. What else is there to change? What else is the present but the past changing?"[39]

Kallen revisited similar ideas six years later in a 1962 *Menorah Journal* article titled "The Promise of the Menorah Idea." In 1962, Kallen was eighty years old, and he used the occasion of returning to the *Menorah Journal* to reconsider the origins of cultural pluralism as well as his own personal history. He moved even further away from biological determinism in this essay than he had in 1954. Reflecting on pluralism as he conceived of it in 1915, Kallen wrote: "At the time I shared the widespread belief—which I no longer hold—that these differences were rooted in race rather than created as cultures."[40]

Kallen then turned to memoir and reflected on his years as an undergraduate at Harvard between 1900 and 1903. He wrote that he "desired to escape the handicaps laid upon one by being known as a Jew" when he first entered Harvard.[41] Calling Jewishness a handicap was not a product of melodramatic hindsight. Remember that when Kallen entered Harvard, he found himself at an institution that historically had been unwelcoming to Jews, and he lived in a national climate of increasing suspicion of ethnic difference.

Kallen also laid a foundation in the essay that allowed him to ask a difficult question, one that he likely was not equipped to ask as pluralism was taking shape during his youth. He wrote: "From my own experience I knew that my Jewish difference, even if it was only a seeming difference, yet could and did cripple my strivings for a life and a living." Kallen wrote in 1962 that it seemed "reasonable" as an undergraduate to "rid myself" of Jewish difference "if I were able." And, Kallen declared: "I *was* able since, unlike the Negro, I could look and act and talk like the model of my choice ... In a word," Kallen wrote, "I could 'pass.'" Finally, he asked himself: "What then was the point of not passing, of suffering the lameness that not-passing entailed?"[42]

Kallen answered this question by seeking to reframe readers' perspective based on the logic of pluralism—cultural difference did not constitute "lameness" but strength. Accepting cultural pluralism rendered passing antidemocratic. For, if pluralists succeeded, nurturing cultural difference would no longer be perceived as un-American but as the very essence of

---

39. Ibid., 23, 24.
40. Kallen, "Promise of the Menorah Idea," 11.
41. Ibid., 9.
42. Ibid., 10. Italics in original.

being American. A renaissance of Jewish culture as Kallen and his fellow Menorah Association founders imagined it would have allowed Jews to escape from feelings of inferiority that made questions about passing or not passing possible, but it also would have demanded that they not escape from Jewishness. In a society that valued cultural difference, promoting Jewish culture would not marginalize Jews but would create opportunities for them to coexist easily within a diverse ethnic landscape. According to Kallen, the cultural viability of the nation itself depended on this diversity.

Kallen made a place for Jewish culture in the United States only by first asking his readers to reconsider the meaning of American culture. As he reminded readers in 1962, the "Menorah Idea," which he defined as promoting a renaissance of Jewish culture, depended fully on the "American Idea," which meant imagining the democratic nation as a federation of nationalities with distinct cultures. There was no absolute "American." Therefore there was no fixed norm to which Jews must assimilate. In an ever-changing, modern nation, attributing a fixed meaning to American identity was nonsensical. And just as American culture had to evolve continually, Jewish culture needed to remain an evolving entity. If Jewish culture hoped to retain its value, it could never remain static. Such dynamism, Kallen continually reminded his readers, was exactly what a "*living* Jewish culture requires."[43]

BIBLIOGRAPHY

Alter, Robert. "Epitaph for a Jewish Magazine: Notes on the 'Menorah Journal.'" *Commentary* (1965) 51–55.

Baldwin, Neil. *Henry Ford and the Jews: The Mass Production of Hate*. New York: Public Affairs, 2001.

Benn Michaels, Walter. *Our America: Nativism, Modernism, and Pluralism*. Durham: Duke University Press, 1995.

Bourne, Randolph S. "Trans-National America." *Atlantic Monthly*, July 1916, 86–97.

Dinnerstein, Leonard. *Anti-Semitism in America*. New York: Oxford University Press, 1994.

DuBois, W. E. B. *The Souls of Black Folk*. New York: Oxford University Press, 2007.

Feiner, Shmuel. *The Jewish Enlightenment*. Translated by Chaya Naor. Philadelphia: University of Pennsylvania Press, 2002.

Feiner, Shmuel, and David Sorkin, eds. *New Perspectives on the Haskalah*. London: Littman Library of Jewish Civilization, 2001.

Fried, Lewis. "Creating Hebraism, Confronting Hellenism: The *Menorah Journal* and the Struggle for the Jewish Imagination." *American Jewish Archives Journal* 53 (2001) 147–74.

———. "The *Menorah Journal*: Yavneh in America, 1945–50." *American Jewish Archives Journal* 50 (1998) 77–108.

43. Ibid., 16. Italics in original.

Gerstle, Gary. "Liberty, Coercion, and the Making of Americans." *Journal of American History* 84 (1997) 524–58.

Greene, Daniel. *The Jewish Origins of Cultural Pluralism: The Menorah Association and American Diversity.* Bloomington: Indiana University Press, 2011.

Grumet, Elinor. "The Menorah Idea and the Apprenticeship of Lionel Trilling." PhD diss., University of Iowa, 1979.

Harap, Louis. "The Menorah Journal—A Literary Precursor." *Midstream*, October 1984, 51–55.

Heinze, Andrew R. *Is It 'Cos I's Black? Jews and the Whiteness Problem.* Ann Arbor: University of Michigan, 2007.

———. "Schizophrenia Americana: Aliens, Alienists, and the 'Personality Shift' of Twentieth-Century Culture." *American Quarterly* 55 (2003) 227–56.

Higham, John. *Strangers in the Land: Patterns of American Nativism, 1860–1925.* New Brunswick, NJ: Rutgers University Press, 1994.

Intercollegiate Menorah Association. *The Menorah Movement for the Advancement of Jewish Culture and Ideals.* Ann Arbor, MI: Intercollegiate Menorah Association, 1914.

Joselit, Jenna Weissman. "Without Ghettoism: A History of the Intercollegiate Menorah Association, 1906–1930." *American Jewish Archives Journal* 30 (1978) 133–54.

Kallen, Horace M. "Alain Locke and Cultural Pluralism." *Journal of Philosophy* 54 (1957) 119–27.

———. *Cultural Pluralism and the American Idea: An Essay in Social Philosophy.* Philadelphia: University of Pennsylvania Press, 1956.

———. *Culture and Democracy in the United States.* New York: Boni & Liveright, 1924. Reprint, New Brunswick, NJ: Transaction, 1998.

———. "Nationality and the Hyphenated American." *Menorah Journal* 1 (1915) 79–86.

———. "Promise of the Menorah Idea." *Menorah Journal* 49 (1962) 9–16.

———. *The Structure of Lasting Peace.* Boston: Jones, 1918.

Klingenstein, Susanne. *Jews in the American Academy 1900–1940: The Dynamics of Intellectual Assimilation.* New Haven: Yale University Press, 1991.

Konvitz, Milton R. "Horace Meyer Kallen (1882–1974)." *American Jewish Year Book* 75 (1974–1975) 55–80.

———, ed. *The Legacy of Horace M. Kallen.* Cranbury, NJ: Associated University Presses, 1987.

———. *Nine American Jewish Thinkers.* New Brunswick, NJ: Transaction, 2000.

Korelitz Seth. "The Menorah Idea: From Religion to Culture, From Race to Ethnicity." *American Jewish History* 85 (1997) 75–100.

Krupnick, Mark. "The Menorah Journal Group and the Origins of Modern Jewish Radicalism." *Studies in American Jewish Literature* 5 (1979) 56–67.

Lewis, David Levering. *W. E. B. DuBois: Biography of a Race, 1868–1919.* New York: Holt, 1993.

Menand, Louis. *The Metaphysical Club: A Story of Ideas in America.* New York: Farrar, Straus & Giroux, 2001.

Meyer, Michael A. *Response to Modernity: A History of the Reform Movement in Judaism.* New York: Oxford University Press, 1988.

Nashon, Edna, ed. *From the Ghetto to the Melting Pot: Israel Zangwill's Jewish Plays.* Detroit: Wayne State University Press, 2006.

Orsi, Robert A. "The Disciplinary Vocabulary of Modernity." *International Journal* 59 (2004) 879–85.
Pappas, Andrea. "The Picture at the *Menorah Journal*: Making 'Jewish Art.'" *American Jewish History* 90 (2002) 205–38.
Posnock, Ross. *Color and Culture: Black Writers and the Making of the Modern Intellectual*. Cambridge: Harvard University Press, 1998.
Ross, Edward Alsworth. *The Old World in the New: The Significance of Past and Present Immigration to the American People*. New York: Century, 1913.
Schmidt, Sarah. *Horace M. Kallen: Prophet of American Zionism*. Brooklyn: Carlson, 1995.
Schorsch, Ismar. *From Text to Context: The Turn to History in Modern Judaism*. Waltham, MA: Brandeis University Press, 1994.
Sollors, Werner. *Beyond Ethnicity: Consent and Descent in American Culture*. New York: Oxford University Press, 1986.
———. "A Critique of Pure Pluralism." In *Reconstructing American Literary History*, edited by Sacvan Bercovitch, 250–79. Harvard English Studies 13. Cambridge: Harvard University Press, 1986.
Strauss, Lauren B. "Staying Afloat in the Melting Pot: Constructing an American Jewish Identity in the *Menorah Journal* of the 1920s." *American Jewish History* 84 (1996) 315–31.
Toll, William. "Horace M. Kallen: Pluralism and American Jewish Identity." *American Jewish History* 85 (1997) 57–74.
Wald, Alan M. "The Menorah Group Moves Left." *Jewish Social Studies* 38 (1976) 289–320.
Weinfeld, David. "What Difference Does Difference Make? Horace Kallen, Alain Locke, and the Birth of Cultural Pluralism." In *Philosophic Values and World Citizenship: Locke to Obama and Beyond*, edited by Jacoby Adeshei Carter and Leonard Harris, 165–87. Lanham, MD: Lexington, 2010.
Westbrook, Robert B. *John Dewey and American Democracy*. Ithaca, NY: Cornell University Press, 1991.
Whitfield, Stephen. "Introduction to the Transaction Edition." In *Culture and Democracy in the United States*. New Brunswick, NJ: Transaction, 1998.

11

Religious Pluralism in Islam

THOMAS MICHEL

THE NOTION OF PLURALISM as applied to religious thought has many dimensions. Fundamental to the concept is the theological question of exclusivity or inclusivity: how do the followers of a given religion regard those outside their community? It makes a great deal of difference whether a community sees outsiders as fellow pilgrims who are headed for the same goal but follow a different path, or as unfortunates who have wandered off the path and are consequently condemned to fumble blindly in the dark and destined for eternal damnation. Are those of another religion seen as prospective partners and collaborators meant to work together on a common task for the sake of a common good, or are they rivals, competitors, even enemies who must be avoided or overcome? For monotheist believers in an Abrahamic tradition, the key question becomes: how does God intend that we treat those outside our community? Do we embrace them, distinguish ourselves from them, shun them, try to convert them, fight against them, or simply adopt a neutral policy of live and let live?

Certainly, the history of each religious group reveals a multiplicity of answers proposed at various times and places, and in this Islam is no different from Judaism, Christianity, and the other religions. How a community answers the theological question has serious practical implications for the way a community lives with others in plural societies. In the first part of this chapter, we will look briefly at the theological issue of what might be called "the salvation of non-Muslims," and then in the second part view the sociological issue of how Muslim groups and movements are engaged in building pluralist societies.

QUR'ANIC INCLUSIVITY

Down through the centuries, Muslim attitudes toward non-Muslims have evolved, although Muslim scholars have always recognized that for any attitude or policy to be considered authentically Islamic, it must be rooted in the teaching of the Qur'an and authentic sayings of the Prophet Muhammad. The late Fazlur Rahman held that the Qur'an consistently offers a more inclusive view of other religions than what is usually found in the writings of later generations of Muslims.

The demands of modern life have prompted leading Muslim thinkers in our day to address the question of pluralism. Many factors account for this. There is the increased mobility that finds Muslims living anywhere from Alaska to Argentina to Korea, along with millions of non-Muslims residing in the nations of the Arabian Peninsula. Another factor lies in the desire of scholars to show the compatibility between Islamic principles and the assumptions of modern democracy, which is reaching global consensus as the form of government most suitable for defending human dignity and establishing social justice. There is also the desire to correct the widespread misapprehension that Muslims are prevented by Islamic precepts from being able to live willingly and peacefully in truly pluralistic situations.

This concern of Muslim scholars to affirm an inclusivist religious outlook must not be seen as a purely defensive posture meant to counteract the accusations of violence and xenophobia that arose after the World Trade Center attacks. Already in 1985, long before 9/11, I published an article in the journal *Islam and the Modern World* in which I studied the writings of thirty-six Muslim scholars who were advocating the involvement of Muslims in building pluralist societies.[1]

Down through the centuries, Muslim attitudes toward non-Muslims have evolved, but Muslim scholars have always recognized that for any attitude or policy to be considered authentically Islamic, it must be rooted in the teaching of the Qur'an and authentic sayings of Muhammad. Fazlur Rahman held that if Muslims were to focus more squarely on the consistent teaching of the Qur'an, rather than upon the formulations of later generations of Muslims, they would find a firmer basis for a more inclusive approach to other religions. He contended that a conceptual basis for "a more positive and a more open Muslim attitude" towards other religions "can only

---

1. Michel, *Islam and the Modern Age*, 37–49.

be achieved by the harkening of Muslims more to the Qur'an than to the historical formulations of Islam."[2]

Perhaps Fazlur Rahman's assessment is overly pessimistic. Recent research into scholars such as Al-Ghazali, Ibn Arabi, Ibn Taymiyya and his disciple Ibn Qayyim al-Jawziyya indicate that even in medieval times, some Muslim thinkers saw the possibility of at least eschatological salvation for sinners and followers of other religions.[3] For Ibn Taymiyya and Ibn Qayyim, the Garden is eternal but the Fire is not. The Fire will be extinguished and those in it released. Mohammad Hassan Khalil concludes: "Ibn Taymiyya avers that those who were once damned will proceed into the only remaining abode, the Garden, "the abode of felicity," where they will enjoy "everlasting pleasure."[4]

Modern Muslim scholars note that the Qur'an appeared in a religiously plural environment and affirm that the Sacred Book lays the groundwork for an inclusivist view of other religions. Amir Hussain avers that the Qur'an presumes a pluralist environment and assumes that Muhammad's hearers were already familiar with the stories of the Jewish and Christian prophets.[5] As a Qur'anic basis for accepting other religions as legitimate paths, if not necessarily on the same truth level as Islam, Mahmoud Ayoub cites Qur'anic verses such as "To everyone we have appointed a way and a course to follow" (5:48) and "For each there is a direction toward which he turns; vie therefore with one another in the performance of good works. Wherever you may be, God shall bring you all together [on Judgment day]"[6] (2:148).

Abdulaziz Sachedina begins from the Qur'anic verse "Mankind was one community. Then God sent forth the Prophets as bearers of good news and as warners. He sent down with them the Book with the truth, that He might judge between people regarding that on which they had differed" (2:213). For Sachedina, the verse presents Muslims with three basic elements of faith that form the starting point for an Islamic pluralism: (1) the unity of humankind under One God, (2) the particularity of religions

---

2. Fazlur Rahman, "People of the Book and the Diversity of Religions," in Griffiths, *Christianity through Non-Christian Eyes*, 110.

3. Khalil, "Muslim Scholarly Discussions on Salvation and the *Fate* of 'Others,'" esp. 105–31.

4. Khalil, *Islam and the Fate of Others*, 85. In his dissertation (n3, above) Khalil treats mainly the views expressed in Ibn Taymiyya's *fatwas* regarding the ultimate fate of non-Muslims. In his published work, he approaches the topic more from Ibn Taymiyya's polemic *Al-Jawab al-Sahih* and his *Radd 'ala qala b-fana' al-janna wal-nar*.

5. Amir Hussain, "Muslims, Pluralism, and Interfaith Dialogue," in Safi, *Progressive Muslims*, 253.

6. Esposito, *Future of Islam*, 176.

brought by the prophets, and (3) the role of revelation in resolving the differences among communities of faith.

He argues that the belief "that 'the People are one community' is the foundation of a theological pluralism, which presupposes the divinely ordained equivalence and equal rights of all human beings."[7] He holds that a community's affirming the possibility of salvation for others than themselves is crucial for a truly pluralist view of other religions. "The acid test of pluralism is whether a religion is willing to recognize members of other religions as potential citizens in the world to come." Then he asks a key question: "Is such citizenship conferred in spite of or because of the person's membership in another religion?"[8]

Commenting on the same verse, Ayoub holds that "What the Qur'an decries is not diversity but discord or conflict. It decries what it calls in Sura 2:213 baghi, meaning hostility, insolence or envy among human individuals and societies. The Qur'an does not condone this. Difference is good, but conflict is evil."[9]

That the Qur'an affirms diversity while condemning hostility is taken up by the *Common Word* initiative. This proposal from the year 2007, which collected the names of over three hundred prominent Muslim scholars and leaders as signers, made a dramatic appeal for unity in building multireligious harmony. "To those who relish conflict and destruction for their own sake or reckon that ultimately they stand to gain through them, we say that our very eternal souls are at stake if we fail to sincerely make every effort to make peace and come together in harmony . . . So let our differences not cause hatred and strife between us. Let us vie with each other only in righteousness and good works. Let us respect each other, be fair, just and kind to one another and live in sincere peace, harmony and mutual goodwill."[10]

Two leading Muslim thinkers who have laid the theological groundwork for pluralism are the Kurdish scholar from Turkey Said Nursi, and the Egyptian scholar Fathi Osman. Nursi affirms that not only Muslims, but also the followers of other religions worship God, each in their own way. If the followers of the earlier religions perform a type of genuine worship of God, there is a kind of spirituality and holiness present in them. In acknowledging "the manifestations of the unseen and epiphanies of the spirit, revelation and inspiration"[11] found in the various religions, Nursi is inviting

---

7. Sachedina, *Islamic Roots of Democratic Pluralism*, 28.
8. Ibid., 38.
9. Ayoub, "Islam and the Challenge of Religious Pluralism," 57.
10. *Common Word between Us and You*, 3.
11. Said Nursi, *Risale-i Nur Külliyatı*, [*Risale-i Nur Collection*], The Rays, "The

Muslims to acknowledge some of the ways in which God might be active also in other religions. If there are genuine elements of holiness and goodness in the other religions, it is proper for Muslims to befriend and love their neighbors of the Peoples of the Book. Throughout his life, Nursi advocated Muslims and Christians working together to promote and defend the values that derive from their respective revelations.

Like the *Common Word* initiative, Nursi's invitation to interfaith cooperation was directed specifically to Christians, but some of those influenced by Nursi's ideas have extended to the followers of other religions as well the invitation to work together to support and pursue pluralistic values. The contemporary Turkish scholar Fethullah Gülen, whose thought was much influenced by Nursi, in a message delivered to the Parliament of World Religions in Capetown, South Africa, in 1999, took up the need for Muslims to cooperate not only with Christians and Jews to instill the values of pluralism into modern societies, but also to engage Buddhists, Hindus, Taoists, and Confucians in implementing the values of love, respect, tolerance, forgiveness, mercy, human rights, peace, brotherhood, and freedom."[12]

Gülen urges Muslims who live in minority situations as in Western Europe, the Americas, Sub-Saharan Africa, and Southeast Asia to consider the regions in which they live not according to the medieval jurisprudential categories of *dar al-salam* and *dar al-harb*, but in the pluralist category of *dar al-hizmet* [Ar. *hidhma*], that is, regions in which Muslims are called to *serve* others in accord with the Qur'anic injunction to Muslims to be a "blessing for the universe." This has led the movement inspired by Gülen to establish schools, communication media, and social institutions. Their schools have been welcomed in the largely Christian Philippines and in Buddhist Cambodia and Myanmar, not as Islamic schools, but as institutions providing a service to the whole, religiously plural, population.

The late Fathi Osman, a former professor at Al-Azhar University in Cairo, demands that Muslims extend true pluralism beyond the People of the Book to Hindus, Buddhists and others. According to him, Muslims are called to live in peace and cooperate not only with "the children of Abraham," as stated in the previous Qur'anic reference of 2:213, but also with all, as stated in the broader injunction of the verse: "Every human being ["the children of Adam"] has his or her spiritual compass, and has been granted dignity by God" (Qr 17:70).[13] The Qur'anic notion of a spiritual compass has shaped the thinking of many Muslim thinkers down through the ages. The

---

Supreme Sign," Second Chapter, First Truth, Istanbul: Sözler Publications, 2004. p. 172

12. Gülen, "Necessity of Interfaith Dialogue," in *Essays, Perspectives, Opinions*, 35.

13. Osman, *Children of Adam*, 7.

famous words of Jalal al-Din Rumi, the great mystical poet, are an example: "We are like a compass, while one leg is firmly fixed on the shari'a, the other traverses the seventy-two nations."[14] This inclusivist view of Rumi has been quoted repeatedly by modern scholars of religious pluralism such as Fethullah Gülen.

Osman is not alone in basing his understanding of a Qur'an-inspired pluralism on the aforementioned verse 17:70. Ali Asghar Engineer lists the pluralist values enjoined by the Qur'an as the formative ideal to be embodied in today's Muslim: "A progressive Muslim is one who is firmly grounded in the Qur'anic values of truth (haq), justice (adl), compassion (rahman), wisdom (hikmah) and does service to others, rather than being served by others ... Progressive Islam not only does not adopt a sectarian approach but must be respectful of entire humanity and human dignity as per Quran 17:70."[15]

After reviewing the Qur'anic teachings and Islamic institutions in history that have displayed the values of pluralism in thought and practice, Osman advocates a greater self-assurance among Muslims in the promotion of pluralist societies. In his analysis, Muslims are hindered in pursuing dedication to pluralism that should be an integral part of the Islamic approach to society, not because of any strictures found in Islamic sources and history, but because of the traumatizing and inhibiting effects of colonial domination. He states: "Muslims have the moral and legal principles of pluralism available in their religious sources and heritages, and they have had a long history of practicing pluralism. They can therefore be a constructive and effective contributor to contemporary global pluralism. They have only to overcome a lack of confidence in themselves that derives from years of stagnation and their lack of trust in others that stems from years of humiliation and exploitation."[16]

To conclude these remarks on the theoretical approach of Muslims to the question of religious pluralism, it should be noted that the view of modern Muslims might more precisely be termed "inclusivism" rather than "pluralism." While these Muslim scholars see the possibility of salvation for the followers of other religions, they view Islam as the most complete, perfect path that exceeds others in truth and goodness. This is clear in Rifat

---

14. Jalal al-Din Rumi, cited in Citlak, *Rumi and His Sufi Path of Love*, 90.

15. Engineer, "Who Is a Progressive Muslim?," on Raheel Raza's blog, and cited by Prateek, "The Phantom of Progressive Islam—What Is at Stake?," 7.

16. Osman, *Children of Adam*, 42.

Atay's critique of John Hick's religious pluralism in his comprehensive and carefully thought-out study of the question.[17]

Mahmut Aydin agrees that the general view of Muslims supports an inclusivist position that is parallel with Christian inclusivist theologies of religions. He holds that "exclusivist and inclusivist Muslims put the teaching of the Prophet Muhammad at the center and evaluate other teachings according to their distance from this center, just as traditional Christians put Christianity, Jesus Christ, or the Church at the center and evaluate the others according to their relation and closeness to this center."[18] However, Aydin then contrasts this inclusivist approach of Muslim thinkers with the more genuinely pluralist approach of the Qur'an "which condemns those Christians and Jews who made exclusive claims about the uniqueness and superiority of their own faiths,"[19] and urges Muslims to rely solely on faith and good deeds in their hope for salvation.

EXPERIMENTS IN PLURALISM

If theoretical formulations concerning pluralism are not put into practice in religiously and ethnically plural societies, such pronouncements remain empty verbiage or propaganda. However, there are today many Muslim individuals, organizations, and movements that are sincerely working to build societies on pluralist principles. I will attempt to describe three such efforts. Of course, it is possible to refer to many similar efforts.

Like the followers of other religions, many Muslims have displayed hesitancy and lack of enthusiasm toward the affirmation and construction of truly pluralist societies. Nevertheless, effective examples can also be offered of Muslim involvement in the establishment of pluralist principles in society, both from countries in which Muslims form minority groups as well as in those states where Muslims are the dominant majority. I will outline several concrete efforts taken from my experience of working together with Muslims in Southeast Asia. There are several reasons for this choice. This is the part of the world with which I am most familiar, and I have had personal involvement in many of the projects I describe. More importantly, some of the most creative and successful programs aimed at transforming society according to pluralist principles are being carried out, in my opinion, in that region.

17. Atay, *Religious Pluralism and Islam*.

18. Mahmut Aydin, "Islam and Diverse Faiths: A Muslim View," in Schmidt-Leukel and Ridgeon, *Islam and Inter-faith Relations*, 36.

19. Ibid., 37.

Southeast Asia is something of a microcosm for examining interactions between Muslims and their neighbors of other religions. Indonesia has the world's largest Muslim population but also sizeable Christian, Buddhist, and Hindu minorities. The Philippines has an overwhelming Christian majority, with minorities composed of Muslim peoples and the followers of traditional religions. Thailand, Myanmar, and Cambodia have large Buddhist majorities and, in each case, important Muslim minorities. In Singapore, Muslim and Christian minorities live in a largely Confucian society. The most religiously and ethnically plural state in the region is Malaysia, with a slight Muslim majority, and sizeable Hindu and Christian minorities as well as many followers of all the religions traditionally practiced in China.

MUCAARD (MUSLIM-CHRISTIAN AGENCY FOR ADVOCACY, RELIEF, AND DEVELOPMENT)

The first movement that I will mention is called MUCAARD, an acronym meaning "Muslim–Christian Agency for Advocacy, Relief and Development." It's an umbrella organization of mosque-and-church-based associations in more than 120 villages in the southern Philippines that has been operating quietly and effectively since 1984. In each village, an interreligious committee operates independently and chooses its projects according to local needs. MUCAARD's mandate, according to its charter is: "To develop sustainable communities where Muslims, Christians and Tribal People can live together recognizing and respecting their different faiths and cultures where there is sustainable environment, political empowerment, economic equity, gender equality, unity and lasting peace."

Muslims, Christians, and the followers of the traditional religion came together after the communal violence that occurred in the 1970s, and they intuited that by working together for the benefit of all, they could help to overcome ethnic and religious suspicion and strife. They began with simple, obvious projects: all-weather roads, pickup trucks to take fish to market, seminars to teach crop rotation and introduce new types of seed and animal species, day-care centers for working mothers, and income generation projects for village women.

Over the years their approach has become more sophisticated, with projects for combating climate change, providing safe water supplies, developing integrated agro-forestry, and microfinance for small- and medium-sized enterprises, all the while promoting peace and harmony between the diverse communities. It is important to note that MUCAARD is not just another rural development agency; it is an organization consciously rooted in the mosques and churches, in worship of God, promoted in Friday and Sunday sermons, and carried forward in lectures and workshops about each other's religions, moments of joint fellowship, and the common celebration of religious and national feasts.

MUCAARD is just one of many examples I could have chosen that are committed to promoting an active pluralism in the villages of Mindanao in the southern Philippines. It is mainly a rural-based organization located in agricultural and fishing villages, but it has its urban counterparts, where Muslims and Christians work together to respond to the needs of squatters and slum dwellers. They run free clinics and schools for the poor and provide legal services to defend those threatened with expulsion from their land and homes.

In the region there is a proliferation of jointly sponsored interreligious projects that attempt to build peace and harmony through joint action for the common good. If space permitted, I could illustrate the work for justice of Zamboanga's Islamic-Christian Urban Poor Association, the work for peace of PAZ (Peace Associates of Zamboanga), the efforts at reconciliation carried out by the Muslim-Christian Interfaith Conference and the Moro-Christian People's Alliance, and the initiatives of the Silsilah group to promote mutual understanding and education for dialogue.

THE BISHOPS-ULAMA FORUM

The historical background of the conflict in the southern Philippines has been studied by many researchers. The broad lines of tension go back to internal migration of Christian Filipinos from Luzon and the Visayas into regions of Mindanao and the Sulu archipelago that had traditionally been populated by Muslims and followers of the traditional religion, a movement which continued throughout the twentieth century. Tensions between the newcomers and the indigenous peoples erupted in widespread fighting in the early 1970s, out of which the Moro National Liberation Front (MNLF) emerged as the leading political and military force of Muslims in opposition to the Manila government.

For twenty-five years the MNLF waged guerrilla warfare against the Philippines government, while army troops and the constabulary were simultaneously active in pursuing and seeking to subdue the rebels. It was not until 1996 that a peace treaty between the government and MNLF was announced, but the accord ran into trouble almost immediately in Mindanao, the very region for which the peace accord was intended.

Aside from the internal lacunae in the agreement itself, the accord was not popular with the people. Christian opposition to the accord was expressed even in the House of Representatives in Manila, and Christian vigilantes in protest set off bombs in Zamboanga and other cities of Mindanao. The Christian clergy were particularly adamant in their opposition and were preaching against the agreement in the churches. The Christians felt that the accord was a "sell-out," a handing over of political control in Mindanao to the Muslims, the first step towards the establishment of Islamic law and the erection of an Islamic state.

The Muslims of Mindanao-Sulu, for their part, were no happier with the agreement. The general view was that the accord was "too little, too late." They felt that the concessions granted were more on the order of "paper benefits" than any concrete plans that would improve their situation. They claimed that the accord profited mainly politicians and office-holders rather than the average man and woman in the street. Moreover, it was claimed that the accord helped some ethnic groups while being basically irrelevant to others. Thus, in the first weeks after the agreement was signed it looked likely that the long-sought peace accord would become a dead letter and, worse, that it might actually give rise to a new round of communal violence.

It was at this point that the religious leaders came together in an initiative to try to convince the people of Mindanao that the agreement, with all its flaws and limitations, was still the best chance for a lasting peace in the region. The leading Muslim ulama, the Catholic bishops, and the leaders of the Protestant churches already knew each other, having taken part in previous regional dialogues aimed at bringing peace and overcoming tensions, or they had served together on various citizens' committees. In July 1996 they formed an organization called the "Bishops-Ulama Forum" whose proximate goal was to explain the benefits of the peace accord to their own people, to overcome suspicions, to answer objections, to take up suggestions for implementation, and to gather proposals for presentation to the civil authorities.

Since that time, for the past sixteen years, the Bishops-Ulama Forum has met regularly every three months. The participants have studied together every aspect of life in the southern Philippines—proposed legislation, cultural affairs, demilitarization, education, sustainable development, environment issues, open-pit mining, gun control, agrarian reform, drug use, and family life. They have made joint calls for cease-fires, condemned the formation of vigilante groups, organized and participated in prayer rallies, designated zones of peace, monitored local and national elections, and sponsored dozens of seminars on the culture of peace for educators, lay and religious workers, youth, and administrators of schools and universities in southern Philippines.

In recent years, the Forum has inspired the formation of sister organizations devoted to the same goals of building a peaceful pluralist society in Mindanao. The Priest-Imam Forum, bringing together local middle-level religious leaders, was formed in 1999, and in 2002 the Alliance of Mindanao Youth for Peace grew out of a peace camp experience of Muslim, Christian and Lumad (traditional culture and religion) young people. The fourth tripartite Mindanao Peace Camp was held in April, 2007, in the Davao region of eastern Mindanao. It is worth noting that all these organizations are consciously religious in their motivation and at the same time committed to pluralist values of participatory democracy, civic responsibility, ethnic and religious harmony, access to legal redress, gender equality, and acceptance of diversity.

To me, the really interesting aspect of the Bishops' Ulama Forum and its sister organizations is their conviction that any truly peaceful and pluralist society can be built only by the participation of all civil society groups in a given region. Pluralism cannot be legislated or imposed by the political, military, economic, or religious leadership, although all have a part to play. Projects can be initiated or sponsored by various groups, but will be successful only through the cooperation of all.

The Bishops-Ulama Forum supports the Mindanao Week of Peace. The annual event, fully supported by the ulama and Christian leaders, includes forums and training programs on the values of pluralism and techniques of peace-building for students, women's groups, educators, labor union officials, government bureaucrats, police, and military. Popular events—art exhibits, handicraft fairs, karaoke contests, basketball tournaments—keep the week from becoming overly didactic. Some features of the Week of Peace, such as the fashion shows, daily rock bands, and traditional dance performances, can present a challenge to Muslims to accept the cultural and religious diversity in which they live. Generally, while holding back from active participation in those features deemed unacceptable in Muslim culture or incompatible with the Islamic way of life, Muslims have not objected to or boycotted such elements of public entertainment and cultural expression.

AMAN (ASIAN MUSLIM ACTION NETWORK)

The previous two experiments in pluralism were cases where Muslims joined together with non-Muslims to further pluralistic values in their societies. The Asian Muslim Action Network (AMAN) differs from them by being a wholly Muslim initiative that has opened all its programs to the participation and even to the membership of non-Muslims. It is also different in that, whereas MUCAARD and the Bishops Ulama Forum were sub-national, regional, organizations aimed at dealing with local issues of pluralism, AMAN is an international association of Muslims.

AMAN has been, from its inception, an international network of Muslims from 18 Asian countries that brings together "individuals, groups and associations of Muslims in Asia subscribing to a progressive and enlightened approach to Islam." Since its foundation in 1990, AMAN has cooperated with Muslim groups and those of other faiths, and worked "with grassroots communities or engaged in research and policy advocacy for the eradication of poverty, environmental protection, human rights, social justice, inter-faith and inter-cultural dialogue, communal harmony and peace."

This self-description gives an accurate picture of the scope of AMAN and its pluralist value system. Founded by a small but influential group of Muslim scholars and social activists, AMAN seeks to respond to the numerous challenges faced by the peoples of Asia "ranging from mass poverty to elite corruption, materialistic life style, increasing ethnic, religious, and communal conflict, violence against women and children, and environmental degradation."

At the Second Plenary Assembly of AMAN, held in Dhaka, Bangladesh, in 2000, Ali Asghar Engineer of Bombay, chairman of AMAN, noted the motivation for creating the network: "With the advent of democracies in South and Southeast Asian nations, awareness about democratic rights, human rights, and women's rights has been growing fast. However, although there was a great deal of secular theorizing on the issue, there was a lack of Islamic thought, and still less of activism."[20] In other words, AMAN is responding to the need felt by progressive Muslims in Asia to reflect on questions of pluralism, such as poverty, democracy, civil rights, human rights, economic sustainability, the status of women, and exploitation of children from an explicitly Islamic point of view. The association conducts training programs for Muslim and non-Muslim activists and organizes seminars for youth leaders to face issues connected with the empowerment of Asia's poor and vulnerable and to promote an activist approach to self-reliant development.

In the twenty-three years since its creation, AMAN has grown quickly. In addition to individual memberships in eighteen Asian countries, seventy-six local and national Muslim organizations in Asia have become members of AMAN, giving the association the character of an umbrella

20. Engineer, *Interfaith Conference on the Culture of Peace*, 6.

organization. Local chapters have been established in Afghanistan, Bangladesh, Cambodia, Indonesia, India, Malaysia, Pakistan, Philippines, and Sri Lanka, and its programs include the active participation of Muslims in China, Iran, Afghanistan, and the Central Asian republics.

The triennial plenary assemblies are not business meetings so much as a convergence of workshops and study sessions. At the Third Plenary Assembly, held in Bangkok in December 2003, participants from twenty-one Asian nations took part. The theme was: "Building a culture of peace," with break-out seminars on: "Multi-ethnic Asia," "Interfaith dialogue," "Women and peace," "Youth for peace," "Poverty and peace," and "HIV/AIDS."

At the fourth plenary, held in November 2006 in Jakarta, the AMAN workshops focused on themes of globalization, ethnic and religious pluralism, human rights, HIV/AIDS, interreligious dialogue, and peacebuilding. Five international commissions were set up to deal with (1) Asian minorities, peace processes, refugees and asylum seekers; (2) women and gender rights; (3) education, research information technology, and interfaith cooperation; (4) civil society, governance and advocacy; (5) representation to regional organizations. Peace missions aimed at disengagement and reconciliation were sent to Indonesia and Sri Lanka as Asian initiatives in the peace process.

The stated concern for the "marginalized and vulnerable" has brought AMAN into the area of human rights. In 2001, the organization set up AMAN Watch as a regional expression of human rights concerns, which monitors human rights violations in predominantly Muslim regions of Asia, as well as the violation of the civil rights of Muslims in both majority and minority situations. AMAN Watch is one of the partner associations in the Hong Kong-based Asian Human Rights Commission (AHRC) and Religious Groups for Human Rights (RGHR).

Parallel to AMAN Watch, AMAN created "Gender Watch" which follows, reports and publicizes exploitation of women and violations of gender equality at the pan-Asian level. Three other projects were approved which were aimed at coordinating a continental approach to pressing problems: (1) humanitarian assistance and care for those living with HIV/AIDS, (2) a study on ecology, economy and sustainable development, and (3) developing contacts in China.

AMAN has published over twenty books on topics of concern, mainly focusing on themes of peace and Islamic renewal in Asia. Its latest project is the monthly AMANA news service, which has, up to now, produced its first six issues.

AMAN is quite open to working together in shared programs with other organizations, as well as with bodies linked with one or another religion in Asia. As such, AMAN has undertaken joint initiatives with Christians on peace education and on questions of justice for ethnic minorities, with the Federation of Asian Bishops' Conferences, a continental association of seventeen Catholic bishops' conferences, and with the Christian Conference of Asia, an ecumenical body composed of over 120 Churches and Synods, of Orthodox and Reformation orientation, in Asia.

AMAN's approach to Islamic practice is what the Malaysian political scientist Chandra Muzaffar calls a "values approach to Islam," which he contrasts to a fiqh [i.e., jurisprudential] approach, with its "rigid religious-secular dichotomy." Muzaffar states: "It is only too apparent that a non-dogmatic approach to Islam which recognizes the primacy of eternal, universal spiritual and moral values while acknowledging the importance of rituals, symbols and practices is the most sane and sensible way of living religion in today's world."[21]

One of the most effective projects of AMAN is its educational work with Asian youth. The organizations conducts training courses and youth camps focused on developing Muslim leadership which can address the principal AMAN concerns of poverty, social justice, environmental degradation, human rights, questions of peace, harmony, and reconciliation, development issues and advocacy on behalf of "marginalized and vulnerable sectors of society such as women, children, and ethnic and religious minorities." Recent seminars and workshops have included the topics of community-based peace education, preventive education on HIV-AIDS, and human rights from an Islamic perspective.

In 2003, AMAN instituted the "School of Peace Studies and Conflict Transformation," an annual course to train peace advocates in the techniques of conflict analysis and reconciliation. AMAN undertakes "training for trainers" workshops to prepare local and national animators and annually awards scholarships for researchers working on questions in the above-mentioned fields; almost eight hundred activists have taken part in leadership training courses over the past nine years.

AMAN has given particular attention to the situations of ethnic and religious minorities. Most countries of Asia have minority groups distinguished by language, religion, race, or cultural background from the majority. Almost invariably, such groups suffer various forms of discrimination: the minority groups are often mistrusted and unwelcome in the dominant national society, treated with bureaucratic resistance and indifference, and in some instances subject to violence and persecution. The fact that their

---

21. Muzaffar, "AMAN: The Challenges Ahead," 21–22.

native language and religion is often not that of the dominant majority further isolates the ethnic minorities.

Unlike some Muslim movements and associations which are inspired by the teaching of charismatic preachers, AMAN has no single intellectual mentor, but is guided by a constellation of prominent Asian Muslim scholars. The association has members drawn without distinction from both the Sunni and Shi'i traditions. Although AMAN is predominantly a Muslim organization based on Islamic principles, the organization accepts non-Muslim members who agree to the ideals and goals of the organization. Its various programs are open to non-Muslim participants and speakers, not only to Christians, which would not be unusual among Muslim associations, but also to Hindus, Buddhists, and non-religious social activists. Thus, the pluralism advocated by AMAN's statements and programs is reflected in its own composition.

I have outlined the activities and outlooks of three Southeast Asian movements through which Muslims seek to promote the values of pluralist societies. They are typical of many efforts occurring today among Muslims, and parallels could be found in other parts of the Muslim world. A commitment to pluralism in society obviously is not the conviction of every Muslim, but the questions raised by pluralism are ones that every thinking Muslim today must confront. What kind of society does he or she want to live in? What are the effective ways of bringing that society about?

Some observers, like John Esposito of Georgetown University's Alwaleed Center for Christian-Muslim Understanding are optimistic that the international Islamic community has the resources to be active agents in promoting societal pluralism. He states: "Reform-minded Muslims, religious and lay, men and women, are working to articulate a progressive, constructive Islamic framework. Informed by a deep knowledge of their religious tradition and modern education in law, history, politics, medicine, economics and the sciences, they are equipped to reinterpret Islamic sources and traditions to meet the challenges of modernization and development, leadership and ideology, democratization, pluralism, and foreign policy."[22]

BIBLIOGRAPHY

Atay, Rifat. "Religious Pluralism and Islam." PhD diss., University of St. Andrews, 1999.
Aydin, Mahmut. "Islam and Diverse Faiths: A Muslim View." In *Islam and Inter-faith Relations*, edited by Perry Schmidt-Leukel and Lloyd Ridgeon, 36. London: SCM, 2007.

---

22. Esposito, *Future of Islam*, 195.

Ayoub, Mahmoud. "Islam and the Challenge of Religious Pluralism." *Global Dialogue* 2 (2000) 55–58. http://www.worlddialogue.org/content.php?id=58.
Citlak, M. Fatih. *Rumi and His Sufi Path of Love*. Somerset, NJ: Light, 2007.
A Common Word between Us and You. Amman: The Royal Aal al-Bayt Institute for Islamic Thought, 2007.
Engineer, Asghar Ali. *Interfaith Conference on the Culture of Peace*. Bangkok: Asian Muslim Action Network, 2001.
———. "Who Is a Progressive Muslim?" Posted September 2, 2011, Raheel Raza's blog. http://raheelraza.wordpress.com/2011/09/02/who-is-a-progressive-muslim-by-asghar-ali-engineer.
Esposito, John L. *The Future of Islam*. New York: Oxford University Press, 2010.
Griffiths, Paul J., ed. *Christianity through Non-Christian Eyes*. Maryknoll, NY: Orbis, 1989.
Gülen, Fethullah. *M. Fethullah Gülen: Essays, Perspectives, Opinions*. Somerset, NJ: Light, 2006.
Khalil, Mohammad Hassan. *Islam and the Fate of Others*. New York: Oxford University Press, 2012.
———. "Muslim Scholarly Discussions on Salvation and the *Fate* of 'Others.'" Unpublished PhD diss., University of Michigan, 2007.
Michel, Thomas. *Islam and the Modern Age*. Delhi: Jamia Millia Islamia, 1984.
Muzaffar, Chandra. "AMAN: The Challenges Ahead." In *Interfaith Conference on the Culture of Peace*. Bangkok: AMAN, 1991.
Nursi, Said. "The Supreme Sign." 2nd chapter, 1st truth in *The Rays*. Risale-i Nur Collection. Translated by Şukran Vahide. Istanbul: Sözler Publications, 2004.
Osman, Mohamed Fathi. *The Children of Adam: An Islamic Perspective on Pluralism*. Occasional Papers series. Washington, DC: Center for Muslim–Christian Understanding, Georgetown University, 1996.
Prateek, Satya. "The Phantom of Progressive Islam—What Is at Stake?" *Amana* (Bangkok) 5 (2011) 7–10.
Sachedina, Abdulaziz. *The Islamic Roots of Democratic Pluralism*. New York: Oxford University Press, 2001.
Safi, Omid, ed. *Progressive Muslims*. Oxford: One World, 2003.
Schmidt-Leukel, Perry, and Lloyd Ridgeon, eds. *Islam and Inter-faith Relations*. London: SCM, 2007.

12

Response to Tom Michel

PAUL L. HECK

SOMETIME TOWARD THE MIDDLE of the tenth century CE, a gifted and philosophically minded *littérateur* by the name of Abu Hayyan al-Tawhidi held a number of evening conversations with the vizier to the Buyid dynasty, Ibn Sa'dan (d. 985), at his court in Rayy (near today's Tehran). One evening the discussion turned to the plurality of religions. Which one is true? At this time, the Abode of Islam, still nominally under the leadership of the Abbasid caliphs in Baghdad, housed Jews, Christians, and Zoroastrians as well as Muslims of varied affiliation. The question was thus not simply academic but quite relevant to the day's social realities.

At one point in the discussion, of which al-Tawhidi left us a record, he refers to a skeptic from Sijistan, a region lying in southeastern Iran. This man had explained his skeptical views to al-Tawhidi's own teacher (a logician by the name of Abu Sulayman al-Sijistani). In fact, he had assumed a kind of skepticism, a belief in the equivalence of contradictory truth claims, as his own creed. This anonymous figure related to al-Tawhidi's teacher how earlier in life he had passionately defended a set of beliefs. However, he began to notice that one day he would have the upper hand in the argument only to be bested by his opponent the next day. He concluded from this that he could no longer honestly judge a belief to be correct simply because it was backed by argumentation: The argument used to support it would invariably be turned against it. He had also read the scriptures and teachings of the various communities but did not find one better than another. It was impossible to say they were all true. How could they be, teaching opposing points of view? Still, he found satisfaction in seeing all as equally plausible even if none could be determined to be singularly true. This, however, had not led him to abandon his own religion, as he explains:

> My own religion is inviolable because I was born and raised in it. I have absorbed its sweetness and am familiar with the ways of its people. I am like a man who enters a caravanserai to seek cover from the heat of the sun. He takes the room given to him without question. While asleep, a cloud takes shapes and sends down buckets of rain, and his room begins to leak on all sides. Looking across the courtyard, he sees all the other rooms in the same condition. He also sees how muddy the courtyard has become and concludes that the best thing to do is to stay in his room, leak and all, rather than splatter his legs in the muck of the courtyard. Yes, like him, it is best for me to stay where I am. I was born with a blank mind. My parents introduced me to this religion without discussion, and when I examined it, I found it to be much like other religions. It is dearer to me to keep it than abandon it. I would only make the choice to leave it for another that offered a more convincing argument for its truths, but I have not found such a one, and so I stick with what the years have made familiar to me.

It is worth pointing out that al-Tawhidi was no relativist. In fact, evidence suggests that he used this and similar stories to poke fun at the religious studies scholars of his day, who loved to regale audiences with their ability to argue a position at what would have been the equivalent at that time of academic conferences but who actually believed nothing themselves. In short, they were sophists, who, consciously or not, endeavored merely to make a mockery of beliefs. In other places in his oeuvre, al-Tawhidi roundly castigates them for their abstruseness and obfuscating ways that only mask their own lack of beliefs and commitments. In the view of al-Tawhidi, what should be mocked is not faith but the skepticism of these sophists: Because they see beliefs as nothing but the product of one's upbringing, they do not take thinking about religion to a deeper level of research and reflection and thus fail to understand what beliefs are altogether.

All of this is by way of comments on Tom Michel's essay, which raises a very significant horizon for the study of religious pluralism. Let us call it ideal pluralism as opposed to practical pluralism, a concept that features in the paper of Paula Fredriksen. With practical pluralism, the idea is that everyone pays homage to the state as existential authority in the public space while expressing their own beliefs at home or within the confines of their particular communities. A problem arises when one community claims to have the truth—belief in a singular deity which cannot coexist with other deities and which all peoples should therefore recognize, even the holders of political power. It is here that practical pluralism has trouble balancing the claims of the state and the truth claims of monotheistic pluralism. Threatened, the state has to suppress the place of beliefs and commitments in public. This is something to take seriously today. Religious pluralism of this kind is implicated in the modality of governance in our societies. One might take the question into the arena of academia. How are religious studies scholars implicated, consciously or not, in the interests of the state to present itself as sole existential authority in society?

In contrast, by surveying a selection of Islam-inspired religiously pluralistic endeavors in Southeast Asia, Tom offers insight into the concept of ideal pluralism. Despite media coverage of Islam, it is important to emphasize that Islam is playing a vital role in this regard. There are certainly contrary winds blowing these days across the global community of Muslims, but Tom offers extensive concrete evidence of a different way of conceiving the relation of belief to the public square. It is something that deserves scholarly attention.

With ideal pluralism, the idea is that people of different faiths come together for joint action in the public sphere without leaving their commitments and truth claims behind. Here, people do not shift faith according to context: "Now I recognize the state as existential authority in my life and pay homage to its deities, and now I do not." Noteworthy among the data that Tom surveys in his essay is the fact that the deepest beliefs and commitments of people are dynamically operative in the public sphere alongside others with different truth claims, and it is precisely this fact (and not in spite of it) that the experience is meaningful and productive. In this way, people of diverse faith commitments come together civilly but without modulating religious accent. This requires a religious affirmation of civility and tolerance (if not actually affection) of the religious other but also a willingness to be exposed to (and enriched by) the beliefs and commitments of others. The model here, drawing upon the work of Hans Joas, could be called cross-religious value communication as opposed to the limited model of overlapping consensus expectation as proposed by John Rawls. Far from watering down the faith experience in public, unexpected surprises in self-insight take place in this way. Here, then, with ideal pluralism, it is through, and not in spite of, religious distinctiveness that meaning is found and formed. What is the nature of this reality? Under what conditions, mental and social, does religious pluralism take ideal rather than practical form? For one, while not requiring hostility to power, it would assume at least benign indifference to the state as singular existential authority in society.

The irony is that practical pluralism (where the state pretends to neutral protection of all faiths) threatens our beliefs and commitments whereas ideal pluralism does not. With practical pluralism, we sense that our deepest beliefs and commitments have no place in public. This can raise anxieties about the truths of those beliefs and commitments. How could they be true if they have no place in public? And so one undergoes a gradual transformation to faith in state policies, taking on non-committed religious sentiment when in public. Anxieties of this kind, I believe, which are engendered in part by practical pluralism, are very much lurking in the background when it comes to the clash of civilizations today or, more precisely, the many instances of tension between state and faith commitment today.

So, the first point is that we need to pay greater attention to the study of ideal pluralism as it is currently being pursued, especially among the rising generation of graduate students. The second point that emerges from Tom's essay is one that calls us to reflect more precisely on what we are doing in the academy in our endeavors to study (and even grasp) the phenomenon of religious pluralism and what this implies for our ability or inability to acquire knowledge of religion, which, as scholars in the academy, is our goal. In other words, religious pluralism is forcing us to reconsider what religion is if we hope to acquire knowledge of it. Are we as scholars of religious pluralism somehow embedded in the agenda of practical pluralism and its relativizing tendencies? As I survey the field (to say nothing of my own research inquiries), I do not find that we are "compromised" in this way but rather that we are very committed to understanding the phenomenon of beliefs and commitments as a constitutive and thus rationally compelling element of the human condition, but we always have to be questioning the status quo as we (for better or worse) represent it, especially when popular opinion can often conceive of religion as personal experience and thus potentially irrational superstition with no objective worth. Tom's essay calls us to greater scrutiny about what we are doing in the academy.

The bottom line is that religious pluralism and religious relativism are closely paired. My own work on the history of skepticism in classical Islam, of which the narratives of al-Tawhidi offer but one example, shows that at that time the Abode of Islam, precisely because of its extraordinary religious pluralism, was also familiar with the concomitant phenomenon of religious relativism—or what was known at the time as the equivalence of evidence (*takafu' al-adilla*) or the idea that all religions are equally compelling (or equally repelling, depending on your viewpoint). It thus makes sense to dismiss—and even make light of—all beliefs. The goal is not ignoble, namely, to find tranquility by affirming ignorance of religious commitments. Is that where we are headed with the study of religious pluralism?

It may not be our job as scholars in the academy to decide where religious truth lies, although we certainly want to invite out students to consider the possibility of a relation with truth. The point is that we are always at risk of falling prey to one agenda or another, whether religionizing or secularizing. Are we sufficiently self-aware as scholars—and teachers—of religious pluralism? I would like to share here a comment of one of my Moroccan graduate students who visited us at Georgetown for a few weeks in March 2011. She was very impressed with her experience in the United States, particularly the fact that the existence of a plurality of beliefs does not threaten stability in society (which is sadly not always the case elsewhere). However, after returning to her country, she wrote to me and had this to say: "In the United States, religions are not studied seriously on their own terms. They are studied selectively for the sake of national harmony (not a bad goal, she admitted in subsequent correspondence), but it comes at the expense of the beliefs and principles of one's own religion." She continued, "Even at Georgetown (with which she was also impressed for its embrace of many faiths), you have to put aside your own religion on its terms and follow the university's approach that marginalizes the scientific basis of religion for the sake of common ground." By "the scientific basis of religion," she meant the idea of viewing religion not simply as curious personal choices but as questions worthy of rational consideration. She concluded, "If relativism is the end goal of your study of religion, you will never understand what religion is."

The impressions of this student are arguably limited, but they do bring us back to Tom's essay—and even to Tom himself, who is a leading scholar of religion and religious pluralism (especially as it involves Islam), but it is well known that he does not approach his study of religions as curious personal choices or accidental products of cultural history, nor does he take up the quasi-anthropological approach of participant observation. Rather, he takes the truth claims of Islam very seriously in his capacity as a Christian and Jesuit priest. The various examples he provides of pluralism raise questions about our approach to the study of religious pluralism and what it means for our ability to understand and acquire knowledge of religion. Could Tom have reached such insight into religious pluralism were he not in active relation with the various groups whose beliefs, commitments, and activities he not only studies but also views as rationally compelling? A plurality of religions need not imply relativism in the case where the various believers view one another's claims as worthy of rational consideration. We could extend the question to scholars of religious pluralism. Is the stream attractive to us? Do our scholarly inquiries have impact on our souls, causing us to think ever anew who we are and what the world is? Do we wonder?

We have to admit that our ability to acquire knowledge of such religiously pluralistic enterprises in the public square as Tom has described would be greatly limited if we were not to see them as occasions for the communication of beliefs and commitments as truths per se. It would arguably be difficult to understand religion as such if we engage the study of religious pluralism as instantiations of personal and thus relative values. In what ways do we classify our study of pluralism as expression of religious relativism?

I'm not sure how we'll maneuver through the vagaries of our discipline and ensure its "scientific basis" (especially when it is easily associated with interreligious dialogue), but I've long been intrigued by the gap between what believers say they are all about and what scholars say believers are all about. I wonder if the study of religious pluralism—specifically along the horizon of ideal pluralism—offers a way to address this gap. Implicit in Tom's paper is a challenge: that the study of religious pluralism is not simply a matter of studying many religions as opposed to one. It demands its own epistemology, one that involves a new way of thinking about our role in the academy and its relation to the peoples whose beliefs we study.

13

One Faith, Different Rites
Nicholas of Cusa's New Awareness of Religious Pluralism

PIM VALKENBERG

IN THIS ESSAY I want to explore the meaning of the words "one religion in a variety of rites" that are used by Nicholas of Cusa in his reflections on the possibility of a peaceful solution to religiously motivated warfare. First, I will discuss how Nicholas is nowadays often seen as one of the first theologians who took religious pluralism seriously to such an extent that he may be seen as the precursor of what is now called the pluralistic approach in the present-day Christian theology of religions. Second, I want to investigate the possibility that Nicholas derived the guiding idea behind the words "one religion in a variety of rites" from Islamic sources. If it can be shown that Nicholas derived this idea indirectly from the Qur'an, we would not only have an interesting historical example of a Christian theologian who was not afraid to derive inspiration from the sacred books of other religious traditions, but also a guideline for contemporary Christian-Muslim dialogue. Even though I do not think that Nicholas can really be seen as a religious pluralist in the modern sense of the word, I do think that he had a remarkable awareness of religious pluralism. He developed this awareness after a remarkable event: the fall or—from a different perspective—the conquest of Constantinople in 1453.

NICHOLAS OF CUSA AND THE FALL OF CONSTANTINOPLE

Nikolaus von Kues (1401–1464) was born in Bernkastel-Kues along the Mosel river. A scholar of theology, philosophy, canon law, mathematics and natural sciences, he served the Church as a diplomat and cardinal, and he was involved in attempts to reunite the Western (Latin) and the Eastern (Greek) Church. In order to facilitate the negotiations about this attempt at reunification, Nicholas visited Constantinople sixteen years before it was conquered by the Ottoman Sultan Mehmet II in 1453. It is quite probable that Nicholas gained some knowledge of Islam during his travels, and therefore the fall of Constantinople provoked two reactions from his side.

Nicholas's reaction, written only a few weeks after the fall, was a fervent plea for peace of faith: *De Pace Fidei*. In this fictitious dialogue between representatives of many religions and cultures, Nicholas tests the possibility for a peaceful agreement in one faith. He introduces a form of utopia, an idea about how the world could be if it were in accordance with the intention of its Creator. It has the form of a council, with which Nicholas was familiar in the form of the Ecumenical Council of Basel (1431) at which he had been present. But it was not a meeting of Christians only; it seemed more like a forerunner of the League of Nations or United Nations, with a big number of representatives of the different nations attending, or a kind of Parliament of the World's Religions presided by the Word, Christ himself. Nicholas introduces his fiction as follows: "There was a certain man who, having formerly seen the sites in the regions of Constantinople, was inflamed with zeal for God as a result of those deeds that were reported to have been perpetrated at Constantinople most recently and most cruelly by the King of the Turks. Consequently, with many groanings he beseeched the Creator of all, because of His kindness, to restrain the persecution that was raging more fiercely than usual on account of the difference of rite between the [two] religions."[1] This man, in whom we might well recognize Nicholas himself, seems to be convinced that violence between religions can be overcome if religious persons realize that their religious rites are in fact varieties of one basic faith: *una religio in rituum varietate*. In the imaginary story of *De Pace Fidei*, the King of heaven and earth receives a number of messengers who bring the stories of religious strives and oppression. One of these messengers asks the heavenly King to manifest His face so that the enmity will end and all people realize that "there is only one religion in a variety of

---

1. English translation according to Hopkins, *Nicholas of Cusa's* De Pace Fidei *and* Cribratio Alkorani, 33.

rites."² So this is the utopian ideal for Nicholas of Cusa: if only God would reveal Godself, we would be able to acknowledge that we worship the same God in a variety of rites, and in that case all enmities between religions would cease. Here we hear a fundamental notion in the work of Nicholas the philosopher: the idea of learned ignorance. We know that ultimately we do not know God, we only know how God is worshipped in a variety of rites. But Nicholas is enough of a politician to add a healthy dose of realism here: maybe it is not possible to eliminate the differences of rites, and in that case let the diversity between religions be a source of greater devotion, so that there be one religion and one true worship of God.³

NICHOLAS OF CUSA AND RELIGIOUS PLURALISM

Nicholas of Cusa is probably one of the few medieval thinkers who are mentioned sometimes in present-day discussions of religious pluralism. I will give two recent examples of the appeal that is made to Nicholas in these discussions. We will see that his name can be used to endorse the common points between Islam and Christianity, but some ambiguity in his texts can also lead to false interpretations.

The first example comes from the Yale theologian Miroslav Volf, who uses Nicholas of Cusa in the context of his plea for common ground between Islam and Christianity. In his recent book *Allah: A Christian Response*, Volf refers to Nicholas's response to the fall of Constantinople.⁴

First of all, Volf reminds us that Nicholas, in contrast to most Christian leaders at that time, argued in favor of a non-violent reaction to the fall of Constantinople. While Aeneas Silvius Piccolomini, the later Pope Pius II, started to make plans for a new crusade, and asked his friend Nicholas to help him in doing so, Nicholas himself discussed the idea of organizing a conference between Christians and Muslims in a letter to another friend, John of Segovia.⁵ It is quite possible that he derived the idea of such a conference from his earlier experiences in ecumenical matters. While the idea of Christian unity—in the form of return to Roman Catholicism—was prevalent in his efforts at the Council of Basel or in his visit to Constantinople, it is the idea of unity of faith in the diversity of rites that is leading him in his description of this interreligious council. So, the idea that all people, even

---

2. Ibid, 35 (no. 5).
3. Ibid. (no. 6).
4. See Volf, *Allah: A Christian Response*, chap. 2: "A Catholic Cardinal and the One God of All," 40–59.
5. Volf, *Allah*, 47.

though their specific rites or religious practices may be different, ultimately worship the one true God, forms the basis of Nicholas's idea of the council that is to contribute to the peace of faith.

In his book, Volf underscores the positive approach to Islam that Nicholas embodies: "First, faced with a powerful enemy, Nicholas offers an alternative to war. It consists in argumentative engagement with Muslims. War, he believes, can never resolve issues between Christians and Muslims. The battle to be won is the battle of ideas, not the battle of swords. Hence he recommends a 'conversation,' a 'council,' a 'dialogue.' . . . Nicholas was by nature a mediator, and much of his professional life was devoted to forging unity between estranged groups within the church, above all between the Christian West and the Christian East, between Rome and Constantinople."[6] After Constantinople became the capital of the Ottoman empire, Nicholas extended this idea of forging unity to the relations between Christians and Muslims, and he could do so because of his theological insight that the Christian confession of the Triune God and the Muslim profession of *Tawhīd* can be bridged by the insight in God's ultimate incomprehensibility. "In this way he hoped to show that Christians and Muslims name 'in different names' and worship in 'different ways' the one true God, while at the same time insisting that the Christian faith offers the most reliable and complete revelation of that one God."[7]

Volf distinguishes between two leading ideas in Nicholas's theological approach to interfaith relations. On the one hand, the idea of "one religion in many rites" belongs to what Volf calls his "overall project," while the idea of "all religions as versions of the final and Christian religion" belongs to his general strategy.[8] In *De Pace Fidei*, the overall project is situated in the utopian—or, in terms of Christian theology, eschatological—possibility of universal peace between religions because of the one God that they seek to know and to worship in different forms, while the general strategy is that the diversity between the religions serves as incitement for greater devotion. In contrast to the ecumenical councils that belonged to the reality in which Nicholas of Cusa lived, the interfaith council on Peace between Religions was a utopian idea that did not become part of historical reality, since Christianity and Islam are still separated by theological differences. Yet, it was the genius of Nicholas of Cusa to come up with this utopian ideal

---

6. Ibid., 57–58.
7. Ibid., 56.
8. Ibid., 50.

in answer to the religious violence of an historical clash between Christians and Muslims.⁹

The second example comes from a recent volume on Catholic engagement with world religions. Here, the authors discuss Nicholas of Cusa not as a model of peaceful theological interactions with Muslims, but rather as an enigmatic scholar who tends to be interpreted as a precursor of pluralism—a tendency that the authors seek to discourage. *Catholic Engagement with World Religions*, edited by Karl Becker and Ilaria Morali, has recently been published by Orbis, a publisher that had issued quite a few works pleading for pluralism in the Catholic theology of religions. The point of departure of this book is that until now most approaches to religious pluralism have been those of individual theologians, but now there needs to be an approach that speaks on behalf of the tradition of the Catholic Church. As Becker and Morali make clear in their preface to this book, it was a Muslim professor of theology who pointed out that he could not find any books containing a complete and solid theology of religions from a Catholic point of view.¹⁰

One of the main arguments in this book is that there has hardly been any pluralist approach in the tradition of Catholic Christianity—with one possible exception: Nicholas of Cusa. In her overview of the Early Modern period, Ilaria Morali significantly dates the beginning of this period in 1453, the fall of Constantinople and therefore, the first work she discusses is Nicholas of Cusa's *de Pace Fidei*. After having sketched its contents, she continues: "In this irenic vision of an utopian harmony among religions tending toward an unique wisdom, is it possible to see an anticipation of the current pluralistic vision that denies the claim of Christian revelation to uniqueness and universality?"¹¹ I agree with Morali that this is not the case: Nicholas of Cusa speaks explicitly as a Christian theologian. He is aware of the fact that no human being is able to comprehend God's infinite being, and therefore all human beings seek God in different rites and call him by different names. Since we are human beings, we all have our different rites and images concerning God. But underneath these differences, there is one faith, and as soon as we become aware of that, we will be able to live in peace and harmony. One may surmise that this one religion will be Christianity, according to which God has manifested himself fully in Jesus Christ, but in the fiction of *De Pace Fidei* this remains just a possibility because all attention is focused on the different rites in which the one God is sought. In that

---

9. See Hösle, *Der philosophische Dialog*, 196.

10. See Becker and Morali, *Catholic Engagement with World Religions*, xxxii.

11. Morali, "The Early Modern Period," in *Catholic Engagement with World Religions*, 71–72. See also the summary treatment by Karl Becker in the chapter "Theology of the Christian Economy of Salvation," ibid., 370.

sense, we may say that this first reaction to the fall of Constantinople clearly is an appeal to dialogue and peaceful conversation in which we try to find what unites us, not to strife and warfare in which we seek to articulate what divides us.

Thus, even though I think that it is not correct to associate Nicholas of Cusa with present-day forms of pluralism in the Christian theology of religions, it is understandable to make this connection since the phrase "one religion in a variety of rites" sounds very much like the ideas of two great contemporary champions of religious pluralism: Wilfred Cantwell Smith and John Hick. Consequently, before we will engage in a historical search for the sources of these words, we will succinctly discuss their apparent similarity with contemporary pluralism.

The idea that behind the many different religious practices and institutions one universal human response to the divine reality can be discerned is, of course, widely disseminated. In the history of interpretation of the words *una religio in rituum varietate*, most scholars have referred to the famous concept of *docta ignorantia*, according to which human beings who try to find true knowledge about God ultimately come to the insight that God, because of God's incomprehensibility, cannot be fully known. This idea that leads Nicholas to say that God infinitely surpasses all names, including such names as Father, Son, and Holy Spirit, has its roots in Neo-platonism and the pseudo-Dionysian tradition of apophatic theology.[12] It represents a form of universalism that emphasizes the common points among the monotheistic religions, and this theory has been popular among philosophers since the Enlightenment.[13] At the same time, the word *ritus* indicates that Nicholas's own experiences in ecumenical overtures may have been instrumental in forging this idea as well.[14]

Today, the words "one religion in a variety of rites" most likely remind one of the theology of religious pluralism proposed by Wilfred Cantwell Smith or John Hick. Wilfred Cantwell Smith (1916–2000), a Canadian scholar of comparative religion, became particularly famous for his reflections on the relation between faith and belief.[15] In one of his earliest publications, he distinguished sharply between faith as a universal human characteristic, and the diverse expressions of this faith in the cumulative

---

12. See Valkenberg, "Learned Ignorance and Faithful Interpretation," 34–52.

13. De Gandillac, *La philosophie de Nicolas de Cues*, 43.

14. Seidlmayer, "Una religio in rituum varietate," 145–207; de Gandillac, "Una religio in rituum varietate," 92–105.

15. See Smith, *Faith and Belief.*

traditions of humankind.[16] This leads him to speak of a "history of religion in the singular" in which different religious communities are constantly interacting.[17]

John Hick (1922–2012) is probably the most famous proponent of the pluralistic thesis in the Christian theology of religions. A British philosopher of religion, Hick lectured in both the United Kingdom (Birmingham) and the United States (Claremont). His definitive and comprehensive interpretation of religion appeared in 1989.[18] His pluralistic hypothesis, according to which the different religions can be seen as different interpretations of what Hick calls the Real, is based on the Kantian distinction between the noumenal and the phenomenal: human beings cannot experience the Real *an sich* (as it is in itself) but can only experience the Real as it appears to us in its different manifestations that are interpreted differently (as personal or impersonal) in the different religious traditions of humankind.[19]

We are confronted here with two types of hypotheses. In Nicholas of Cusa's utopian dialogue, the idea that there is one religion in a variety of rites would be seen as true if God would come and reveal the truth. As a servant of the Church, Nicholas knows that God has already come to reveal this truth in Jesus Christ. Yet his literary fiction represents an eschatological desire phrased in prayer: If only God would come and teach us the truth about which we differ, we could live together peacefully. Nicholas's hypothesis is different from that in Smith and Hick which is developed to do justice to religious diversity. Even though they were Christians, Smith and Hick as scholars of religion propose a theology of religions different from that of Nicholas.

More importantly, the awareness of religious pluralism in the twentieth century is different, not only in dimensions but also in nature from that of the fifteenth century. It is therefore not possible to speak of Nicholas of Cusa as a pluralist in the contemporary sense of this word, even though his terminology sometimes sounds strikingly pluralistic. Yet there is unmistakably a form of pluralism behind the notion of "one religion in a variety of rites." If it is not the kind of pluralism that we encounter in the contemporary Christian theology of religions, what kind of pluralism might it be? Another work by Nicholas of Cusa in which he again uses the same phrase might give us an interesting clue.

---

16. Smith, *Meaning and End of Religion*.
17. Smith, *Towards a World Theology*, 3–20.
18. Hick, *Interpretation of Religion*.
19. Ibid., 246–47.

THE ISLAMIC SOURCES OF
"ONE FAITH—DIFFERENT RITES"

While *De Pace Fidei* was Nicholas's first reaction to the fall of Constantinople, he came back to this event later with a second reaction in which he again uses the same idea about the variety of rites and the one faith. This he did seven years later, in a much larger and more explicitly theological book in which he wanted to give a Christian interpretation of the Qur'an, in order to provide Pope Pius II with some materials for a letter to Sultan Mehmet. This book, the *Cribratio alkorani* or "Sifting of the Qur'an," is often seen as a book with a much more polemical approach to Islam than the peaceful setting of *De Pace Fidei*.[20]

While its literary form is different, as the *Sifting of the Qur'an* is an approach to the holy book of Islam with the mindset of a Christian theologian, the same form of pluralism is operative here. More importantly, Nicholas here identifies a specific Islamic way to look at the plurality of messengers and at the guidance given by God to humankind. It is this Islamic view on the history of prophecy and revelation that is behind Nicholas's phrase: "one religion in a variety of rites."

At the beginning of the first book of the *Cribratio alkorani*, Nicholas explains this Islamic point of view on religious plurality as follows:

> [Followers of Muhammad] also say that God sent to all nations indigenous messengers and that [through them] He admonished these nations regarding what they had to believe and had to do in order to be numbered, on the day of judgment, among those who are good and in order to attain unto the Paradise full of joy. [. . .] Accordingly [followers of Muhammad] conclude that if the variety of laws and of rites is found to be present in the identity-of-faith that is exhorted within the various nations by the messengers of God, then indeed this kind of diversity cannot at all prevent one who is obedient from obtaining a fitting reward at the hands of the most gracious and most just Judge.[21]

As in *De Pace Fidei*, the one religion is present in a variety of nations as a hidden guidance that will be fully uncovered by God on the Day of Judgment. In the meantime, the diversity serves as an incitement to do good and in this way arrive at eternal bliss.

It is not difficult to detect the text from the Qur'an that corresponds with what Nicholas of Cusa summarizes here. It is from *surat al-ma'ida*

---

20. See, among others, Daniel, *Islam and the West*, 307.
21. *Cribratio Alkorani*, I.2 (no. 27), trans. Hopkins, 88.

(Qur'an 5:48), often mentioned by Muslims as an important source for their thinking about religious pluralism[22]: "We have assigned a law (*shir'ah*) and a path (*minhaj*) to each of you. If God had so willed, He would have made you one community (*ummatan wahidatan*) but He wanted to test you through that which He has given you, so race to do good: you will all return to God and He will make clear to you the matters you differed about."[23] The Qur'anic idea is that God sent different messengers to different nations that each have their own "belief systems" (to borrow Wifred Cantwell Smith's term) in order to emulate one another in doing good—and God will in the end pass judgment over their differences.

Did Nicholas of Cusa get this idea about the God-given meaningfulness of religious plurality from the Qur'an? Yes, he did, but indirectly. In order to show how, I have to outline the complicated but interesting story of the first encounters between the world of Islam and the world of the Latin West. This story will take us back from Nicholas of Cusa in the fifteenth century to Peter the Venerable and Hermann of Dalmatia in the twelfth century, and finally, to Abdallah ibn Salām who is believed to be an early Jewish convert to Islam in the seventh century and to none other than Prophet Muhammad himself in conversation with Abdallah ibn Salām.

We begin with Nicholas of Cusa and his copy of the Qur'an. In the introduction to the *Cribratio Alkorani* he tells us that he has made quite an effort to obtain a good Latin translation of the Qur'an.[24] Since he could not read Arabic and his efforts to commission a Latin translation failed, in the end he had to settle for the twelfth-century translation by Robert of Ketton that was part of the so-called Toledan collection: that is, the translations commissioned by Peter the Venerable, Abbot of Cluny, in Toledo around 1140.[25] Interestingly, Peter's translation project was inspired by the same idea as Nicholas's *De Pace Fidei*: to prefer the battle of words over the battle of arms—the Crusades—as reaction to the emerging political power of Islam.[26] The Toledan collection was for a long time the main instrument for the Christian West to become acquainted with the world of Islam, and it has been reprinted many times since its first printing in 1543 by the Reformed

---

22. See Valkenberg, *Sharing Lights on the Way to God*, 152–62.

23. Qur'an 5:48 in the interpretation by Abdel Haleem, *Qur'an: English Translation and Parallel Arabic Text*, 117. I added a transliteration of the most important Arabic words in this text.

24. *Cribratio Alkorani*, prologue (nos. 2–4), translation Hopkins, pages 75–76.

25. See Kritzeck, *Peter the Venerable and Islam*.

26. Kritzeck, *Peter the Venerable and Islam*, 21.

theologian Theodor Buchmann or Bibliander in Basel, with introductory essays by Martin Luther and Philipp Melanchthon.[27]

Writing a century earlier, Nicholas of Cusa used a manuscript that can still be consulted today since it has been preserved in his own personal library. The Toledan collection did contain the first Latin translation of the Qur'an by Robert of Ketton, but also a few other works that shed some light on the history of Islam, among them a work entitled *Doctrina Machumet*, or the Teaching of Muhammad, translated by Hermann of Dalmatia in 1143.[28]

It is in this book on the teaching of Muhammad that Nicholas of Cusa made a marginal note: *fides una, ritus diversus*: one faith, different rites. This marginal note indicates, according to scholars Erich Meuthen and Ludwig Hagemann, that Nicholas of Cusa derived his idea of the diversity of rites coexisting with one universal faith from the world of Islam.[29] The word "derived" might suggest too much, since Nicholas could not have noticed the importance of the phrase in the text translated by Hermann of Dalmatia if he had not had similar notions in his mind dating from his earlier studies of Canon Law and his experiences at the Council of Basel.[30] But there is clear textual evidence that an Islamic source occasioned him to make a note that would have—in its rephrasing in *De Pace Fidei*—such a lasting influence.

What is this book whose Latin translation inspired Nicholas of Cusa to write down the association that—according to Hagemann—would lead him to his famous *una religio in rituum varietate*? The work is known in its Arabic original as the *Masā'il* or "Questions" attributed to Abdallah ibn Salām. The genre of this book is well-known in early Islamic apologetics: a group of Jews (or Christians, for that matter) come to Prophet Muhammad and pose him some questions the answers to which, according to their tradition, are

---

27. Ibid., viii. A somewhat later edition from 1550 is reproduced on the internet by the *Bibliothèque Nationale de France*: gallica.bnf.fr. The first part of the title in Latin is: *Machumetis Saracenorum principis ejusque successorum vitae, doctrina, ac ipse Alcoran*. The text is reprinted by *Les Mondes Humanistes* (GRAC—UMR 5037) in 2010.

28. See Pijper, *Het boek der duizend vragen*, 4.

29. See Meuthen, "Der Dialogus concludens Amedistarum errorem ex gestis et doctrina concilii Basiliensis," 11–114, in an historical note on pp. 58–62. Ludwig Hagemann discusses the origin of the formula in *Nicolai de Cusa Cribratio Alkorani*, 223 (in a note on the text quoted earlier from book I.2 [no. 27]): "*Verba 'fides una, ritus diversus' a Nicolao in margine adscripta magni ad illam Nicolai sententiam 'religio una in rituum varietate' (De Pace 1 n.6) momenti sunt. Si quaeremus, quibus e fontibus ea doctrina hausta sit, dubium non potest esse, quin Doctrina fons et origo illius sententiae sit.*" A short description also in Biechler, "Interreligious Dialogue," 270–96, here 279.

30. This is the point that Erich Meuthen makes in MFCG 8, 61: "Sehr verschiedene Wurzeln speisen also die Frucht der cusanischen >Toleranz<-Idee."

known only to a true prophet. Of course, in the Muslim tradition, Muhammad provides the answers and, as a result, the Jews convert to Islam.

The author of the *Masā'il* is Abdallah ibn Salām, who was well-known and was mentioned quite a few times in early Islamic sources such as the *hadith* collections.[31] Unfortunately, the contents of such works as of the *Masā'il* are not very stable because copyists and editors in the Arabic world tended to add questions of their own into the text. Because the Latin text of the translation by Hermann of Dalmatia is made of a relatively old version of the text, it is often considered to be the most reliable textual basis of this work.[32]

The *Doctrina Mahumet* describes how Muhammad in Medina is informed by Gabriel that a delegation of four Jewish religious leaders, led by *Abdia iben Salon* (Abdallah ibn Salām), is about to visit him.[33] Abdia explains that he has come to question Muhammad about things that are not clear in their Jewish faith. The first question is: "Are you a prophet (*propheta*) or a messenger (*nuncius*)?" Muhammad replies: "God has made me both a prophet and a messenger." Abdia asks: "Do you preach your law or the law of God (*lex Dei*)?" When Muhammad answers that he preaches the law of God, Abdia asks what this law is, and Muhammad answers: "Faith (*fides*)." When asked which faith, Muhammad responds with the two basic tenets of monotheism and resurrection of the dead. Abdia then asks: "How many laws of God are there?" Muhammad responds: "There is one law of God." "But what about the prophets that have come before you?," asks Abdia. Muhammad responds: "The law or the faith of the prophets is one, but the rites of the different ones were of course different."[34] The discussion then goes on about whether people can attain paradise by faith (*fides*), by certain beliefs (*credulitas*), or by works (*opere*). This discussion in the *Doctrina Mahumet* comes close to the context and the terminology of the qur'anic *surah al-ma'ida* that Nicholas of Cusa quoted at the beginning of his *Cribratio Alkorani*: God could have made us one community, but He has given us different rites and customs in order for us to rival one another by doing good, and in the end God will pass judgment about the differences.

---

31. See, for instance, the footnote added in the Qur'an-translation by Muhammad Muhsin Khan and Muhammad Taqi-ud-Din Al-Hilali, Riyadh: Darussalam, 1996, 165–166 with reference to Qur'an 5:66, from *Sahih al-Bukhari*, 5/3938.

32. Pijper, *Het boek der duizend vragen*, 40. Kritzeck, *Peter the Venerable and Islam*, 73–74, describes a manuscript (MS 1162 of the *Bibliothèque de l'Arsenal*) that he believes to be the original Toledan collection, written in Spain before 1150 and bound in Cluny shortly thereafter.

33. Latin quotations are from the Bibliander edition, fol. 189–90.

34. *Lex quidem, siue fides, omnium una, sed ritus diuersorum nimirum diuersi.*

After this short discussion of these fundamental issues in Islamic theology, the Latin text of the *Doctrina Mahumet* continues with a discussion of the book that Muhammad claims to have received from God, and then it goes on with a number of seemingly unconnected issues: questions about the meaning of numbers, about God's creation of the heavenly bodies, and riddles such as "what woman came forth only from a man, and what man only from a woman?" What these seemingly disparate matters have in common is that regular human beings do not know the truth about them, but a true prophet knows how to answer the questions and riddles. Since Muhammad succeeds in responding to Abdallah's challenges, the Jewish delegation accepts his being a true Prophet and consequently converts to Islam.[35] This means that the remark about the one law or faith and the diversity of rites also functions in the context of what we may call Islamic "prophetology" which has always been one of the foremost issues in dialogues and apologetics between Muslims and Jews, for instance in the *Kuzari* by Judah Halevi.[36]

In order to know what the phrase in Islamic theology was that Hermann of Dalmatia translated as *Lex / fides una, sed ritus diversi*, we need to go back to the Arabic text of the *Masā'il*, but as I already indicated, there is as yet no critical edition of this text, and the history of this text is very unstable.[37] I was able to find an Arabic text version on the Internet, but this version clearly represents a much later version of the text and a stricter form of Islamic apologetics than the text translated by Hermann of Dalmatia. Yet we may assume that the basic concepts have been preserved even if the theological context in this Arabic version represents a later development.

When we retrace the Latin phrase about the one *lex* or *fides* and the diversity of *ritus* back to its Arabic roots, we will find that it matches perfectly with Islamic prophetology: Muslims believe in a plurality of prophets and scriptures, because God has revealed God's guidance through different rites. Yet, at the same time, there is only one true faith that is—in accordance with the apologetic style of the text—immediately identified with the religion of Islam. In Muhammad's answer to Abdallah Ibn Salām's question about the message that he brings as prophet and messenger, we find Muhammad saying, according to the Arabic text:[38] "There is one *dīn*," a word that is usually

35. See Kritzeck, *Peter the Venerable and Islam*, 91–93 (The solution of the riddle is: Eve—from Adam—and Christ—from the Virgin Mary).

36. See the introductory remarks by Barbara Roggema, Marcel Poorthuis, and Pim Valkenberg in *The Three Rings: Textual Studies in the Historical Trialogue of Judaism, Christianity and Islam*.

37. See Kritzeck, *Peter the Venerable and Islam*, 89.

38. I quote a contemporary Arabic version on the Internet, which represents a more advanced stage of Islamic theology, as most Arabic text versions do (see Pijper, *Het boek*

translated as "religion," but it can be translated as "Law" as well, because it is the Law of God. In the medieval reception of Islam in the West, we often see that these terms, *religio* and *lex* are used interchangeably. Muhammad continues: "The religion of the prophets was the pure religion of God, the religion of His angels, and the religion of Islam."[39] When Abdallah ibn Salām asks, how many religions (or Laws) of God there are, Muhammad answers: "One religion, and that is Islam."[40] In this later version of the text, the word *islām* in Arabic is interpreted as referring to the institutionalized religion of Islam, rather than as an attitude of faith as submitting (or rather: aligning) oneself to God's will and guidance. But in older versions of the *masā'il*, the attitude of faith might be the subject of discussion, since the text makes the famous distinction between *islām* as the enacting of the five pillars of Islam and *imān* as believing in the six basic tenets of the faith.

After this discussion, Abdallah wants to know how many paths or ways there were—the question "how many?" refers back to similar questions concerning the number of prophets. He uses the Arabic word *shir'ah*, which literally refers to the path to the water well, which is essential for survival in the desert—the word *shari'ah* is derived from the same root.[41] Muhammad answers: "There were different paths (or laws) with the peoples of the past."[42] Thus we have two words, *dīn* and *shir'ah*, that can both be translated as "law." Precisely this ambiguity is characteristic of the issue at hand between Abdallah and Muhammad, and it creates a tension that is germane to Islamic theology: there are many customary laws (plural: *sharā'i*) while there is one Law of God at the same time. Again, in the context of Jewish-Muslim dialogue one is reminded of the role of *halakhah*, the "way to walk" and enact the Torah of God.

Even though the theology in this Arabic text is clearly not pluralist since it immediately identifies the one religion or *dīn* of the prophets with the established religion of Islam, we can still recognize the Qur'anic theology of religions from *surah al-Ma'ida* (5:48) here, in the verse that gave Nicholas of Cusa occasion to make his remark about *fides una, ritus diversus* in his *Cribratio Alkorani*. "If God had willed, He could have made you one community, but He has given each of you a law and a way, and He will judge about the differences on the day of the resurrection." So, *fides una, ritus*

---

der duizend vragen, 39). The text quoted can be found on: cb.rayaheen.net/showthread.php?tid=27739.

39. 'ala dīn Allah al-khālis wa dīn malākatihi wa dīn al-islām
40. Qāla: ya Ibn Salām dīn wāhid wa-huwa al-islām
41. kam kānat al-sharā'i?
42. kānat mukhtalifa fi al-umam al-mādiya

diversus is a translation of *dīn wāhid, sharā'i'* (or *manāhij*) *mukhtalifa*. There is one religion revealed by God, but there are different ways or customs or rites in which this religion is enacted by the different peoples.[43]

Being the latest of the three monotheistic or Abrahamic religions, the religion of Islam had to relate itself to the other two Abrahamic religions from the beginning, and therefore we find a distinct representation of their relationships in the Qur'an. On the one hand, it is clear that the different heirs of Abraham have different ways in which they see themselves be guided by God towards salvation. These different rites or customs go back to the different prophets that were sent to the different nations in the past. On the other hand, there is one pure Law or religion revealed by God to guide humankind. Of course Muslims will generally say that this one religion is perfectly embodied in the Qur'an as God's message to Prophet Muhammad, and in Islam, while it is less perfectly embodied in Judaism and Christianity insofar as they do not preserve God's guidance in *Taurat* and *Injīl* unadulterated. There is a plurality of Prophets and a plurality of Scriptures, and consequently a plurality of religious customs and rites about which God will tell the truth on the Day of Judgment. Yet there is one true *dīn*, one religion that consists of human beings aligning themselves to the will and guidance of the one true God. And, according to the majority of Muslim theologians, this one religion exists in the religion of Islam. In a similar way the Church of Christ is said by the Second Vatican Council to subsist in the Catholic Church. In both cases, these concepts can be interpreted in a pluralist sense, though historically, they usually have been interpreted in an inclusivist way. This explains how present-day Islamic theologians can use this distinction between the one universal faith and the different belief systems of the different religions, referring to the unity of *dīn* on the one hand, and to the plurality of laws and ways on the other, as a qur'anic support for a pluralist or universalist theology of religions.[44] When Nicholas of Cusa plays with this idea in his *De Pace Fidei*, he plays with an idea that he apparently picked up during his study of the Toledan collection. And it is of course not coincidental that Wilfred Cantwell Smith formulated his idea of

---

43. Cuypers, *The Banquet: A Reading of the Fifth Sura of the Qur'an*, 242 remarks that the word *minhaj* ("path") in 5:48 "in its technical meaning of 'religious custom,' way of life, is borrowed from rabbinical language." The same is true for the entire *Masā'il*: Muhammad responds to Jewish questions about religion and laws.

44. See, for instance, the Iranian scholar of qur'anic exegesis Sayyid Muhammad Husayn al-Tabataba'i in his twenty-volume *al-Mizān fī tafsīr al-Qur'an*, Beirut 1973–74. Also, Akrami, "Particularity and Universality in the Qur'an," 3–13. For a universalist rather than pluralist interpretation, see Shah-Kazemi, *The Other in the Light of the One*.

the one basic faith and the multiplicity of religious belief systems during his study of Islam as well.

Does that make Nicholas of Cusa a pluralist in the modern sense of the word? I think that it would be anachronistic to think so. For Nicholas, the one religion of God was clearly revealed in Christ who as the Word presided over Nicholas' congress of faiths, similar to the way that the later Arabic text of the *Masā'il* of Abdallah ibn Salām clearly identifies the one religion of God with Islam. Neither of them were pluralists in the modern sense of the word. But they were at least aware of the fact of religious plurality and of the role of this plurality in God's plans with the world.

The conquest of Constantinople by the Ottomans made Nicholas of Cusa think about the difference between the ideal world in which God would reveal Godself and we would all realize that there is one faith in a variety of rites, and our present-day reality in which a full knowledge of God's plans with the world escapes us and we are left with rival religions that seem to betray true faith by engaging in strife and warfare. This awareness of the difference between the eschatological ideal, sketched so powerfully in *De Pace Fidei*, and the reality of religious rivalry engaged Nicholas in deeper study of the Qur'an in order to understand better the nature of the rival religion. While doing so, he discovered how the Qur'an offers another rivalry that might bring us closer to the God who will in the end pass judgment about our differences: the endeavor to emulate one another in doing good. Even though he was a scholar and not a peace activist, it might have been this form of pluralism that inspired Nicholas in his phrasing "one religion—many rites": there are many different ways to do good and serve others in order to come closer to God during our lives here on earth, knowing that we do not know the full truth and that God in the end will tell us about the true sense of our differences. It is significant that Nicholas was stimulated in his thinking by a text from the Qur'an that still is used by many contemporary Muslims as source of inspiration for their engagement in promoting interfaith dialogue.

BIBLIOGRAPHY

Abdel Haleem, Muhammad A. S. *The Qur'an: English Translation and Parallel Arabic Text*. Oxford: Oxford University Press, 2010.

Akrami, Seyed Amir. "Particularity and Universality in the Qur'an." Pt. 1, chap. 1 in *Communicating the Word: Revelation, Translation, and Interpretation in Christianity and Islam*, edited by David Marshall. Washington, DC: Georgetown University Press, 2011.

Becker, Karl J., and Ilaria Morali, eds. *Catholic Engagement with World Religions: A Comprehensive Study*. Maryknoll, NY: Orbis, 2010.

Bibliander [Theodor Buchmann], ed. *Machumetis Saracenorum principis ejusque successorum vitae, doctrina, ac ipse Alcoran*. Basel: Oporinus, 1550.

Biechler, James E. "Interreligious Dialogue." Chap. 9 in *Introducing Nicholas of Cusa: A Guide to a Renaissance Man*, edited by C. M. Bellitto et al. New York: Paulist, 2004.

Cuypers, Michel. *The Banquet: A Reading of the Fifth Sura of the Qur'an*. Miami: Convivium, 2009.

Daniel, Norman. *Islam and the West: The Making of an Image*. Oxford: Oneworld, 1993.

Decorte, Jos. Introduction to *Nicolaas van Cusa: Godsdienstvrede*, translated from the Latin by Jos Lievens, 7–46. Kampen: Agora, 2000. Originally written 1453.

De Gandillac, Maurice. *La philosophie de Nicolas de Cues*. Paris: Aubier, 1941.

———. "Una religio in rituum varietate." In *Nikolaus von Kues als Promotor der Ökumene*, edited by Rudolf Haubst, 92–105. Mainz: Matthias-Grünewald, 1971.

Elliott, Neil. "From 'The Heresy of the Saracens' to 'The War against the Turks': A Study of Later Medieval Understandings of Islam from Peter the Venerable to Martin Luther." Occasional papers 9. Centre for the Study of Islam and Christian-Muslim Relations, University of Birmingham, 2001.

Esposito, John L. *The Future of Islam*. Oxford: Oxford University Press, 2010.

Glei, Reinhold, ed. *Petrus Venerabilis: Schriften zum Islam*. Altenberge: CIS, 1985.

Hagemann, Ludwig, ed. *Nicolai de Cusa Cribratio Alkorani*. Opera Omnia 8. Hamburg: Meiner, 1986.

Hick, John. *An Interpretation of Religion: Human Responses to the Transcendent*. London: Macmillan, 1989.

Hopkins, Jasper. *Nicholas of Cusa's* De Pace Fidei *and* Cribratio Alkorani: *Translation and Analysis*. Minneapolis: Banning, 1990.

Hösle, Vittorio. *Der philosophische Dialog*. München: Beck, 2006.

Kritzeck, James. *Peter the Venerable and Islam*. Princeton: Princeton University Press, 1964.

Kutleša, Stipe. "Croatian Philosophers I: Hermann of Dalmatia (1110–1154)." *Prolegomena* 3 (2004) 57–71.

Lamarque, Henri. "Vies et doctrine de Mahomet, chef des Sarrasins et de ses successeurs, avec le Coran proprement dit: Présentation." *Les Mondes Humanistes* (GRAC – UMR 5037), septembre 2010, i–iii. http://sites.univ-lyon2.fr/lesmondeshumanistes/wp-content/uploads/2010/09/Le-Coran-latin-de-Bibliander1.pdf.

Meuthen, Erich. "Der Dialogus concludens Amedistarum errorem ex gestis et doctrina concilii Basiliensis." *Mitteilungen und Forschungsbeiträge der Cusanus-Gesellschaft* 8 (1970) 11–114.

Morali, Ilaria. "The Early Modern Period." In *Catholic Engagement with World Religions: A Comprehensive Study*, edited by K. J. Becker and I. Morali, 69–90. Maryknoll, NY: Orbis, 2010.

Pijper, Guillaume F. *Het boek der duizend vragen*. PhD diss., University of Leiden, 1924. Leiden: Brill, 1924.

Ricci, Ronit. "A Jew on Java, a Model Malay Rabbi and a Tamil Torah Scholar: Representations of Abdullah Ibnu Salam in the *Book of One Thousand Questions*." *Journal of the Royal Asiatic Society*, series 3, 18 (2008) 481–95.

Roggema, Barbara, et al., eds. *The Three Rings: Textual Studies in the Historical Trialogue of Judaism, Christianity and Islam*. Publications of the Thomas Instituut te Utrecht n.s. 11. Leuven: Peeters, 2005.

Seidlmayer, Michael. "'Una religio in rituum varietate': Zur Religionsauffassung des Nikolaus von Cues." *Archiv für Kulturgeschichte* 36 (1954) 145–207.

Shah-Kazemi, Reza. *The Other in the Light of the One: The Universality of the Qur'an and Interfaith Dialogue*. Cambridge: Islamic Texts Society, 2006.

Smith, Wilfred C. *Faith and Belief*. Princeton: Princeton University Press, 1979.

———. *The Meaning and End of Religion: A New Approach to the Religious Traditions of Mankind*. New York: Mentor, 1964.

———. *Towards a World Theology: Faith and the Comparative History of Religion*. London: Macmillan, 1981.

Valkenberg, Pim. "Learned Ignorance and Faithful Interpretation of the Qur'an in Nicholas of Cusa (1401–1464)." Chap 2 in *Learned Ignorance: Intellectual Humility among Jews, Christians, and Muslims*, edited by James L. Heft et al. New York: Oxford University Press, 2011.

———. *Sharing Lights on the Way to God: Muslim–Christian Dialogue and Theology in the Context of Abrahamic Partnership*. Amsterdam: Rodopi, 2006.

Volf, Miroslav. *Allah: A Christian Response*. New York: HarperOne, 2011.

14

Lateral and Hierarchical Religious Difference in the Qur'an
Muslima Theology of Religious Pluralism

JERUSHA TANNER LAMPTEY

How does the Qur'anic discourse depict the phenomenon of religious diversity, specific other religions and, more generally, the religious "other"? While seemingly simple, this question, in fact, is rife with significant theological and practical implications. Theologically, it is intimately connected to the understanding of God and God's action in the world. It is also intertwined with the understanding of humankind and the purpose of human creation. In fact, this complex question in many ways defines the theological relationship between God and humankind; the Qur'ān's depiction of religious otherness and the religious "other" is also—and always—a depiction of God and the religious "self."

Practically, the depiction of the religious "other" assumes great importance in light of the uniqueness and ubiquity of the modern reality of religious diversity. Today, we encounter diversity in a more intimate and intricate manner. Such encounters frequently prompt inquiry into convergences and divergences in belief and practice, and discussions of appropriate forms of interreligious interaction. Moreover, ongoing waves of religious violence and oppression force us to ask difficult questions about the relationship between depictions of religious diversity, other specific religions, and religious "others," intolerance, and oppression. Although there is not an automatic and direct connection between negative depictions of the religious "other" and intolerant actions, negative depictions can easily be coopted to further incite intolerance and even violence among individuals and groups.

THE "RELIGIOUS OTHER" IN THE QUR'AN

In addition to its enduring theological and practical import, the question of how the Qur'an depicts the religious "other" is also inherently complex. The Qur'an explicitly and extensively discusses the topic of religious difference, sometimes referencing specific groups, such as the *al-naṣārā*, *yahūd*, and *ahl ul-kitāb* (commonly translated as the Nazarenes/Christians, the Jews and the People of Scripture) but also using more general terminology, such as believers, hypocrites, disbelievers, and submitters. However, throughout this discourse, the Qur'an does not consistently depict religious otherness as acceptable or unacceptable. At times, otherness is positively evaluated and at others, it is blatantly scorned:

> Those who believe, the Jews, the Nazarenes, and the Sabians—all those who believe in God and the Last Day and do good—will have their reward with their Lord. No fear for them, nor will they grieve.[1]

> We have assigned a law and a path to each of you. If God had so willed, He would have made you one community, but He wanted to test you through that which He has given you, so race to do good: you will all return to God and He will make clear to you the matters you differed about.[2]

> The hypocrites will be in the lowest depths of Hell, and you will find no one to help them.[3]

Moreover, the extensive—and seemingly ambivalent—discussion of religious otherness is tangled together with repeated Qur'anic affirmations of continuity and commonality (or sameness) between religious communities, revelations and prophets:

1. Qur'an 2:62.
2. Qur'an 5:48 (excerpt).
3. Qur'an 4:145.

> We have sent other messengers before you—some We have mentioned to you and some We have not—and no messenger could bring about a sign except with God's permission . . .[4]

> We sent to you [Muhammad] the Scripture with the truth, confirming the Scriptures that came before it, and with final authority over them.[5]

These various elements of the Qur'anic discourse on religious otherness have prompted the articulation of a variety of hermeneutical approaches, all of which aim to address—or make sense of—this complexity and apparent ambiguity. While one possible approach would be to deem the text inconsistent and thereby account for the apparent mixed messages, this strategy has not been employed by most historical or contemporary Islamic scholars, scholars who largely approach the Qur'an as the inerrant Word of God. Rather Islamic scholars have largely preferred hermeneutical strategies that rely upon notions such as chronology, progressive revelation, abrogation, distinctions between particular and universal verses, and prioritization of Qur'anic principle or values. These strategies, with varying degrees of authority, have resulted in and continue to result in diverse depictions of the overarching Qur'anic view of the religious "other."

The contemporary Islamic discourse in the United States bears witness to this hermeneutical diversity, with scholars voicing interpretations of the Qur'anic discourse that can be grouped into two dominant trends: first, there are those that prioritize the message of religious sameness, downplaying—even ignoring—Qur'anic discussions of difference. This trend is evident, for example, in the writings of Asghar Ali Engineer and Abdulaziz Sachedina. Concerned with providing a theological justification for human rights and civil pluralism, Engineer downplays the particularities of the Islamic tradition and advances a view that the Qur'an is primarily concerned with general ethical action not specific tenets of belief or practice.[6] Sachedina argues that the shared human nature bestowed on all at the time of creation takes precedence over and reduces the importance of the particular—and conflict-producing—religious differences introduced through revelation.[7]

Comprising the second major trend are those interpretations that aim to simultaneously account for both religious sameness and difference, but are able to do so only through models that depict religious communities as

---

4. Qur'an 40:78 (excerpt).
5. Qur'an 5:48 (excerpt).
6. Engineer, "Islam and Pluralism."
7. Sachedina, "Qurān and Other Religions."

isolated or hierarchically ranked. Two prominent examples of this trend are found in the work of Seyyed Hossein Nasr and Muhammad Legenhausen. Nasr draws an analogy to solar systems, arguing for the integrity of different religious universes and their particularities. This approach manages to uphold both sameness and difference, but does so only by treating religious universes as if they are homogeneous wholes that exist in isolation from one another.[8] Critiquing most pluralistic views of religious diversity for devaluing religious practice and religious imperative, Legenhausen distinguishes between questions of truth, salvation and correct religion and argues that, while other religions may be true and salvific, only Islam is the correct religion—the divinely commanded religion—in contemporary times.[9]

TWO CONCEPTIONS OF THE "RELIGIOUS OTHER"

Without delving further into the nuances and many valuable insights of these interpretations, what is central to note is that—irrespective of their ultimate evaluation of the religious "other" or of religious diversity—both trends are premised upon a common conception of difference. In the majority of these interpretations, difference is conceived of as that which unambiguously divides humanity through the erection of clear and static boundaries. In the first trend—the prioritization of sameness—such boundaries are seen as impediments to the ultimate goal of tolerant interaction; boundaries and difference create conflict. Thus difference is downplayed, while sameness is emphasized. In the second trend—the attempt to simultaneously affirm sameness and difference—divisions and boundaries are upheld in an effort to address Qur'anic messages on the value and divine intentionality of difference. Religions are therefore depicted as bounded wholes that either do not—or ideally would not—interact at all or are related only through some sort of evaluative hierarchy, such as supersession or completeness. Separation and hierarchical evaluation uphold boundaries and difference, and, although sameness is acknowledged, it is not permitted to eradicate or blur such boundaries.

This conception of religious difference as being intimately tied to boundaries, however, is problematic for two primary reasons. First, it leads to an excessive focus on the boundaries themselves and on the process of identifying that which demarcates a boundary. The boundary assumes great prominence as the symbol and marker of the division between insiders and

---

8. Nasr, "Religion and Religions."

9. Legenhausen, "Muslim's Non-reductive Religious Pluralism." Legenhausen previously wrote on this topic in *Islam and Religious Pluralism*.

outsiders, a symbol or marker that is depicted as clear, static, and unambiguously defined. This sort of definition is only achieved through the identification of a *simple* and *singular* threshold criterion. In the contemporary discourse, some such criteria are recognition of Muhammad as a prophet or adherence to the specific rituals of Islam. While these are certainly important components in the Qur'anic discourse on religious otherness, they are not the only components. Therefore, an excessive focus on boundaries necessary leads to a reduction or simplification of the complexity of the Qur'anic discourse, as well as of the nature of religious identity and interaction.

The second reason why the shared conception is problematic is that it presupposes a certain genre of religious "other." If religious difference creates clear and static boundaries, then the religious "other" in this scenario is one that is wholly discrete, clearly identified, clearly bounded. It is an "other" that is unmistakably distinct from the religious "self." However, this genre of religious "other"—not to mention religious "self"—again reduces the complexity of the Qur'anic discourse. The religious "other" of the Qur'an is unique and perplexing in that it is an "other" that is simultaneously the same as and different from the "self."

Some insights drawn from the work of Jonathan Z. Smith can help to clarify this distinction. Smith acknowledges this boundary-focused view of the "other" when he discusses the binary opposition of WE/THEY, or IN/OUT.[10] This stark dualism is characterized by a preoccupation with clearly defined, impenetrable boundaries, limits, thresholds, and pollution. As such, the primary mode of interaction depicted by this binary is a double process of containment, that is, keeping in and keeping out. However, Smith contends that "othering"—the process whereby we make sense of the "other"—is much more complex than the basic opposition of us and them. Othering actually involves multiple possible relations with the "other." Intriguingly, the deepest intellectual issues arise when the other is "too much like us," when the other is the *proximate* other in distinction from the distant other. Distant others are so clearly distinguished that they are insignificant and voiceless; since they are easily defined and contained, they require minimal exegetical effort. The proximate other, though, is much more complex and amorphous; it is the "other" who claims to be "you." As such, the proximate other presents a direct and perpetual challenge to the worldview and identity of the "self," forcing ongoing modification, reconsideration, and redrawing of boundaries. Proximate difference does not erect discrete and static boundaries, but on the contrary provokes questions about dynamic and multiple relations between the self and the other.

---

10. Smith, *Relating Religion*, 230.

In my view, the Qur'anic religious "other" is *this* genre of other; it is the proximate religious other. As such, neither of the two prominent trends in contemporary Islamic discourse effectively accounts for both the proximity *and* the otherness of the proximate religious other. The trend of prioritizing sameness partially addresses proximity, but neglects otherness by devaluing difference. The attempt to affirm both sameness and difference, conversely, neglects the full complexity of proximity by establishing clearly defined and bounded religious wholes.

This inability to effectively account for both proximity and otherness arises from the shared, underlying conception of difference evident in both trends in contemporary Islamic thought. Therefore, it is essential to identify and articulate an alternative conception of religious difference. It is necessary to *think differently about difference itself.*

THE "RELIGIOUS OTHER" AND PIETY (*TAQWĀ*)

In my research, I draw resources for this "rethinking" of difference from Muslim women's interpretation of the Qur'an—primarily the hermeneutical and theoretical approaches of Amina Wadud, Riffat Hassan, and Asma Barlas[11]—and feminist theology. While neither field is primarily concerned with religious difference, both fields offer pointed critiques of dominant paradigms of human difference (specifically sexual difference). In doing so, they provide significant insights into and conceptual fodder for the articulation of alternative models of difference. These insights and raw conceptual materials can be generalized and critically extended to the topic of religious difference. In the remainder of this essay, I will highlight one such extension drawn from Muslim women's reinterpretation and its rich implications for reinterpreting the Qur'anic discourse on the religious "other."

Wadud and Barlas maintain that the only basis for differentiating hierarchically between individuals is *taqwā*, or piety. In her work on the Qur'an, sex and gender, Asma Barlas draws a distinction between difference that differentiates laterally and difference that differentiates hierarchically. Her main contention is that sexual difference (that is, biological difference) is divinely intended and purposeful, and as such should be acknowledged, rather than ignored or downplayed. However, she contends, divinely intended sexual difference only differentiates "laterally"—meaning it distinguishes

---

11. Wadud, *Qur'an and Woman*; Hassan, "Feminism in Islam," 248–78; and Barlas, *"Believing Women" in Islam.*

individuals without ascribing value.[12] Individuals, therefore, cannot—or should not—be assessed on the basis of their sexual biology.[13]

In addition to this non-evaluative form of difference—lateral difference—Barlas identifies another genre, hierarchical difference, which *is* associated with evaluation and assessment. Citing Surah 49, āya 13,[14] Barlas argues that hierarchical difference is evaluated only with respect to the concept of *taqwā* (God consciousness, or piety). *Taqwā* is tied to and assessed on the individual level, rather than based on affiliation with a particular group, that is, men or women. This, however, does not mean that an individual can strive for or achieve *taqwā* in isolation. *Taqwā* is always defined in the context of multiple relationships. Every individual is capable and responsible for him or herself, but capacity and responsibility can only be actualized relationally and socially. In arguing for the distinction between lateral and hierarchical difference, Barlas aims to illuminate the fact that there *are* multiple genres of difference and to challenge the pervasive conflation and static linking of the two.

Building upon Barlas' distinction, it is possible to outline defining characteristics for both genres of difference, beginning with hierarchical difference. First, hierarchical difference is connected with accountability, judgment, rewards, and punishments; it is evaluative. Second, evaluation is carried out only on the basis of conformity or non-conformity with the concept of *taqwā*. Third, the evaluation of *taqwā*—or hierarchical difference—is performed on the individual level. It is, however, always connected to social and relational manifestations. In other words, every person is assessed individually, but that assessment is integrally related to the individual's interactions with others, both divine and human.

There are also three defining characteristics of lateral difference. First, lateral difference is a group phenomenon. It does not primarily refer to individual particularities, but rather to patterns and trends of difference at the group level. The fact that lateral difference is a group phenomenon, however, does not mean that lateral groups are completely discrete; groupings that denote lateral difference can overlap, intersect and even be inclusive of other lateral groups. Second, lateral difference is divinely intended. Lateral difference, therefore, is not the result of degeneration, human error, or corruption. It is willed by God for a teleological purpose and, as such, should

---

12. Barlas, *"Believing Women" in Islam*, 145.

13. Ibid., 11.

14. Qur'an 49:13: "People, We created you all from a single man and a single woman, and made you into races and tribes so that you should know one another. In God's eyes, the most honored of you are the ones most mindful of Him [has the most *taqwā*]: God is all knowing, all aware."

not be targeted for eradication or homogenization. Third, lateral difference never serves as the basis of evaluation. Evaluation is not tied to difference that is divinely intended. Moreover, evaluation is not conducted at the group level. It is important to clarify that this does not mean that there will be *no evaluation* whatsoever within groups of lateral difference; rather, it implies that a singular evaluation will not be uniformly ascribed to an entire group solely on the basis of membership in that group. As a result, in seeking to identify groups of lateral difference within the Qur'anic discourse, the goal is not to find groups that are *never evaluated*, but rather groups that are *partially* and *diversely* evaluated.

HIERARCHICAL AND LATERAL DIFFERENCE

The distinction between lateral and hierarchical difference and the outline of the defining characteristics of both provide a novel roadmap for navigating the Qur'anic discourse on religious difference. By rereading the Qur'anic discourse with an eye to identifying the two genres and understanding the relationship between them, certain pivotal nuances are illuminated. Perhaps the most striking and thought-provoking is that the delineation between hierarchical and lateral difference corresponds with a distinction in terminology.

Hierarchical difference (that is, evaluative, *taqwā*-based, individual difference) is connected to terms and concepts, such as *īmān* (belief), *kufr* (disbelief), *nifāq* (hypocrisy) and *islām* (submission), in all of their various grammatical forms. As the result of comprehensively tracing these concepts throughout the discourse, it becomes apparent that they denote various—and *particular*—manifestations of *taqwā* or the lack thereof. In the Qur'an, the central evaluative role of *taqwā* expressed in 49:13 is coupled with explanations of the multifaceted content of *taqwā*, for example:

> True goodness does not consist in turning your face towards East or West. The truly good are those who believe in God and the Last Day, in the angels, the Scripture, and the prophets; who give away some of their wealth, however much they cherish it, to their relatives, to orphans, the needy, travelers and beggars, and to liberate those in bondage; those who keep up the prayer and pay the prescribed alms; who keep pledges whenever they make them; who are steadfast in misfortune, adversity, and times of danger. These are the ones who are true, and it is they who are **conscious of God** (muttaqū n).[15]

15. Qur'an 2:177.

Hierarchical religious concepts, including *īmān* (belief), *kufr* (disbelief), *nifāq* (hypocrisy) and *islām* (submission), are then continuously juxtaposed to these central features of *taqwā*:

> True **believers** (mu'minūn) are those whose hearts tremble with awe when God is mentioned, whose faith increases when His revelations are recited to them, who put their trust in their Lord.[16]
>
> But **those who believed** (alladhī na āmanū), did good deeds, and humbled themselves before their Lord will be companions in Paradise and there they will stay.[17]
>
> The **disbelievers** (alladhīna kafarū) will remain in doubt about it until the Hour suddenly overpowers them or until torment descends on them on a Day devoid of all hope.[18]
>
> When man suffers some affliction, he prays to his Lord and turns to Him, but once he has been granted a favor from God, he forgets the One he had been praying to and sets up rivals to God, to make others stray from His path. Say, "Enjoy your ingratitude (kufr) for a little while: you will be one of the inhabitants of the Fire."[19]

Moreover, manifestations of the *taqwā*-related concepts of belief, submission, disbelief and hypocrisy are assessed individually:

> You who believe, you are responsible for your own souls; if anyone else goes astray it will not harm you so long as you follow the guidance; you will all return to God, and He will make you realize what you have done.[20]

They are also tied closely to praise and disdain, as well as promises of reward or punishment:

> Who could be better in religion than those who submit ('aslama) themselves wholly to God, do good, and follow the religion of Abraham, who was true in faith (ḥanīf)?[21]

---

16. Qur'an 8:2.
17. Qur'an 11:23.
18. Qur'an 22:55.
19. Qur'an 39:8.
20. Qur'an 5:105.
21. Qur'an 4:125 (excerpt).

> The worst creatures in the sight of God are those who reject (kafarū) Him and will not believe.[22]

> In fact, any who submit ('aslama) themselves wholly to God and do good will have their reward with their Lord: no fear for them, nor will they grieve.[23]

> We shall send those who reject Our revelations (kafarū) to the Fire. When their skins have been burned away, We shall replace them with new ones so that they may continue to feel the pain: God is mighty and wise.[24]

In distinction from the hierarchical concepts of religious difference, lateral religious difference (that is, group difference that is divinely intended, and not the basis of evaluation) is associated with terminology that refers to specific groups, such as *al-naṣārā* (Nazarenes, Christians), *yahūd* (Jews), and *ahl ul-kitāb* (People of Scripture). Tracing these terms throughout the Qur'an, it becomes apparent that they refer to diverse communities that exist as a result of God's will:

> We have assigned a law and a path to each of you. If God had so willed, He would have made you one community, but He wanted to test you through that which He has given you, so race to do good: you will all return to God and He will make clear to you the matters you differed about.[25]

> We have appointed acts of devotion (mansak) for every community (umma) to observe, so do not let them argue with you [Prophet] about this matter. Call them to your Lord—you are on the right path—and if they argue with you, say, "God is well aware of what you are doing."[26]

More notably—and the cause of many interpretive debates—these groups are *partially* and *variously* evaluated. This is highlighted through common refrains that, for example, describe "*some* among the people of the Book" (that is, a part of the larger group) as praiseworthy and others as blameworthy:

---

22. Qurān 8:55.
23. Qur'an 2:112.
24. Qur'an 4:56.
25. Qur'an 5:48 (excerpt).
26. Qur'an 22:67.

> Some of the People of the Scripture believe in God, in what has been sent down to you and in what was sent down to them: humbling themselves before God, they would never sell God's revelation for a small price. These people will have their reward with their Lord: God is swift in reckoning.[27]
>
> Some of the People of the Scripture would dearly love to lead you astray, but they only lead themselves astray, though they do not realize it.[28]

Since such evaluations are partial and diverse, they cannot be prompted by lateral difference, by the communitarian identity. If they were, then they would be holistically and homogeneously applied to the entire group. These evaluations, rather, are prompted by the manifestations of particular forms of hierarchical difference among individual members of the lateral group. This is made even more explicit in other Qur'anic verses that reprimand, for example, those who *disbelieve* (manifest *kufr*) among the People of the Book.[29]

Although this is a very brief and limited introduction to the delineation between hierarchical and lateral religious difference within the Qur'anic discourse, it is enough to indicate certain weighty implications. To begin, the coexistence of divergent assessments of religious "others" has been typically explained through abrogation, chronology, or specification of Qur'anic praise to a very small contingent of the People of the Book or other communities. The reconceptualization of religious difference as consisting of two genres, however, presents an alternative and unique hermeneutical option. The divergent assessments are no longer contradictions, but rather *multiple possible intersections* of lateral and hierarchical difference.

Additionally, if hierarchical and lateral difference are separate genres, they should not be conflated or treated as synonymous. No one hierarchical category (including believers or disbelievers) can be treated as an automatic synonym for a lateral community. People of the Scripture, for example, are not automatically disbelievers based upon their communal affiliation as People of the Scripture. If they are described in this fashion, as disbelievers, it is due to the fact that they manifest disbelief. Conversely if they are described as believers, it is not necessarily because they are rare exemplars or covert converts to the path of Prophet Muhammad; rather, they may be

---

27. Qur'an 3:199.
28. Qur'an 3:69.
29. Qur'an 98:1: "Those who disbelieve (*kafarū*) among the People of the Scripture and the associators were not about to change their ways until they were sent clear evidence."

described as believers because they simply manifest belief. Similarly, yet provocatively, members of Prophet Muhammad's community are not believers because they are members of his community, but rather because—and only if—they manifest belief.

Hierarchical evaluation is never fixed or holistically applied to an entire lateral religious group because it is not ascribed on the basis of communal affiliation; hierarchical religious evaluation is individually assessed. Therefore, while there is hierarchical assessment of *taqwā*, this assessment is not confined to or defined by the boundaries between divinely intended lateral communities. In fact, hierarchical difference is uniquely characterized by its lack of denotative stability. It does not denote or correspond exactly and statically with specific groups. It can cut across and through *all* categories of lateral religious difference, creating various intersections and challenging the notion of discrete and fixed boundaries.

However, the lack of denotative stability in reference to lateral communities should not be misconstrued as indicating that *taqwā* and its related concepts lack definite content. In the Qur'an, hierarchical concepts are specific, evaluative and social; certain actions, behaviors, and beliefs in relation to God and other humans are positively evaluated and others are negatively evaluated. In fact, it is by delineating between the two distinct, yet dynamically interrelated genres that it is possible to navigate between two objectionable extremes, between exclusivism and relativism. By distinguishing between hierarchical and lateral religious difference, it is possible to avoid the presentation of *taqwā* as confined to one reified, lateral community, and also to avoid the depiction of *taqwā* as a relativistic and nebulous form of belief.

It is also by distinguishing between hierarchical and lateral religious difference that it becomes possible to more holistically comprehend the complexity of the proximate religious other. Difference is no longer conceived of as that which divides humanity through impermeable boundaries. Difference is rather the dynamic intersections that produce various (perhaps even infinite) combinations of proximity and otherness. As such, the choice is no longer between prioritizing sameness and proximity to the detriment of otherness, or neglecting the intricacies of proximity through isolation and linear hierarchies. With this reconceptualization, with this rethinking of difference, the primary choice is to focus on the dynamic intersections themselves without collapsing the two genres, without depicting them in a static or exclusive relationship, and without returning to a reliance upon oversimplified threshold criteria.

However, an acknowledgement of and focus on the dynamic intersections will also necessitate that we deeply probe the intricacies of hierarchical difference itself. In order to avoid reverting to reliance on the notion of static, distinct boundaries between groups, we will need to obtain a more robust view of what the evaluative concepts and overarching Qur'anic discourse actually entail. If belief and disbelief are no longer ascribed on the basis of communal affiliation, then what exactly are belief and disbelief? How exactly do they conform to or diverge from the central evaluative standard of *taqwā* in all of its dynamic, social and relational complexity?

BIBLIOGRAPHY

Akrami, Seyed Amir. "Particularity and Universality in the Qur'an." Pt. 1, chap. 1 in *Communicating the Word. Revelation, Translation, and Interpretation in Christianity and Islam*, edited by David Marshall, 3–13. Washington, DC: Georgetown University Press, 2011.

Barlas, Asma. "Amina Wadud's Hermeneutics of the Qur'an: Women Rereading Sacred Texts." In *Modern Muslim Intellectuals and the Qur'an*, edited by Suha Taji-Farouki, 97–124. London: Oxford University, 2006.

———. *"Believing Women" in Islam: Unreading Patriarchal Interpretations of the Qur'an*. Austin: University of Texas, 2002.

Engineer, Asghar Ali. "Islam and Pluralism." In *The Myth of Religious Superiority: A Multifaith Exploration*, edited by Paul Knitter, 211–19. Maryknoll, NY: Orbis, 2005.

Hassan, Riffat. "Feminism in Islam." In *Feminism and World Religions*, edited by Arvind Sharma and Katherine K. Young, 248–78. Albany: State University of New York, 1999.

———. "Feminist Theology: The Challenges for Muslim Women." In *Women and Islam: Critical Concepts in Sociology*, edited by Haideh Moghissi, 195–208. London: Routledge, 2005.

———. "Muslim Women and Post-Patriarchal Islam." In *After Patriarchy: Feminist Transformations of the World Religions*, edited by Paula M. Cooey et al., 39–64. Maryknoll, NY: Orbis, 1998.

Legenhausen, Muhammad. *Islam and Religious Pluralism*. London: Al Hoda, 1999.

———. "A Muslim's Non-reductive Religious Pluralism." In *Islam and Global Dialogue: Religious Pluralism and the Pursuit of Peace*, edited by Roger Boase, 51–73. Surrey: Ashgate, 2005.

Nasr, Seyyed Hossein. "Religion and Religions." In *The Religious Other: Towards a Muslim Theology of Other Religions in a Post-Prophetic Age*, edited by Muhammad Suheyl Umar, 59–81. Lahore: Iqbal Academy Pakistan, 2008.

Sachedina, Abdulaziz. *The Islamic Roots of Democratic Pluralism*. Oxford: Oxford University, 2001.

———. "The Qur'an and Other Religions." In *The Cambridge Companion to the Qur'an*, edited by Jane Dammen McAuliffe, 291–309. Cambridge: Cambridge University, 2006.

Shah-Kazemi, Reza. *The Other in the Light of the One: The Universality of the Qur'an and Interfaith Dialogue*. Cambridge: Islamic Texts Society, 2006.

Smith, Jonathan Z. *Relating Religion: Essays in the Study of Religion*. Chicago: University of Chicago, 2004.

Wadud, Amina. "Alternative Qur'anic Interpretation and the Status of Muslim Women." In *Windows of Faith: Muslim Women Scholar-Activists in North America*, edited by Gisela Webb, 3–21. Syracuse: Syracuse University, 2000.

———. *Inside the Gender Jihad: Women's Reform in Islam*. Oxford: Oneworld, 2006.

———. *Qur'an and Woman: Rereading the Sacred Texts from a Woman's Perspective*. New York: Oxford University, 1999.

15

Outside *de jure* Religious Pluralism No Dialogue

A Critical Socio-Theological Assessment of Christian-Muslim Dialogue in Post-Colonial Sub-Saharan Africa

MARINUS C. IWUCHUKWU

IN LIGHT OF THE social-political reality in many parts of contemporary sub-Saharan Africa, Johann Haafkens was correct in predicting several years ago that "polarization along religious lines could seriously jeopardize the future of this part of the world; the maintenance of good neighborly relations between Christians and Muslims therefore is a matter of considerable importance."[1] Haafkens also underscored the extent and serious consequences of the existing polarization between the adherents of these two religions not only in some sub-Saharan African communities but also in the entire African continent. This chapter embarks on a constructive and critical review and evaluation of the relations between Muslims and Christians in post-colonial sub-Saharan Africa. It will identify some of the main reasons for the conflicts and the challenges confronting effective Muslim–Christian dialogue, provide constructive suggestions for restoring the normative cultural and religious pluralism of African communities, and

---

1. Johann Haafkens, "Direction of Christian-Muslim Relations in Sub-Saharan Africa," in Haddad and Haddad, *Christian-Muslim Encounters*, 300.

advocate implementation of the dialogue of life and the dialogue of action as means to effectively engage in Muslim–Christian dialogue.

The estimated population of sub-Saharan Africa is over 1 billion people. The region consists of a plethora of languages and cultures with multiple religions. However, Christianity and Islam are the dominant religions in most parts of Africa. According to a 2011 Pew Forum religion and public life analysis and poll, sub-Saharan Africa has about 500 million Christians and about 234 million Muslims.[2] The once dominant indigenous religions have lost majority of their adherents in most sub-Saharan African societies to the aggressive missionary activities of Christians and Muslims. Ironically, in the search for numerical superiority, Muslim and Christian missionaries have become rivals (and in some communities ferocious antagonists) more to each other than to the African religions that were originally, in most places, the primary focus of their mass conversion missions.

Christian-Muslim relations in post-colonial Africa fall into three relationship types: in some countries the relationship is gravely volatile; in some, there is appreciable peaceful coexistence; and in others, religious differences have no apparent significant social consequence. Countries in the first type include Nigeria, Egypt, the Sudan, Kenya, Central African Republic, and parts of Uganda. Countries represented by the second type include Senegal, Tanzania, Ethiopia, South Africa, and Ghana.[3] Countries in the third type include Botswana, Angola, Namibia, Morocco, and Rwanda. In the countries belonging to the third type, the presence of either Islam or Christianity is so overwhelmingly dominant that adherents of the other religion constitute 5 or less percent of the total population; hence, there is a marginal social tension resulting from religious differences.

PRIMARY CAUSES OF MUSLIM–CHRISTIAN CONFLICTS IN AFRICA

In those parts of Africa where Muslim–Christian conflicts are perennial, a number of reasons are adduced to account for the conflicts. While some of

---

2. See Pew, "Global Christianity," and Pew, "Tolerance and Tension."

3. Although Christian-Muslim relationships in these countries have been generally peaceful, there have been occasional incidents of violence and conflicts between followers of the two religions. For instance, Lawrence Mbogoni alludes to three major incidents of Christian-Muslim conflicts in Tanzania since the sixteenth century. The last was the riot at the Mwembechai mosque on February 13, 1998. The rarity of such violent conflicts explains why the relationship between Christians and Muslims in Tanzania and other countries in this category is considered peaceful. See Mbogoni, *Cross versus the Crescent*, 2ff.

the immediate reasons that lead to such conflicts are often smokescreens or symptoms (and there are myriads of such reasons), this chapter will focus on what the author considers primary causes of the conflicts. These are the preexisting conflicts between Christians and Muslims in Europe and the Middle East, and between Christian denominations; the discrediting of African traditional religions by foreign evangelizers; the breakdown of pacts between colonial rulers and Muslim leaders after independence; the tension between Islam and Enlightenment European secularism; and the rise of Islamic revivalism and fundamentalism.

Those countries in Africa that experience grave volatile relationships raise the greatest concern. They raise concern because of the frequent occurrences of violence, which affect not only Muslims and Christians at the epicenter of the violence but also entire country and even the world at large. Hence, it is imperative to constructively and critically identify the possible primary causes of Muslim–Christian violent conflicts.

First, the African continent, especially the sub-Saharan region, has become the new arena for Christians and Muslims to play out their age-old rivalry, resentment toward each other, and efforts to either triumph over or impede the growth of the other. Such hostile rivalry had defined Christian-Muslim relationships in Europe and the Mediterranean world prior to their engaging each other in sub-Saharan Africa. Students of history will recall the *reconquista* in Spain, the crusades against Muslims, and the dominance of the Turks over many parts of Christian Eastern Europe. They will also recall the influence of European colonial authorities over many Islamic countries, including Egypt, Syria, Palestine, Lebanon, Libya, and Saudi Arabia, from the eighteenth century. Given the long history of acrimony and rivalry between Arab Muslims and Western Christians, it is not surprising that, as both engaged in the campaign to convert Africans, they were destined to collide; to be haunted by the ghost of their past relationship. In African countries where the Western and Arab ideologies prevail strongly and where African religious and cultural values have been significantly eroded, the tension between African Christian and Muslim converts tends to perpetuate the hate and acrimony endemic to the relationship of Christians and Muslims in Europe and the Middle East.

Describing this historical fact, Haafkens writes: "For the missionaries, who came mainly from Europe, influenced by centuries of rivalry between Christianity and Islam in the Mediterranean area, Islam in Africa was clearly seen as a danger and a force to be combated."[4] Rasmussen also describes the hostility on the part of European missionaries in Africa toward Islam:

4. Haafkens, "Direction of Christian-Muslim Relations," 303. At a synod meeting

> The early missionaries in Northern Nigeria and Tanganyika . . . reflected the polemical attitude to Islam in Europe. In all probability, they had hardly heard or read anything positive about Islam. Rather, they had heard about a "fatalistic" religion full of superstitious ideas, bereft of any real spirituality, and socially backward to a degree that was totally obstructive to development and civilization. It was such medieval notions about "a religion of violence" that characterized the missionaries' views of Islam in Tanganyika and Nigeria.[5]

Haafkens traces the roots of Christian-Muslim conflicts in Africa to their acrimonious history in northeastern Africa through the nineteenth century caused either by largely external factors or by the reenactment in the African milieu of global Christian-Muslim antagonisms. He writes: "Of course there . . . have been times of confrontation and war. It is noteworthy that several such conflicts were directly related to the tensions in the Christian-Muslim relationship in the Mediterranean and actually involved people from outside Africa."[6]

Post-colonial Christian-Muslim relations in the Sudan, northern Nigeria, parts of Kenya, and Uganda are rife with incidents of violent conflict. It is no coincidence that these countries, former colonies of Great Britain, bear the trademark of the British colonial authorities. The United Kingdom was a noted site of interreligious conflicts and violence within Europe.[7] Features of these conflicts played out vividly in a number of countries ruled by the British across the world, especially in Africa. The paradigm of antagonism and rivalry dictated the Christian missionary enterprise in Africa as it was carried out by the various denominationally backed missionary organizations. As Rasmussen recounts, "It was not only the Muslims who had to be fought. Both in Northern Nigeria and Tanganyika the Catholics also constituted some kind of menace to the Protestant missions, and there was fierce competition between Catholic and Protestant missions."[8]

---

in 1908 of the Anglican Diocese of Western Equatorial Africa, one of the speakers in response to the spread of Islam in Yoruba land said, "The Church must face this fact as a country faces an enemy, and determine upon a definite plan of campaign." See Gbadamosi, *Growth of Islam among the Yoruba*, 230.

5. Rasmussen, *Christian-Muslim Relations in Africa*, 36.

6. Haafkens, "Direction of Christian-Muslim Relations," 302.

7. Post-Reformation history in Great Britain (and many other European countries) is replete with widespread incidents of violent conflicts. The huge migration of religious minorities like the Puritans, Quakers, and Methodists to the United States is evidence of the religious conflicts that prevailed in the United Kingdom.

8. Rasmussen, *Christian-Muslim Relations in Africa*, 39.

Second, as Haafkens points out, "Where relationships [between Muslims and Christians] were harmonious this may have been due, in a large measure, to resources and circumstances within the sub-Saharan African community itself which seem to make it possible for people to live together peacefully in culturally and religiously plural societies."[9] Historically, Islam predates Christianity in many sub-Saharan African societies. In most places Muslims lived peacefully with their relatives who believed in and practiced the African traditional religions. Muslim converts in many parts of sub-Saharan Africa found ways to uphold and constructively integrate African cultural and even religious values into their lives.[10] Haafkens accurately notes that "there were long periods in the history of Islam in Africa when Muslims lived peacefully together with adherents of African traditional religions."[11] It is also historically true that until the coming of Islam, in most of North Africa Christianity had existed largely peacefully with indigenous religious adherents.

Given the fact that both Islam and Christianity are foreign religions to most sub-Saharan African countries, they were initially transmitted primarily by foreigners, either by the activities of merchant clerics, as was the case with Islam, or by professional clerics under the aegis of colonial authority and supervision, as with Christian missionaries. It is incontrovertible that these foreign evangelizers lacked substantial appreciation and respect for the African traditional religions and in many instances treated African cultural values with condescension. Sanneh critically reviews the low esteem in which both Christian and Islamic missionaries held African cultures. And he argues that the local cultural structures and values presented appreciable resistance to both Christianity and Islam, which resulted in watering down the application of some Islamic doctrines and dogmas in many African communities.[12] It is logical to see that the negativity toward African culture with which Christian and Muslim missionaries approached the evangelization of Africans would in the long run boomerang and/or exacerbate ongoing tension and conflicts.

Third, the coming of Christianity into most sub-Saharan African societies was orchestrated and supervised by the European colonizers. This is precisely the case for most of West, Central, and East African countries. The case of Angola typically reflects this paradigm, since the Portuguese colonizers exclusively enlisted the Roman Catholic Church as their main ally

9. Haafkens, "Direction of Christian-Muslim Relations," 302.
10. Ibid.
11. Ibid., 303.
12. Ibid., 11ff.

in the administration of the colony.¹³ Consequently, Christian missionaries were seen by many Africans as tools of the colonial authorities. This symbiotic relationship and identification of Christianity with colonial authorities was evident at the early stages of the colonial era. The colonialists in places like northern Nigeria and the Sudan signed pacts with Muslim leaders to exempt the Muslim-dominated areas from Christian evangelization.¹⁴ According to Matthew H. Kukah, there was a conscious effort to separate or at best minimize contacts of Christian missionaries with African Muslims.¹⁵ It is, therefore, reasonable to speculate that the absence of serious conflicts between Muslims and Christians during the colonial era is due to the absence of direct encounter in most places (western Nigeria, Senegal, and Tanzania are notable exceptions.¹⁶ Ironically, these places have maintained an impressive model of Muslim–Christian peaceful relationship in Africa). While these pacts were meant to avert Muslim–Christian conflicts during the colonial era, the propensity toward antagonism was building. After independence, with the absence of colonial authorities' restraint on religious missionary activities, Christian and Muslim missionaries crossed paths and sought followers from the same communities. This development, sadly, set the scene for eventual interreligious conflicts that would ravage communities in northern Nigeria, Kenya, and the Sudan. However, it is necessary to continue to highlight the fact that the normative pre-Islamic and pre-Christian African societies practiced religious pluralism.

Fourth, modern African states, or rather post-colonial independent African countries, are the products of Enlightenment European imperialism. Given that the Enlightenment European social-political order had a

---

13. For more information on the exclusive privileges enjoyed by the Roman Catholic Church in Angola, see Sanneh, *Piety and Power*, 91ff.

14. Signing this pact was a measure for securing the loyalty of northern leaders while avoiding any form of Islamic revolution, which the British considered potent. See Rasmussen, *Christian-Muslim Relations in Africa*, 18ff.

15. Hassan Matthew Kukah, "Managing Christian-Muslim Relations in Africa," in Falola, *Christianity and Social Change in Africa*, 391–411.

16. Haafkens also arrives at this conclusion. See Haafkens, "Direction of Christian-Muslim Relations," 304. In addition, it has to be stated that although the agreement not to proselytize in Muslim-dominated areas, or rather not to seek converts among Muslims, existed between Muslim leaders and the colonialists, there were Christian missions at different parts of northern Nigeria. However, such missions were established to provide for the spiritual and religious needs of Christians who had relocated to the north from the south, for non-Muslim, indigenous religious people, or for those in leprosia, some of whom were Muslims. In some of the Muslim-dominated cities like Kano and Sokoto, separate suburbs were carved out to accommodate the non-Muslim urban dwellers. Hence, such suburbs were named *sabon gari* (new city area). See Bunza, *Christian Missions among Muslims*, 73ff.

strong leaning toward secularism, the social-political structures that the colonialists bequeathed to their African colonies are those of the secular state.[17] In contrast, African Muslim leaders[18] have vociferously rejected the fundamental principle of secularism, namely, the separation of religion and politics. Not surprisingly, controversies between Muslims and Christians in many modern African states have resulted from polarized reception of the principle of secularism.[19]

One aspect of the debate over the secular state is the question of the Shari'a and its application. Shari'a is required legal jurisprudence for Muslims. The three indispensable tools for promoting a robust and faithful Muslim life within a society are the Qur'an, the Hadith, and the Shari'a.[20] The application of the Shari'a, according to Muslims, guarantees the positive influence of religion in a state. The separation of church and state, which is a product of the Enlightenment Age and the epitome of secularism, is not a virtue but rather a social vice. Sanneh reflects the thoughts of a former leading Islamic scholar, Al-Muqaddimah Ibn Khaldún, as he writes: "Christianity is not a true 'missionary religion' because, unlike Islam, it does not embrace religion as a state idea, and without the state religious truth lacks the necessary political instrument to establish and maintain it."[21] The Shari'a and its application, in the assessment of non-Muslims, are a major factor in the tendency for conflict between Muslims and Christians. Christians, aware of the minimal recognition and respect the Shari'a accords them compared to Muslims and of the fact that they are likely to be measured by a religious standard unacceptable to them, *ipso facto* object to and resist the application and adjudication of the Shari'a as a state legal system.

---

17. Jan H. Boer refers to this approach of the British colonial era as a post-Victorian age philosophy. See Boer, *Missionary Messengers of Liberation in a Colonial Context*, 71.

18. It should be noted that the religious forebears of these Muslims leaders inhabited many parts of Africa before the advent of European Christian missionaries, functioning in the capacity of imperial authorities in some parts of Africa.

19. Sanneh provides an extensive history and analysis of the secular state as an inherited colonial legacy. His argument underlines the fact that post-colonial African states are modeled after the statecraft for which they were groomed and which they inherited. Moreover, the African countries we have today (with very few exceptions) are the direct result of the machinations of European colonizers, cooked and served from the kitchen of the February 1885 Berlin Congress, chaired by then German Chancellor Prince Otto von Bismarck. Invariably, post-colonial independent African states operated on the only political state model they were designed to replicate, namely secular statehood. See Sanneh, *Piety and Power*, 85ff.

20. Ibid.

21. Ibid., 10.

Finally, the rise of Islamic revivalism and fundamentalism, which began in the eighteenth century but crested with the Iranian Revolution of 1979 and the terrorist attacks of September 11, 2001, has significantly and directly influenced Muslim–Christian conflicts in sub-Saharan Africa. As a religious political development, which began with the growing rejection of Western colonialism and its secularist principles in Muslim-dominated countries of the Middle East, Islamic revivalism contributed to the birth of the Wahhabi movement in Saudi Arabia and the Islamic Brotherhood in Egypt.[22] Sub-Saharan Africa, Islamic revivalism produced the Uthman Dan Fodio jihad in northern Nigeria and the Mahdist movement in the Sudan.[23] Islamic revivalism eventually gave birth to Islamic fundamentalism, which gained global recognition in the Iranian Revolution of 1979[24] led by Ayotollah Khomeni, the September 11, 2001 terrorist attacks in the United States, and other terrorist activities across the globe. The influence of Islamic revivalism and subsequent Islamic fundamentalism gradually but persistently came to prevail in different parts of sub-Saharan Africa, especially in northern Nigeria, the Sudan, Kenya, Uganda, Somalia, Central African Republic, etc. This explains the existence of terrorist cells in different parts of Africa today.

CHALLENGES TO ENDURING MUSLIM–CHRISTIAN RELATION/DIALOGUE

Following the identification of some of the primary causes of Christian-Muslim conflicts in many parts of post-colonial sub-Saharan African, it is necessary to highlight some of the major challenges facing attempts to end these conflicts. As the causes of the conflicts are many and varied, so are the challenges. It suffices to underscore some of the more significant

22. For more information about this development, see Ayoob and Kosebalaban, *Religion and Politics in Saudi Arabia*.

23. The Mahdist movement was strong in the Sudan. It is the equivalent in Islam of the return of the Messiah in Judaism. Although theologically this concept is often associated with the eschaton, certain charismatic leaders in Islamic tradition are sometimes considered or give themselves away as the precursor to the coming Mahdi. This idea gathered significant traction and sympathy in the Sudan. Last, *Sokoto Caliphate*, 90ff, and Adeleye, *Power and Diplomacy in Northern Nigeria*, 11ff.

24. Incidents of Islamic radicalism and social violence in different parts of Africa, especially in northern Nigeria, have been attributed to the impact of the 1979 Iran Revolution. Substantiating this observation is the rise of Shi'ite radical movements in northern Nigeria led by Ibrahim Al-Zakzaky. See Bunza, *Christian Missions among Muslims*, 140, and Muhammad Sani Umar, "Islam in Nigeria: Its Concept, Manifestatioins and Role in Nation-Building," in Atanda et al., *Nigeria since Independence*, 88–89.

challenges—globalization, the post-9/11 war on terror, exclusivist theologies, lack of grassroots participation in dialogue, geographical divisions, failure to standardize the rule of law, and the implementation of Shari'a law.

Of primary importance today is the challenge of globalization, which has made it increasingly untenable for cultures and religions that previously lived apart to remain isolated from each other. Globalization brings about greater integration between peoples and religions of the world. This global development has exponentially promoted migration and immigration. Because Western countries control major portions of the world economy and have a higher standard of living, they have invariably become dominant centers of attraction for immigration. As a result, many Muslim immigrants from different parts of the world, including sub-Saharan Africa, have emigrated to the West in search of better living conditions.

Since Western societies have evolved under the influence of Christianity and its worldview, many of these Muslim immigrants feel marginalized in the West, where Islam is a minority religion. As a result, some Muslim extremists, under the mantle of Al Qaeda, the Taliban, and their operatives, have openly declared their disdain and hatred for the West and Christianity.[25] Francis Robinson describes how Islamists have made connections between the view of Europe and America as demons and the development, beginning in the nineteenth century, of an "active pan-Islamic consciousness in the Muslim world."[26]

As a result, Muslim extremists, including those in sub-Saharan Africa, have associated with African Christians some of the political and military activities spearheaded by Western countries that affect Muslims in different parts of the world. There have been violent attacks on Christians in Egypt, Nigeria, Kenya, the Sudan, and Algeria for events that took place in different parts of the Western world, including the Danish cartoon of Prophet Mohammed, the American-led wars in Iraq and Afghanistan, the ongoing Israeli-Palestinian conflict, etc. Insofar as some Muslims continue to express resentment and ill feelings toward the West, Muslim–Christian relations in Africa remain in jeopardy.

The impact of the post-September 11, 2011 war on terror and reactions from African Muslims also constitute a major challenge to the relationship between Muslims and Christians in sub-Saharan Africa. Many Muslims in Africa think that the American and Western European led war on terror is specifically meant to antagonize Islam and Muslims. Given that the United

25. Akbar S. Ahmed, "Islam and the West: Clash or Dialogue of Civilisations?" in Boase, *Islam and Global Dialogue*, 112–13, and Francis Robinson, "Islam and the West: Clash of Civilisation?" in Boase, *Islam and Global Dialogue*, 81.

26. Robinson, "Islam and the West," in Boase, *Islam and Global Dialogue*, 79ff.

States and Europe are commonly identified as Christian regions, Muslims conclude that this is a modern equivalent of the crusades.[27] To associate religion with criminal activities is inimical to social order and especially to the peaceful coexistence of Muslims and Christians anywhere in the globe. Conversely, it is in the interest of the common good, social order, and security to support justified and responsible government responses to any form of crime, even when that crime has a religious motive.

Supercessionist and exclusivist theological viewpoints pose another serious challenge to Muslim–Christian dialogue and relations. The exponential growth of Pentecostalism and exclusivist evangelical positions among Christians and the growth of militant and extremist Islamic radicals have given rise to antagonistic polarization between African Muslims and Christians. The polarization has increased tension between adherents of both religions and the incidence of violence.

Effective interreligious dialogue is also hampered by the overt focus of dialogic exercises on religious leaders. Although places of worship are often targeted during Muslim–Christian conflicts and some religious leaders have suffered casualties, most of the victims of the conflicts are innocent, ordinary citizens. Some of them are attacked in their homes and others in their businesses or places of work or even on the streets. Yet efforts toward dialogue and resolution of the conflicts are focused exclusively around religious leaders. The exclusive concentration of dialogic activities on the contributions and social influences of the overtly religious as agents for effectively ending ongoing interreligious conflicts is a myth. As Kukah rightly states,

> Dialogue in many African countries has tended to focus on Christian leaders teaming up with Muslim leaders, holding hands and smiling while the cameras click and click around the corridors of the powerful. These pictures are then sent out through the media and they are supposed to send out signals to the effect that if ordinary Christians and Muslims see that their leaders are working together in peace and harmony, they would follow suit. These cycles of dialogue have been going on in Nigeria for many years and yet, as it is clear, the violence has not relented. If anything, in the last few years, religiously induced violence has claimed thousands of lives in the country.[28]

27. Ibid., 81.

28. Kukah, "Managing Christian-Muslim Relations in Africa," in Falola, *Christianity and Social Change in Africa*, 397–98.

Effective interreligious dialogue in sub-Saharan Africa between Christians and Muslims must involve the active participation and support of religious leaders, the political class, academics, the full range of social and economic classes, and especially the rank and file members of both religions. The rank and file members of both religions bear the direct brunt of persistent acrimony and are used as canon fodder by the perpetrators of the antagonism and violence. Forums need to be created to access their contributions and insights toward effective dialogue between Christians and Muslims.

The differences in the understanding of the modern principle of separation of religion and state between Christians and Muslims is a substantial challenge to effective interreligious dialogue in sub-Saharan African. Significant populations of Muslims believe that the principle of separation of religion and state is a Western ideology, not healthy for Muslims, and it is anti-Islamic. According to Sanneh, "Classical Islamic sources deny any strict distinction between religion and politics."[29] He goes on to state the basis of the conventional Islamic understanding, namely, that "the Caliph (*khalifah*), the earthly sovereign, as the Prophet's successor, is one charged with the 'power to bind and to loosen,' and is furthermore commanded to restrain people from bloodshed and to ensure their welfare in this world and in the future life."[30]

Notwithstanding this classical position, moderate Muslims and some conservatives advocate the principle of the separation of church and state, albeit with some modifications.[31] The failure to arrive at a healthy compromise on the understanding and application of the separation of religion from politics among Christians and Muslims poses a major hindrance to effective interreligious dialogue.

During the period of colonization, many colonial authorities created clearly marked regional administrative boundaries along religious lines in some parts of sub-Saharan Africa. Two good examples are the Sudan and Nigeria. The British created a north/south geographical demarcation based on Muslim north and Christian/animist south. While the south in both cases had the special privilege of Western education, the colonial authorities leaned politically more toward the north and ensured that power was handed over to the north at their departure. This model and policy invariably resulted in a conflict that divided the countries into Muslim north and

---

29. Sanneh, *Piety and Power*, 98. Also see Bunza, *Christian Missions among Muslims*, 161f.

30. Sanneh, *Piety and Power*, 98.

31. Ibid., 97–108.

Christian south. The creation of these geographical divisions has become a major challenge to interreligious dialogue. In light of such demarcations, Kukah calls for a rethinking of what is called Muslim–Christian conflict in Africa. According to him, "these crises are largely the crises generated by the structural weakness and inefficiency inherent in the post-colonial state."[32] Where such structural weakness persists, dialogue between Muslims and Christians is seriously inhibited.

The absence of standard state structures of law and order in some African societies is yet another challenge to effective resolution of Muslim–Christian conflicts. Some countries lack the will to standardize the implementation and promotion of the rule of law. Many have observed the concomitance of this absence and endemic corruption within the political class. Consequently, the standard principles of a modern state are compromised and the primary function of promoting and sustaining the rule law, which is a basic ingredient of a modern state, is either marginalized or completely ignored.[33] This failure facilitates the mayhem and anarchical intent of violence-oriented fundamentalists and bigots, be they Christians or Muslims. And the prevalence of incidents of violence in the name of religion makes effective dialogue between Muslims and Christians near impracticable. It is the primary duty and responsibility of every modern state to protect and defend the lives of its citizens. Two of the five challenges John N. Paden identifies as militating against effective nation-building in Nigeria are "consolidating rule of law" and "developing capacities for conflict resolution."[34] It is difficult for citizens to have confidence in their governments if religiously motivated violence remains perennial, while the perpetrators are not apprehended and due processes of prosecution and indictment not invoked. Nigeria alone has recorded over fifteen thousand human casualties, hundreds of thousands of people displaced or injured, and billions of dollars worth of property damage and losses between 1990 and the present.[35] The incidence of violence from religiously motivated conflicts is growing almost unabated in certain parts of Africa. From Egypt to Nigeria to Sudan, terror cells and insurgent groups are increasing—Joseph

---

32. Kukah, "Managing Christian-Muslim Relations in Africa," in Falola, *Christianity and Social Change in Africa*, 401.

33. Ibid., 401ff.

34. Paden, *Faith and Politics in Nigeria*, 58–65.

35. Marinus Iwuchukwu provides data and information, covering about two decades, regarding the cost and casualties of Muslim–Christian violent conflicts in Northern Nigeria. See Iwuchukwu, "Revisiting the Perennial Religious Conflicts in Northern Nigeria, 1990–2010," in Iwuchukwu and Stiltner, *Can Muslims and Christians Resolve Their Religious and Social Conflicts?*, 3–37.

Kony's Lord's Resistance Army from Uganda, Al Shabaab from Somalia, and Boko Haram in Nigeria.[36]

The Islamic Shari'a legal system and how it is applied in society constitutes one of the greatest challenges to effective interreligious dialogue. The establishment and application of a Shari'a legal system in different parts of Africa, especially in the Sudan (1983) and Northern Nigeria (2000), remain very problematic. The introduction of strict application of the Shari'a in these countries has left in its wake incidents of catastrophic violence and conflicts between Muslims and Christians, making it very difficult for Christians and Muslims to engage in healthy dialogue. For most non-Muslims, especially Christians, their fundamental objection to the Shari'a is that the Shari'a legal system is *ab initio* designed to serve the religious interest of Muslims. Hence, the application of the Shari'a in multireligious societies of modern states (typical of the average African society) is inherently problematic. Addressing the impact of Shari'a application in Africa, Sanneh writes: "What has happened is that, beginning in the mid-1970s, Muslim political activism erupted into the open, demanding national attention. The Shari'ah has been a catalyst for this. Muslims have organized behind it with calls for its adoption as public law, with little experience of running a religious state."[37]

In the case of Nigeria, in spite of the many times discussion about the Shari'a has been a regional or national focus, there has never been a conclusive, amicable decision (as is evident in the debates of the 1940s, 1960, and 1978).[38] In 1999, with the ascension to power of a federal civilian administration under the leadership of President Olusegun Obasanjo (a Christian from southwestern Nigeria), the legislative assemblies of twelve northern states, led by Zamfara state, passed into law the application of the Shari'a legal system in their states. This development led to widespread violence and clashes between Muslims and Christians. In the case of the Sudan, the approval of Shari'a legislation in 1983 sparked off the second civil war

---

36. Al Shabaab and Boko Haram are currently two of the most violent terrorist organizations operating as Islamic insurgents, with the intent of installing Islamic theocratic governments. Kony's Lord's Resistance Army is engaged in guerrilla war against not only the government of Uganda but also those of the neighboring countries, with the intent of establishing a Christian theocracy. All these insurgent groups attack innocent civilians as well as government security personnel and security establishments. They use all forms of weapons available to them including assault rifles and different kinds of bombs.

37. Sanneh, *Piety and Power*, 21.

38. For a summary on the Shari'a debates in Nigeria see, *Sharia Debates in Africa*, "Sharia Debates and Their Perception by Christians and Muslims in Selected African Countries"—"Nigeria," An International, Multidisciplinary and Comparative Research Project at University of Bayreuth, 2007.

between the SPLA (Sudan People's Liberation Army), fighting on behalf of the Christian/Animist southern Sudan, and the central political authority of the Sudan under Islamist political leadership. The war between the southern Sudan people and the central government eventually culminated in the secession of southern Sudan in July 2011.

According to the latest record, over twelve African countries observe some form of Shari'a regulation, ranging from a very strict application, as in Mauritania, the Sudan, and Nigeria, to minimal application as in Uganda. All the North African countries apply the Shari'a legal system in some significant fashion, thus diminishing the religious dignity of non-Muslims in those countries.[39]

LOOKING AHEAD FOR BETTER MUSLIM-CHRISTIAN RELATION IN AFRICA

Sanneh insightfully states:

> The fact is that Christian and Muslim Africa is for the most part enfolded within the larger setting of the old Africa, with its deep-rooted hospitality, tolerance, and generosity, and it will be surprising if nothing of that admirable heritage did not survive in the new religions. Both sides are involved in a creative transformation process, and it cannot be stressed enough how much Christian and Muslim Africans owe to traditional Africa, whatever the rhetoric of religious propaganda.[40]

Sanneh reflects the nostalgia of many Africans. Like Sanneh, many African scholars wonder where the glorious days of Africa as a people who love and cherish one another have gone. They are nostalgic for the return to what one may describe as the nascent and uncorrupted African society. Such expectations may be a mirage, for while most pre-Islamic and pre-Christian African societies were not entangled in interreligious conflicts and antagonism, they had extensive experience of conflicts and violence based on ethnic and communal differences and other social-political problems. For a return to the pre-Islamic and pre-colonial/pre-Christian social and communal cohesion to be realistic, the goal should not be to return to that *physical* world but to an earlier *ideology*, and to recapture a worldview.

---

39. For details on the Shari'a law application in Africa and globally, see, "What Countries Use Sharia Law?," *Answers.com*, http://wiki.answers.com/Q/what_countries_use_sharia_law (accessed December 29, 2011).

40. Sanneh, *Piety and Power*, 24.

Africans can evolve ways of restoring peace, brotherhood, a communal sense of harmony, concord, hospitality, generosity, and religious pluralism. To achieve these goals, all Africans—Muslims and Christians—should consider traditional ethos and modern social values that could enhance the search for a new social order.

One of the tools modern society offers is the pragmatic adoption of the bill of rights, especially the right to freedom of religion. This fundamental human right has been embraced and advocated by most mainline Christians. Beginning with the World Council of Churches' Declaration on Religious Liberty of August 1948[41] to the Catholic Church's *Dignitatis Humanae* of the Second Vatican Council (1965),[42] Christians have affirmed the irrevocable rights of all to choose or reject religions, free from any institutional pressure. From the Islamic perspective, Ahmad S. Moussalli clearly articulates the Islamic basis for freedom of religion. "The Qur'an is very clear on a fundamental principle, which is the freedom to believe or not to believe."[43] Muslims have the injunction, enshrined in the Qur'an, to respect every individual's freedom of religion: "There is no compulsion in religion" (Q. 2:256). Also in the Qur'an, God addresses the following rhetorical question to Mohammed: "And had your Lord willed, those on earth would have believed—all of them entirely. Then, [O Muhammad], would you compel the people in order that they become believers?" (Q. 10:99).

Once freedom of religion is genuinely and imperatively respected across Africa, both Christians and Muslims will be fully disposed to appreciate and practice cultural and religious pluralism, which are major pre-Islamic and pre-colonial African social values. When Africans apply the principle of pluralism within the multicultural and multireligious reality of African cosmopolitan communities today, it will be a major step toward ending Muslim–Christian conflicts and antagonism.

Religious and cultural pluralism as a worldview is indispensable not only to enhancing mutual appreciation between people of different religions but also between people who subscribe to the same religion. In Africa, both Islam and Christianity have rancorous diversity within their ranks. In Egypt, Muslim moderates, radicals, and conservatives contest against each other in the same religious communities. In Nigeria, the Muslim population consists of the Tijaniyya, Qadariyya, Izala, Ahmadiya, and Ansar Ud-Deen, some of whom are pitted against each other. Among Christians, there are ongoing rivalries between Catholics, Protestants, Pentecostals, and Independent

---

41. See World Council of Churches, "Declaration on Religious Liberty."
42. Paul VI, "Declaration on Religious Freedom."
43. Moussalli, *Islamic Quest for Democracy, Pluralism, and Human Rights*, 84.

African Churches in all parts of Africa. At the same time, these various brands of Christianity are often locked in rivalry and antagonism against Muslims in their communities.

Upholding and advocating cultural and religions pluralism will significantly minimize the rhetoric of hate, prejudice, and resentment which Muslims and Christians use against each other (and even against groups within their own ranks). Growth in this direction will ensure more harmonious African communities, regardless of how many religious affiliations exist among the people. The adoption of a religious and cultural pluralistic worldview would guarantee peace among Christian and Muslim Africans and among Africans of all religions and cultures. Sanneh affirms this fundamental assumption by urging, "If we are to hope for any progress in interfaith relations, we must resist the view that our particular tradition [religion] is superior."[44]

If Muslim and Christian Africans adopt the principle of cultural and religious pluralism, incidents of violent conflicts based on ethnic and religious differences will be reduced. More importantly, Muslims and Christians will be able to engage in more meaningful, effective, and successful dialogue among themselves, with each other, and with the rest of the society.

If the forum and disposition for genuine dialogue are established, the different types of dialogue will have higher possibilities of attaining their goals. Of the four types of dialogue (dialogue of life, dialogue of action, dialogue of theological exchange, and dialogue of religious experience), the most effective for sustaining social order are the dialogue of action and dialogue of life. These two types of dialogue will ultimately ensure the survival of the communal spirit, generosity, hospitality, and pluralism that are the hallmarks of African spiritual and cultural values.

A dialogue of action will require that Muslim and Christian organizations collaborate on providing and supporting the common good of the society. Members of these two religions would jointly embark on projects like health care, education, and other charitable activities to serve the needs of all in their immediate communities, regardless of religious affiliation or lack thereof. When such collaborative ventures are successfully undertaken, the African value of empathy and care for the needy in one's neighborhood will prevail.

A dialogue of life promotes and advocates civility and altruism toward one's neighbor. People will be welcome to reside and work anywhere in the community and to receive the support and protection of their interests in the most civilized and friendly way. Religious difference will no longer be a

---

44. Sanneh, *Piety and Power*, 114.

factor in determining where one lives or works, as is the case today in some African communities where religiously motivated violence persists.

These two types of dialogue fit into the normative African social and communal living paradigm. Africans are acquainted with collaborative projects among different tribes, villages, clans, and families for the benefit of the larger community. There is a higher potential of success when Muslims and Christians collaboratively explore and execute projects, provided both are open to the principles of religious pluralism. In the same vein, Muslim and Christian Africans are more likely to respect and appreciate each other as neighbors and coworkers if they open up to each other with respect and dignity.

CONCLUSION

It is imperative to urge the Western Christian and Arab Muslim worlds to honor and respect the religious and cultural pluralism that Africans adopt. Africans are faced with criticism from both the Arab and Western worlds, and are often under pressure to adopt the kind of Islam or Christianity that replicates what exists in the Middle East and the West respectively. These pressures are unproductive for Africans, who must constructively and critically develop their own culturally conditioned Christian or Islamic religions.

It is very important that both the West and the Arabs who have overseen the spread of Christianity and Islam in sub-Saharan Africa learn to respect the principles of cultural and religious pluralism. They should learn to appreciate the ingenuity and authenticity of how Africans choose to become Christians or Muslims. If Africans independently develop the religious and cultural pluralism most adaptable to their world, relationships between Muslim and Christian Africans will coalesce into a new social order that can effectively confront the many social, economic, and political challenges communities in the sub-continent have been facing.

Ultimately, sub-Saharan African problems need solutions that are authentically African and adaptable to post-colonial sub-Saharan African state and social structures. The rest of the world, especially the Western and Arab countries, need to learn that a truly global cultural and religious pluralism cannot be attained if the expectation or desire is to annihilate or marginalize the religious culture of any group of people on planet earth. The pre-Islamic and pre-Christian African social value of religious pluralism needs to be firmly reestablished in all post-colonial African societies, thus ensuring the success and effectiveness of efforts toward Muslim–Christian dialogue in all parts of the sub-Saharan African region burdened by persistent Muslim–Christian conflicts.

BIBLIOGRAPHY

Adeleye, R. A. *Power and Diplomacy in Northern Nigeria 1804–1906: The Sokoto Caliphate and Its Enemies*. New York: Humanities, 1971.

Atanda, J. A., et al., eds. *Nigeria since Independence: The First 25 Years*. Ibadan, Nigeria: Heinemann Educational Books, 1989.

Ayoob, Mohammed, and Hassan Kosebalaban. *Religion and Politics in Saudi Arabia: Wahhabism and the State*. Boulder, CO: Rienner, 2009.

Boase, Roger, ed. *Islam and Global Dialogue: Religious Pluralism and the Pursuit of Peace*. Burlington, VT: Ashgate, 2005.

Boer, Jan Harm. *Missionary Messengers of Liberation in a Colonial Context: A Case Study of the Sudan United Mission*. Amsterdam: Rodopi, 1979.

Bunza, Mukhtar Umar. *Christian Missions among Muslims: Sokoto Province, Nigeria, 1935–1990*. Lawrenceville, NJ: Africa World Press, 2007.

Falola, Toyin, ed. *Christianity and Social Change in Africa: Essays in Honor of J. D. Y. Peel*. Durham, NC: Carolina Academic, 2005.

Gbadamosi, T. G. O. *The Growth of Islam among the Yoruba, 1841–1908*. London: Longman, 1978.

Haddad, Yvonne Yazbeck, and Wadi Zaidan Haddad, eds. *Christian-Muslim Encounters*. Gainesville: University Press of Florida, 1995.

Iwuchukwu, Marinus C., and Brian Stiltner. *Can Muslims and Christians Resolve Their Religious and Social Conflicts? Cases from Africa and the United States*. Lewiston, NY: Mellen, 2013.

Last, Murray. *The Sokoto Caliphate*. New York: Humanities, 1967.

Mbogoni. *The Cross versus the Crescent: Religion and Politics in Tanzania from the 1880s to the 1990s*. Dar es Salaam, Tanzania: Mkuki no Nyota, 2005.

Moussalli, Ahmad S. *The Islamic Quest for Democracy, Pluralism, and Human Rights* Gainesville: University Press of Florida, 2001.

Paden, John N. *Faith and Politics in Nigeria*. Washington, DC: US Institute of Peace, 2008.

Paul VI. "Declaration on Religious Freedom." Declaration on religious freedom, promulgated December 7, 1965. http://www.vatican.va/archive/hist_councils/ii_vatican_council/documents/vat-ii_decl_19651207_dignitatis-humanae_en.html.

Pew Research Center. "Global Christianity: A Report on the Size and Distribution of the World's Christian Population." Pew Forum on Religion and Public Life. December 19, 2011. http://www.pewforum.org/2011/12/19/global-christianity-regions.

———. "Tolerance and Tension: Islam and Christianity in Sub-Saharan Africa." Pew Forum on Religion and Public Life. April 15, 2010. http://pewforum.org/executive-summary-islam-and-christianity-in-sub-saharan-africa.aspx.

Rasmussen, Lissi. *Christian-Muslim Relations in Africa: The Cases of Northern Nigeria and Tanzania Compared*. New York: British Academic, 1993.

Sanneh, Lamin. *Piety and Power: Muslims and Christians in West Africa*. Maryknoll, NY: Orbis, 1996.

Sharia Debates in Africa. "Sharia Debates and Their Perception by Christians and Muslims in Selected African Countries" [Nigeria]. An International, Multidisciplinary and Comparative Research Project at University of Bayreuth, 2007. http://www.sharia-in-africa.net/pages/project/nigeria.php.

World Council of Churches. "Declaration on Religious Liberty." Adopted at the first assembly of the World Council of Churches, Amsterdam, August 1948. http://www.religlaw.org/content/religlaw/documents/wccdecreliglib1948.htm.

16

The Shifting Significance of Theologies of Religious Pluralism

S. MARK HEIM

IN THIS PAPER I will sketch the shifting significance of theologies of religious pluralism, from the perspective of a Christian theologian. In brief, this story traces the migration of the theology of religion from an adjunct role focused on a specialized task to a more prominent thematic focus as a response to a troubling challenge and then to an integral place in the constitutive work of systematic or foundational theology. In that later phase, this involves consideration of the nature of comparative theology as distinct from but related to theologies of religious pluralism. Along the way, we shall also have occasion to consider very telling objections that have been raised to the whole project of theologies of religious diversity, and to discuss whether it is a project shared with other religious traditions. Finally, I will say something about the specific case of the rise of Trinitarian theologies of religious pluralism, a development that I suggest is in fact directly stimulated by the shift I am describing. I will argue that Christian Trinitarian theologies of religion correlate most fruitfully with a "differential pluralism" approach to religious diversity.

SHIFTING SIGNIFICANCE

Christian theology's treatment of religious pluralism (what has been called theology of religions) was at one time a discipline primarily connected with a practical task, the work of Christian mission. Theology of religions, insofar as it constituted a distinct discipline, was largely devoted to explicating the conditions under which other religions were or could be bridges to Christian faith. In more recent times, theology of religions become oriented to a thematic challenge. Theologies of religious pluralism, including "pluralist" theologies, have been driven by concern for religious diversity as an intellectual and perhaps apologetic problem. How can Christians account for the existence, the power and the virtues of other religious traditions? Why do these traditions not call into question distinctive Christian claims and assumptions? In both of these cases—as a field for mission or a challenge to Christian universality—religious diversity figures primarily as a difficulty to be negotiated. In the first case it is negotiated with a strategy to overcome that diversity with Christian evangelization. In the second case it is negotiated with an interpretive analysis that explains the ways in which various faiths can function as contributory branches of the Christian way of salvation or with a revisionist analysis that argues they independently constitute their own paths to human fulfillment in relation to ultimate reality. These three modalities of theology roughly correspond to the well known typology of exclusivist (replacement), inclusivist (fulfillment) and pluralist (equality) perspectives.[1]

This shift has also affected the location of theologies of religious pluralism (hereafter TRP). As an adjunct of Christian mission, such theology had a specialized, practical task which compared religious traditions and Christian revelation to assess the best way to seed the gospel into the religions. As a response to the spiritual and intellectual challenge of religious diversity, TRP has become the interest of a much wider constituency. In addition to its application in mission or in formal interreligious dialogue, it is of increasing relevance for those living in pluralistic social environments. In Christian history, theologies of religion were in large measure *a priori*. In the contemporary situation these theologies—whether developed out of close contact with religious others or not—are subject to much more ready testing against peoples' first hand experience of interreligious encounter or even double belonging and against peoples' greater knowledge of the textual and spiritual depth of other traditions.

The types of TRP I have just described are very much with us. A further shift is under way, characterized by a turn toward the positive meaning of religious difference. Diversity is not a problem to be negotiated, but a richness to be explored. In this sense TRP becomes not a specialized theory for a particular practice, nor the systematic answer to a particular theological

---

1. See Knitter, *Introducing Theologies of Religion*.

question, but programmatic for the entire syllabus of theology. The key shift is toward taking the content of other religions as sources for Christian theological reflection, as well as objects of theological interpretation. This shift is basic to the rise of comparative theology as a discipline. Such a move itself depends upon certain theological arguments, and it is at this point that Trinitarian theologies of religious pluralism have come to the fore. If the diversity of religions is rooted in the diversity of the divine life itself, then the heart of the religions, their insights and realizations, become permanent parts of the content of Christian theology even though the privileged access to this content lies outside the traditional sources of Christian theology. The implications of this conclusion are enormous, though they are also as yet unclear and undeveloped. We will return to this matter toward the end of our discussion.

OBJECTIONS

As TRP has shifted in the ways we have described, it has been dogged by hesitations and objections voiced against the earlier versions and continuing against later variations. We can summarize some of the most powerful of these. The entire TRP project may appear incoherent because of the underlying conceptual confusion of its categories. "Theologies of religions" take religion as their subject, in the singular or the plural, and this is inherently ambiguous. The Christian theologian in this discipline will, of necessity, work from a Christian point of view (and probably a rather nuanced one) as the frame of reference, but will almost inevitably take as his/her subject a field of much more reified and homogenized units like "Buddhism." Such units are highly problematic, as recent discussions of the study of "religion" illustrate.[2] A second order discourse that depends on these units as its playing pieces builds from shaky foundations an even flimsier structure. A related criticism objects not so much to the monolithic treatment of the traditions as to the monochromatic treatment of adherents, stressing the hybridity of religious identity in individuals and groups.[3] That hybridity may involve the conjunction of a religious tradition with culture, gender or social location but it may well also involve a mixture of religious influences, practices and commitments. Neither religions nor their adherents "stand still" enough to be addressed in this way.

It seems secondly that theologies of religions are illegitimate, for they must inevitably interpret the material of other religions in the terms of their

2. See Thatamanil, "Comparative Theology after 'Religion.'"
3. See Fletcher, *Monopoly on Salvation?*

own confession. Such an effort is intrinsically biased and imperialistic. Its methods of understanding distort by their very nature, and serve an apologetic purpose. No tradition or faith that becomes the object of this discipline can fully agree with its conclusions. Whether explicitly coopted by schemes of social domination or naively deployed as a kind of cultural chauvinism, the study is poisoned at its roots.

The condemnation of theologies of religious pluralism as immoral is only slightly softened by the observation that they seem to have the compensatory failing of being impossible. Even if the evaluative and interpretive judgments they contemplate are conceivable in principle, they would still be beyond the means of any individual or team of persons to realize in practice. To do so would require a comprehensive knowledge—experiential as well as cognitive—of the religions involved, on a level one might argue is even beyond that required to faithfully practice them as a devotee. Therefore, some maintain that even if TRP is legitimate in principle, the very least that methodological prudence demands is a moratorium on such grandiose efforts until such time as we have a better level of mutual knowledge and less conflicted social conditions.[4]

The power of these critiques cannot be denied. I reject their conclusion not because its premises are groundless, but because there are equally powerful but opposing considerations. The theology of religions is a vital undertaking despite these concerns, but can never be fully secure against them.

First, it is necessary because it is unavoidable. We all have theologies of religion, whether we choose to reflect upon them or not. In this sense, TRP is an exercise in self-awareness, both for communities and for individuals. It makes explicit what is operative.[5] In fact, in a teaching context this can be one helpful way to approach the subject. Have people survey their own behaviors. What patterns of avoidance or revulsion mark their attitude toward participation in or valuation of a variety of religious practices and traditions? What incidents of positive interaction or personal relations involving individuals or elements from various faiths can they name in their own experience? Then ask them what assumptions can account for the combination of these behaviors and experiences in their lives. In such a way, one can "retroject" an operative theology, though it may never have been explicitly articulated.

---

4. James Fredericks has eloquently made this case. See for instance his discussion in his introduction to Clooney, *New Comparative Theology*.

5. See Nicholson, "New Comparative Theology."

Second, the nature of our existing TRP is either an impetus toward interreligious learning or an obstacle to it. Interreligious learning happens in many inadvertent ways, but sustained interreligious learning—especially as a community activity more than just an individual one—is unlikely to happen without a rationale for why it is important and even integral to the practice of one's own tradition. Theology articulates why interreligious engagement is part of the normal Christian life.

Third, such theology is the necessary "docking mechanism" that allows what is learned from the religious other to find a place within the ongoing life and wisdom of my tradition and practice. However powerful the experience or insight gained from engagement with religious pluralism, if there is no intellectual and imaginative framework within which this can be recognized and even serve to modify and reconstruct our previous understandings, there is a tendency for those insights to evaporate or fade, on the one hand, or for their acknowledgement to lead to estrangement from one's own tradition, on the other. It is difficult to integrate wisdom from these disparate contexts without any imaginative setting.

Fourth, in a pluralistic environment and particularly for those who themselves have a hybrid religious background or multiple religious affinities, such a theology is not an optional embellishment. It is the very heart of any operative theology or faith structure. In fact, there are some people for whom it may be said that an operative theology of religious pluralism is the closest thing they have to a core religious orientation or a "home" tradition. There are people, in other words, who would have a hard time saying what if any religion they belong to, but who would readily give an account of the way in which they sift and gather elements from various traditions in their own lives. A "theology of religions" may be the closest they have to a determinable religion. In any event, it is inescapeably continuous with being religious at all.

Finally, in a society marked by religious pluralism TRP has an important public role. When conflict and violence are linked to religion, it is common to hear leaders in different communities argue that the exclusivist or pejorative rationales used by their coreligionists to justify violence are illegitimate. But the materials for such justification lay ready at hand in all our traditions, and often what is markedly lacking is an affirmative alternative teaching that would affirm the value of the religious other, precisely as religious. One of the most helpful things religious communities or religious individuals can add to the public discourse about diversity is a positive statement about the value of religious others from the viewpoint of a particular tradition.

TRP AND COMPARATIVE THEOLOGY

As I have described it, TRP for the most part frames the need for learning from other religious traditions or accommodates the results of such learning. It does not exemplify that learning concretely. In recent years alongside theologies of religion a practice of comparative theology has arisen.[6] In addition to the three forms of TRP we discussed earlier (exclusivism, inclusivism, pluralism), another has appeared that Paul Knitter calls the "Acceptance" approach, unified mainly by its resistance to the level of closure for religious diversity represented by any of the other three.[7] In this category he sees three primary divisions, the first being what he calls "postliberal" TRPs, the second being my TRP, and the third being the approach of comparative theology.

In fact, it would seem that comparative theology is somewhat outside the box of TRP. Comparative theology *per se* takes no consistent position on TRP. It simply applies itself to deep interreligious learning and the attentiveness this requires. As its title suggests, its substance crosses the genres of comparative religion and systematic theology. Unlike religious studies, comparative theology is a religiously committed project. Unlike systematic theology, it already accepts the authoritative sources of another religion as sources in confessional theology. It works across texts, rituals or experiences within one religious setting and those of another religious setting. It is extremely sophisticated in the scholarly demands placed on its practitioners regarding language and history. But it is open-ended and *ad hoc* in its expectations and claims. It seeks resonances that arise when two faiths converse and each uses its own language, an attempt to translate in two directions. Theology of religions learns about the other to interpret it in terms that come pervasively from the home tradition. In comparative theology, one is interpreted back. As Frank Clooney puts it, "We need a home from which to go forth, yet must actually go forth, learning from another religious tradition, hearing questions to which we do not already

---

6. See Clooney, *Comparative Theology*. For illustrations of contemporary variety in the practice of comparative theology see Clooney, *New Comparative Theology*. Clooney traces the origins of comparative theology back three hundred years, but in the terms that I discuss it here, it is a recent academic arrival.

7. Knitter, *Introducing Theologies of Religion*, part 4.

have answers."[8] This challenging balance of openness and commitment has to be struck in a deeply personal way, and it may not be done in the same way from one comparative theologian to another. This leaves such scholars somewhat "marginal persons," in Clooney's phrase, whose relation to the religions they connect in their study remains a question for the communities on either side. If what they do is not to be entirely and ineffably individual, it must mean something to the traditions whose integrity comparative theologians so respect, something to those within them who do not do this work. And this reconnects us to theologies of pluralism.

The line between TRP and comparative theology is not and need not be clear. Indeed, any serious effort at one will involve some of the other. Comparative theology comes in several primary forms.[9] Its religiously engaged inquiry can be explicitly grounded in a particular confessional identity or it can take the form of a more eclectic intellectual quest for religious truth.[10] It can take an open-ended form, where the questions and conclusions are left to emerge from a thematic exploration, or it can be focused around an acknowledged problem in one's own tradition for which light is sought in another.[11] The work of comparative theology is essential to the shift I believe is currently underway. That is, it is comparative theology that holds the promise of moving theology of religious pluralism from an esoteric subdiscipline to an integral feature of theology proper. Just as the distinct disciplines of biblical studies and historical studies have become necessary features of the systematic treatment of virtually any theological topic, so too will a comparative religious treatment become foundational. No systematic theologian need be a disciplinary expert in those areas. But no theologian can be competent without some formation in these fields, and she or he must regularly depend on the work of others who focus in those areas. Just so, it will come to be with comparative theology (hereafter, CT). But we are at a relatively early stage in that process.

---

8. Clooney, *Comparative Theology*, 155.

9. This description is taken from an unpublished talk by Catherine Cornille, "Approaches and Methods in Comparative Theology," at the Harvard Center for the Study of World Religions, April 20, 2012.

10. Keith Ward's work would be an example of this. See Ward, *Concept of God*; Ward, *Religion and Revelation*.

11. Francis Clooney would be an example of the first. See his description of his approach in Clooney, *Comparative Theology*. John Keenan would be an example of the second, in his study of Buddhist sources with the purpose of transposing Christology from what he sees as problematic metaphysical assumptions. See Keenan, *Gospel of Mark*. Paul Knitter articulates this approach very clearly in the personal account found in Knitter, *Without Buddha I Could Not Be a Christian*.

The Shifting Significance of Theologies of Religious Pluralism 249

TRP AND CT IN MULTIPLE RELIGIOUS TRADITIONS

I have been speaking explicitly of Christian theology. But are the TRP and CT projects reciprocal ones? Is TRP or CT done from other religious perspectives? Could these actually be cooperative interreligious projects? Are the very terms of TRP and CT so much set by Christian assumptions and needs (or by modern and postmodern Western assumptions) that they are destined to be a one way street? Comparative theology is, to this point, an overwhelmingly Christian endeavor. As is often remarked of interreligious dialogue, Christian enthusiasm (even if found among a minority of Christians) is rarely reciprocated at the same level. There are two primary issues here, the first set by the mediating role of academic scholarship and the second by the distinctive character of the religious traditions themselves.

On the first point, Parimal Patil, responding to Clooney's *Hindu God, Christian God*, describes the "asymmetrical demands" on the Hindu scholar who might wish to produce a mirrored version of that study, a Hindu study which would be "interreligious, comparative, dialogical and confessional."[12] Patil pointed out that current comparative theology must move through at least three mediations, dealing with one's own tradition, another religious tradition and the scholarly community. There is asymmetry for the Hindu scholar at each step.

For the Christian comparative theologian, the relevant sources in Christian tradition are readily available and her/his own discipline (theology) and the Western scholarly community have been mutually conditioning each other for centuries. Comparative theology may be a novel undertaking, but its primary components are close at hand. The distinctive addition is the study of another religious tradition as a theological source. For the Hindu scholar, even access to the materials from her/his own tradition (particularly in a form that can be referenced in scholarly terms) is often problematic. Doing comparative work in such a way that it "counts" with the scholarly guild is crucial for those whose livelihood is academic and not supported by a religious institution. And yet, as we have seen, Christian theology and Western intellectual traditions have been through such a long period of mutual formation that the Hindu comparative thinker may feel the academic mediation itself already seems like encounter with a different religious tradition. The Hindu comparative thinker encounters both of these obstacles before even taking up the study of the dialogue tradition. Of course, in the case of Christianity, it may be true that it will have been

---

12. Parimal G. Patil, "Hindu Theologian's Response," in Clooney, *Hindu God, Christian God*, 186.

hard for the Hindu thinker to have avoided some familiarity with Christian thought.

This imbalance is reflected in the fact that by the nineteenth century, Christian missionaries in India tended to deploy against Hinduism the criticisms that they had learned (they believed) to defend themselves against at home. In this respect, theology had taken on a strongly apologetic quality, in which it expounded basic Christian ideas in the face of presumed objections. It was driven by what representative intellectuals in the tradition regarded as the most threatening or challenging forms of thought in their cultural context. For post-enlightenment theology these were scientific thought, historical study and psychological analysis. This also meant that the academy of the twentieth century was formed in a kind of mirror image of the Christian apologetic outlook: the academic study of religion was the place where the most prominent and most distinctively Western challenges to religion (but preeminently to Christianity) were given pride of place. Other religious traditions were subject to a double mediation—partly constructed on the model of Christianity as "religions" *per se* and then subject to the same forms of study that defined critical reason in the West. Because of this history, "theology" will always be a problematic term for the task we are describing, when undertaken in another tradition (though the word is adopted by some as practically functional).

So the first problem is that the Hindu comparative thinker is constrained by a somewhat alien framework: the comparative discussion has been shaped by the concerns that come naturally to Christians. The second problem is to ask what (perhaps quite different) comparative concerns come naturally to Hindus or whether in fact they arise at all, in this sense. What would it mean to have a "comparative theology" based on dynamics intrinsic to Hindu life and thinking? If Christian comparative thinkers frame their thought around topics like revelation or incarnation or church, what would it mean for Hindu thinkers to formulate analogous projects on more traditional Hindu terms?

In other words, the "theology" in comparative theology is itself a site for comparative reflection. By which I mean that "theology" designates a set of issues and practices that constitute a dynamic within Christian history and life: issues around passing on the tradition from one generation to another, forming individuals and communities in its essentials, addressing conflicts and anomalies that arise in its life, and relating its key elements to other types or sources of knowledge and wisdom. Rather than looking for a Hindu analogue to the way Christians have done these things, it is helpful to ask first, what kinds of things seem similarly important for Hindu tradition and practice and second what ways of doing these things are most prominent? What comparative issues arise from that foundation? Interestingly, there are some Hindu thinkers who now are seriously approaching the topic from this perspective.[13]

Even the somewhat generic things I named—like passing the tradition from generation to generation or forming individuals in a life practice—have a nongeneric form in Christian theology that stems from the implicit assumption of a church, a single social body encompassing the members, and a largely shared set of rituals and beliefs which are passed on alike to all. This all looks very different where no such assumptions are in place. It is to such issues that we are continually returned when we deal in specifics. The Hindu epics, for instance, strike a Christian observer by virtue of their ubiquity in the lived tradition, similar to the universality of biblical stories in the Christian tradition. But parallels quickly break down, as the Vedas (in a narrow sense, śruti) have more the revelation character Christians associate with the Bible, while knowledge and interpretation of them may belong to particular groups for particular purposes that have no direct analogues in Christianity. Thus even to say that there are texts/scriptures and commentaries on them in both religions does not serve to identify a common activity, serving the same purposes.

This was brought home to me very helpfully a few years ago when I was invited to the meeting of a group of eminent Jewish scholars who were considering a joint project/publication that would explore Jewish forms of the "theology of religions." I was asked to give a brief talk about the development and nature of Christian theologies of religion, partly perhaps as a model, perhaps largely as a cautionary tale (they were too polite to say).

In thinking about what to say to such an audience, and in the discussion itself, I was struck very strongly with just how contingent the Christian theology of religious pluralism is. It is hard to imagine the Christian theologies of religious pluralism apart from their intellectual forerunners in the theology of mission and, equally, apart from the realities of the global mission movement. If theology of mission considered religions as abstract objects for Christian correction or replacement, the actual practice of mission brought the beginnings of actual knowledge of the traditions, exposure to the direct encounter and the authentic materials that could eventually require one to take account of the religions in their own right. In explaining how and why Christians do this kind of theological reflection, it was inevitable to say something about where it came from. And in rehearsing

---

13. See for instance Long, "(Tentatively) Putting the Pieces Together," in Clooney, *New Comparative Theology*. Francis Clooney has organized a small, ongoing consultation around this question at the Harvard Center for the Study of World Religions.

that, I was freshly aware at each step how this would or (mostly) wouldn't be relevant in a Jewish consideration of these questions.

This is summed up in the conclusion that group reached following the meeting, which was not to go forward with the project. I remember the variety of views that were expressed in the discussion. Some said that the Noahite laws were a perfectly adequate view of other religions and that the task was already done. Others said that a Jewish theology of religions was a nonstarter because there was no such thing as a Jewish theology to host it. Yet others noted that an informed knowledge of the teaching of other religions was at times a life and death matter for a persecuted minority, which did not have the luxury of being ignorant of the other—thus a certain kind of theology of religions was already a part of Jewish history. Some said new reflection was needed to correspond to the numbers of Jewish persons who manifested some kind of "double belonging" in connection to other traditions. That is, there was a practical need for some assessment of these traditions (like Buddhism) to be helpful in discerning the value or limits to such doubleness. From some of the participants I gathered a sense that the project of interpreting and assessing other religions on the basis of one's one was a presumptuous activity, and one for which there was, thankfully, no internal impetus in Jewish tradition.

Though no book was forthcoming, I'm very grateful for that meeting and what I learned from it, which was just how different the questions looked from this perspective. It was unclear that we were actually talking about the same questions. In defense of the defense of TRP that I outlined above, however, I will note that there was a sequel to this story. A later meeting of many of the same scholars did result in the production of a book that has just appeared.[14] Though the questions may vary, many of the concerns that I listed in that defense appear to be shared across traditions.

TRINITARIAN THEOLOGIES OF RELIGIOUS PLURALISM

We can say that religious pluralism is not the same reality or does not present the same kind of question to all traditions. TRP involves reflection on what it is in any single faith—intrinsic to it—that most characteristically frames issues of difference and thus the encounter with the religious other. CT involves explorations of how what is thus taken to be most constitutive of one's own tradition might itself be altered by that encounter. In Christian circles this has played out around the role of the Trinity in TRP.

14. Goshen-Gottstein and Korn, *Jewish Theology and World Religions*.

The Trinity is Christian theology's understanding of the internal ground for the diversity in God's economy of salvation, the modes of God's relation with creation. Connecting this inner ground of diversity with the reality of external religious pluralism seems to me now a marriage made in heaven. And a renewal of Trinitarian theology in the late twentieth century thought stood ready to support this reflection.[15] But this renewal did not connect sooner with the upsurge in attention to the theology of religions precisely because that connection waited on the shift that we have already described.

My own writing is a paradigm example. In my first book on religious pluralism, I am chagrined to note that Trinity merited only a couple of references in the index.[16] The shift I am describing had not yet taken place for me. So long as religious diversity was seen as a "problem" of the types we described, and above all as an issue defined around the access to salvation among those of various faiths, there was little need to make this connection. And most Christian writers did not do so, though their approaches to religious diversity tended to mirror different aspects of Trinitarian thought (a natural theology of creation, a logos Christology or a focus on the Spirit blowing where it wills).[17]

A Trinitarian theology of religions interprets religious pluralism. But the value of a Trinitarian theology for this task becomes apparent only under certain understandings of pluralism. A generically positive view of other religions is not sufficient for this purpose. It is only where the contrasts among religions are themselves valued that this dynamic can truly develop. As theologies of religion began to approach the traditions as bearing intrinsic value rather than serving strictly provisional functions as delivery vehicles, Trinity came more to the fore. It is only when the distinctive content of other traditions is viewed in a sufficiently positive light that theologians think to ground that content in the Trinitarian nature. Though it is stated as a generic abstraction, still it is accurate to say of the doctrine that it affirms intrinsic, fruitful difference in fullest unity. So long as the religions are seen either as conflictual difference or as degrees of repetition, the connection to Trinity is largely superfluous.

The promise of Trinitarian theology is its focus on the dialectic between the universal and the particular. Any Christian idea of Trinity will be inevitably constituted by the particularity of Christ at the same time that

---

15. This was an ecumenical Christian phenomenon, represented by Karl Barth in Protestantism, Karl Rahner in Catholicism and John Zizioulas in Orthodoxy. See for instance Peters, *God as Trinity*.

16. Heim, *Is Christ the Only Way?*

17. See Heim, *Grounds for Understanding*.

it in some sense relativizes that particularity. Christians do not arrive at a Trinitarian idea of God except through a maximalist understanding of Jesus' unity with God. And yet once arrived at, this same understanding of God necessarily implies that Jesus Christ cannot be an exhaustive or exclusive source for the knowledge of God nor the exhaustive and isolated act of God to save us. This is what Gavin D'Costa means in stating his thesis that "a Trinitarian theology guards against exclusivism and pluralism by dialectically relating the universal and the particular."[18] Of course, actually doing that relating is difficult, and we all may be seen to incline more toward one end than the other—as Raimundo Panikkar, for instance, is often seen to have universalized the trinity to the point of losing its particularistic basis and D'Costa himself seen by others as leaning equally heavily toward the Christological and even ecclesiological particularity. The broad benefits of a Trinitarian approach are argued effectively by D'Costa and others.[19] I share their conclusions, though I take a further step which is not so widely shared and connect Trinity with a diversity of religious ends.[20]

I believe there is an elective affinity between Trinitarian theologies and what David Griffin calls "differential pluralism." Griffin notes that pluralism has often been defined in line with one of its possible interpretations, what he calls "identist pluralism." This view holds that "all religions are oriented toward the same religious object . . . and promote essentially the same end."[21] This conflation is encouraged by the terminological convention that has come to unequivocally designate many holders of this view as "pluralists." Griffin says this is unfortunate, in that these "pluralists" do not differ from so-called inclusivists or exclusivists as to the assumption of one ultimate divine object and one human goal in adjustment to that object. They differ only over the extent to which particular religions succeed in realizing this orientation and its aim. Exclusivists would hold all religions but one strive in vain to do so. Inclusivists would say that several may do so, to the extent that they draw implicitly on sources revealed more explicitly in one or a few. And pluralists would say that many (or all) do so independently. All of these are to be contrasted with what he calls "differential" or deep pluralism, which holds that "religions promote different ends," perhaps by virtue of orienting themselves to different ultimate reference points. They cannot be

---

18. D'Costa, "Christ, the Trinity and Religious Plurality," 18.
19. See Kèarkkèainen, *Trinity and Religious Pluralism*.
20. See particularly Heim, *Salvations: Truth and Difference in Religion*.
21. Griffin, "Religious Pluralism: Generic, Identist and Deep," 24.

interpreted along only one axis. Such deep pluralism is "pluralistic soteriologically and perhaps also ontologically."²²

I believe that the logic of trintarian theologies of religion fits particularly well with differential pluralism. I say this, understanding that some significant trinitarian theologies of religion reject such pluralism and some differential pluralists do not frame their thought as trinitarian.²³ It is my contention that rich Trinitarian theologies of religion tend to arise precisely in the area where "differential pluralism" overlaps with that part of the spectrum of inclusivist theologies of religion we might call "differential inclusivism." In its Christian form, differential inclusivism would see other religious paths not only as possible avenues toward the Christian end but at the same time as distinct paths to their own. Trinitarian approaches to religious diversity respond to the ironic lack of concrete pluralism in identist pluralist writers, and to the banality of inclusivism when it affirms in other traditions only what can be found in one's own.

Trinitarian TRPs are fueled by the recognition that what is true includes what is different. Much turns on what we mean by the word "true" in that sentence. Often we mean that the maximally and definitively true also includes (on a lesser level) the relative and transitionally true. There may even be necessary transitory truths, the stuff of "skillful means" in Buddhist thought for instance, but these stand on a lower plane in a distinct hierarchy. The word "true" is being used in two quite distinct ways. Relative formulations are truly different from the ultimate, but not equally true in the same sense as the more definitive accounts. Truths of the this sort are meant to collapse or be dispelled, but those of the second sort endure. If we mean something stronger than that when we call different, apparently contrasting things "true," then it seems there are only two directions we can go. One is a radical incommensurability of plural ultimates and the other is some kind of coinherence in a complex ultimate (in Christian terms, the Trinitarian option). The truth that God is one includes the different (but not opposed nor transient) truth that God is relational.

This is a commonplace in traditional Trinitarian theology, where the diversity in the divine economy—evident for instance in the contrast between the monotheistic revelation of God's unity and the Christological revelation of God's incarnation—is referred to a root in the real diversity

22. Ibid., 24. Griffin uses both "differential pluralism" and "deep pluralism," but prefers the latter. He sees such pluralism as pioneered by John Cobb and advanced in Heim, *Salvations: Truth and Difference in Religion*.

23. Gavin D'Costa would be an example of the first. See D'Costa, *Meeting of Religions and the Trinity*. John Cobb is an example of the second. See Cobb, *Beyond Dialogue*; Cobb and Mobilization for the Human Family, *Christian Faith and Religious Diversity*.

or complexity in God's own nature. No part of the historical economy is entirely replaced or dispensed with by another (Hebrew scriptures in the Christian Bible are a sign of this): they depend upon each other. The shorthand statement "the economic trinity is the ontological trinity" expresses this idea. The various features of the historical economy are grounded in the internal economy of the self-giving love within the divine life. There can be different equally authentic dimensions of relation of God to the world because there are different types of relation encompassed within God's communion nature.

Some parts of that historical story are indeed contingent and conditional, but the bare fact of plurality in the roles and faces of God in that story is not such. That plurality is an authentic reflection of the divine process or nature. Religious differences cannot exhaustively be attributed to culturally conditioned responses to an identical divine datum. They are in part funded by differential response to a complexity of dimensions in the divine life and relations with the world. The shift I have been describing above points toward the conclusion that religious diversity is part of the divine economy (not the object of a particular practical mission task, or the subject for an apologetic or revisionist argument). It means that at least some religious differences are rooted, like differences in the traditional economy of salvation, in the divine nature of a complex God.

This raises many questions, but here I would lift up just one aspect of this approach, in connection with the task of comparative theology described earlier. We noted in that discussion the particular (and difficult) balance comparative theologians strike between openness and commitment. Though individual comparative theologians demonstrate an extraordinary ability to realize this balance, I believe it cannot be sustained by the Christian community without a basis that goes as deep in its theological identity as this balance goes in the biographies of many of these theologians. And the Trinitarian theology I have described promises to offer such a basis.

In fact, I see the criticisms raised against it as reassuring in this regard. My own TRP is criticized on one side as a chastened but still imperialistic imposition of Christian Trinitarian terms on others (a hyper-particularity). It is criticized on another side as an importation of so much pluralism into the content of trinity as to explode its Christian identity.[24] Both criticisms frequently focus on the same eschatological theme. They find an ambiguity in my writing. The ambiguity comes in the combination of two things. The first is an affirmation that those who follow a Buddhist or a Hindu path may

24. For the first, see Perry Schmidt-Leukel, "Transformation of Christian Self-Understanding in Relation to Buddhism." For the second see Kèarkkèainen, *Trinity and Religious Pluralism*.

realize the religious ends concretely sought by those traditions, in distinction from the salvation Christians might seek. The second is a hope based on my conviction that those ends are feasible only because they are rooted in real dimensions of the Trinitarian God's relation with the world, and those dimensions are themselves rooted in the divine relational nature itself. That hope is that those adherents and their ends might find their way into the communion with God and others that is salvation. This would of course involve compromise of any supposed "one and onlyness" of these ends, though no compromise of their ultimacy. And the Christian end, on the other hand, would necessarily involve an intrinsic diversity, a "co-ultimacy" involving the religions that is parallel to the Trinity itself.

In regard to my first affirmation, some critics hold I have surely departed from an essential feature of Christian faith, which is the conviction that all will be unambiguously united in the Christian end according to the divine purpose. In regard to the second hope, other critics find the smoking gun that proves I do not respect the integrity of religious others. A full discussion of these objections would constitute another paper. Perhaps a different type of Trinitarian theology of religious diversity will prove more adequate than this one. My primary purpose here is not to defend my own among all others, but to use it as an example to illustrate the trajectory we have described. This alleged ambiguity and the suspension between these two types of criticism, seem to me to mark a position that is ideal for the practice of comparative theology, supporting that peculiar combination of commitment and openness it requires. They also appear to me deeply consistent with the positive Trinitarian faith and eschatological mystery that are found in Christian sources.

I have described a shift in theologies of religious pluralism, from an adjunct role in the work of mission to a topical, more apologetic role in theology's account of religious diversity to an integral role in the understanding of central Christian doctrines. This change in the place of a TRP has run parallel with the rise of Trinitarian forms of TRP, a fact I have argued is far from coincidental. I believe that in such forms we will find the best response to the many legitimate concerns about TRP described earlier. And I believe we will find also find them the best basis on which to integrate the work of comparative theology as a permanent facet of all theological reflection. These theologies already exemplify that development, in that Trinity is not only used to interpret the religions, but the religions prove key to understanding the nature of Trinity.

BIBLIOGRAPHY

Clooney, Francis X. *Comparative Theology: Deep Learning across Religious Borders*. Malden, MA: Wiley-Blackwell, 2010.

———. *Hindu God, Christian God: How Reason Helps Break Down the Boundaries between Religions*. New York: Oxford University Press, 2001.

———. *The New Comparative Theology: Interreligious Insights from the Next Generation*. London: T. & T. Clark, 2010.

Cobb, John B., Jr. *Beyond Dialogue: Toward a Mutual Transformation of Christianity and Buddhism*. Philadelphia: Fortress, 1982.

Cobb, John B., Jr., and Mobilization for the Human Family. *Christian Faith and Religious Diversity*. Minneapolis: Fortress, 2002.

D'Costa, Gavin. "Christ, the Trinity and Religious Plurality." Chap. 2 in *Christian Uniqueness Reconsidered: The Myth of a Pluralistic Theology of Religions*, edited by Gavin D'Costa. Maryknoll, NY: Orbis, 1990.

———. *The Meeting of Religions and the Trinity*. Faith Meets Faith. Maryknoll, NY: Orbis, 2000.

Fletcher, Jeannine Hill. *Monopoly on Salvation? A Feminist Approach to Religious Pluralism*. New York: Continuum, 2005.

Goshen-Gottstein, Alon, and Eugene Korn, eds. *Jewish Theology and World Religions*. Portland, OR: Littmann, 2012.

Griffin, David Ray. "Religious Pluralism: Generic, Identist and Deep." In *Deep Religious Pluralism*, edited by David Ray Griffin, 3–38. Louisville: Westminster John Knox, 2005.

Heim, S. Mark, ed. *Grounds for Understanding: Ecumenical Resources for Responses to Religious Pluralism*. Grand Rapids: Eerdmans, 1998.

———. *Is Christ the Only Way? Christian Faith in a Pluralistic World*. Valley Forge, PA: Judson, 1985.

———. *Salvations: Truth and Difference in Religion*. Faith Meets Faith. Maryknoll, NY: Orbis, 1995.

Kèarkkèainen, Veli-Matti. *Trinity and Religious Pluralism: The Doctrine of the Trinity in Christian Theology of Religions*. Aldershot, UK: Ashgate, 2004.

Keenan, John P. *The Gospel of Mark: A Mahayana Reading*. Faith Meets Faith. Maryknoll, NY: Orbis, 1995.

Knitter, Paul F. *Introducing Theologies of Religion*. Maryknoll, NY: Orbis, 2002.

———. *Without Buddha I Could Not Be a Christian*. Oxford: Oneworld, 2009.

Long, Jeffrey. "(Tentatively) Putting the Pieces Together: Comparative Theology in the Tradition of Sri Ramakrishna." Chap. 8 in *The New Comparative Theology: Interreligious Insights from the Next Generation*, edited by Francis X. Clooney. London: T. & T. Clark, 2010.

Nicholson, Hugh. "The New Comparative Theology and the Problem of Theological Hegemonism." Chap. 3 in *The New Comparative Theology*, edited by Francis X. Clooney. London: T. & T. Clark, 2010.

Peters, Ted. *God as Trinity: Relationality and Temporality in the Divine Life*. Louisville: Westminster John Knox, 1993.

Schmidt-Leukel, Perry. "The Transformation of Christian Self-Understanding in Relation to Buddhism." *Current Dialogue* 51 (2011) 25–37.

Thatamanil, John. "Comparative Theology after 'Religion.'" In *Planetary Loves*, edited by Stephen D. Moore, 238–57. New York: Fordham University Press, 2010.

Ward, Keith. *The Concept of God*. Oxford: Blackwell, 1974.

———. *Religion and Revelation: A Theology of Revelation in the World's Religions*. New York: Oxford University Press, 1994.

17

From Soteriology to Comparative Theology and Back

A Response to Mark Heim

PETER C. PHAN

IN HER ESSAY "THINKING 'Religion': The Christian Past and Interreligious Future of Religious Studies and Theology," Jenny Daggers, professor of Theology & Religious Studies at Liverpool Hope University, links Professor Heim and me together as proponents of a theology of religions that honors both universality and particularity.[1] While deeply honored by such—quite undeserved—association with a theologian as distinguished as Mark Heim, I am even more so to be a respondent to his paper on the recent developments of the Christian theologies of religious pluralism.

There are many fruitful ways of approaching Professor Heim's informative presentation, one of which is to peruse it as Heim's own theological autobiography. The shifting movements in contemporary theologies of religions reflect Heim's own pilgrimage from an inclusivist stance to what David Griffin calls "differential pluralism" or "deep pluralism." This shift is nicely bookended by two of Heim's works on the theology of religions, namely, *Salvations: Truth and Difference in Religion* (1995)[2] and *The Depth of the Riches: A Trinitarian Theology of Religious Ends* (2001).[3] In the first,

1. *Journal of the American Academy of Religion* 78 (2010) 961–90, esp. 982–83.
2. Maryknoll, NY: Orbis, 1995.
3. Grand Rapids: Eerdmans, 2001.

Heim uses "salvations," in the unusual plural form, to emphasize that an adequate theology of religions must take into account the fact that there are many distinct religious aims, each meaningful and valid in itself. In the second, Heim argues that the Christian doctrine of the Trinity as the one God subsisting in three persons or relations, that is, Father, Son, and Spirit, may be used to represent distinct religious aims such as those propounded by Buddhism, Advaita Vedanta, and Islam.

Moving beyond the by now familiar threefold types of theologies of religions—exclusivism, inclusivism, and pluralism—Professor Heim recognizes the need of developing what is been termed "comparative theology." While some of these comparativist theologians such as James Fredericks have become skeptical of the value of the theology-of-religions enterprise,[4] Professor Heim continues to defend, as I myself have done elsewhere, its usefulness and even necessity. But, he rightly insists that comparative theology is a the next necessary step in constructing a Christian theology that not only takes non-Christian religions as objects of study but uses their beliefs and practices as data or *locus theologicus* for theological reflection on the Christian faith.

In so doing Professor Heim draws attention of students of religious pluralism to the at times irreconcilable differences among religions. His vivid account of the dialogue with Jewish scholars on the possibility of "Jewish theology of religions" serves as an opportune cautionary tale. With this deep awareness of religious differences, Heim is irrevocably committed to a double proposition: First, "those who know only their own religion, know none"; and second, "those who are not decisively committed to one faith, know no others."[5]

Heim himself is aware that his theology of religious pluralism on the basis of the Christian doctrine of the Trinity, as developed in his book *The Depths of the Riches* mentioned above, has been criticized on the one hand as being "a chastened but still imperialistic imposition of Christian Trinitarian terms on others" and on the other as "an importation of so much pluralism into the content of [the] Trinity as to explode its Christian identity." This is not the place to evaluate the validity of Heim's attempt to relate the Christian doctrine of Father, Son, and Spirit to the distinct religious aims proposed by the three religions mentioned above. Nor is it opportune to respond to the charge that either Heim's theological construal remains still too much Christian (from the liberal side) or retains too little of it (from the conservative

---

4. See Fredericks, *Faith among Faiths*.
5. *Salvations*, 1.

side). Interestingly, that Heim's proposal is objected to from the opposite sides of the theological spectrum is a good sign that it has something true to say.

Rather I would like to explore further Heim's suggestion that "comparative theology" should be the next step in the dialogue among religions. There has been a general agreement that the threefold category of exclusivism, inclusivism and pluralism, while helpful as a general roadmap to recent developments in the theology of religions and to characterize the theological position of one's own religious tradition toward other religions, does not yield a fruitful constructive theology of religions. For one thing, it focuses on the issue of the possibility of salvation for the followers of other religions and assumes a univocal concept of salvation. More importantly, it tends to view other religions a priori and from the perspective of one's own religion rather than as the other religions see themselves. Despite their differences, the three approaches, as Heim himself has persuasively argued, share a common hegemonic stance toward other religions.[6] For all practical purposes we have reached an impasse in the theology of religions built on this threefold category. Hence, Heim's suggestion of a comparative theology.

By no means a newly minted invention, "comparative theology" has recently been promoted and practiced by a group of (mostly Roman Catholic) theologians headed by Francis Clooney and James Fredericks.[7] Eschewing a priori judgments on the salvific value of non-Christian religions and refraining from constructing overarching theories of religion, practitioners of the "new comparative theology" seek to think "interreligiously" and to carry out limited and focused comparisons between selected Christian "texts" (including sacred writings, rituals, liturgical performances, ethical and ascetical practices, etc.) and those of other religious traditions with the ultimate goal of constructing a new understanding of the Christian faith itself in the light of these non-Christian data. Though related to the nineteenth-century apologetical comparative theology, comparative religion, the theology of religions, and interreligious dialogue, the new comparative theology is distinct from all of them in that it is both unabashedly confessional and rigorously academic. Furthermore, it does not intend to serve the purposes of demonstrating the superiority of Christianity and converting non-Christians but aims at understanding the teachings of *one's own faith* better with the insights gained from a close reading of the "texts" of the other religious traditions. In this way, comparative theologians are guided by two apparently conflictive postures, namely, in James Fredericks's

---

6. See Heim's critique of John Hick and Paul Knitter in his *Salvations*. The same thesis is argued by Hugh Nicholson in his *Comparative Theology and the Problem of Religious Rivalry*.

7. See Clooney, *Comparative Theology* and *New Comparative Theology*.

expressions, "commitment to the home tradition" and "a 'vulnerability' to the truth of another religious tradition."[8] Again, according to Fredericks, comparative theology understands itself as "a procedure which is normative, constructive, and revisionist, and which is done by believers for the benefits of believers, even as it includes the academy of scholars as a public to be addressed as well."[9]

The proof of comparative theology, as with any pudding, is in the eating. Fortunately, there has already been an impressive corpus of scholarly works by a cohort of younger theologians (notably, A. Bagus Laksana, Kristin B. Kiblinger, Hugh Nicholson, David A. Clairmont, Daniel Joslyn-Siemiatkoski, Michelle Voss Roberts, Tracy Sayuki Tiemeier, Jeffrey Long, John N. Sheveland, Thomas Cattoi, Anh Quoc Tran, Erika Seamon, Jerusha Lamptey, Maureen Walsh, etc.) that show the fruitfulness of the new discipline. Together with the first generation of comparative theologians (chief among whom, Francis Clooney, James Fredericks, John Berthrong, David Burrell, Catherine Cornille, Peter Feldmeier, John Keenan, Leo Lefebure, and Pam Valkenberg), these theologians have shown that Heim's proposal has become a reality, and a very promising one. The Graduate Program in Theology of Georgetown University, with religious pluralism as its object of study, is proud to be able to contribute to the building-up of this new comparative theology.

BIBLIOGRAPHY

Clooney, Francis X. *Comparative Theology: Deep Learning across Religious Borders*. Malden, MA: Wiley-Blackwell, 2010.

———. *The New Comparative Theology: Interreligious Insights from the Next Generation*. London: T. & T. Clark, 2010.

Fredericks, James L. *Faith among Faiths: Christian Theology and Non-Christian Religions*. New York: Paulist Press, 1999.

Heim, S. Mark. *The Depth of the Riches: A Trinitarian Theology of Religious Ends*. Grand Rapids: Eerdmans, 2001.

———. *Salvations: Truth and Difference in Religion*. Faith Meets Faith. Maryknoll, NY: Orbis, 1995

Nicholson, Hugh. *Comparative Theology and the Problem of Religious Rivalry*. New York: Oxford University Press, 2011.

---

8. Fredericks, introduction to Clooney, *New Comparative Theology*, xii.
9. Ibid., xiii.

18

What Has Renaissance Polyphony to Offer Theological Method?

JOHN N. SHEVELAND

How can believers approach experiences of difference and otherness in ways that encourage learning and solidarity rather than defensiveness or half-measures of inclusion amounting to little more than domestication?[1] In this essay I propose the musical, aural experience of "polyphony" as an interdisciplinary model for reimagining interreligious encounters as scenes of beauty and reconciliation. Specifically, I argue that the model of polyphony creates imaginative and moral space for religious believers to inscribe religiously distinctive voices within their identity rather than to postulate and refine various theories of inclusion that perpetuate weak forms of inclusion that keep otherness external, distanced, and thus non-reconciled. Comparative theology as an experience of polyphony is an enterprise that can, heuristically, construe religiously distinct voices as beautiful and reconciled while preserving their distinctiveness. A theological appropriation of musical polyphony can reorient the theological task as conceived in the theologian's imagination away from judgment of others—typified in

---

1. Stating the liabilities of domestication, Anne Clifford, working with language from Emmanuel Levinas and Michael Barnes, SJ, writes, "The other cannot become an object of knowledge or experience. If it does, 'egology' results and the 'I' becomes a 'living from' that uses up the other in order to fulfill its own needs and desires. For Levinas ethics is situated in an 'encounter' with the other that cannot be reduced to a symmetrical 'relationship.'" Clifford, "Global Horizon of Religious Pluralism and the Local Dialogue with the Other," 171.

many theologies of religions however well-intentioned—to an appreciation of them, and away from comparison predicated on latent competition to comparison predicated on aesthetic appreciation and moral identification.[2] In short, polyphony prizes theological aesthetics over antagonism, and dynamic human voices imbedded in history over reified religious concepts or declarative statements of an abstract nature. Solidarity is the intended outcome of this proposal, first as an intellectual virtue[3] conditioning theological thinking and speech, and second as a moral virtue[4] capable of healing the effects of domestication of religious others.

In defending this new space of imaginative and moral solidarity, this chapter makes three arguments and provides a list of cautions for prudent use of the category. The chapter argues that polyphony achieves unity among voices while preserving their distinctiveness, that the category recalls the

---

2. Peter Phan's clarification is instructive. Theologies of religions like Inclusivism (a "Fulfillment" model) and Pluralism (a "Mutuality" model) are best understood not as ill-fated attempts at interreligious dialogue upon which a moratorium should be imposed, but as examples of a preliminary, *intra*-religious dialogue in which the Christian community discerns the scope and limits of Christian doctrine in the light of religiously diverse persons and communities. Phan's observation is useful for two reasons. It preserves a limited appropriateness of theologies of religions by clarifying their function as discourses internal to the Christian community *about* religious difference and therefore, implicitly, never designed or equipped to empower concrete human encounter. It also preserves the basic critique registered against these models by comparative theologians like Clooney and Fredericks who rightly worry about the ineluctable inhospitality of abstract, *a priori* conceptualizations of the other, however well intended, a critique which can be deepened by postcolonial discourses surrounding homogenization, domestication, and violence against religiously different persons and traditions. Cf. Phan, "Praying to the Buddha," 14. For a review of improvements made by theologies of religions advocates, see Kiblinger, "Relating Theology of Religions and Comparative Theology," 21–42.

3. David Hollenbach defines intellectual solidarity as "a willingness to take other persons seriously enough to engage them in conversation and debate about what makes life worth living, including what will make for the good of our deeply interdependent public life . . . [intellectual solidarity] differs radically from pure tolerance by seeking positive engagement with the other through both listening and speaking." Hollenbach, "Is Tolerance Enough?," 13.

4. Solidarity as a moral virtue transforming personal and collective lives toward justice has been defined by James F. Keenan, who writes that "solidarity is not first and foremost a principle for action; solidarity is affective and spiritual union with others whose life situations are also being challenged and compromised. From that union we are called to act in justice. Solidarity is then first a fundamental, existential, deeply felt sense of union; but secondly it is a call to engage in certain moral practices to better the life situation of the other." Keenan, "Impasse and Solidarity in Theological Ethics," 50. For additional projects on solidarity and polyphony, see: Sheveland, "Solidarity in Three Sacred Texts," 33–45; "Solidarity through Polyphony," 171–90; and *Piety and Responsibility*.

aesthetic dimensions of voices rather than their merely cognitive or rational features, that the category accomplishes moral solidarity, and finally that several cautions should be noted in order for this new interreligious category to become ascendant.

POLYPHONY PRESERVES DISTINCTION-IN-UNITY

The musical genre of polyphony—also called counterpoint—flourished in the Renaissance and Baroque periods in the Latin West and grew out of the more simplistic Gregorian Chant, specifically, the style of harmonized chant called *Organum*, the sung prayer of Christian monks. A composer in this genre brings together multiple voices sounding their own individual melody lines.[5] It is important to note that each voice, rather than being a mere harmonic part in relationship to a dominant melody, represents a distinct melody with its own integrity and musical logic that could feasibly refrain from interaction with other melodies. But in this genre, three, four, five and rarely six melody lines are combined deliberately to produce an emergent structure of greater depth than any single melody line could produce on its own.[6] One commentator remarks that "[i]t is hard to write a beautiful song. It is even harder to write several individually beautiful songs that, when sung simultaneously, sound as a more beautiful polyphonic whole."[7]

Clearly the difficult compositional task of combining multiple melodies, beautiful individually in their own right, can give rise to more beauty than could be perceived in temporally isolated soundings of those melodies. Multiple melody lines superimposed on each other create an aural experience for the listener in which the voices mutually self-refer and self-modify to create a polyphonic whole more beautiful than the sum of its parts. Again:

> The internal structures that create each of the voices, separately must contribute to the emergent structure of the polyphony, which in turn must reinforce and comment on the structures of the individual voices. The way that is accomplished in detail is . . . "counterpoint."[8]

---

5. Leading composers included Jacob Obrecht (*d.* 1505), Josquin des Prez (*d.* 1521), Giovanni Pierluigi da Palestrina (*d.* 1594), and William Byrd (*d.* 1623), and later, Johann Sebastian Bach (*d.* 1750).

6. Copland, *What to Listen for in Music*, 86.

7. Rain, *Music Inside and Out*, 177.

8. Ibid., 177.

Not only do individual voices when combined give rise to a more beautiful emergent structure. That emergent structure also bends back, reflexively, as a movement that now sheds further light on the individual voices comprising it. An individual voice changes *while it sounds* as a consequence of the movement's other voices.[9] As Zuckerkandl explains, "The musical meaning of a tune is affected and may be changed by the other tonal motions that go on at the same time."[10] The emergent structure or polyphonic chord offers the hearer a new vantage point, a new aural context or set of resources with which to appreciate individual voices. That new vantage point affords unexpected insight into the previously isolated voices. Rather than assaulting the ear with dissonance, polyphony reveals consonance.[11] Parallel motifs, tensions, and disagreements among the voices are sharpened in the chord. A previously unobserved quality in a given melody line breaks through more clearly on account of a separate voice contrapuntally drawing out its quality by way of contrasting with it. Contrast functions as a heuristic tool training the ear to appreciate both the emergent structure of the whole and the irreducible particularity of the voices constituting that structure. Indeed, contrast and even tension between voices represents the condition for the possibility of consonance. To articulate the point somewhat more starkly, one hears an impoverished version of a given voice when it remains isolated within its own logic.

Transposing all of this to a comparative theological discussion involves recognizing that an audience understands an individual religious speaker with greater nuance and sophistication when her speech is heard communally in a shared context with other speech. Pluriformity thus enriches experience and enhances the conditions for the possibility of understanding rather than poses a theological problem that, for example, must be addressed through the home tradition's interpretive or doctrinal criteria. Polyphony resists the temptation to caricature other voices or pass over their real differences; it relies on texture and difference as the condition of its possibility. So too, comparative theology acknowledges difference as a *sine qua non* for engaging the other with hospitality and integrity. The

---

9. Zuckerkandl, *Sense of Music*, 149.

10. Ibid., 150.

11. "The theologically minded musicians of the Middle Ages saw in the two states of consonant and dissonant sound the tonal counterpart of Good and Evil: That Which Should Be, and That Which Should Not Be. One thing the two pairs certainly have in common: the distinction as such of consonance and dissonance has been questioned as little as the distinction of good and evil; but as to the specific question as to what sounds should be called consonant, what dissonant, the opinion of the ages differ just as much as they do about specific moral questions." Zuckerkandl, *Sense of Music*, 152.

dynamics of counterpoint within polyphony support the moral imperative of taking our companions in dialogue seriously precisely in their difference, but not isolation, from us.

Comparative or interreligious theologians recognize, value, and preserve distinctions while attending to emergent structures of intelligibility that can motivate and reward the making of comparisons. They do so by underscoring the real differences, contrasts, and tensions between voices in order to resist domestication, caricature, and hegemonic discourses. On the other hand, they are keenly interested in the possible emergence of a unitive framework of intelligibility making comparison both possible and profitable. Polyphony encourages theologians to pursue both tasks, with the additional benefit of underscoring the aesthetic qualities imbedded in the emergent structure of intelligibility which impact the listener and drive her to continue the exposure and value it as aesthetically meaningful. This task is demanding both in music and in the theological application. As Aaron Copland indicates,

> Music that is polyphonically written makes greater demands on the attention of the listener, because it moves by reason of separate and independent melodic strands, which together form harmonies. . . . Polyphonic texture implies a listener who can hear separate strands of melody sung by separate voices, instead of hearing only the sound of all voices as they happen from moment to moment."[12]

The demand placed on musicians and listeners of which Copland speaks is strongly analogous to the demands placed upon theologians and religious communities in today's religiously plural and hyper connected world. Musically, if polyphonic texture requires a listener capable of hearing and parsing separate if related strands of melody sung by individual voices, then similar demands can be said to obtain for religious speech today: not only must it be attuned to distinctions and otherness where these surface, but there must be also a corresponding resistance against the urge to homogenize the pluriform voices of today's religious landscape, an urge through laziness, indifference, or convenience to refuse the patient listening that parses distinctions between voices as well as possible grounds for analogical relationships between them. The inhospitality hovering above discourses of *homogeneity* tends to be compounded by *hegemonic* discourses within and about religious voices.

Examples of hegemonic discourses within and about religions are supplied by various theologies of religions which, however diverse,

12. Copland, *What to Listen for in Music*, 84–85.

well-intended and focused on inclusion of others they may be, tend overwhelmingly to include otherness by demonstrating power over it through self-referential categorization of otherness. This mode of categorization notes similarities or affinities but also imputes varying degrees of error, limitation, or incompleteness. Strategies of inclusion in many theologies of religions function like hegemonic discourses because they fail to attend adequately to the richly textured particularity of the other who, though determined to be fit for inclusion, becomes absorbed into or fulfilled within the normative structures of the home tradition, the same tradition which generated the terms of inclusion in the first place and employed in-house doctrinal criteria as the standard of interpretation and assessment. In a climate wherein such theological tendencies are evident and increasingly neuralgic, the category of polyphony functions to interrupt hegemonic categorization by soliciting a generously patient listening to the voices available to experience. Polyphony encourages in listeners greater levels of personal and communal comfort with the supposition that each voice or melody is fundamentally non-reducible to external criteria of interpretation, even as each voice exists alongside other voices and can be interpreted reciprocally alongside them.

POLYPHONY AMPLIFIES THE AESTHETIC EXPERIENCE OF THEOLOGICAL COMPARISON

The transportation of polyphony into comparative theological method contributes a new, aesthetic understanding of interreligious dialogue and learning that deliberately eschews reductive modes of comparison which stress the cognitive or rational features of theological speech and even doctrinal language. Aesthetic features ground the latent potential of texts, traditions, and voices to induce an affective appreciation of the new vocal tone and its effects on the new communal tone. Not only are the texts, voices and traditions viewed as species of beauty, but the sound they create together in the new listener is apprehended as beautiful. The overworked speculations concerning the status of another religion's truth claims vis-à-vis those of one's own become less urgent in this model and replaced by a readiness to be edified by the voices and language of the dialogue and the learning it produces. These voices and languages now occupy public and shared space characterized by a principal of non-competition since musical polyphony depends on multiple melody lines combined in a non-competitive fashion for the production of beauty. To be sure, at various points in a score of music certain voices become more emergent or prominent than others. But no single voice in polyphony is continually dominant or even continually present; dynamics of augmentation, diminution, and rest apply to all voices.[13] Each voice represents a melody that cannot be reduced to a mere subsidiary harmonic relationship to another's dominant melody. Precedence and subsequence are replaced by musical dynamics such as augmentation and diminution, which focus the audience on contextual relationships of interaction, on the (re)discovery of one's own familiar voice as a member of a community of voices, and on the emergent beauty of the whole.

The analogy with comparative theology is clear. No one speaker should be self-preoccupied in ways which exclude other voices or construe some voices in terms of static, normative positions of precedence and subsequence relative to other voices. While a theologian does learns from colleagues and texts in other traditions, she does well to consider the affective or aesthetic component of the sound produced in community and heard in an even wider community. This common sound (to use an aural image) or this public square (to use a spatial image) functions in the first instance as the condition for the possibility of comparison. She does well to let her ear become trained, sensitive to, and accountable to the larger whole of which her voice is a part. It is not a dialogue over which she exercises control but one of unpredictable development, of reciprocal illumination, and surprising edification consistent with the dynamism of human voices imbedded in community and history. This dialogue can, just like polyphony, be marked by a great complexity of voices educating the careful listener, and it can also be marked by great tension begging for resolution. She will perceive this tension and valorize—not flatten out or domesticate—its place in the theological community as voices contributing to a complex score of music, each of which speak to the irreducible mystery grasping and shaping them. The polyphony model can shift the theologian's attention away from theological learning as information gathering and transfer leading to conformity—away from implementation of predetermined conceptual norms—toward appreciation of the dynamics of relationship and beauty among and between voices.

POLYPHONY CONTRIBUTES A NEW METAPHOR TO IMAGINE THE SOLIDARITY OF ALL IN ENCOUNTER

This third proposal suggests that theological speakers are bound together in a common enterprise or symphony *because of* their diversity, which has now become not a problem to be solved but a richness to be preserved and

---

13. Ibid., 134. See Cornille, *Im-possibility of Interreligious Dialogue*, 9–58.

promoted. My neighbor's voice not merely communicates new information about her to me; it also contributes to my own self-understanding, increases the parameters of my own identity, and helps me to locate myself in solidarity with her in a global community of dynamic religious encounter. Our differences and distinctions no longer relegate us to a competitive zero-sum' game of differential and non-relational self-understanding but instead find shelter together under a larger rubric of unity, though not identification.

This change in the perception of religious difference is considerable. If this sort of corporate endeavor seizes the theological imagination, the prospects for interreligious learning and conflict resolution are encouraging. The change in perception would spell humility in the best sense of the word: an awareness of our individual limits and gifts coupled with a willingness to learn from others who have now become resources ignored at our own peril, voices whose diminishment signals a lost opportunity to deepen wisdom and understanding. In short, the polyphony model renders "enclave theology" a peculiar contradiction in a world that is better described as an interactive commons wherein no voice sounds or is heard alone.[14]

Solidarity is a principle virtue and vocation which may help to describe this interdependence and relational self-understanding. It represents a thick species of empathy and action for others that bear some modest relation to what John Paul II referred to as the experience of "interdependence" that characterizes modern persons in today's globalized world.[15] While interdependence is a virtue which all persons can understand and enact, the depth of meaning of solidarity requires additional vocabulary. Its meaning in the Christian community is to be found in qualities of Christian faith and life which regard one's neighbor "as the living image of God the Father, redeemed by Jesus, and placed under the action of the Holy Spirit."[16] To date, the elaboration of solidarity in Catholic Social Teaching has privileged the interdependence of human persons and societies, linking it to social, economic, and political justice.

Yet the principle of solidarity obtains meaningfully in contexts of interreligious encounter, too. Insofar as one can be trained gradually to hear and appreciate distinct voices in musical polyphony, augmenting one's range

---

14. "By enclave theology I mean a theology based narrowly in a single tradition that seeks not to learn from other traditions and enrich them, but instead to topple and defeat them. . . . Whether openly or secretly it is not really interested in dialogue but in rectitude and hegemony. . . . It is in danger of what Paul rejected as 'party spirit' or 'works of the flesh,' namely, enmity, strife, and factionalism (Gal. 5:20)." Hunsinger, *Eucharist and Ecumenism*, 1.

15. John Paul II, *Sollicitudo rei socialis*, §38.

16. Curran et al., "Commentary on *Sollicitudo rei socialis*," 429.

of affect, sensitivity, and even sense of identity so that, consequently, one seeks to hear, learn from, and incorporate yet more exposure to religiously different voices, so too with solidarity. For in Christian experience, solidarity is both an intellectual and moral virtue. It is an intellectual virtue when the other's voice makes a demand on me to be heard and is given space and place to be so. Solidarity is a moral virtue when spontaneous empathy for and action on behalf of other persons flows from the Christian experience of self and other being together the subjects of divine grace and reconciliation. Rather than mere pragmatic assent to the *de facto* interdependence of persons and communities today that attends globalization, solidarity more profoundly enacts a species of love (*caritas*) for neighbors that fundamentally recalculates their human goodness in keeping with who they are as subjects of divine action.[17] As Curran, Himes, and Shannon noted, "[s]olidarity in this understanding has dimensions of total gratuity, forgiveness, and reconciliation. The neighbor is a living image of God the Father, redeemed by Jesus, and placed under the action of the Holy Spirit."[18] As these actions define and lend depth to the dignity of such persons, solidarity is a virtue which simply is in keeping with their identity as persons who are subjects of divine action. It is, therefore, a vocation to be realized and embodied in a world where the perception of these realities is often unclear, where the moral action required of solidarity is often refused, and where the call to solidarity prepares one to lose oneself for the sake of the good of others rather than exploit or instrumentalize them for one's own ends.[19] If such solidarity must be retrieved in today's troubled climate of global and local religious encounter, polyphony as a model for interreligious encounter is one heuristic that can help, principally by preserving the autonomous dignity of all voices, by inviting each voice to hear and be heard by others interdependently, and by fostering the development of a more capacious sense of identity made possible by encounter.

---

17. I have suggested elsewhere that solidarity is "an active empathic response to neighbors near and far which senses them as dear and spontaneously gives rise to active resistance of structures of oppression. Far more than a passive sentiment of sympathy for the other, solidarity is active, transformative, and valorized by specifically theological commitments. That is, it is a spiritual virtue predicated on the radical, objective unity of persons with each other as constituent members of the reconciled body of Christ whose vocation it is to *re-member* that body, such that all members of that body are treated as "somebodies" rather than "nobodies," indeed, as "somebodies" to whom I am spontaneously responsible." Sheveland, "Solidarity in Three Sacred Texts," 33.

18. Curran et al., "Commentary on *Sollicitudo rei socialis*," 429.

19. John Paul II, *Sollicitudo rei socialis*, §38.

REDEEMING THEOLOGICAL IMAGINATION

An interdisciplinary offering of this sort can complicate matters and place significant demands on those who would apply it to theological reflection. While this essay's use of polyphony is meant to reinvest interreligious encounter with aesthetics, affect, and solidarity, it also brings with it some potential stumbling blocks, as do all highly particular methodological constructs. I list five of these now as a caution and indicator of nuance yet to be teased out for the model to be satisfactory. If sufficiently named and avoided, these five points of caution create greater imaginative space for theological reflection on religious others to carry on in ways that are redeemed or liberated from ideological tendencies that preserve power for some by distorting others.

Superficiality. It will not do to enlist the model without adequate compliance to the demands of music as an independent field of original application. The theologian-composer will need to acquire a working knowledge of polyphony, including its historical antecedents, development, ecclesial context, and possible non-Western and non-Christian parallels. She might also *experience* musical polyphony by listening to actual examples of this type of music in order to train the ear better to hear the complexity of vocal polyphony, voices' similarity-in-difference, tensions, consonance, dissonance, resolutions, and other meaningful dynamics of a musical score. With that aesthetic grounding one can then imagine if and how theological voices might similarly be arranged.

Incommensurability. Neither in music nor in interreligious encounter is polyphony designed to tolerate unlimited degrees of difference, nor relativism. Where even marked differences can be organized and understood as polyphony, we need theologian-composers sensitive to harmonic depth in the voices and texts being compared and who are able to anticipate possible resolutions to movements marked by tension or even dissonance. Where harmonic depth and resolution of dissonance into consonance elude the listener, we need patient and attentive theologian-composers who can rest in and navigate through that tension through a deeper listening that may resist finality of interpretation, knowing, too, that no properly theological subject matter ever receives finality of interpretation. A deeper listening may not, in all cases, render unnecessary the application of theological norms to determine the line of demarcation between on the one hand differences that together create polyphonic consonance and, on the other, differences which together lack resolution and are dissonant. Just as not all tension can or should find resolution, nor should companions in dialogue be expected to reduce their confessional stance or delimit their understanding of what counts as true and real.[20] Thus, one must ask how comparative theologians should navigate the important demands of communal norms while not sacrificing the hospitable and solidaristic outcomes polyphony envisions.[21]

Reception. How will my companions in dialogue and all people of good will receive my construal of their voices according to this model? Is this interdisciplinary musing, like so much theology to date, plagued by a Western cultural hegemony, however aesthetic and well-intentioned? Theologian-composers must tend to concerns that this method prioritizes a norm alien to the traditions to which it is being applied and that it is just one more cloaked version of a Western or Christian imperialism indifferent to the perception of those to whom the metaphor is meant peaceably to apply. While no speaker should have to apologize for her particularity it is also wise to wield that particularity prudently, sensitively, dialogically, and with historical consciousness. In such cases of methodological failure, the comparativist bears the responsibility of clearly stating the model's irenic intentions with respect to intellectual and moral solidarity and accepting the possibility that in these cases the model may serve those intentions inadequately.

Verification and Multiple Attestation. The merit of polyphony as an organizing principle for interreligious encounter will stand or fall on the basis of its capacity to characterize the dynamics of theological comparisons in meaningful and edifying ways. Comparative theologians will need to test its fitness as a principle capable of organizing the independent voices of companions in dialogue. Multiple experiments are needed which deal in highly specific subject matter in order for the model to gain credence by passing the test of multiple attestation, that is, by organizing multiple sets of discrete comparisons. Such attestations will speak to the fitness of the model and its promise for future efforts, especially if polyphony can be appreciated retroactively to organize theological voices meaningfully rather than to precondition and thus control their utterances prior to the encounter.

Rigidity. Use of this interdisciplinary metaphor should be suggestive, imaginative, and heuristic. It should not be absolute or rigid. One will meet with little success by rigidly transporting the many rules entailed in musical polyphony directing into theological comparison as though their relationship is one of univocity or one-to-one correspondence, as though theological voices resemble fixed, static sounds rather than dynamic and

---

20. Clooney, "Comparative Theology," 662.

21. Zuckerkandl, *Sense of Music*, 146, 155. "The inevitably and permanently dialogical character of an interreligious and comparative theology does not mean that such a theology always eventuates in mutual agreement and understanding. Such a theology can remain confessional, even apologetic." Clooney, "Comparative Theology," 662.

developing tones subject ineluctably to change in history, community, and through encounter with the other. Far from a predetermined template fitted onto theological voices, polyphony should function heuristically to represent the promise of consonant voices, the promise of dissonant voices finding consonance in the one chord, and the promise associated with multiple voices sounding together complexly and richly in such a way as to change how all voices are heard. Polyphony should be imported into comparative theological reflection as an aesthetic and even moral paradigm but not as a system of fixed rules voices are then promptly deemed to comply with or deviate from. The model is proposed to serve real human beings imbedded in concrete histories, interactions, and liabilities, by shifting the paradigm for encounter toward these aesthetic and moral commitments; it does not in the first instance seek to satisfy specialists in either academic field.

In these ways the model of polyphony, not yet adequately verified but replete with potential, may contribute an interdisciplinary model by which theologians can be dialogical, that is, aware of differences contrapuntally and aesthetically rather than antagonistically, and in so doing help us to move toward the transformative experiences of intellectual and moral solidarity to which our traditions rightly call us.[22]

BIBLIOGRAPHY

Clooney, Francis X. "Comparative Theology." In *The Oxford Handbook of Systematic Theology*, edited by John Webster, 653–59. New York: Oxford University Press, 2007.

Clifford, Anne. "Global Horizon of Religious Pluralism and the Local Dialogue with the Other." In *New Horizons in Theology*, edited by Terrence W. Tilley, 162–81. Maryknoll, NY: Orbis, 2004.

Copland, Aaron. *What to Listen for in Music*. New York: Penguin Classics, 2002.

Cornille, Catherine. *The Im-possibility of Interreligious Dialogue*. New York: Crossroad, 2008.

Curran, Charles E., et al. "Commentary on *Sollicitudo rei socialis (On Social Concern)*." In *Modern Catholic Social Teaching*, edited by Kenneth R. Himes, 415–35. Washington, DC: Georgetown University Press, 2005.

Hollenbach, David. "Is Tolerance Enough? The Catholic University and the Common Good." *Conversations on Jesuit Higher Education* 13 (1998) 5–11.

Hunsinger, George. *The Eucharist and Ecumenism: Let Us Keep the Feast*. Current Issues in Theology. Cambridge: Cambridge University Press, 2008.

---

22. *In Memoriam*, Roger O. Doyle, D.M.A. (1939–2012), Emeritus Professor, University of Portland. I am grateful to Thomas Tweed, Peter Phan, and Daniel Madigan S.J. for their remarks at the conference, and to Joseph Mudd for comments on an earlier draft of the essay.

John Paul II. *Sollicitudo rei socialis* [On social concern]. http://www.vatican.va/holy_father/john_paul_ii/encyclicals/documents/hf_jp-ii_enc_30121987_sollicitudo-rei-socialis_en.html.

Keenan, James F. "Impasse and Solidarity in Theological Ethics." *Catholic Theological Society of America Proceedings* 64 (2009) 47–60.

Kiblinger, Kristin Beise. "Relating Theology of Religions and Comparative Theology." In *The New Comparative Theology*, edited by Francis X. Clooney, 21–42. New York: T. & T. Clark, 2010.

Phan, Peter. "Praying to the Buddha: Living amid Religious Pluralism." *Commonweal*, January 26, 2007. http://commonwealmagazine.org/praying-buddha-0.

Rain, John. *Music Inside and Out: Going Too Far in Musical Essays*. Singapore: G+B Arts International, 2001.

Sheveland, John N. *Piety and Responsibility: Patterns of Unity in Karl Rahner, Karl Barth, and Vedanta Desika*. Burlington, VT: Ashgate, 2011.

———. "Solidarity in Three Sacred Texts." *Vidyajyoti Journal of Theological Reflection* 74 (2010) 33–45.

———. "Solidarity through Polyphony." In *The New Comparative Theology: Interreligious Insights from the Next Generation*, edited by Francis X. Clooney, 171–90. New York: T. & T. Clark, 2010.

Zuckerkandl, Victor. *The Sense of Music*. Princeton: Princeton University Press, 1959.

19

Karl Rahner's "Anonymous Christianity" in Light of Pluralism and Contemporary Theology of Religions in Asia

TODD E. JOHANSON

KARL RAHNER IS ARGUABLY the most significant and influential Catholic theologian of the twentieth century. He played a major role in shaping the theology of Vatican II, bringing the Catholic Church fully into the modern world. In fact, Herbert Vorgrimler argues that Rahner played a major role in shaping all of the Vatican II documents except four.[1] One document that he directly helped to draft and that strongly bears the mark of his theology is *Nostra Aetate*, the Church's declaration on its relationship to non-Christians. That groundbreaking document remains the cornerstone of post-Vatican II Catholic inclusivist theologies, as does Rahner's form of inclusivism in general.[2] Rahner's position epitomizes the dominant form of inclusivism in Catholic theology to this point, particularly in the post-Vatican II magisterium.[3] His work is at the heart of the emerging inclusivist theology that

1. Vorgrimler, *Understanding Karl Rahner*, 100.

2. For a succinct overview and analysis of the pertinent Vatican II documents in general, and *Nostra Aetate* in particular, see Karkkainen, *Introduction to the Theology of Religions*, 111–22.

3. Although Rahner brought an unprecedented openness to the Church via his "liberal" push for renewal and modernization as reflected in Vatican II in general and *Nostra Aetate* in particular, his inclusivist stance of "anonymous Christianity," while novel

continues to develop in the Church in light of our pluralistic, globalizing context. Jeannine Hill Fletcher asserts that "it is hard to name a theologian who has singularly influenced the contemporary discourse on religious pluralism more than Karl Rahner."[4] A perennial issue in that context is how to account for God's gracious activity outside of the visible Church, which is foundational in determining the Church's relationship to non-Christian religions. Rahner's inclusivist theology gave rise to the idea of "anonymous Christianity" as an expression that epitomizes his inclusivism. Asian theologians have been influenced by Rahner's thought, and in their interaction with it in that pluralistic context, they have both appropriated his theology and challenged it and its limitations for the Church in Asia today. In the interaction between the predominant Eurocentric tradition (as expressed in the magisterium and in Rahner's thought) and the emerging Asian theology of religions, two of the key issues are interreligious dialogue and multiple religious belonging. The identity and role of Christ is a critical underpinning of both issues. I will explore these issues in assessing how the interaction between Rahner and Asian voices can further our understanding of religious identity and interaction in developing Catholic inclusivist theology, in light of both the uniqueness of traditional claims about Christ and their applicability in a diverse contemporary context such as Asia. I will attempt to show that Rahner's inclusivist theology is still highly relevant for today, but that it is also in need of further exploration, contextualized appropriation, expansion, and transformation in order for the Church's inclusivism to adequately address the realities and needs of the contemporary pluralistic world.[5] I will suggest some key ideas in his theology that merit further exploration, and begin to explore those ideas myself. In short, Rahner provides an essential foundation, but we need more to stay in fruitful dialogue with non-Christians in ways that can help Christians and non-Christians alike to seek truth, grow in healthy interrelationships, and pursue justice and peace together. My test case for Rahner's applicability will be primarily Peter Phan's appropriation of Rahner in the context of contemporary Asian theology of religions.

Rahner expressed the essence of his inclusivism with the phrase "anonymous Christianity," a term that he coined and to which he referred in

---

and significant, is nonetheless Christocentric, Eurocentric, and largely dogmatically deferent to the Church's tradition. Rahner's influence is also evident in post-Vatican II magisterial documents such as *Dialogue and Proclamation* and *Dominus Iesus*.

4. Hill Fletcher, "Rahner and Religious Diversity," 235.

5. This sentiment is widely expressed in contemporary theology; see, e.g., Bell, "Constraints on the Theological Absorption of Plurality."

multiple writings.⁶ Since Rahner affirmed that Jesus Christ is the universal, singular, absolute Savior, all who receive salvation do so through Christ. However, by virtue of his theology of grace in conjunction with his universal theological anthropology of transcendence, Rahner also affirmed that this can be accomplished unthematically.⁷ Rahner's theology resides in the tension of a dialectic: on the one hand, Jesus Christ is the absolute Savior, and faith and the Church are necessary for salvation; on the other hand, there are degrees of membership in the Church, and the bestowal of grace is made effective for salvation in all who move toward God in transcendent openness and embrace grace. This could be entirely unthematic; someone simply needs to accept the offer of grace implicitly by accepting her own being. Nonetheless, the openness that does not explicitly say "no" to God, but remains open to the movement of grace, is still in the grace of Jesus Christ and continues to seek after God. Thus, there is a continuous movement toward God in grace-enabled openness that will keep driving toward an explicit faith in Jesus Christ in whatever way life circumstances allow.⁸ Rahner accepted that the world's religious traditions are concrete mediations of transcendental grace and revelation, and are often insightful and fruitful. They are also positively divinely willed, and are therefore means of encountering grace in concrete history; it must be so, because grace is only experienced categorically. Additionally, since humanity has an innate openness to the other, this experience of grace is realized in our relationships with others in which love is expressed. There is a fundamental unity between love of neighbor and of God, and God is both the object and ground of all love. Thus, to love is to move in transcendence toward the goal of union with God as salvation, and to show implicit faith.⁹ This transcendent movement is Christological in character, and is brought about universally by the Spirit of God.¹⁰

Rahner's theology has received much criticism. That criticism has been particularly focused on his idea of the anonymous Christian.¹¹ Whether the term itself is useful, the critical question is this: Is the universal, transcendental, inclusivist perspective that the term represents still viable, particularly

---

6. See, e.g., "Anonymous Christians" and "Observations on the Problem of the Anonymous Christians."

7. Rahner, *Foundations of Christian Faith*, 176.

8. Rahner, *Theological Investigations*, 6:390–98.

9. Duffy, "Experience of Grace," 52–53.

10. Pandiappallil, *Jesus the Christ and Religious Pluralism*, 103.

11. For a detailed discussion of the critique of Rahner's idea of anonymous Christianity, see Crowley, "Encountering the Religious Other," 567ff. See also Hill Fletcher, "Rahner and Religious Diversity," 235–47.

in non-European and multi-cultural, multi-religious contexts today? The answer is yes, at least for the Church in many parts of Asia. Rahner himself recognized the need for the integral, inculturated, internal development of non-Eurocentric theologies in non-European cultures, admitting that they not only can develop in that way, but in fact they must.[12] The fact that a Japanese translation of *Foundations* was produced, and with a new foreword by Rahner, is a tell-tale sign of his global influence.[13] Rahner's thought has found a fresh reception in the Church in Asia, promoting considerable creative appropriation. Rahner's theology has had a significant influence on the Federation of Asian Bishops' Conferences, including in issues around inculturation, interreligious dialogue, and the option for the poor.[14] Asian theologians in general are also showing an openness to and an interest in Rahner, particularly around ecclesiology, theological method, and mission. The main mission strategy of the Asian Church is to address Asian cultures, religions, and the poor through mutual dialogue. Even the concept of the anonymous Christian has been better received there than in the West.[15] A major appropriation has been the idea of transcendence as a vehicle for positive social and religious change, as well as a personal affirmation of the individual's value and her responsibility. A prominent Asian theologian today who has been influenced by Rahner is Peter Phan.

Phan's work epitomizes the incorporation of Rahnerian theology into an Asian approach to theology. Rahner's influence is evident in Phan's work regarding multiple religious belonging and interreligious dialogue in the encounter with the complex, pluralistic world of Asia.[16] Regarding the concept of multiple religious belonging in the Church in Asia, Phan makes a positive appropriation of Rahner. Phan notes the ubiquitous nature of multiple religious belonging in Asia, and how it is becoming much more common in the West. It poses serious challenges to Christian identity and mission as well as to dialogue, but nonetheless he sees it as strongly positive.[17] He discusses it in terms of those who are raised Christian, but in a pluralistic setting. He defines it as including but going beyond inculturation and dialogue. In such a hyphenated religious identity, Christians accept both doctrines and

---

12. From the foreword to a 1981 Japanese translation of *Foundations*, quoted in Griener, "Rahner and the Pacific Rim," 54.

13. Ibid.

14. Ibid., 58–59.

15. Ibid., 61.

16. While I acknowledge the prominence that Phan gives to liberation theology in addition to multiple-religious belonging and interreligious dialogue, I have largely bracketed that issue for this chapter due to space considerations.

17. Phan, *Being Religious Interreligiously*, 60.

practices of another religion, and live those beliefs, values, and practices in their daily lives. He asks whether such a hyphenated identity is theologically possible as authentically Christian. He gives a positive answer, but notes that with Christianity's strong, universal truth claims, a theology of religions that can incorporate it must be carefully delineated.[18] Phan identifies eight essential characteristics of such a theology. First, upholding the truth of Jesus Christ as the unique and universal Savior does not exclude non-Christians from salvation. Second, the fact of Jesus as the absolute Savior[19] does not prevent acknowledging the goodness and truth in other religions, nor their function as ways of salvation. Phan's concepts, and even his particular language here, are quite reminiscent of Rahner.[20] Phan even discusses in a long footnote how Rahner supported this view with the idea that God positively willed other religions and that others are saved through those religions via their embodiments of grace.[21] Third, that function of other religions is carried out by both the Logos and the Spirit. The Logos is identical with Jesus, but not exhausted by him. The Logos and the Spirit are intimately connected, but distinct, and at times the Spirit operates beyond the Logos in saving presence beyond Christianity.[22] The idea that Jesus does not exhaust the Logos is both theologically and logically sound. If the Logos is divine, and divinity is characterized by omnipotence, omniscience, and omnipresence, then clearly the person and work of Jesus Christ does not exhaust the Logos due to the finitude of his humanity. As long as it is affirmed that the Logos was fully and uniquely present in Jesus, the Logos would still be fully present and active everywhere else too-otherwise, the Logos would not be God. However, the separation of the economic activity of the Logos and the Spirit is problematic from a Catholic dogmatic perspective. While the Logos and the Spirit are distinguishable, they are ultimately intimately intertwined and inseparable; *Dominus Iesus* specifically rejects the idea that the work of the Spirit is beyond the scope of the Logos.[23] Additionally, any working

---

18. Ibid., 61–63.

19. For Phan, absolute does not mean exclusive, but inclusive, constitutive, reciprocal, relational, participatory, and mutually fulfilling, albeit with a certain primacy given to the Christian side of the dynamic. See *Being Religious Interreligously*, 60–101, and 137–46.

20. Ibid., 64–65.

21. Ibid., 64.

22. Ibid., 65.

23. *Dominus Iesus* 6 and 12. Phan contends that *DI* 6 does not condemn the perspective that he elucidates, but he does not mention *DI* 12, which seems to give a clear rebuttal of the position he takes. Explaining more fully how his perspective is compatible with *DI* in general, and 12 in particular, would strengthen his case.

of the Spirit beyond the Logos is contrary to the Logos' omniscience, omnipresence, and universal saving mission to the cosmos, as well as to the perichoretic union of the Logos and the Spirit. Besides, it is not necessary to posit a working of the Spirit beyond the Logos for other religions to have meaningful teaching and dialogue for Christians, nor for there to be room to be surprised by what the Spirit may reveal through religious others. The infinity of the Logos can be just as creative and surprising in bringing us to new or deeper realizations of faith and practice. The economic unity of the Spirit and the Logos then does not diminish the case for a Christian theology and practice of multiple religious belonging. Rahner's perspective is helpful with this issue; grace is always Christological in character, but it is also always inclusive, ubiquitous, and brought about by the Spirit as the truly loving, saving, universal self-communication of God, even if the Christological character of it remains unthematic.

Fourth, religious pluralism is to be accepted both in fact and in principle, since God in grace has included other religions in salvation history; they have a positive, particular role to play in their own right, and not as mere stepping stones or seeds destined to be fulfilled by Christianity.[24] Some tension with Rahner emerges here; Rahner clearly held that other religions and their adherents were still transcendentally seeking the ultimate fulfillment in Christ via explicit Christianity. Rahner did not anticipate the idea that someone who was a committed Christian may also want to self-identify with another religion. This is an example of how everyday reality can chafe against his somewhat overly theoretical and philosophical Christocentric transcendentalism. In holding primarily to theorizing and leaving it to historians of religion and others to do the field work, Rahner's ability to speak to diverse situations and contexts is somewhat limited. Fifth, the autonomy of non-Christian religions does not detract from either the fact of Jesus as the unique and universal Savior, nor of the Christian Church as the sacrament of Christ's salvation. Christ's uniqueness is constitutive and relational, meaning that he is the only one who opens access to God for all people, but since the other religions are a part of God's salvific plan, with Christ as the culminating point, they are related to Christ and each other.[25] Here, Phan is upholding the dialectic of autonomy and relationality in an essential unity; such a use of dialectic is typically Rahnerian, as is the language that Phan uses in this section. Sixth, there is therefore a reciprocal relationship between Christianity and other religions; they mutually complement and enrich each other. Dialogue is essential to them bearing fruit in and for each

---

24. Phan, *Being Religious Interreligiously*, 65–66.
25. Ibid., 66.

other. Seventh, there is also a reciprocal relationship between Jesus Christ and other savior figures. Those other figures complement the revelation and salvation of Jesus by "God's self-revelation and redemption manifested in other savior figures and non-Christian religions."[26] Again, the influence of Rahner is evident, although the idea of other savior-figures gives pause for thought. However, as long as the salvific mediation of those other figures is a participated one that is dependent on the Logos, and only one incarnation is affirmed in distinction to multiple instantiations, this idea is not problematic for Catholic doctrine. In fact, the eighth point confirms just that: there is an "asymmetricality" to those other figures, which means that "Jesus mediates God's gift of salvation to humanity in an overt, explicit, and fully visible way, which is now continued in Christianity, whereas other savior figures and religions, insofar as they mediate God's salvation to their followers, do so through the power of the Logos and the Spirit."[27] This perspective fits well with Rahner's idea of the categorical revelation in Christ versus the transcendental revelation in other religions, although it does move beyond Rahner; he did not address participated mediation or multiple instantiations of the Logos. As long as incarnational revelation is distinguished from instantiational, this idea is acceptable and fruitful in creating room for a more positive assessment of revelation and salvific mediation in other religions, as well as granting more of an equal footing and a positive role for them to play. Finally, Phan emphasizes that the best starting point for developing a Christian theology of religions and the best basis for a positive assessment of multiple religious belonging is the experience of those who have pioneered it, such as Aloysius Pieris, who insists that an integral component of authentic theology and praxis is liberation of the poor. The criteria that Phan proposes come from their experiences, including living in the tension of the dialectic between Christianity and the other religion with which one is identifying in an *advaita* or mystical union.[28] Rahner's mystical experience was at the heart of his theology, and so was the idea of starting with experience in general. Apparently, this contextualized theology comes from a strong Rahnerian influence as well, although again we see how it is moving beyond it, such as in the application to liberation theology and in the appropriation of the Hindu concept of *advaita*.

A second critical issue in the context of the pluralistic Asian Church that Phan addresses is interreligious dialogue. Once again Rahner's influence is evident, but Phan also challenges and moves beyond Rahner as he

26. Ibid., 66–67.
27. Ibid., 67.
28. Ibid., 70–75.

applies aspects of Rahnerian theology to praxis, and thus reevaluates and modifies principles. Interreligious dialogue is another area where Christian claims to absolute, exclusive truth become problematic, and can easily lead to an impasse. One such claim that Phan deals with in dialogue is the claim of Jesus Christ as the absolute, universal, unique Savior. He asks whether such a claim should be maintained in dialogue, or bracketed and set aside, or abandoned altogether. Phan's answer is that it should be positively maintained and asserted in dialogue; Jesus Christ as the absolute Savior is essential to Christian theology and approaching dialogue with integrity, so it is impossible to avoid. Otherwise, one is being disingenuous and erecting an obstacle to sincere dialogue. However, the basic approach should be inclusive, not exclusive.[29] Phan has a good point if one holds to the traditional, dogmatic position that Jesus Christ as God and the only Savior is essential to Christian faith. Since this teaching is what is the most distinctive and truly unique in Christianity, it makes sense. Rahner's influence is again evident here in the concept of the absolute Savior. Next, Phan says that while the assertion of the absolute claim of the uniqueness and universality of Jesus Christ must hold, the same claim for the Church must be abandoned. There is a fundamental difference between Jesus Christ and the Church that must be maintained, or else it is idolatry. The theological difference between Jesus and Christianity or the Church must be maintained; Jesus is divine, the Church is human. Furthermore, the Church always exists as a concrete, historical, inculturated, diverse, and evolving entity. It is a mixture of good and bad, having done much good, but also having caused much suffering. This strongly mitigates against the idea that the Church is the absolute or exclusive vessel of divine revelation or grace, or that it has an absolute uniqueness or universality.[30] Phan makes a strong and interesting point. Rahner's theology has a certain affinity toward Phan's perspective regarding the universal, transcendent nature of revelation and grace beyond the Church. Rahner's move of focusing on universal, transcendental grace and the attaining of salvation through openness to that, even if totally unthematic, pushes away from an ecclesial perspective with an emphasis on dogma and baptism, and toward a more experiential and existential approach, yet maintaining the insistence on the absoluteness of Christ. Phan then further elaborates on what contributes to positive, mutual dialogue. One must distinguish between a claim and its justification. The claim to absolute uniqueness and universality is a faith-claim, and cannot be deduced by reason or argumentation alone. It cannot be empirically demonstrated. Therefore, while not relativized, others

29. Ibid., 85–92.
30. Ibid., 91–95.

may make such claims in principle as well. But does this necessarily lead to an impasse? Not if the proper goal and intent of dialogue is kept in mind. Dialogue should initially be a dialogue of theological exchange, where the goal is neither conversion nor constructing a universal theology of religions based on a universal, core body of religious experience. Rather, the goal is simply "seeking understanding of the other faiths and one's own faith in light of other faiths."[31] This mutual, open exchange will also lead to the dialogues of life (living together in harmony), action (working for justice and peace), and religious experience (cultic praxis). Combining a high Christology with a low ecclesiology and a focus on experience is a very helpful method for good dialogue.[32] An analysis of Phan demonstrates that he has appropriated some key doctrines and concepts from Rahner, and applied them in his own context in a fruitful manner that both affirms an essential foundation and moves beyond it in light of the contemporary situation of pluralism. In the next section, I will turn to my own analysis of how Rahner's theology can be further explored and applied fruitfully in contemporary theology of religions.

Vatican II was a watershed in the development of Catholic theology, and its spirit of reform and openness toward the world are unprecedented in the history of Catholicism.[33] Two areas where the documents of Vatican II are relatively vague, and also where Rahner engaged positively in moving beyond their scope, are: the question of whether other religious traditions themselves are salvifically mediating, and the closely related question of exactly how and to what degree they contain revelation.[34] Rahner did affirm that other religious traditions themselves are salvific, so religious others are saved through (and not in spite of) their traditions. He also affirmed that other traditions have real revelation as a work of the Spirit in grace. In order to appropriate and build upon Rahner in fruitful ways for contemporary theology of religions in the West in keeping with the spirit of Vatican II, these are promising areas for further inquiry and theological development.[35] Phan's work is moving Rahner in a positive direction in these areas. Another area for further development from Rahner's thought is the mystery of God's gracious, self-communicative, self-giving, universal love as a key concept

---

31. Ibid., 98–99.
32. Ibid., 92–101.
33. Karkkainen, *Introduction to the Theology of Religions*, 111.
34. Ibid., 114–18; Dupuis, *Christianity and the Religions*, 59.
35. In addition to Phan, a prominent example of this kind of further development in Catholic theology of religions based on Rahner's work is the theological project of Jacques Dupuis. See *Christianity and the Religions* and *Toward a Christian Theology of Religious Pluralism*.

in moving toward a more open, pluralistic inclusivism in Catholic theology of religions.[36] Now I will begin to explore how Rahner's concepts of revelation and divine love can be further developed for potentially advancing the discussion in Western theology of religions.

Rahner asserted that the incarnation of Jesus Christ is the ultimate historical mediation of God's revelation. He also posited that in Christ, the human potential for union with God reaches its perfect climax in history. As the God-man, Jesus brings God down fully to humanity, and raises humanity fully up to God. The incarnation is unique both in degree and kind as categorical revelation. However, Rahner also asserted that no religious tradition, not even Christianity nor even Catholicism, exhausts or perfectly receives or communicates revelation in its fullness. All religions are imperfect, because they all have a strong human element of finitude. This leads to the conclusion that not even the Church has the fullness of revelation in the sense of all possible revelation, although it has the fullness of what has been revealed. But even what has been revealed is not fully or perfectly understood or communicated.[37] This is fully in line with the magisterial perspective on revelation. *Dei Verbum* teaches that the revelation of God's word as the Bible is the revelation of Christ, but nonetheless it is God's word in human form, and through human mediation. The Bible is God's inspired word, and is inerrant, but under three specific conditions: (1) in reference to the original documents only, (2) in the context of the original culture and in line with the sacred authors' intent, and (3) regarding faith and morals, or what pertains to salvation only.[38] For Rahner, the incarnation and the Bible are both categorical revelation, and are distinguished from the transcendental, unthematic, universal, general revelation present in all times and places to everyone. But, there is a qualitative difference to biblical revelation compared to the incarnation. In the incarnation, Jesus' humanity is substantially united to the divine Logos or the Son. It is a unique, full, and perfect union of the human and the divine that is integral to the person of Jesus Christ as the God-man. The revelation in the Bible, while mediated by the Spirit of the Logos, is not substantially united with the sacred authors through whom it comes. Although there is a preexistent and innate move of grace in their humanity (as in everyone's), clearly that is distinct from the revelatory union of God and humanity in Jesus Christ. So only in the incarnation, or incarnational revelation, is there a direct, full, explicit, tangible,

---

36. Rahner made a "recurring appeal to the radical incomprehensibility of God, who is encountered ultimately only in love." Quoted in Griener, "Rahner and the Pacific Rim," 58.

37. Rahner, *Foundations of Christian Faith*, 176–228.

38. *Dei Verbum* 1–6 and 11–13.

and perfect revelation of the divine in the human, as a singular event in history. Biblical revelation has an implicit, indirect, symbolic aspect to it, as something coming to humanity from without, that is distinct from incarnational revelation (although closely related to it). The humanity that received biblical revelation was neither perfect nor substantially united to the divine. The giving of biblical revelation was a gradual process of both historical givenness and development in understanding; there is a progression to it. Thus, there is more of a distance there than in the incarnation. One can therefore argue that incarnational revelation is of a different degree and kind compared to transcendental revelation, but biblical revelation is only a difference of degree (although a much higher degree of revelation). After all, all revelation comes via the Spirit of Christ to an enworlded humanity. In that case, one can still distinguish incarnational revelation, biblical categorical revelation, and general transcendental revelation. But, there is perhaps more of an affinity between biblical and general revelation than has been traditionally accorded them in Catholic theology.[39] Also, all revelation is ultimately united as the revelation of God; there is an inherent unity to all revelation, whether incarnational, biblical, or transcendental, as it all has one and the same source. There is a parallel here to Rahner's perspective on the human aspect of the incarnation. Jesus Christ's fulfillment of humanity *qua* human is a difference of degree compared to ours, even a radically different degree, but not of kind.[40] Our *telos* is the same fulfillment that we are moving toward in freedom, openness, and transcendence, just as our source is the same created source from the eternal divine intent of the Creator. Jesus achieved his fulfillment in his humanity categorically, whereas ours will come eschatologically in the beatific vision in the end. The stronger working of the divine in Jesus via his substantial union with the Logos made this fulfillment possible. This idea can be applied to non-incarnational revelation. The stronger working of the Spirit of Christ, in which God's revelatory work is more active or manifest, led to the biblical revelation as an immediate consequence of the incarnation.[41] It is like God is doing more of the work Godself, resulting in a much higher degree of revelation. The human finitude of those through whom God was revealing did not interfere as much, although they were still active and cooperating by grace with God. In the rest of humanity, the revelatory work is more human, and thus less

---

39. For a similar kind of argument in more detail, see Jacques Dupuis' Rahner-influenced theology of open revelation in which there is a decisive word in Jesus Christ, but initial or seminal words in other religions, in *Christianity and the Religions*, 114–62.

40. Kilby, *Karl Rahner: A Brief Introduction*, 16–21.

41. This idea is suggested by the connection between Jesus, the Spirit, and the Apostles in John 14:15–26; 15:26–27; and 16:4–15.

revelatory and more prone to error, vagueness, etc., due to our imperfect finitude. Perhaps this idea could be envisioned as a spectrum of revelation vis-à-vis humanity, that is, if we consider revelation from the human side of it. (Of course, the spectrum would not apply to the incarnation considered as a whole, since it is unique as a hypostatic union; thus, the idea is very limited and somewhat artificial in isolating the humanity of the incarnation, but perhaps still useful for illuminating the concept that I am attempting to elucidate). The spectrum would go from the incarnation to those in whom revelation remains highly unthematic and not consciously realized or processed. Perhaps a better image is that of a stone dropped in a pond. The impact of God becoming human produces a universal, categorical ripple that moves out from that singularity, which is unique, yet the ripple effect in its totality, even when relatively weak and far removed from the original splash in time and space, remains connected to it and is a direct result of it. In this image, the stone-splash would be the incarnation, the strongest ripple effect would be biblical revelation, and the continuing effect would be transcendental revelation. Once it moves beyond biblical revelation, some people access or appropriate it more fully, such as the Buddha; most others, less so, and to varying degrees.[42] This idea lends itself to a more positive assessment of religious others and their truth and goodness, but still gives a unique primacy to the incarnation, and the religious tradition that came from that event. The Church and the Bible maintain the highest position, but more space is created for a positive assessment of religious others that reduces that privileging of Christianity and moves toward a more generous, affirmative assessment of other religions and their relationship to God.

This kind of intentional move toward a more pluralistic, open inclusivism allows for successfully living in the tension of both affirming the essential doctrines of one's tradition, thus maintaining the integrity of the tradition and a robust particularity of belief, and at the same time being intentionally, maximally affirming of and generous in one's assessment of religious others. The goal of this pluralistic inclusivism is to be as open and generous as possible in actively seeking the goodness, truth, and work of the Spirit in religious others and their traditions, while intentionally remaining within the bounds of traditional orthodoxy. But, rather than a defensive guarding of orthodoxy with an emphasis on epistemology (being correct

---

42. Of course, I realize that the Buddha lived long before the Christ-event categorically, but the incarnation still takes logical precedence and priority as the climax of divine revelation, and is already the climax in timeless eternity in the divine mind and intent for creation before the advent of the Buddha. The timeless, transhistorical nature of Christ's christic presence in the Logos is still the ultimate source of all revelation, regardless of its categorical sequence.

in knowledge as the most essential thing) that comes at the expense of diminishing our view of and closing ourselves to religious others, it is an open push to see how far we can go in affirming others without knowingly, willingly compromising essential doctrine. A couple of key principles here are acknowledging our own epistemic limits, and taking seriously the theological ideas that religious others are also created in the image of God, and that the Spirit of Christ is generously, mercifully, and surprisingly at work in a grace-filled world. We must be humble enough to acknowledge our own limits, and let our guard down enough to be open to being surprised by how much the Spirit is at work in others. If we take seriously that there is this kind of wideness to God's mercy and to God's generous, gracious self-giving and self-communication in the world, this will help to strengthen our own faith and knowledge of the truth, and to keep Christianity as a relevant, vibrant, and positively influential faith for today. It will also help to work for understanding, forgiveness, reconciliation, justice, and peace in a world in desperate need of those things.

The shift in focus from an epistemology of theological correctness to a praxis of charity based on the humble acknowledgment previously described will help make this ideal a reality, and Rahner's theology has a large, positive contribution to make to such a pluralistic inclusivism.[43] Of course, it becomes its best and reaches its maximal potential as it is appropriated, critiqued, and modified to meet the needs of our postmodern, globalizing world in specific, local, inculturated contexts. The intersection of Rahnerian theology and inclusivism with contemporary Asian theology of religions, such as in the work of Peter Phan, is one such fruitful context. I will now turn to the question of whether the concept of charity or love can help an inclusivist perspective to move beyond the difficulties created by the exclusive truth claims that it maintains.

In the West, a challenging issue at the forefront of discussion and debate is the impasse in theology of religions and interreligious dialogue created by competing absolute truth claims. One proposed solution to the problem is to adopt a *de jure* pluralism. In pluralism, the solution is to deny these absolute truth-claims; they are relativized under the one and only absolute, the Absolute. Religious concepts, including absolute truth-claims, are attempts by human minds and reasoning to account for the experience of this Absolute, each according to her own worldview and experiences. All absolute faith-claims are subsumed under the one Absolute, as

---

43. For example, Rahner's theology gives primacy to love over knowledge, and emphasizes that love is primarily an act that demonstrates our openness and surrender to God's grace; in other words, love has primacy, and is primarily about a loving praxis. See DeCrosse, "Rahner's Ethics and the Pacific Rim," 134–35.

limited, culture-specific conceptions which are conceived in the mysterious interface between the human mind and the ineffable Ultimate.[44] But that is highly problematic from a Catholic perspective, because logically it requires the denial of dogma. Central truths must be rejected, and thus, traditional orthodoxy must be abandoned. Therefore, Catholics must give up traditional revelation and even the most central dogmas with soteriological implications, e.g., the Trinity and the salvific mediation of the Logos. The truth claims that God is one in three, only one, many, and nothing at all are all equally valid (and hence equally invalid); the claims that Jesus is the way, a way, and no way at all are also equally (in)valid. This results in the eradication of dogma categorically. But is it possible to affirm the Catholic Church's inclusivism, particularly with its Rahnerian Christocentrism and absolute truth claims, and still have deeply meaningful, mutual dialogue and other significant interreligious interaction? Even pushing toward a more pluralistic and holistic openness still leaves the Christian inclusivist with affirming that Jesus Christ is the only ultimate salvific mediator, and that others' experiences of the divine and salvation come via the Spirit of Christ. This position is necessary to affirming truth-claims and not falling into a *de jure* pluralistic relativism, so to a certain degree it is unavoidable, but one can minimize the impact of this epistemological privileging and possibly find a way through the impasse via a pluralistic inclusivism that emphasizes engaged, charitable praxis in ongoing, meaningful interreligious relationships, whether in formal theological dialogue or next door neighbors relating to each other in their daily lives. One must affirm truth and truth-claims to maintain the integrity and robust particularity of one's tradition, but for the pluralistic inclusivist, the emphasis on love-based practice helps to mitigate the barriers this may erect by minimizing the inherent privileging that inclusivism entails and seeking to be maximally open and generous in our estimation of the work of the Spirit in the world at large.

Another way to state this thesis is to say that in order to get past the impasse, it must be embraced. Only by embracing it (and not trying to avoid it in either other-denying exclusivism or a *de jure* pluralism)[45] will

44. See, e.g., Hick, *Interpretation of Religion*, and Hick, "Next Step beyond Dialogue," 3–12.

45. Exclusivism is a denial of the religious other through denying that her religion mediates the divine, and is salvific or liberating. Pluralism is also a denial of the religious other through denying the validity of the other's truth claims, and all religious truth claims (except for the claim that there is only one Absolute as ineffable mystery). Both of these positions attempt to avoid the impasse through denying truth (either the exclusivistic denial of the other's truth, or the pluralistic denial of all particular truth). While inclusivism is somewhat susceptible to these critiques as well, a shift toward a pluralistic, charity-based praxis can greatly minimize the negative impact, significantly

we be able to truly begin to move through it. Some key principles to this crucial move are as follows. First, humbly acknowledging our own epistemic limits, and the epistemic justification of the other as just as valid. Of course, the epistemic particulars cannot always be held as equal, but can be held as always equally justifiable based on the other's epistemic location. Second, shifting the focus from an epistemology of correct knowledge of the divine to a praxis of love from the divine. Third, shifting away from a strong Christocentrism and more toward a pneumatological perspective that actively seeks the gracious work of the Spirit in the world at large.[46] From a Catholic point of view, the Spirit is still ultimately acknowledged as the Spirit of Christ, but also as the Spirit of God who is speaking to and working in and through religious others and their traditions. This Spirit-focused move helps to broaden theology of religions in the West beyond the narrow, strongly Christocentric, soteriological issue toward a more comprehensive, holistic approach. Rahner's theology, although tending to more strongly emphasize Christ, also puts significant emphasis on the Spirit in his theology of religions. Veli-Matti Karkkainen contends that Rahner's inclusivist approach "is distinctively pneumatological in that it is the Spirit who enables human reception of divine grace and the self's experience of existential transcendence."[47] Although the climax of this revelation or divine, gracious self-communication is in Christ, it is still the Spirit who mediates transcendental revelation in the historical contexts of other religious traditions and individuals. Therefore, all religious traditions have a positive, real revelatory value and are potentially salvific in their reception and expression of revealed truth mediated by the Spirit. Other religions are valid ways of receiving and communicating revelation, and Christ is present in non-Christian believers, who have implicitly accepted him through the Spirit (although in varying degrees and always less than the fullness of revelation in Christ and his presence in Christianity).[48] Perhaps Rahner's pneumatological theology is promising for further development in a more expansive, holistic Christian theology of religions based more strongly on

---

more so than what is possible in either exclusivism or pluralism. Inclusivism is not an ideal answer, but it is the best answer or the ideal compromise in the sense of maximally allowing for both robust particularity and robust engagement with the other in a pluralistic world. Exclusivism more strongly denigrates otherness, and pluralism more strongly denigrates particularity. Both therefore more strongly denigrate meaningful engagement in dialogue with religious others.

46. For a fuller explanation of this idea from an Asian perspective, see Yong, *Beyond the Impasse*.

47. Karkkainen, *Introduction to the Theology of Religions*, 194.

48. Ibid., 194–96.

the Spirit, yet without losing its Christological character. These three essential principles will help to acknowledge the goodness, truth, and work of the Spirit present in the other in an attitude of pluralistic openness. As we apply these principles, mutual openness, respect, and recognition of the other's dignity can be strengthened, allowing dialogue and understanding to progress further. Of course, this is essential in moving toward reconciliation, solidarity, and peace building.

A pluralistic inclusivist theology is about an emphasis on a pluralistic praxis of love in the Spirit, but it is not an abandoning of principle, nor even an ignoring or bracketing of it in favor of pragmatics. On the contrary, the focus becomes a praxis of love, because it is based on the deepest and strongest principle-the truth that God is love.[49] To put it in biblical terms: we love because God first loved us, and offered his only Son as an atoning sacrifice for our sins.[50] To put it in Rahner's terms: love is the relational principle or dynamic force that gives rise to God's self-communication to us and all creation as a grace-filled world created in love and always moving toward its ultimate fulfillment and end in love. To put it in Jean-Luc Marion's terms: if Love is God's first name and first philosophy, and if we are given to ourselves or given our subjectivity as an iconic love-gift from Love, then love is the essence of who we are, as the image of God-is-Love. For Marion, a saturated phenomenon is something that gives itself so excessively that it floods or overwhelms intuition, defies conceptual mastery, and opens upon an infinite hermeneutical horizon.[51] In Marion's application of the concept of saturated phenomena to his Catholic theology, it is akin to Rahner's idea of Mystery as the infinite horizon of absolute transcendence that leads us toward the ultimate *telos* of beatific vision. For Marion, the double saturation or ultimate saturated phenomenon is revelation, and the paragon of revelation, the quintessential givenness of all four saturated phenomena at once in their ultimate expression, is the incarnation.[52] Whether considered biblically, from Rahner's modern perspective, or in Marion's postmodern terms, the essence of reality is that God is love, and love is the most profoundly revealed in the incarnation, death, and resurrection of Jesus Christ. If we are created in the image of love and redeemed by love, then we are love, and love takes its rightful place of primacy, in both principle and practice. So God loves, the world worlds, and then we love. Love is the unifying prin-

---

49. 1 John 4:16.

50. 1 John 4:10.

51. For a fuller explanation of Jean-Luc Marion's phenomenological theology of saturation, see *God Without Being* and *Being Given*.

52. The four saturated phenomena are flesh, event, idol, and icon. For a detailed explanation of how Marion applies them to the incarnation, see *Being Given*.

ciple of everything, the first principle or principle of principles, and thus the ground of all true principles and all authentic praxis as well. Love is also something that is necessarily active or dynamic, always pushing out from the self and toward the other in relationality, as well as returning to the self and prompting growth in love via relationships. If love is God's gracious self-communication to us for redemption and salvation, then a grace-filled world is a love-filled world. The one who came as incarnate Love has declared that love is the principle of principles, and is expressed ultimately in action for the good of others.[53] Love is abundantly available and infused in humanity via grace and our creation in God's image, and is fostered in grace by the Spirit in our lives, even where thematic, categorical, revelatory knowledge may be relatively lacking. It is developed in us universally through habituation in our daily experiences of God's grace-filled world.

The way through the impasse created by competing doctrinal claims in theology of religions and in interreligious dialogue and living is to embrace the impasse and move through it by acknowledging the truth that God is love and therefore we are love. Of course, the epistemological difficulties remain. But, love is a universal principle and language that all can therefore relate to, regardless of exactly how the concept is expressed in various cultures or languages or philosophies or theologies, due to our common nature as spirit in the Spirit. Love is inherent to our nature and infused in us by God-is-Love, as well as developed in us by God's Spirit through our open, seeking freedom in daily living. Is there actually some real difference or distinction between Christians loving their neighbors as themselves, and Buddhists practicing non-hate and non-greed (stated positively as loving-kindness or unconditional, non-self interested seeking of others' welfare, and generous giving for others' needs)?[54] Phenomenologically speaking, love may give itself and show itself in an innumerable richness and variety of ways, opening up onto an endless hermeneutical horizon as icon of the divine. But the underlying unity is still recognizable, perhaps even experientially intuitive. The epistemological difficulties arising from plurality can be embraced as necessary to affirm the truth of love based on one's own understanding of it and ultimate reality, thus maintaining the integrity of one's tradition and giving love a contextualized, conceptual foundation, yet the mountain of those epistemological difficulties can be transformed into a mole hill through the practice of love based on our universal experience of it in myriad ways. Love is a powerful symbol and vehicle for maximizing our ability to absorb and deal with plurality in healthy, life-affirming, and other-

---

53. Matt 22:34–40; John 15:9–17.
54. See Harvey, *Introduction to Buddhist Ethics*.

affirming ways. Love is the universal language through which we can all engage in the dialogue of life and mutual self-discovery. The ways in which it can be experienced and expressed are as limitless as our creative capacity to learn and grow in relationships. Love is what unites us to God, God to us, and us to each other. If there is such a thing as a principle of principles in the postmodern, globalizing world, love is the best candidate. It is the ultimate enworlded and embodied expression of God's self-communication for our good and fulfillment.

In spite of Rahner's groundbreaking work, there is a widely recognized need in contemporary Catholic theology to push beyond the limitations of his position, particularly in light of our postmodern, postcolonial, globalizing context where the premium is on praxis rather than theory, such as in interreligious dialogue and religious practices in multicultural, multireligious contexts like Asia, where people of varying cultures, faiths, and practices interact daily, and the boundaries around varying faith traditions and cultures are fluid. There is a need to push beyond the Rahnerian form of inclusivism, in both expanding beyond the soteriological question and moving toward praxis in an interreligious context. To this point, Christian theology of religions has mainly been an intrareligious endeavor with a focus on the theoretical. The time has come to challenge ourselves to push further toward a holistic, open, practical, and pluralistically inclusive theology of religions that does not settle upon merely considering whether non-Christians can receive salvation and how, but considers more broadly how God is active in the world religions and the world's people as a whole. The best way forward to achieve this goal is to focus on a love-based praxis that acknowledges the divine and the work of the Spirit in the other, and in surprising ways from which we can truly learn and grow, and not merely as a poor facsimile or seed of what we in Christendom already possess. In other words, Christian theology of religions must become less narrowly theoretical and soteriological, and more broadly practical and truly theological in the widest sense. Only then can it fully engage with those of other religions in mutual dialogue for growth, unity, reconciliation, and peace in the world. Christianity's relevance as an engaging and vibrant world faith for today is at stake in this. I have attempted to show that Rahner's inclusivism is still an essential foundation that remains relevant, but also that it needs further development and contextualized appropriation and transformation to continue speaking adequately to the postmodern world. The contributions of non-Eurocentric Catholic theologians such as Peter Phan are indispensible to such continuing development of and transformation of Rahnerian thought for today.

BIBLIOGRAPHY

Bell, Catherine. "Constraints on the Theological Absorption of Plurality." In *Rahner beyond Rahner: A Great Theologian Encounters the Pacific Rim*, edited by Paul G. Crowley, 39–44. Lanham: Rowman & Littlefield, 2005.

Crowley, Paul G. "Encountering the Religious Other: Challenges to Rahner's Transcendental Project." *Theological Studies* 71 (2010) 567–85.

DeCrosse, David. "Rahner's Ethics and the Pacific Rim." In *Rahner beyond Rahner: A Great Theologian Encounters the Pacific Rim*, edited by Paul G. Crowley, 133–36. Lanham, MD: Rowman & Littlefield, 2005.

Duffy, Stephen J. "Experience of Grace." In *The Cambridge Companion to Karl Rahner*, edited by Declan Marmion and Mary Hines. New York: Cambridge University Press, 2005.

Dupuis, Jacques. *Christianity and the Religions: From Confrontation to Dialogue*. Maryknoll, NY: Orbis, 2002.

Griener, George E. "Rahner and the Pacific Rim." In *Rahner beyond Rahner: A Great Theologian Encounters the Pacific Rim*, edited by Paul G. Crowley, 53–72. Lanham: Rowman & Littlefield, 2005.

Harvey, Peter. *An Introduction to Buddhist Ethics*. New York: Cambridge University Press, 2000.

Hick, John. *An Interpretation of Religion*. 2nd ed. New Haven: Yale University Press, 2004.

———. "The Next Step beyond Dialogue." In *The Myth of Religious Superiority*, edited by Paul F. Knitter, 3–12. Maryknoll, NY: Orbis, 2005.

Hill Fletcher, Jeannine. *Monopoly on Salvation? A Feminist Approach to Religious Pluralism*. New York: Continuum, 2005.

———. "Rahner and Religious Diversity." In *The Cambridge Companion to Karl Rahner*, edited by Declan Marmion and Mary Hines. New York: Cambridge University Press, 2005.

Karkkainen, Veli-Matti. *An Introduction to the Theology of Religions*. Downers Grove, IL: InterVarsity, 2003.

Kilby, Karen. *Karl Rahner: A Brief Introduction*. New York: Crossroad, 2007.

Marion, Jean-Luc. *Being Given*. Stanford: Stanford University Press, 2002.

———. *God Without Being*. Chicago: University of Chicago Press, 1991.

Pandiappallil, Joseph. *Jesus the Christ and Religious Pluralism: Rahnerian Christology and Belief Today*. New York: Crossroad, 2001.

Paul VI. *Dei Verbum*. Dogmatic constitution on divine revelation. Vatican Council II. Promulgated November 18, 1965.

Phan, Peter. *Being Religious Interreligiously: Asian Perspectives on Interfaith Dialogue*. Maryknoll, NY: Orbis, 2004.

———. *Christianity with an Asian Face: Asian American Theology in the Making*. Maryknoll, NY: Orbis, 2003.

Rahner, Karl. "Anonymous Christians." In *Theological Investigations*, 6:390–98. Baltimore: Helicon, 1969.

———. *Foundations of Christian Faith*. New York: Crossroad, 1978.

———. "Observations on the Problem of the Anonymous Christians." In *Theological Investigations*, 14:280–94. New York: Seabury, 1976.

Ratzinger, Joseph. *Dominus Iesus*. Declaration on the sanctity and salvific universality of Jesus Christ and the Church. Ratified June 16, 2000, by Pope John Paul II.

Vorgrimler, Herbert. *Understanding Karl Rahner*. New York: Crossroad, 1986.

Yong, Amos. *Beyond the Impasse: Toward a Pneumatological Theology of Religions*. Grand Rapids: Baker Academic, 2003.

20

Relativism, Universalism, and Pluralism in the Age of Globalization
A Reflection on Raimon Panikkar's Approach

YOUNG-CHAN RO

INTRODUCTION

One of the most serious issues we are facing today is cultural diversity and religious pluralism on one hand, and "globalization" of the world on the other, the emergence of a unique phenomenon of "diversity" in combination of an attempt for "globalization." It appears to be that we are trying to achieve these two conflicting goals at the same time. On one hand, we witness the growing trends of cultural diversity, religious pluralism, and ideological relativism. On the other hand, however, we also recognize that the world is rapidly becoming "one" big place in an attempt to unify and globalize in establishing a universal system, norm, and values. This paper is a reflection on Raimon Panikkar's approach to some of fundamental issues involved in understanding pluralism, especially in clarifying issues involved in cultural and religious diversity, relativism, universalism, and pluralism in light of globalization. One of the most urgent issues humanity is facing today is how to deal with religious conflict and cultural diversity in the process of globalization. On the one hand, we are facing the globalizing process in every aspect of life today including economic cooperation, international trade, and technological development. On the other hand, we also face the trend of universalizing the globe in terms of language, culture, and ways of knowing and thinking. As the world is becoming one, we see a danger of political and economic imperialism, and cultural colonialism; one system or institution has become the norm and one culture has become a dominant force invading every corner of the globe. In this respect, the paper will clarify some fundamental concepts and ideas such as "relativism," "relativity," "universalism," "plurality," and "pluralism" in order to elucidate a deeper implication of cultural diversity and religious pluralism. Furthermore, this paper will discuss tension and conflict between "relativism" and "universalism," and try to find an approach, beyond the dichotomy of "relativism" and "universalism," to expound the significance of "pluralism." The paper will focus especially on the idea of pluralism not only in the social and cultural context but also in understanding the fundamental nature of humanity and reality, beyond the cultural and social phenomena of modern world.

ATTEMPT FOR GLOBALIZATION

The main thrust of this paper is to discuss issues involving "relativism," "universalism," "pluralism," etc. in light of Raimon Panikkar's[1] unique approach in dealing with these issues. Globalization process is not only a modern or contemporary human attempt to make the world one big house or *oikos* with one standard system, rule or *nomos* but also it has a long historical root. Time and again, we human beings have repeated the same attempt without success. We see numerous examples of this attempt in both the West and the East. From the Roman Empire to the British Empire, from the Spanish imperial claims to the Qin China and the Imperial Japan, human beings have tried tirelessly to build powerful kingdoms, empires, and nations. It has been a common tendency of the people or nation with a power to dominate the world, to make the world one big country or nation with the one ideology, system, language, religion, and culture. This tendency has a mythic origin found in the story of the Tower of Babel in the Book of Genesis:

---

1. I am deeply in debt to Raimon Panikkar (1918–2010) who expounded the idea of pluralism in light of religious and cultural diversity. Raimon Panikkar was one of the leading scholars and original thinkers tackled this vital issue throughout his entire life. Among numerous books he wrote, *Invisible Harmony*, *Intra-Religious Dialogue*, and his last book, *Rhythm of Being*, are representative in dealing with these issues.

> Now the whole earth had one language and the same words. And as they migrated from the east, they came upon a plan in the land of Shinar and settled there. And they said to one another, "Come, let us make bricks, and burn them thoroughly." And they had brick for stone, and bitumen for mortar. Then they said, "Come, let us build ourselves a city, and a tower with it top in the heavens, and let us make a name for ourselves; otherwise we shall be scattered abroad upon the face of the whole earth." The Lord came down to see the city and the tower, which mortals had built. And the Lord said, "Look, they are one people, and they have all one language: and this is only the beginning of what they will do; nothing that they propose to do will now be impossible for them. Come let us go down, and confuse their language here, so that they will not understand one another's speech." So the Lord scattered them abroad from there over the face of all the earth and they left off building the city. Therefore it was called Babel, because the Lord confused the language of all the earth: and from there the Lord scattered them abroad over the face of all the earth. (Gen 11:1-9, NRSV)

According to Raimon Panikkar who interpreted this myth in light of his idea of pluralism, human beings, time and again, have repeated the dream of making one world without success: "In any case, after sixty centuries of human memory in the history realm, is there no way for us to awaken to the futility of this realm? What would happen if we simply gave up wanting to build this unitarian tower?"[2] Throughout history, we have attempted at globalizing the world. It has been attempted in terms of the extension of space, geographical territory, political power, commercial dominance, etc. Beyond the idea of the expansion of space, it has also been tried in terms of building a political or religious empire such as Christendom or an expansion of missionary institutions. In modern times, globalization has also been ideological dominance such as Marxism, Communism, Capitalism, or Democracy. Although Democracy is an institution rather than ideology, it has been conceived as an ideology in some parts of the world and has become yet another form of the Western and especially American dominance. Democracy, however, is primarily an institution not an ideology. Once we try to superimpose Democracy to all other parts of the world and cultures, it

---

2. Raimon Panikkar has been one of the most inspiring thinkers and scholars advocating the pluralistic view of reality. I am much indebted to his profound insight. For his interpretation of the myth of the Tower of Babel, see Panikkar, "Myth of Pluralism: The Tower of Babel," in *Invisible Harmony*, 53-54. The original version of this article was published as "Myth of Pluralism: The Tower of Babel—A Meditation on Non-Violence," *Cross Currents* 29 (1979) 197-230.

becomes yet another form of ideology. Once we absolutize and universalize one system, it becomes an ideology. Democracy is profoundly a "cracy" (institution) not an "ism (ideology)." Communism, Socialism, and Marxism as ideologies had strong ambitions to make their ideologies the absolute and global. Once the zeal for globalizing one's conviction becomes so powerful and urgent, it compels a sense of mission for globalizing their conviction. In this sense, ideology and religion are very close to each other in absolutizing and universalizing their belief system. Democracy, however, resists this temptation. Democracy by nature accepts and recognizes the limitation and imperfectness of its own system. It rejects the idea of making its own idea as the absolute. In fact, democracy is based on the premise of human fragility and propensity toward evil, and thus it tries to prevent the human from the temptation of making his or her belief system or ideology absolute. The American theologian and political thinker Reinhold Niebuhr (1892–1971) has expounded the democratic institutions based on the Christian assumption of human nature. "Man's capacity for justice makes democracy possible and man's inclination to do injustice makes democracy necessary."[3]

The globalization process has also been found in human attempts to standardize as in making one form of measurement or system as global. The human desire for universality in terms of communication, transportation, and even ways of thinking has become more and more apparent these days. Since the Enlightenment in the West, individual human rights, reason and rationality have become global phenomena. Logic, reason, and rationality, for example, have become the universal standard for ways of knowing and judging truth, thus making reason as the absolute global criterion in establishing a global understanding. The term "global understanding" is problematic and in fact, it is a misnomer. Understanding assumes "standing-under" the spell of the other in allowing us to stand under the specific circumstance or situation of "other." When we create a certain system, method, and criteria for "understanding" other, we already betray the very nature of understanding. Because we are using this specific "framework," "system," or "method" of our "understanding" for understanding other. In this case, we are already imposing "my yardstick" to "understand" you. This is not "standing-under" in the genuine sense of the word to allow myself in order to see, to listen from "other's" perspective. In this respect, the "standard," the "global" understanding is not possible without imposing our own standard consisting of certain criteria or framework of thinking we have created as

---

3. Reinhold Niebuhr, for example, understood democracy in relationship with human nature, as he expound in *Children of Light and the Children of Darkness*, xiii.

the objective and universal criteria, and impose them to others in order to understand them. This is "overstanding," as Panikkar aptly put it.[4]

The notion of global perspective may also sound great in overcoming provinciality and partiality. This, however, is also misleading. Simply put no one has the perfect 380 degree-vision to see the whole globe at once. We only look at the globe seen from one particular angle. We all have a global vision from a partial and particular perspective. Nonetheless, we still try to build an illusory tower in the hope that we will be able to look at the whole globe. Again, the Tower of Babel is a powerful representation of human desire for external expansion, to cover the globe, to conquer the world, to own the universe, etc. This desire for spatial and external expansion has motivated human beings to go higher, further, and see more in believing that we will someday be able to see the whole globe at once. The spatial concept of globalization has resulted in political hegemony, economic monopoly, and cultural imperialism. In this respect, "globalization" means "Westernization" and "Americanization." In fact, the "modernization" process was almost identical with the Westernization process. This world, again, is becoming one world, with one language, one system, and one universal standard. On one hand, this is an inevitable process especially due to the rapid development of technology. On the other, however, we see that we are involved in the same process that has resulted in dismay. The powerful Qin dynasty that unified the whole of China for the first time in Chinese history and tried to impose one universal standard, one culture, one legal system, etc. lasted only 13 years. One of the longest dynasties with one monarch, one ideology, and one system was the Chosŏn Dynasty in Korea (1292–1910). This dynasty, however, was confined to a small peninsula with no ambition to expand their empire to make it universal or global as found, for example, in the Roman Empire.

The current financial crisis in Europe and America may be an indication, a sign, or a symptom of human desire for global expansion and universalizing a particular system of values, institution, and ways of thinking, is reaching to its limit. In fact, we no longer have the "East" and the "West" because the East is rapidly becoming the "West." The whole world is now rapidly becoming the "West."

There is an indefatigable human desire and effort to expand ourselves to farther and farther and to possess the globe and the universe. It seems to me that we are reaching to the point where we can no longer push ourselves to that direction without breaking both the globe and the human.

---

4. Panikkar discussed this idea of "overstanding" vs. "understanding" extensively in "Pluralism of Truth," in *Invisible Harmony*, 92–95.

An ecological crisis and the phenomenon of global warming is yet another serious indication of the human limit of expansionism.

WHOLE AND PART

We need a different way of thinking and understanding the globe and the universe. The globe and universe are not only external entities as a physical matter, but also have to be internalized and spiritualized in terms of the human relationship to them. The whole and the part are no longer in dichotomy but in unity. The globalizing process is not mere an external expansion, a physical process, but an internal process of crystallizing one's own experience, a spiritual process of relating to the world and the universe. We have long forgotten the wisdom and insight: The whole is in part, *totum in parte*. The whole is not sum of the parts but each part exists for the sake of the whole.[5] Globalization is not simply an objectifying of the globe but subjectively experiencing the world, not only simply externalizing the globe but also internalizing the globe and the world in relationship to us. Modern science, the analytical mind, and the scientific method have helped us treat the globe as a detached entity, an object for our observation, use, even abuse. The globalizing process has become a tangible and material process and has lost the spiritual dimension in making the globe and the universe as parts of our own being, an *internalizing* process. In the physical process of extension, there is no intrinsic relation or unity between individuality and totality. The relationship between individuality and totality, particularity and universality, the local and the global is neither dualistic nor monistic but is non-dualistic because these are neither divided in two separate entities nor totally identifiable one entity.[6]

It is not my intention to discuss the nature of non-duality or "a-duality" (*advaita*) in full spectrum but it would suffice to say that the issue of globalization in understanding the world as one or many is not a proper approach. Western culture has been dominated by a dualistic way of thinking in dividing matter and spirit, mind and body, and the global and the local under the influence of scientific approach, rational and logical thinking. So globalization in this sense has been heavily influenced by Western scientific thinking and universalizing Western standards and values.

---

5. Panikkar, *Experience of God*, 75.

6. Non-dualism or a-dualism is English translation of Sanskrit word, *advaita*. Raimon Panikkar has expounded the notion of non-dualism based on the Hindu idea of *advaita*. For more about Panikkar's explanation on the notion of *avaita*, see his last book, *Rhythm of Being*, 216–17.

RELATIVISTIC ATTITUDE

There are various strong movements resisting the globalization process. Against universalism and the globalization process, relativism is concerned with a uniqueness and irreducibility of individual being. The Enlightenment mentality or thought, which has had a great influence in shaping modernity, deeply influenced the modern West in advancing democratic ideas and institutions. One of the founding fathers of America, Thomas Jefferson (1743–1836), for example, was heavily influenced by this Enlightenment thought as he laid the ideological foundation of the United States of America. Individualism is one of the hallmarks of modern thought. The Individual is an *un-dividable* last entity, a sacred atom (unsplitable). This individualism, however, also caused a dialectical tension with community, society, and nation. Every individual has become an atom, an unsplitable entity. In this respect, we may observe the rise of relativism. Relativism, unlike globalism, does not try to build one universal empire, kingdom, and universal city. Relativism, however, believes that every entity is complete in itself and does not need others to be its own being. Here we may see two issues: one is an ontological assertion that each being is on its own, and second, the sense of value of every being is equally and uniquely belongs to each separate being. In this sense, there is no need or desire for the other in terms of knowledge or being, an epistemological and ontological solipsism.

Relativism is a form of reaction to universalism in relation to globalization. The risk and danger of globalization has prompted various forms of reaction, among those, relativism may be the strongest and the most direct reaction against universalism. Since universalism has been the underlying assumption for globalization, relativism has been expressed in the form of nationalism or sometimes exclusivism. Modern mentality and democratic ideals have also contributed to this tendency of individualism. Once this individualism becomes extreme, it has a tendency to absolutize individual uniqueness. This tendency can bring conflict and clash between different individualities, cultures, religions, etc. It also can bring indifference to other individualities including religion and culture. An extreme form of individualism has resulted in relativism. Relativism resists universalism and globalization, and relativizes the world, the globe, truth, and reality. There is no absolute universal standard for anything. Relativism when pushed, however, has a tendency to become indifferent to others and totally self-centered. Relativism, thus, may become yet another ideology since it is a form of belief (relative-ism) to reject any attempt at relating to "other" systems, cultures, religions, and values.

What we see here is two phenomena of modern mentality: individuation and relativization. On one hand, individuality has the most valuable entity, an irreducible last entity, and thus their own individuality is absolute but once they discover "others" may have the same kind of sense of "absolute," they may become relativistic. In this assumption humanity is nothing but the total sum of individual beings. Here humanity is defined in terms of number and quantity but not quality. Humanity is more than just total sum of the people on earth in terms of number. Beyond the concept of number and quantity, humanity concerns the quality of being a human. The process of extreme individuation and relativism will eventually produce indifference, cynicism, solipsism, and skepticism toward the human efforts of seeking unity, truth, and reality.

The sense of skepticism and relativism discourages human efforts for seeking the universal truth. They may not feel any need for "universal" truth. In fact, for them truth may not be universal. In this sense, each individual constructed a little universe of their own and there is no need to interact with each other. Human being is an isolated individual and living in his/her own solipsistic universe.

RELATIVITY AND RELATIVISM

We have to make a clear distinction between "relativity" and "relativism." As discussed above, relativism does not need the other. This is certain belief system in asserting individuality and particularity without relating to universality or even unity with other beings. It asserts its own independence. Relativity, however, is a notion emphasizing the nature of inter-independence of every being. This affirms that each being is in need of the other in the sense that no single being can exist independently. Relativity is an ontological constitution of all beings. Relativity is a way of recognizing the intrinsic relatedness of each being. Relativity is in this sense has nothing to do with relativism but is a way of describing the "relationship" found in all beings. Every being is in relationship with other beings to become its own being. No single being exists in isolation without being related to other beings. In this sense, relativity is the very nature of being. The two words, relativity and relativism are entirely unrelated. The word relativity has been used in expressing the nature of the radical interdependence of every being, "radical relativity." One of the best examples of relativity is found in the idea of *yin* and *yang*. In order to be *yin*, it requires *yang*, and *yang* requires *yin*. At the same time, *yang* is not an independent being apart from *yin*, or *yin* independent of *yang*. In fact *yang* is found in *yin* and *yin* is in *yang*. Relativity is not to assert an "extrinsic *connection*" of one being to other but it is rather an "intrinsic *relation*" of every being. Every being exists in relation to other beings. In this sense, relativity is nothing but an affirmation of the relatedness of every being to other beings in an intrinsic way. Relationship is not to be understood as an external string binding one being to another being, but it expresses the idea of the intrinsic relatedness of one being to another being. In this respect, relationship is the foundation that allows each being to be found in existence both epistemologically and ontologically. A father, for example, is not a father without having to relate to his son. A son cannot become a son until he enters into the relationship with his father. A son is a son in relative to his father and vice versa. This is the relativity of a being. Father becomes a father in relative to a son, a son to a father. A being is defined in relationship with other being. In this sense, relationship is a constitutive element of becoming a being.

Relativity found in relationship is neither dualistic nor monistic. A true relationship does not assume a dichotomy of separating two beings. Once a relation becomes dualistic, it becomes a mere extrinsic connection in binding two different entities, and thus, relation becomes either formal or functional. In this context, relationship loses a dynamic interaction and interpenetration between two beings and it has no intrinsic awareness of others in its own being or the presence of others in his/her own being.

On the other hand, however, when a relationship becomes monistic, it becomes monolithic. This relationship becomes totally one sided, one dominates the other because the object must eventually succumb to the subject, and the subject and the object become one and the same. In this context, a relationship does not exist. Once we lose relativity, we lose relationship. Relativity is both the core and defining characteristic of relationship. For this reason the nature of relativity is fundamentally non-dualistic. Relationship must possess relativity as the intrinsic nature of being.

Here the idea of non-dualistic is an important way of understanding relativity. It is neither one nor two as discussed above. The non-dualistic character of relativity allows relationship, vital, dynamic, and creative. Thus, relativity is the most construct of the components of every being in relationship with other beings.

PLURALISM

Relativity is not yet pluralism. The word pluralism has become a fashion now, religious pluralism, cultural pluralism etc. The meaning of pluralism, however, has to be clarified. To begin with the whole issue of pluralism, we must start with the observation that there are many different things, not just one thing. This is an affirmation that there is plurality, rather than singularity in the world. In other words, plurality is a simple recognition of our observation stating that there are many different things in the world. For example, when we recognize the fact that there are more than one culture or one religion exist, this means plurality, the plurality of religion and culture. We must first accept the fact that I am not the only human being in this world, my culture is not the only culture nor is my religion the only one in this world. This is a serious step toward pluralism; however, it is not yet pluralism. Plurality is the factual foundation for pluralism. We sometimes confused plurality with pluralism in thinking that the recognition and acceptance of plurality is pluralism. From the socio-political perspective, pluralism, often, is used in describing various social, ethnic, religious groups. Pluralism, in this sense, is a way of accepting diversity of people, religious affiliation, and cultural heritage. This is the level of plurality, but it is not pluralism yet.

Pluralism, unlike plurality, is a way of understanding reality, a form of reflection on how a being is related to other beings in terms of basic structure of being. Pluralism is not a way of accepting that there are more than just one being, the awareness of many. Pluralism does not seek a unity among many. Recognition of many, plurality, does not mount to pluralism. It does not seek to find unity by reducing each particularity to a common ground. Pluralism does not believe unity as essential or even indispensible ideal.

Pluralism does not to seek a universal system. As discussed above, building a universal system, making a universal path, constructing a universal tower is all destined to fail. Pluralism, on the other hand, allows incompatibility, incommensurability among pluralities. In fact, pluralism arises at the moment of experiencing incompatibility. Pluralism does not attempt to reduce the incompatibility of the differences between two beings into "rational" and "logical" formula by appealing to reason, i.e., rational reductionism. Reason and rationality can definitely provide a common ground for universality. This is the power of reason that can transcend cultural barriers and religious diversity. Rationality has become the most effective means of communication because of the universality of reason. Religious and cultural diversities, however, should not be reduced to rationality or reason alone. For this reason, pluralism makes us aware of human contingency, the non-rational element, and the mystical aspect of reality. On the other hand, however, pluralism does not reject intelligibility but understands intelligibility beyond reason alone. There is more than one form of intelligibility, the intelligibility based on reason alone. Human being has an ability to know more than through reason and rationality. Reason is not the only way to monopolize human intelligibility.

Furthermore, intelligibility is not the only way to seek a common understanding or agreement among different entities and beings. Pluralism tries to reach intelligibility as much as possible but it allows the dimension of unintelligibility. It is an existential attitude and genuine openness toward truth and reality. Pluralism should not to be understood as an ideology in absolutizing a particular system but as an *attitude* that listens and discerns the nature of reality and being. In this sense, pluralism is a way of understanding that every being is pluralistically oriented and structured.

Here we see two dimensions of pluralism. From an individualistic point of view, pluralism is the fundamental structure and way of being. Each and every being is already pluralistically composed to become its own being. From the communal and collective point of view, pluralism is a way of recognizing that the nature of reality and being are mutually dependent on each other (*pratitiyasamudpada*).[7] These two dimensions, however, are not separable. Pluralism assumes the interdependence of all beings as both an external relationship to other beings and an intrinsic structure of every being. Pluralism in this sense is not an artificial superstructure or system to measure, not an ideology to impose, not a universal philosophy to educate, not a universal religion or ethics encompassing different religious beliefs, but it is an existential *attitude* of openness to others, to nature and heaven and earth. Beyond the dichotomy of relativism and universalism, pluralism is a way of discerning the nature of reality and being. It is a way of finding wisdom to comprehend how to relate to each other without losing one's own being and identity. Pluralism allows us to engage in dialogue, not a dialectical dialogue but a dialogical dialogue.[8] Dialectical dialogue is based on the dichotomy of either or logic, and once we reject one we must affirm the other. Dialogical dialogue, however, based on idea of "dia-logical," or "through the logos" is a mutual understanding of the *logos* of each other at the risk of mutual transformation.

---

7. This is a Buddhist notion in explaining that each and every being exit interdependently as known, the doctrine of "dependent co-origination." According to this doctrine, each being, when it arises as a being, it already interdependently exists. This means that origination of any being requires "interdependency."

8. Panikkar used these terms in various contexts in his writings. For an example how he used these terminologies, see his *Rhythm of Being*, 310.

BIBLIOGRAPHY

Beneke, Chris. *Beyond Toleration: The Religious Origins of American Pluralism.* New York: Oxford University Press, 2006.

Cobb, John, Jr., and Ward M. McAfee. *The Dialogue Comes of Age: Christian Encounters with Other Traditions.* Minneapolis: Fortress, 2010.

Eck, Diane. *A New Religious America: How a "Christian Country" Has Become the World's Most Religiously Diverse Nation.* San Francisco: HarperSanFrancisco, 2001.

Fredericks, James L. *Faith among Faiths: Christian Theology and Non-Christian Religions.* New York: Paulist, 1999.

Niebuhr, Reinhold. *The Children of Light and the Children of Darkness: A Vindication of Democracy and a Critique of Its Traditional Defence.* New York: Scribner, 1944.

Panikkar, Raimon. *The Experience of God: Icons of the Mystery.* Minneapolis: Fortress, 2006.

———. *The IntraReligious Dialogue.* Rev. ed. New York: Paulist, 1999.

———. *Invisible Harmony: Essays on Contemplation and Responsibility.* Edited by James Cargas. Minneapolis: Fortress, 1995.

———. *The Rhythm of Being.* Gifford Lectures. Maryknoll, NY: Orbis, 2010.

Contributors

Charles Bernsen is Adjunct Professor of Religion, University of Memphis. He spent 27 years as newspaper reporter and editor. He holds a Ph.D. in Religion from Vanderbilt University. This essay is based on research for his dissertation.

Francesca Cho received her PhD in the History of Religions, with a specialization in East Asian Buddhism, from the University of Chicago Divinity School. Her last book was Everything Yearned For: Manhae's Poems of Love and Longing (Wisdom Publications, 2005). She is currently preparing monographs on the topic of Buddhism and film, and Buddhism and science.

Paula Fredriksen is the Aurelio Professor of Scripture emerita at Boston University and Distinguished Visiting Professor of Comparative Religion at the Hebrew University, Jerusalem. She is the author of *Augustine on Romans* (Scholars Press, 1982) and the award-winning *From Jesus to Christ* (Yale Governors' Award for Best Book, 1988; 2000); she has also published *Jesus of Nazareth, King of the Jews* (Knopf, 1999), which won a 1999 National Jewish Book Award. Her most recent work investigates the ways that ideas about God, humanity, and the world shift and grow during the charged period between Jesus and Augustine in *Sin: The Early History of an Idea* (Princeton University Press, 2012).

Daniel Greene is an Adjunct Professor of History at Northwestern University, and Guest Exhibition Curator at the U.S. Holocaust Museum. He is the author of *The Jewish Origins of Cultural Pluralism: The Menorah Association and American Diversity* (Indiana University Press, 2011).

Paul L. Heck is a member of the Department of Theology at Georgetown University. His research addresses questions of religious ethics, spirituality, political theology, and the foundations of religious knowledge, especially in relation to Islam. His most recent monographs are *Common Ground: Islam,*

Christianity, and Religious Pluralism (Georgetown 2009) and *Skepticism in Classical Islam: Moments of Confusion* (Routledge 2013).

S. Mark Heim is the Samuel Abbot Professor Christian Theology at Andover Newton Theological School in Newton Centre, Massachusetts. He is deeply involved in issues of religious pluralism, Christian ecumenism and the relation of theology and science. His books include *Salvations: Truth and Difference in Religion*, *The Depth of the Riches: A Trinitarian Theology of Religious Ends* and *Saved From Sacrifice: A Theology of the Cross*. He holds a B.A. from Amherst College, a Master of Divinity from Andover Newton Theological School, and a Ph.D. in systematic theology from Boston College. He is a member of the American Theological Society and has received both a Pew Evangelical Scholars Research Fellowhip and a Henry Luce III Fellowship in Theology. He is an ordained American Baptist minister and has represented his denomination on the Faith and Order Commissions of the National Council of Churches and the World Council of Churches. He has taught, studied and lectured in India, Israel, China, Europe, Malaysia, Thailand, and the Fiji Islands.

Marinus Chijioke Iwuchukwu is an Associate Professor of Theology at Duquesne University, Pittsburgh, Pennsylvania. He specializes in Interreligious Dialogue, Religious Pluralism, and Media and Religion. His two monographs are *Media Ecology and Religious Pluralism: Engaging Walter Ong and Jacques Dupuis Toward Effective Interreligious Dialogue and Muslim-Christian Dialogue in Post-Colonial Northern Nigeria* and *The Challenges of Inclusive Cultural and Religious Pluralism*. He has also co-edited a book with the title, *Can Muslims and Christians Resolve their Religious and Social Conflicts? Cases from Africa and the United States*. He has several journal articles published in different peer review journals and some book chapters. He is the current chair of Duquesne University Christian-Muslim Dialogue committee, a consortium of scholars from different disciplines who are invested in promoting and advocating active and progressive.

Todd E. Johanson is a PhD candidate and an adjunct faculty member in the theology department at Duquesne University in Pittsburgh, PA. His primary area of interest and research is in interreligious work. His other recent publications include an article titled, "Charity as Virtue in Non-Christians: A Positive Assessment in Light of Augustine, Aquinas, Pope Benedict XVI, and the Catholic Church's Inclusivism," in the *Global Virtue Ethics Review*, and a forthcoming article in the *Journal of Ecumenical Studies* titled,

"Pluralistic Inclusivism and Christian-Muslim Dialogue: The Challenge of Moving Beyond Polite Discussion Toward Reconciliation and Peace."

Charles B. Jones earned a Master of Theological Studies degree from the Divinity School at Duke University in 1988, an M.A. in History of Religions from the University of Virginia in 1992, followed by the Ph.D. in 1996 with an emphasis on East Asian Buddhism. He has been on the faculty of the School of Theology and Religious Studies at The Catholic University of America since 1996, where he currently serves as associate professor and associate dean for graduate studies. His research involves Buddhism in Taiwan, Late Ming Dynasty gentry religion, Pure Land Buddhism, and Jesuit-Chinese interactions in the late Ming and early Qing periods (1550–1700).

Jerusha Tanner Lamptey is an Assistant Professor of Islam and Ministry at Union Theological Seminary in New York City, where she teaches courses on Islam, the Qur'an, feminist theology, and religious pluralism. She previously taught at Georgetown University, where she also received her PhD in Theological and Religious Studies with a concentration on religious pluralism. She is the author of *Never Wholly Other: A Muslima Theology of Religious Pluralism* (Oxford University Press, 2013).

Matthew W. Maguire is Associate Professor of History and of Catholic Studies at DePaul University, and the author of *The Conversion of Imagination* (Harvard University Press, 2006). He is completing a new book entitled *The Revolutions of Charles Péguy*.

Thomas Michel, SJ is Senior Fellow at the Alwaleed Center for Muslim-Christian Understanding and the Woodstock Theological Center, both at Georgetown University. He received a doctorate in Islamic theology at the University of Chicago, and has taught Islamic Studies and Christian Theology in Indonesia, Thailand, Turkey, Malaysia, and the Philippines. Fr. Michel has also served as the Vatican's Head of the Office for relations with Muslims, as well as the Executive Secretary for the Office of Interreligious and Ecumenical Affairs. He is the recipient of the International Tschelebi Peace Prize from the Zentralinstitut-Islam-Archiv-Deutschland in Soest, Germany.

Joseph M. Murphy is the Paul and Chandler Tagliabue Professor of Interfaith Studies and Dialogue in the Theology Department at Georgetown University. He is the author of *Santería: An African Religion in America, Working the Spirit: Ceremonies of the African Diaspora*. With Mei-Mei

Sanford he has edited the volume *Osun across the Waters: A Yoruba Goddess in Africa and the Americas.*

Peter C. Phan holds the Ignacio Ellacuria, SJ Chair of Catholic Social Thought at Georgetown University. He holds three doctorates and two honorary doctorates. He is the author and editor of some 30 books and of over 300 essays on various aspects of theology. He is the founder of the Graduate Program in Theology at Georgetown University.

Jonathan Ray is the Samuel Eig Associate Professor of Jewish Studies at Georgetown University. He is the author of *The Sephardic Frontier: The Reconquista and the Jewish Community in Medieval Iberia* (Cornell University Press, 2006), and *After Expulsion: 1492 and the Making of Sephardic Jewry* (NYU Press, 2013), as well as several articles on Jewish history and culture in the medieval and early modern world.

Young-chan Ro is Professor of Religious Studies and Director of Korean Studies Center, George Mason University. He authored *The Korean Neo-Confucianism of Yi Yulgok* (SUNY Press, 1987) and co-authored *The Four-Seven Debate: The Most Famous Controversy in Korean Neo-Confucianism* (SUNY Press, 1995). He also published several book chapters in Neo-Confucianism including, "Ecological Implications of Yi Yulgoks cosmology" in *Confucianism and Ecology* (Harvard University Press, 1998), and "Morality, Spirituality, and Spontaneity in Korean Neo-Confucianism," in *Confucian Spirituality* (Crossroad, 2004). He has published many articles in Korean studies, Confucian studies, and comparative religion. He has written several book chapters and articles on Raimon Panikkar including "Panikkar's Universe: Beyond Scientific View of the Universe" (*CIRPIT Review*, no. 3, 2012) and "Cosmogony, Cosmology, and Kosmology" (*CIRPIT Review*, no. 4, 2013) and currently working on Panikkar's epistemology and ontology. He received his Ph.D. in Religious Studies from the University of California at Santa Barbara.

John N. Sheveland is an Associate Professor of Religious Studies at Gonzaga University. He is the author of *Piety and Responsibility* (Ashgate, 2011) and serves as the comparative studies area book review editor for *Religious Studies Review*. His current research centers on Asian theological method and comparative theological responses to religious violence.

Thomas A. Tweed holds the Harold and Martha Welch Endowed Chair in American Studies, with a concurrent appointment in History, at the University of Notre Dame, where he also is a Fellow in the Institute of Latino

Studies and the Kroc Institute for International Peace Studies. He previously taught at the University of Miami, the University of North Carolina at Chapel Hill, and the University of Texas at Austin. He is the author of *The American Encounter with Buddhism, 1844–1912: Victorian Culture and the Limits of Dissent* (1992), *Our Lady of the Exile: Diasporic Religion at a Cuban Catholic Shrine in Miami* (Oxford, 1997), which won the American Academy of Religion's Award for Excellence, and *Crossing and Dwelling: A Theory of Religion* (2006). He edited *Retelling U.S. Religious History* (1997) and coedited *Asian Religions in America: A Documentary History* (Oxford, 1999), which *Choice* named an "outstanding academic book." Tweed's latest book, *America's Church: The National Shrine and Catholic Presence in the Nation's Capitol* (Oxford, 2011), also won the AAR's Award for Excellence. In 2012, he was elected vice president—and future president—of the American Academy of Religion.

Pim Valkenberg is Professor of Religion and Culture at The Catholic University of America. He has taught at the Catholic University of Nijmegen, the Catholic University of Leuven, St. Augustine's College in Johannesburg, and the University of Notre Dame and Loyola University of Maryland, as well as universities in Belgium and South Africa. His publications include *Words of the Living God* (Leuven, 2000), *The Three Rings* (Leuven, 2005), and *The Polemical Dialogue* (Saarbrücken, 1997). His most recent book in English is *Sharing Lights on the Way to God: Muslim–Christian Dialogue and Theology in the Context of Abrahamic Partnership* (Rodopi, 2006), which contains reflections on Muslim-Christian dialogue and readings of texts by Thomas Aquinas, Jalaluddin Rumi, al-Ghazali, Said Nursi, and Fethullah Gülen.

Abraham Velez de Cea is Associate Professor of Buddhism and Comparative Religion in the Department of Philosophy and Religion at Eastern Kentucky University. His research interests include the historical Buddha, Buddhist ethics, comparative theology of religions, and Buddhist–Christian Studies (contemplative practices in Theravāda Buddhism and Catholicism with special emphasis on the Buddha of the *Pāli Nikāyas* and sixteenth-century Spanish mysticism). He is the author of *The Buddha and Religious Diversity* (Routledge, 2013). At present, he is working on a book about discipleship in early Buddhism and early Christianity, exploring the question of dual religious belonging and the possibility of being a disciple of Buddha and Jesus without contradiction.

Index

Addams, Jane, 154
Africa, 223–41
Agustine, Saint, 91, 132
Al Qaeda, 231
Al Shabaab, 235
Al Sijistani, Abu Sulayman, 186
Aleni, Gialio, 81
Alexander the Great, 91
Alexander VI, Pope, 29
Al-Ghadzali, 172
Alliance of Mindanao Youth for Peace, 180
Al-Tawhidi, Abu Hayyan, 186, 189
American Indian Movement (AIM), 8–9
American Pragatism, 163–64
Ames, Roger, 74
Amstutz, Galen, 76, 80
Angels, 97
Aniconism, 97
Anonymous Christianity, 277–96
anti-Semitism, 121, 124, 126, 159
anti-Zionism, 137
Arius, 108
Asian Human Rights Commission (AHRC), 182
Asian Muslim Action Network (AMAN), 180–84
Atay, Rifat, 176
Athanasius, 108
Augustine, Saint, 120
Aydin, Mahmut, 176
Ayoab, Mahmoud, 172–73

Baird, Robert, 42

Barlas, Asma, 214–15
Barres, Maurice, 121
Becker, Karl, 196
Benedict XVI, Pope, 41
Bergson, Henri, 124
Bernard-Lazare, 121–22
Bernstein, Richard, 79
Berthrong, John, 263
Bhaba, Homi, 41
Biagioli, Mario, 75
Bi-religiousness, 31
Bishops-Ulama Forum, 179–81
Bloy, Leon, 121
Bocu, 32
Boko Haram, 235
Botanica, 28, 29, 33, 34, 36, 39, 40, 41, 44
Bourne, Randolf, 161
Bremer, Frederika, 36
Brockey, Liam, 66
Brujeria, 30
Buchmann, Theodor, 201
Buddhism, 46–65, 288, 307
Burrell, David, 263

Caecilian, 108
Canby, Peter, 38
Carlsen, Robert, 37
Cattoi, Thomas, 263
Chango, 32, 34, 36, 40, 43
China
    Han Dynasty, 79
    Ming Dynasty, 66, 75, 78
    Qin Dynasty, 298, 301
    Qing Dynasty, 66, 75, 78

Song Dynasty, 79
Xia Dynasty, 70
Yin Dynasty, 70
Christian Brothers, 7
Chu, Ping-Yi, 66, 73, 75
Circumcision, 106
Clairmont, David A., 263
Claver, Pedro, 30
Clio, 123
Clooney, Frank, 247, 249, 262–63
Cofradia, 37–38
Cohen, Elliot, 157
Comhaire-Sylvain, Suzanne, 41
Common Word Initiative, 173–74
Comparative Theology, 248–49, 261–63, 267–70
Confusianism, 70, 74, 77, 81
Congreation for the Doctrine of the Faith, *Dominus Jesus*, 281
Connelly, John, 120, 132
Constantine, 108–9
Constantinople
  Estrangement from Rome, 195
  Fall of, 192–194, 196–97, 206
Conversion, 103, 106
Copeland, Aaron, 268
Cornille, Catherine, 263
Council of Basel, 193–94, 201
Creolization, 41
Crusades, 200, 232
Cult, 89, 95, 97–98, 106, 109
Culture, xii, 5, 6, 67, 71–72, 74–75, 81, 124, 151–55, 166
Cummings, E. E., 75
Curran, Charles E., 272

Dalai Lama XIV, 46–65
D'Costa, Gavin, 254
De la Charme, Alexandre, 81
De Lubac, Henri, 119–20
De Sahagun, Bernardino, 30
De Santa Cruz, Bishop Morell, 35
"Deep" Pluralism, 260
Demons, 96, 104, 108
Desmangle, Leslie, 41
Dewey, John, 161
Dharma, 64–65
Diaspora, 91–92, 94, 98, 103, 107

Diversity, 4, 6
Divine kinship, 88–89, 104, 107, 127, 130
Docta Ignorantia, 197
Donaldson, David, 70
Donatus, 108
Dreyfus affair, 119–34
Droogers, Andre, 43
Drumont, Edouard, 121
Dubois, W.E.B., 162
Dunne, George, 66

Eitel, Ernst J., 77
Eleggua, 40
Engineer, Asghar Ali, 181, 211
Eskimos, 69
Espiritismo, 33
Esposito, John, 184
Ethnicity, 89
Evil tongue, 136–40, 143, 145, 147–48

Feiner, Shmuel, 158
Feldmeier, Peter, 263
Feminist Theology, 214
Feyerabend, Paul, 71
Fletcher, Jeannine Hill, 278
Ford, Henry, 159
France, Anatole, 128
Fredericks, James, 261–63
Frederikson, Paula, 120
Fredriksen, Paula, 187

Gadamer, Hans-George, 71, 79–80
Galileo, 75
Geertz, Clifford, 72
Geluk School, 59–65
Gender Watch, 182
Gernet, Jacques, 67, 74
Globalization, xiii–xiv, 13, 231, 271, 278, 297–303
Goldwater, Barry, 136
Gonzalez-Wippler, Migene, 33
Green, Garrett, 72
Griffin, David Ray, 42, 43, 254, 260
Griffiths, Paul, 75
Gulen, Fethullah, 174

Haafkens, Johann, 223, 225–27

Hagemann, Ludwig, 201
Halevi, Judah, 203
Hall, David, 74
Hasidism, 141, 148
Haskalah, 158
Hassan, Riffat, 214
Hatuey, 29, 30
Heim, Mark, 61
Hermann of Dalmatia, 200–203
Hick, John, 176, 197–98
Himes, Michael, 272
HIV/AIDS, 182
Hobbes, Thomas, 132
Hopi Indians, 69–70
Hurwitz, Henry, 157
Hussain, Amir, 172
Hybridity, 41

Ibn Arabi, 172
Ibn Qayyim al-Jawziyya, 172
Ibn Taymizza, 172
Inka, Manken, 30–31
Intercollegiate Menoral Association (IMA), 156–61
Iranian Revolution, 230
Islam, 115, 170–85, 192–96, 199–206, 209–22, 223–41
Islamic Brotherhood, 230
Israel, Jonathan, 132

James, William, 163
Jefferson, Thomas, 303
Jesuits, 66–86
Joan of Arc, Saint, 127–130, 132
Joas, Hans, 188
John Paull II, Pope, 271
Joslyn-Siemiatkoski, Daniel, 263
Judaism, 119–34, 135–50, 151–69

Kabuddha, Pacce, 60
Kagan, Rabbi Israel Meir, 137–50
Kallen, Horace M., 151–53, 155–56, 159, 161–69
Kant, Emmanuel, 198
Kaplan, Rabbi Mordecai, 158
Karkkainen, Veli-Matti, 291
Karma, 58, 62
Keenan, John, 263

Ketton, Robert, 200–201
Khaldun, Al-Muqaddimah Ibn, 229
Khalil, Mohammad Hassan, 172
Khomeni, Ayotollah, 230
Kiblinger, Kristin B., 263
Kimelman, Reuven, 136
Knitter, Paul, 247
Kony, Joseph, 235
Korea, Choson Dynasty, 301
Ku Klux Klan, 151, 159
Kubin, Wolfgang, 73
Kuhn, Thomas, 71
Kukah, Matthew H., 228, 234
Kumarajiva, 82
Kusi, Titu, 30

Laksana, A. Bagus, 263
Lamptey, Jerusha, 263
Latinos in America, 28–45
Laudet, Fernand, 127–28
Lefebure, Leo, 263
Legge, James, 70, 77
Levin, Meyer, 158
Lewisohn, Ludwig, 158
Liberation Theology, 283
Lilla, Mark, 132
Linguistic Relativity, 68
Little Traditions, 31, 33
Liu, Lydia H., 81
Liu, Yu, 66–67, 78
Locke, Alain, 162–63
Long, Jeffrey, 263
Longobardo, Nicolo, 77
Lord's Resistance Army, 235
Lowenthal, Marvin, 157

Mahdist Movement, 230
Malotki, Ekkehart, 70
Mang, Wang, 79
Marion, Jean-Luc, 292
Marsden, George, 5
Maximon, 37–39, 43, 44
Maynard, Thierry, 74
Mehmet II, Sultan, 193, 199
Melanchton, Philipp, 201
Melting pot, 154, 161, 164
Menoral Journal, 156–60, 166
Methodology, 12–17, 80–83

Meuthen, Erich, 201
Midrash, 141–42
Migration, 13–14, 15
Mindanao Peace Camp, 180
Mindanao Week of Peace, 180
Minorities, xiv
Mishnah, 136–37, 146
Monotheism, 88, 99, 103
Moore, Laurence, 5
Morali, Ilaria, 196
Moro-Christian Peoples' Alliance, 178
Moro-National Liberation Front (MNLF), 178
Muhammad, Prophet, 171, 176, 200–204, 211, 213, 219–20, 231, 237
Mungello, David, 66
Musar movement, 141–42
Music
  Counterpoint, 266–68
  Gregorian Chant, 264–76
  Polyphony, 264–76
Muslim-Christian Agency for Advocacy, Relief and Development (MUCAARD), 177–78, 181
Muslim-Christian Interfaith Conference, 178
Muzaffar, Chandra, 183
Mysticism, 122, 131–32

Nasr, Seyyed Hossein, 212
Neo-Platonism, 197
New Mexico
  Acoma Pueblo, 1
  Analco Indians, 7
  Arch Lake Woman, 11, 13
  Clovis, 11
  El Santuario de Chimayo, 11
  Fiesta, 6–8, 14
  Juan de Onate, 9
  La Conquistadora, 7
  Pueblo Revolt, 7
  Puye Cliffs, 11
  San Miguel's Chapel, 6–8, 13, 14, 18, 19
  Santa Fe, 6–11, 13, 14, 15, 16, 19
  Soldier's Monument, 6, 8–10, 16
  Taos Pueblo, 11
Nibbana, 60

Nicholas of Cusa
  Cibratio Alkorani, 199–200, 202, 204
  De Pace Fidei, 195–96, 199–201, 205–6
Nicholson, Hugh, 263
Niebuhr, Reinhold, 300
Nikayas, Pali, 46, 58, 62–64
Nirvana, 59
Nursi, Said, 173–74

Obasanjo, President Olusegu, 235
Ochun, 35, 36, 39, 40, 43, 44
Openness, 54–56
Orishas, 32, 35, 36, 40
Osman, Fathi, 173–75
OTMIX, 54–56, 58–59, 63

Paden, John N., 234
Panikkar, Raimundo, 254, 297–308
Parliament of World Religions, 174
Pascal, Blaise, 132
Patil, Parimal, 249
Paul, Saint, 90, 98–108
Peace Associates of Zamboanga (PAZ), 178
Peguy, Charles, 119–34
Peter the Venerable, 200
Phan, Peter C., 260–63, 265, 275–76, 278, 280–85, 289, 294–95, 312
Piccolomini, Aeneas Slvius, 194
Pieris, Aloysius, 283
Piety, 214–17, 220–21
Pius II, Pope, 194, 199
Polytheism, 88, 94, 97, 104–5, 109
Practical pluralism, 187, 189
Pragmatic pluralism, 90, 108, 145, 148
Priest-Imam Forum, 180
Pullum, Geoffrey, 69
Pu-Tai Buddha, 40

Qur'an, 171–75, 199–202, 209–22, 229, 237

Rahner, Karl, 277–96
Rasmussen, Lissi, 225–26
Rattman, Fazlur, 171
Rauls, John, 188

Reagan, Ronald, 135–36, 148
Red scare, 159
Redfield, Robert, 31
Relativism, 303–5
Religious Groups for Human Rights (RGHR), 182
Religious Other, 209–13
Rescher, Nicholas, 73
Ricci, Matheo, 67, 81, 83
Rilaj Mam, 37
Roberts, Michelle Voss, 263
Robinson, Francis, 231
Roosevelt, Theodore, 154
Rorty, Richard, 72
Rosenzweig, Franz, 126, 132
Ross, E.A., 153
Rostas, Susanne, 43
Rumi, Jalal al-Din, 175

Sachedina, Abdalaziz, 172, 211
Sacrifice, 105, 125
Sa'dan, Ibn, 186
Said, Edward, 82
Salam, Abdallah Ibn, 200–204, 206
Salmon, Yosef, 142
Salvation, xi–xii, 37, 42–43, 59, 139, 170, 212, 253, 261–62, 279, 281–84, 291
San Simon, 37–39, 40, 43, 44
Sanneh, Lamin, 229, 231, 235–36
Santa Barbara, 32
Santayana, George, 162
Santos, 28, 32, 34–38, 43, 44
Sapir-Whorf Hypothesis, 70, 72
Scholem, Gerschom, 120
Seamon, Erika, 263
Sefer Chafetz Chaim, 135, 137–39, 141–43, 147–50
Shahn, Ben, 1–4, 17, 18
Shango, 32
Shari'a, 229, 231, 235–36
Sheveland, John N., 263
Slavery, 30, 35
Smail, Daniel Lord, 13
Smith, Jonathan Z., 213
Smith, Wilfred Cantwell, 197–98, 200, 205
Solidarity, 265–66, 271–72

Spinoza, Baruch, 132
Standaert, Nichola, 79
Steiner, George, 75
Sudan People's Liberation Army (SPLA), 236
Sun, Yuming, 73
Symbiosis, 41
Syncretism, 40–42, 44

Taliban, 231
Talmud, 136, 139
Taylor, Charles, 132–33
Technology, 15
Temple tax, 97
The "Other," 269
Theology of Religious Pluralism (TRP), 242–59
Tiemeier, Tracy Sayuki, 263
Tolerance, xv, 89–90
Tran, Anh Quoc, 263
Trilling Lionel, 158
Trinity, 242, 252–57, 261, 271, 282, 290

Ubelhor, Monika, 79
United States Government, 2–3, 153
Upaya, 50
Uthman Dan Fodio Jihad, 230

Valdez Luis, 33
Valkenberg, Pam, 263
Vatican II, 277, 281, 285–86
   Dei Verbum, 286
   Dialogue and Proclamation, 76
   Nostra Aetate, 277
Verbiest, Ferdinand, 81
Virgen de la Caridad, 32, 35, 36, 39, 43, 44
Virgin birth, 73
Virgin of Guadalupe, 40
Virtue, 4
Von Balthasar, Hans Urs, 120
Von Bell, Johann Adam Shall, 81
Von Kues, Nikolaus, 192–208. *See also* Nicholas of Cusa

Wadud, Amina, 214
Wahhabi Movement, 230

Walsh, Maureen, 263
War, 3
Wardy, Robert, 70, 74
Whorf, Benjamin, 69
Wiggins, James, 42
Witchcraft, 30
Wolfson, Harry, 157
World Aqudat Yisrael, 137

Yazi, Seiichi, 81
Yeshiva movement, 141
Yezierska, Anzia, 158
Yoruba people, 32, 35

Youngblood, Nathan, 10

Zambaanga's Islamic-Christian Urban Poor Association, 178
Zamfara State, 235
Zangwill, Israel, 154
Zhang, Qiong, 66, 78
Zhixu, Ouyi, 78
Zionism, 160
Zongjiao, 81
Zuckerkandl, Victor, 267
Zurcher, Erik, 67–68, 77

www.ingramcontent.com/pod-product-compliance
Lightning Source LLC
Chambersburg PA
CBHW052146300426
44115CB00011B/1542